YEARS	LITERATURE	PHILOSOPHY
1000 B.C.	Homer	
	Dionysian festivals; Sophocles, Aristophanes, Euripides	Socrates, Plato, Aristotle, Epicurius, Zeno
1 A.D.	Horace, Cicero, Vergil, Plutarch	
500		Boethius
1100		Abelard
1200	Dante	Thomas Aquinas
1300	Petrarch, Boccaccio	R. Bacon
1400	Chaucer	
1450	Ariosto	
1500	Rabelais, Spenser	Machiavelli, More,
	Marlowe, Shakespeare	Luther, Erasmus,
		Montaigne
1600	Cervantes	F. Bacon, Descartes, Grotius,
	Pepys	Hobbs, Spinoza,
	Milton	Locke
1700	Pope, Swift,	Voltaire
	Defoe, Gray,	
	Goldsmith, Fielding,	Hume,
1750	Burns, Goethe,	Rousseau,
	Schiller,	Kant
1800	Coleridge, Wordsworth, Scott,	
	Byron, Austen, Shelley,	Hegel,
	Keats, Pushkin, Heine,	Mill,
	Cooper, Balzac, Hugo,	Comte,
	Stendhal, Sand, Lytton,	Kierkegaard,
	Dickens, Poe, Dumas, Thackeray,	Schopenhauer,
1850	Longfellow, Hawthorne,	Marx,
	Melville, Stowe,	Engels,
	Whitman, Tennyson,	Thoreau,
	Eliot, Tolstoy, Dostoevski,	Spencer, T. H. Huxley,
	Browning, Mark Twain,	Emerson,
	Ibsen, Stevenson,	Haeckel,
	Wilde, H. James,	Nietzsche,
	Maeterlinck, Zola, Kipling,	Bergson,
1900	G. B. Shaw, Masefield, Mann,	Dewey, Pierce,
	Lawrence, Frost, Maugham,	W. James, Spengler,
	Lewis, T. S. Eliot, Joyce,	Russell,
	Dreiser, Fitzgerald, France,	Santayana
	Malraux, Hemingway,	
	O'Neill, A. Huxley,	
	Benét, Faulkner, Sandburg,	Sartre, Camus
1950	Stein, Steinbeck, Thomas,	
	Williams, Miller, Orwell,	
	Cummings, Auden	

The Understanding of Music

of

Music

Second Edition

THE WADSWORTH MUSIC SERIES

MUSIC LITERATURE

English Folk Song, Fourth Edition by Cecil J. Sharp
Five Centuries of Keyboard Music by John Gillespie
The Musical Experience by John Gillespie
The Musical Experience Record Album by John Gillespie
Scored for the Understanding of Music—Supplemented Edition by Charles R. Hoffer and Marjorie Latham Hoffer
Scored for the Understanding of Music Record Album by Charles R. Hoffer
Talking about Symphonies by Antony Hopkins
The Search for Musical Understanding by Robert W. Buggert and Charles B. Fowler
The Understanding of Music, Second Edition by Charles R. Hoffer
The Understanding of Music Record Album by Charles R. Hoffer
The Understanding of Music Enrichment Record Album by Charles R. Hoffer

MUSIC FOUNDATIONS

Basic Concepts in Music by Gary M. Martin
Basic Resources for Learning Music by Alice Snyder Knuth and William E. Knuth
Foundations in Music Theory, Second Edition with Programed Exercises by Leon Dallin
Introduction to Musical Understanding and Musicianship by Ethel G. Adams
Music Essentials by Robert Pace
Music Fundamentals by Howard A. Murphy with John F. Park

MUSIC SKILLS

Advanced Music Reading by William Thomson
Basic Piano for Adults by Helene Robinson
Basic Violin for Adults by Albert Lazan
Intermediate Piano for Adults, Volume I by Helene Robinson
Intermediate Piano for Adults, Volume II by Helene Robinson
Introduction to Ear Training by William Thomson and Richard P. DeLone
Introduction to Music Reading by William Thomson
Keyboard Harmony: A Comprehensive Approach to Musicianship by Isabel Lehmer
Keyboard Skills: Sight Reading, Transposition, Harmonization, Improvisation by Winifred K. Chastek
Music Dictation: A Stereo-Taped Series by Robert G. Olson
Music Literature for Analysis and Study by Charles W. Walton
Music Reading through Singing by Charles W. Walton and Harry Robert Wilson
Steps to Singing for Voice Classes by Royal Stanton

MUSIC THEORY

Harmony and Melody, Volume I: The Diatonic Style by Elie Siegmeister
Harmony and Melody, Volume II: Modulation; Chromatic and Modern Styles by Elie Siegmeister
A Workbook for Harmony and Melody, Volume I by Elie Siegmeister
A Workbook for Harmony and Melody, Volume II by Elie Siegmeister

MUSIC EDUCATION

Exploring Music with Children by Robert E. Nye and Vernice T. Nye
First Experiences in Music by Lyman C. Hurd, III, and Edith J. Savage
Help Yourself to Music, Second Edition by Beatrice P. Krone and Kurt R. Miller
Music in the Education of Children, Third Edition by Bessie R. Swanson
Planning for Junior High School General Music by William O. Hughes
Singing with Children, Second Edition by Robert E. Nye, Vernice T. Nye, Neva Aubin, and George Kyme
Teaching Music in the Secondary Schools by Charles R. Hoffer
Toward World Understanding with Song by Vernice T. Nye, Robert E. Nye, and H. Virginia Nye
Toward World Understanding with Song Record Album by Vernice T. Nye, Robert E. Nye, and H. Virginia Nye

The Understanding of Music
Second Edition

Charles R. Hoffer

Indiana University

Wadsworth Publishing Company, Inc.
Belmont, California

Acknowledgments

Photographs, paintings, and music examples are reproduced with permission from the
following sources.

Photographs and Paintings

Robert J. Armer: page 451.
Art Institute of Chicago: color plate 10.
Art Reference Bureau, Inc.: pages 60 (Archives Photographiques), 100, 110 (Marburg),
    113 (*Chartres*-Marburg), 130 (Alinari), 131 (Alinari), 133, 135 (Archiv für Kunst
    und Geschichte, Berlin), 219, 226 (Archiv für Kunst und Geschichte, Berlin), 240,
    242, color plates 1, 6, 7.
ASCAP: page 417.
Milton Babbitt, Princeton University: page 431.
BMI Archives: page 390, 410.
Boosey and Hawkes, Inc.: page 406.
The Bettman Archives Inc.: pages 82, 116, 123, 163, 228, 267, 275, 281, 295, 302, 315,
    334, 337, 345, 351, 369, 388, 391, 405.
Columbia Records: page 91.
Finnish National Travel Office: page 5.
Ewing Galloway: pages 31, 37, 39.
The Solomon R. Guggenheim Museum Collection: color plate 12.

Music Examples

Preface

This book seeks to achieve three goals in the area of music appreciation. One objective is to provide information about music—its literature, styles, forms, vocabulary, and other aspects that contribute to a basic knowledge of the art. A second goal is to develop the student's ability to listen to music intelligently and sensitively; he needs to hear what is happening as the sounds progress. The third objective is to increase his liking for music.

How does this book attempt to reach these objectives? First, it provides basic information that opens up the diverse field of music in a way that is both appealing and technically accurate. All major historical periods are presented, as are various forms and performance media—keyboard music, chamber music, art songs, electronic music, and so on. Jazz and many types of ethnic and popular music are also included.

Selection of the materials in this book was based on consideration of content and method—the "what" and the "how" of organizing the information. These considerations have led to a successful way of teaching music appreciation that might be called the "post-hole" approach. It is similar to setting up a fence or a series of telephone poles. Into the holes are set "posts," representing fundamental topics. Between them are strung "lines," which represent less intensively studied subjects designed to relate one major topic to another. Rather than a broad general study of many topics, an in-depth study of a few representative topics promotes clearer understanding and provides a reference point for new items of information.

This book seeks to present the information in a clear and vigorous style, with limited technical vocabulary, careful explanations of new words, and a logical order of presentation. After the initial chapters, the book adheres to a chronological approach. A non-musician might easily be confused if he is required to jump from Chopin to Wagner to Mozart and then to Schoenberg, and he will find it hard to trace trends such as the gradual breaking away from tonality or the increased interest in orchestration and sounds per se.

Teachers of music appreciation respond in various ways to the question, "Does a non-music major need to read notation?" In deference to the valid shadings of instructors' opinions on this subject, notation is presented in a sizable appendix. There it does not interrupt the line of thought in any chapter, but it is readily available for instructors who wish to teach notation and for readers who want to review it. Information about musical instruments is also presented in an appendix.

Because the understanding of music is strengthened by placing musical works in the appropriate cultural and artistic setting, this book is organized according to stylistic periods. This gives the reader a basis for organizing his thinking about works of music, and as long as false parallels are not drawn among the arts and historical events, it is a useful approach.

The second objective of this book is to encourage sensitive listening. The presentation of any information about music should be preceded or accompanied by the study of actual musical works, *through listening*. The student is not expected to read a list of characteristics of the Baroque before knowing how Baroque music sounds. Instead, the listening experience and the mastery of factual learning occur together, so that each supports the other. To recognize specific features of music—cadences, for example—the student needs not only to hear them, but also to know how various composers use them, how the chord choices affect the music, and how cadences relate to various styles. Both types of activity, aural and academic, are necessary for a full understanding of music. The achievement of listening skills can be promoted by using the supplementary book and the recordings created for use with this textbook.

The third objective—the attainment of a positive attitude in the student—is difficult to measure. There is no way to guarantee that a person will like anything, including music. Generally, a positive, varied, no-nonsense approach to the subject is most successful, and this book tries to provide such an approach. Because people usually like what they know and dislike what they don't know, the student's increasing competence and knowledge in music encourage a favorable reaction. The development of positive attitudes is also aided by presenting appealing musical works from the beginning of the course, and by avoiding tedious listening exercises, overly technical explanations, musically meaningless topics, and pompous wording.

The most significant change in the second edition of the textbook itself is the addition of a chapter on ethnic and functional music. This chapter broadens the musical coverage and provides the student with a better perspective from which to consider all kinds of music. Other changes in the book include the replacement of the Mozart Bassoon Concerto with his Fifth Violin Concerto; Roy Harris' Third Symphony has been replaced by the Fourth Symphony of Alan Hovhaness; and substitutions have been made in the Palestrina motet and the Morley madrigal. The Brahms' Clarinet Quintet and a number of music examples have been eliminated in order to reduce the length of the book. The chapter on contemporary music has been updated and enlarged, and the material on opera has been divided and placed in appropriate chapters according to style.

New materials have been designed to supplement the textbook. They include:

1. *Scored for the Understanding of Music—Supplemented Edition*—a book of line scores containing only works that are explained in the textbook. It gives the student something to follow as he listens, thereby keeping his attention on the music and providing visual reinforcement of what he hears.

2. Two new record albums—one of them called the *Enrichment* album, and the other designed especially for *Scored for the Understanding of Music*. The latter album includes all the works contained in the book of the same title. Between them, the two albums include all the musical works discussed in the textbook. Because it contains a good basic selection of music discussed in the text, the original album entitled *The Understanding of Music* is being continued. All three albums allow for individual listening outside of class time, and they can serve as an inexpensive beginning to quality personal record collections.

3. "Learning to Listen" booklets—included in the *Enrichment* and *Scored* albums. They are designed to guide the student's listening practice on a self-instructional basis.

4. The new *Instructor's Guide*—suggestions for teaching, class activities, test items, and a list of books and films.

These materials offer the instructor a wide range of options, so that he can build the course according to his own preferences. The in-

structor may also determine whether the student will be requested to purchase more than the textbook. At least the book of line scores and one or
more of the record albums should be made available in bookstores for the
students who wish to get more out of the course.

I would like to thank all those who encouraged me in my efforts
to be a teacher and writer. I am indebted to the many students in my music
appreciation classes, from whom I learned much about how to aid them
in their understanding of music. Thanks are due to Indiana University for
the use of its library, to Walter Kaufmann and Austin Caswell of the Indiana
University School of Music faculty for their suggestions regarding the
chapter on ethnic music, and to Audrey Lozier, formerly of Ohio Dominican
College, for her ideas about the material on Gregorian chant. I am especially
grateful to the many instructors who took the time to complete and return
the questionnaire regarding the revision of this book. For their reviews of
the book and manuscript I would like to thank C. Thomas Barr, State University College (New Paltz, New York); Robert N. Benson, Miami-Dade
Junior College; Nelson E. Bonar, Fullerton Junior College; Jack Cassing-
ham, Wisconsin State University (Whitewater); Irving H. Cohen, West
Chester State College; Dale B. Fisk, Concordia College (Portland, Oregon);
Robert W. Hartwell, Eastern Kentucky University; Burton L. Karson, California State College (Fullerton, California); Fredric Kurzweil, Queens-
borough Community College; David H. Watkins, Indiana State University;
and Etzel Willhoit, Central Connecticut State College. Special commendation and thanks are due Ellen Bell for her editorial and production efforts.

Finally, thanks beyond the power of words to express are due my
wife, Marjorie, who, as a teacher of music appreciation courses, offered
many valuable suggestions. With gratitude I pay tribute to her editorial
advice and the typing of the manuscript.

Charles R. Hoffer

Contents

1

The Substance of Music   1

The Nature of Music   1
Pitch   2
Melody   3
Counterpoint   6
Harmony   10
Time   13
Dynamics   18
Tone Color   19
Combining the Elements: Music   20

2

Ethnic and Functional Music   23

Some Uses of Music   24
Folk and Ethnic Music   26

Jazz   45
The Current Scene   52

3

Music as a Fine Art   55

Music and Aesthetics   55
The Importance of Aesthetic Experiences   59
Learning about Music   61
Music and Culture   63
Meaning in Music   64
The Evaluation of Music   66

4

Listening to Music   69

Attitude   70
Intellect and Emotion in Music   71
Planes of Listening   72
Listening Techniques   75
Tests of Good Listening   80
Knowing What to Listen For   81

5

Musical Performance   83

Factors Affecting Performance   84
Financial Support of Musical Groups   93
The Role of Music Education   95
Reviews of Musical Events   96

6

Early and Renaissance Music   99

Gregorian Chant   101
Secular Music   106
Polyphony   106
Musical Styles and Periods   107
The Gothic Period and the Motet   109
The Renaissance Era   111
Renaissance Music   114

7 Baroque Vocal Music 129

Characteristics of the Baroque Style 131
Baroque Music 134
George Frideric Handel 134
The Oratorio 136
The Chorale 150
The Cantata 151

8 Baroque Instrumental Music 159

Johann Sebastian Bach 161
The Organ 164
The Fugue 166
Other Organ Forms 171
The Suite 172
The Harpsichord 175
The Baroque Sonata 179
The Concerto Grosso 179
Other Baroque Composers 185

9 The Classical Period 189

The Rococo Subperiod 189
The Classical Attitude 190
Wolfgang Amadeus Mozart 193
The Symphony 195
The Concerto 209
Comparing Stylistic Periods 214

10 Classical Opera and Chamber Music 215

The Elements of Opera 216
Appreciating Opera 218
Early Opera 218
Chamber Music 223
Franz Joseph Haydn 226
The String Quartet 228

The Sonata   236
Other Common Chamber-Music Groups   236

11   Beethoven   239

The Piano   245

12   Early Romanticism   263

Characteristics of Romanticism   263
Franz Schubert   267
The Song   268
Frédéric Chopin   274
Piano Music   276
Franz Liszt   280
Program Music   285
Robert Schumann   288
Felix Mendelssohn   289
The Direction of Romanticism   289

13   Late Romanticism   293

Peter Ilich Tchaikovsky   294
Johannes Brahms   301
Richard Strauss   310
German Romantic Opera   314
Richard Wagner   314
Italian Romantic Opera   320
Giuseppe Verdi   320
Giacomo Puccini   321
Franck, Fauré, and Saint-Saëns   327

14   Nationalism, Impressionism, and Post-Romanticism   331

Nationalism   331
The Russian Five   332
Other Nationalistic Composers   341

Impressionism   343
Claude Debussy   344
Maurice Ravel   350
Post-Romanticism   351

15

Twentieth-Century Music   355

Modern Society and the Creative Artist   355
Igor Stravinsky   357
Neo-Classicism   363
Arnold Schoenberg   368
Bela Bartók   373
Dmitri Shostakovich   380
Other Twentieth-Century Composers   384
Twentieth-Century Opera   390
The Twentieth Century in Review   395

16

American Music   399

The Nineteenth Century   401
The Twentieth Century   403
Charles Ives   404
Aaron Copland   405
William Schuman   409
Alan Hovhaness   413
Other American Composers   416
Musical Comedy   419

17

The Present and Future of Music   423

Further Development of Tone-Row Techniques   424
Microtonal Music   428
Mathematics   428
Timbres   429
Electronic Music   430
Computer Music   434
Chance Music   434
New Sources   436
Eclecticism—Consolidation   436
The Future for the Listener   437

Appendixes   441

A Glossary   443
B Musical Instruments   447
C The Notation of Music   457
D The Harmonic Series   469

Index   471

to Marjorie

The Substance
of Music

1

What is music? What is it that you will be reading about, listening to, and studying?

Music is one form of sound. Quite a lot is known about sound. A stimulus acts to set in motion the molecules in the air. The molecules bump into one another, something in the manner of billiard balls, each setting the next in motion. This chain reaction continues until it strikes the ear drum, where the nervous system picks up the impulses and transmits them to the brain. But not all sounds are music, so this does not answer the question "What is music?"

THE NATURE OF MUSIC

What must sounds have to be placed in that special classification "music"? Stated briefly, the sounds must be organized and meaningful. The letters c-c-h-r-t-a-s are all letters in the alphabet, but unless unscrambled into s-c-r-a-t-c-h, they have no meaning. They are not organized.

In music, organized sounds are planned to occur in a certain sequence in a prescribed space of time. Random sounds cannot be music except by sheer accident, although in some types of music the performer is given some choice of what to do and/or when to do it.

Most musical sounds possess pitch (recognizable levels of highness and lowness) as well as a planned sequence in time. However, all musical sounds need not have pitch. The snare drum and the cymbal have been recognized members of the orchestra for over a century and a half, yet these and a few other similar instruments are incapable of producing discernible pitches. In recent years much work has been done synthesizing sounds on tape recorders and electronic equipment, and here, also, pitch may be a negligible factor. Music, then, is a composite of sounds that are organized and meaningful, occurring in a prescribed space of time and usually having pitch.

Music is made of sounds. What a composer does with and to sound is crucial to the success of the final product. Sounds are to music what cloth is to a piece of clothing. Just as a tailor can cut and form goods to create an article of clothing, a composer can manipulate and form sounds to create a musical composition. A composer can do several things to sound. He can make it high or low. He can place it before, after, or among other sounds in a series. He can combine sounds so that several are heard simultaneously. He can regulate the duration of a sound, and he can make it stronger or weaker. He can change the quality of a sound in countless ways. Finally, he can work with combinations of these six possibilities.

For somewhat different reasons, both the composer and a person learning about music need to consider how sound is controlled and transformed into music. The composer considers what can be done with sound because that is the substance with which he has chosen to work. You need to learn a few basic terms that describe the various ways in which sounds are manipulated. The terms are useful in discussing music in both classroom and out-of-class situations. But even more important to you is their value in aiding your thinking about music. In all areas of life, words are implements that permit us to classify objects and ideas, and in general organize our thinking. For example, if you understand the word "timbre," you can consider more effectively why one particular quality of sound was chosen over another for a certain musical passage. When you are conscious of his choices, you will be thinking along the same paths as the composer, and you can then begin to evaluate and appreciate his actual musical decisions.

PITCH

In musical terminology the degree of highness or lowness of sound is referred to as *pitch*. Pitch can be measured scientifically, since it is determined largely by frequency of molecular vibrations, with a more rapid vibration giving the sensation of higher pitch. Highness as the word is used in music has nothing to do with height in terms of space, so it is perhaps an unfortunate term for the concept. In many non-Western cultures the word that refers to highness has the connotation of smallness, and in some cases, femininity. Among young children in America, the prevailing misconception seems to be that "high" means "loud" and "low" means "soft."

Musicians use the term *interval* to describe the distance between two pitches. The most fundamental interval is the *octave*. It gets its name from the fact that the duplicate of any note in the scale is eight notes away from the original, and it is therefore given the same letter name. The two pitches, if sounded together, blend so well that they sound almost like one note. The naming of intervals is discussed in Appendix C. Recognition and identification of intervals help clarify the relationship between pitches. Intervals are rarely heard in isolation. In musical works they appear in the context of melodies and chords.

MELODY

Melody refers to pitches sounded one after another in a logical, meaningful series. It is an organized group of pitches strung out sequentially to form a satisfying musical entity. Sometimes the term *line* is applied to this concept.

Melody occurs in music in a variety of guises and circumstances. The most common occurrence of melody is in simple, short pieces of music that exist primarily because their melodies are pleasing to hear, play, or sing. The average individual recognizes and responds to countless melodies, ranging from "The Star-Spangled Banner" to folk tunes and popular songs. (The word *tune* is often used as a less formal synonym for melody.) There are also many pieces of a more serious, complex nature that are valued largely for the quality of their melodies. Such works in both the light and serious veins tend to be short, usually not more than a few minutes in length. Although long works such as operas appear to refute the idea of melodic brevity, most of them are actually made up of shorter segments, each with a distinctive melody.

There is, however, another aspect of melody, one that is not so familiar. This concept considers not only the melody itself but, more importantly, what happens to the melody in the course of the musical work. The manipulation of melodies is one of the hallmarks of music composed for artistic value. A melody can thus become the springboard for a long work of music. Such a melody is often called a *theme*, to indicate its place as a central musical idea for the piece.

A theme may or may not be a highly attractive series of pitches; that is, it need not be "tuneful" in the customary sense. The literature of music abounds with examples of mediocre tunes that have become the central idea for great works of music. In other words, a theme is good not so much because of *what it is* but because of *how it is developed and what it becomes*. One of the best-known examples is the short theme from the first movement[1] of Beethoven's *Symphony No. 5:*

The three G's and an E flat that constitute the theme can hardly attract much attention on their own merits. But what Beethoven does with this melodic figure is nothing short of genius, and it makes for some exciting listening.

To illustrate how melodies form the backbone of a large musical work, the fourth movement of *Symphony No. 2* by Jean Sibelius (Yon Sih-*bay*-leeus) will serve admirably. Although the movement is of majestic proportions, it is built almost entirely around four melodies or themes. There are only a few moments during which one of the four themes is not being played. The first and most important theme starts out like this:

There is a short contrasting center section, followed by a repetition of the first phrase. Twice when the theme is heard, Sibelius suspends all forward motion while he interjects an exciting passage for the trumpets and an answer in the French horns—all while the listener waits for the melody to resume. The delay not only holds the listener's attention but tends to prove the adage "Absence makes the heart grow fonder" by making the theme seem especially satisfying when it resumes.

After some minutes, Sibelius shifts almost abruptly to another theme:

---

[1] A *movement* is a large, independent section of a musical composition.

Jean Sibelius.

This one is more transitional in character. That is, it gives the impression not of being important in itself but rather of leading to other musical ideas.

Then begins the second important theme. First it is heard in the oboe part and then the clarinet. When performing this work, most professional-quality orchestras delay the sounding of the second note of the theme for a split second and also give that note a little more stress.

Sibelius slowly builds to tremendous climaxes using this theme, sometimes in a slightly varied form.

The fourth melody is again more transitional:

As the movement progresses, Sibelius takes the first six notes of the first theme and has that fragment played in contrast to some of the other themes.

Notice that often the melodies are played against a background of orchestral sound that has a swirling, nervous, moody quality. This background persists in a stubborn sort of way. All of these features, when added to the driving repetition and interplay of melodies, make this work an exciting and virile piece of music.

Melodies do not exist in a vacuum; for several reasons, they are heard as part of a total musical work. First, melodies are played on an instrument or sung with a voice. Inevitably, the features of the voice or instrument—its tone quality, its adaptability to the requirements of the melody—contribute to or detract from the effect of the melody itself. A melody that is well suited for the violin may be a poor one for the flute, and vice versa. Second, since melodies must exist in a dimension of time, they all have rhythm. Thus the duration of the notes and their placement in time are as vital as their pitch. One awkwardly placed rhythmic value can ruin an otherwise good melody; conversely, a distinctive rhythmic pattern can enhance a rather average tune that would not otherwise be remembered. Third, almost all melodies have other pitches sounded with them. The kind of accompaniment given a melody, or the quality of melodies occurring simultaneously, again has a decided effect on the musical result. Fourth, other music usually precedes and follows the melody. The right kind of musical buildup can make an everyday melody sound like a gift from the gods. Fifth, most melodies tend to center about one particular pitch. There is a sense in which the music moves away from and returns to a "home" pitch. More will be said about this important fact in the discussion of harmony.

The student who is exploring the melodic aspect of music will soon see that melodies come in a wide variety of shapes and sizes. Some are long, giving the impression of ever-flowing melody that never quite repeats itself, even though it has much unity. Others seem to be a collection of short fragments. Melodies have no standard length. Some are easily sung, while others are impossible to perform except on a particular instrument. Strangely, some melodies are not easily remembered. These melodies occur particularly in modern music, in which the pattern of sounds is unfamiliar. All of these considerations point to the fact that the listener's concept of melody should be broad and liberal.

COUNTERPOINT

A third way to alter a sound, in addition to regulating its pitch level and placing it in a consecutive series, is to combine one or more sounds with it. This can be done in either of two ways. One technique is to sound two melodic lines simultaneously. This method is called *counterpoint.* The word comes from the Latin *punctus contra punctum,* meaning "point against point." (In medieval times, notes were called "points.") The adjective form of the word is *contrapuntal.* So contrapuntal music is that which has two or more melodic lines sounding simultaneously in contrast to one another.

Counterpoint is essentially linear music. That is, the composer intends for the listener to perceive these sounds as concurrent melodies— horizontal lines of music. The sounds are not to be thought of vertically, as chords, even though harmonies are produced as the counterpoint progresses.

Since melody and rhythm preceded other musical elements, counterpoint was an earlier invention than the melody-plus-accompaniment that is so common today. Surprising as this may seem at first, it is logical. The use of several pitches sounding as a unit requires a higher degree of musical sophistication than the mere addition of another melody. This is not to say that counterpoint is simpler than music with accompaniment. Far from it. While it was easier *at first* to combine one melody with another, composers soon found that skillfully written counterpoint is equally demanding.

All that was said in the previous section about melody also applies to counterpoint. Whatever is true of a single melody can also be true of melodies when sounded together. Rhythm, instrumental or vocal characteristics, and musical context are all involved. Like a single melody, countermelodies vary greatly in their makeup.

An example of counterpoint in which the lines are easily distinguished is a section from the *Cantata No. 140, "Wachet auf, ruft uns die Stimme"* ("Wake Up, Call the Voices"), by J. S. Bach. In the fourth section, which begins with the words "Zion hears the watchmen calling," one melody is played by the strings in the orchestra. Try singing the melody, or play it on an instrument. Performing the melody will help you remember it. If nothing else, follow the notated music closely as you listen to the piece. Observe that most of the notes of the melody are of short duration, so that the melody conveys the impression of easy and graceful motion.

After the melody in the strings has been played in its entirety, Bach brings in the chorale melody upon which three sections of the cantata are based. (A *chorale,* pronounced "coh-*rahl,*" is a Lutheran hymn tune. Bach did not compose the chorale melodies.) The melody is sung by the tenor section of the chorus.

Again, try singing or playing the chorale melody yourself, or humming along with a recording, even though some of the notes may be a little out of your range. Notice that the melody is slow, strong, and stately. Each note seems to stand like a block of granite, making a good contrast for the other, more gentle melody. Listen to a recording of this section so that you can hear how the two melodies fit together. In fact, two hearings are advisable: on the first hearing, listen selectively for the chorale; the second time, center your attention on the contrasting line.

CANTATA NO. 140

Fourth Section

Ihr Freund kommt vom Him - mel präch - tig,
Her Friend comes from Heav'n in splen - dor,

von Gna - den stark, von Wahr - heit mäch - - - -
in mer - cy strong, in truth al - might - - - -

tig,
y,

ihr Licht wird hell, ihr Stern geht
her light grows bright, her star ap -

auf.
pears.

HARMONY

Another way to combine sounds is to add subordinate sounds to enhance the quality of the main sound. The practice of adding enriching sounds is called *harmonizing*. Harmonizing is well illustrated when a folk song is sung with guitar accompaniment. The folk song may consist of a nice melody, but sung alone it is likely to seem a bit barren. The element of harmony contributed by the guitar provides an appropriate setting and enriches the effect of the song.

The word "harmony" itself is sometimes confusing, due no doubt to its somewhat different use in everyday language. If the girls in a dormitory get along well, they can be said to be living together harmoniously. In music, harmony refers *only* to the simultaneous sounding of pitches, regardless of whether the chords sound pleasing or not.

The difference between counterpoint and harmony is largely one of viewpoint. Counterpoint reflects a linear, horizontal view of music. *Harmony,* on the other hand, stresses the vertical aspect, the effect of sounds heard simultaneously. But counterpoint and harmony are not as distinct as the viewpoints might indicate. In writing counterpoint, the composer must still consider the fact that the lines of music do form simultaneous combinations of sound. In writing harmony, he must bear in mind that every group of vertical sounds occurs in relation to other groups that have preceded and will follow it. In music there is almost always an element of the horizontal (the progression of music in point of time) and the vertical (the effect of sounds at any particular instant). The difference between harmony and counterpoint, therefore, lies in the degree of emphasis given to each dimension.

The term *texture* as it is used in music refers to whether the music is essentially linear or chordal. Texture might be expected to refer to the degree of smoothness or roughness of sound, but such is not the case. Linear music is called *polyphony* (po-*liff*-o-nee); chordal music is known as *homophony* (ho-*moff*-o-nee). These textures will be examined more thoroughly in Chapters 6 and 7.

An understanding of harmony can be aided by defining a few basic terms. One is the word *chord.* A chord is the simultaneous sounding of three or more pitches. Chords form the basis of harmony. The most frequently used chord consists of three notes selected on the basis of an alternating pattern somewhat like the black and red squares on a checkerboard. If you go to the piano and play every other white key, the first three sounds you play will form a chord of some type. In the notation of music, such a chord can be written so that the notes appear in a line-line-line or space-space-space arrangement. (Spaces as well as lines have value in the musical staff.)

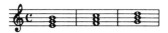

The "every-other" pattern can further be observed in the alphabetical names of pitches in a chord, such as A C E, or B D F.

Sometimes the same three notes in a chord are rearranged. For example, a low C may appear as a high C instead. This "reorganization" may hide the basic pattern from the eye of a person looking at the notation, but the ear can hear the similarity, and the chord is still essentially the same.

The "every-other" pattern of chord construction is so basic that it is frequently found outlined in melodies as well as in chords. The first seven notes of "The Star-Spangled Banner" are an illustration of this fact.

If the sounds give the listener the impression of repose, equilibrium, or agreement, they are called *consonant*. If they give the impression of harshness, tension, disequilibrium, they are called *dissonant*. But words are inadequate to describe these two concepts. They are understood only through the hearing of actual chords, and even then there is no clear-cut distinction between consonance and dissonance. Since any judgment of these elements must be subjective, involving individual taste, it is more accurate to speak of *degrees* of consonance and dissonance. The interplay between these contrasting effects is vital to the art of music.

Chords are heard not only as units containing greater or lesser tension but also as single sensations of sound. Composers, especially in the last one hundred years, have sometimes added tones to chords to achieve a desired "color." An example of this practice occurs in some arrangements of popular songs that end with an especially colorful chord. The effect is one not of tension but of highly enriched sound.

It was mentioned briefly in connection with melody that most music tends to relate to a pitch center. This tendency is especially evident in harmony. Chords are particularly successful in establishing a sense of relationship with the home tone, which is called the *key center* or *tonic*. A chord away from the center gives the feeling of wanting to go to it. Music thus reveals a continual ebb and flow away from and to a key center, and this process establishes a sense of *key* or *tonality*. Interruption of the forward movement within a key gives the listener a feeling of dissatisfaction, and yet predictable motion can become dull if it is never varied. Therefore the composer cannot select chords in a haphazard manner. He must imaginatively control the forward motion of chords to and from the tonic so that the relative degrees of consonance and dissonance occur at the desired places. He must also achieve enough harmonic variety to sustain the listener's interest.

Even while chords are being heard as units, they are implying horizontal motion as well. For this reason, a series of chords is called a *progression.* Here is a simple chord progression in which the sensation of forward motion is evident. Play it or have someone play it for you.

During one playing, stop at the checkmark without sounding the last chord. The incomplete feeling that is created will be readily apparent.*

The purpose of harmony in music is to enhance the musical effect. To return to the folk singer for a moment: if he strums the wrong chords on his guitar, he can ruin the impact of his singing. For example, if he sings an important note in the melody, say a B, but strums an A C E chord, he will create a severe dissonance. Or he could play in A C E chord when C E G is needed to return to the tonic. In a more sophisticated musical work with more complex harmony, the appropriateness and skillful handling of chords are just as crucial. Harmony is comparable to the setting for a play. The effectiveness of the actors' lines in Shakespeare's *Macbeth,* for example, depends much on whether the scenery and costumes indicate the location as twentieth-century America or a gloomy medieval castle. The harmony and the melody must jibe; they must complement each other.

To delve further into the topic of harmony at this point would require lengthy and technical discussion. If you wish to pursue further aspects of harmony, the material in Appendix C will be helpful.

Let us again refer to the chorale melody Bach used for his *Cantata No. 140.* Typically, the last section of a cantata is the singing of the chorale melody by the congregation and performers. (The cantata as a musical form will be studied in Chapter 7.) Bach takes the same melody to which he previously gave contrapuntal emphasis and now presents it with chordal treatment. In other words, he applies two concepts—counterpoint and harmony—to the same melody, but in different situations.

In this harmonization, the melody itself is in the top notes, in the *soprano* part. The three remaining parts, reading downward, are called *alto, tenor,* and *bass* (pronounced "base").

---

* A demonstration of harmonic motion and tonality is included in the *Enrichment* album.

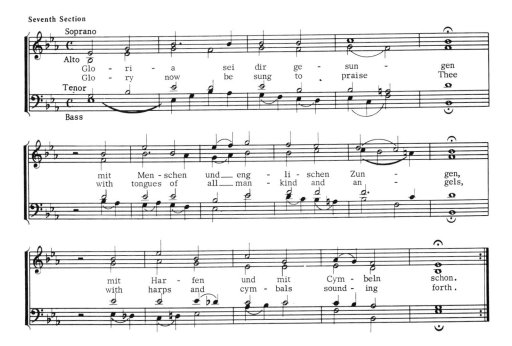

If you can sightread the alto or tenor lines, or hear them performed without the other parts, you will notice that they lack the melodic interest of the chorale melody. It is clear that these inner parts are subservient to the main melody. The bass line is quite a bit more interesting. Even though its wide interval leaps make it seem less stable than the chorale melody, it does have character in a melodic sense. The outer voices (soprano and bass, representing the highest and lowest parts) are more easily heard by the listener, so it is not surprising that these parts are made more interesting by the composer.

TIME

Three dimensions of sound have been explored thus far: pitch, the formation of a consecutive series (melody), and simultaneous combinations (counterpoint and harmony). A fourth way to manipulate sound is in terms of time. Time can be controlled in two ways: (1) by altering the length (duration) of a sound and (2) by adjusting its occurrence in relation to sounds occurring before and after it. The organization and management of time and rhythm in music is of utmost importance, since music is an art that must progress through the dimension of time.

Time can be a difficult concept. We speak of the future and the past, but both are intangible, because the past is memory and the future is prediction. Even the present is nebulous—an instant that is gone before it can be fully assessed. In attempting to understand time, therefore, a person must deal with memory, anticipation, and the search for meaning in a procession of events. Even though it might be said that one musical sound is three seconds long and another three-tenths of a second, these facts contribute little to an understanding of time in a musical composition.

Rhythm

In music, the term *rhythm* refers to those elements that relate to the sensation of ongoing movement, as contrasted with factors of pitch, loudness, or tone quality. It does not refer only to a recurrent pattern, orderly movement, or repeated situation, as it sometimes does in everyday usage.

In a calculated, intellectual study of music, one can easily overlook the sensuous appeal of rhythm. But it is an aspect of music that combines both motor responses and intellectual understanding. Appreciating it will require the listener to feel rhythm physically while attempting to understand how the rhythmic effect is achieved.

Beat

Probably the most fundamental component of rhythm is the *beat,* the recurrent pulse found in most music. The beat is that to which you dance, clap your hands, or tap your foot. It is in some respects comparable to your heartbeat: it is a pulse or throb that is sensed rather than sounded, and it recurs regularly. A beat is not necessarily present in all music. It is not a factor in some Oriental music; nor is it found in Gregorian chant or certain portions of operas, oratorios, and some concertos. In most music, however, the beat is a subtle and pervasive aspect of rhythm.

There may be subdivisions and multiples of the pulse that are perceived along with it. The beat and its less obvious aspects are something like a large wave on the ocean. Not only is there the main swelling of water; there are also numerous smaller formations apparent on the wave, and larger tides affecting all the waves.

The beat remains basically steady, like a heartbeat. A heartbeat that is unaccountably erratic, jumping from a couple of fast beats to a few slow ones and then to one or two fast beats again is a sign of physiological disorder. Music with an unstable beat is equally disturbing and unpleasant. (Try to sing a familiar song while purposely distorting the beat. The effect is irritating and unsettling.) Upon occasion, of course, it may be desirable to change the beat suddenly, but only for reasons that the composer and performer deem musically valid.

The beat and rhythm are not one and the same. A piece with a throbbing, pounding beat may have little rhythmic interest, at least to the musician, while a quiet-sounding work may have an elaborate rhythmic structure. The beat is the simple pulse found in almost all the music familiar to us. Rhythm is a larger concept, including the beat and everything that happens to sounds in relation to time. The beat is mentioned often in the discussion of rhythm because it is so intertwined with other phases of rhythm.

The beat is the unit of measurement by which the duration of a musical tone is judged. In music a tone is not judged as lasting for "three seconds" or "one-half minute." It is regarded as lasting for several beats, one beat, or a fraction of a beat. The appearance of a note tells how much time is allotted to it in relation to the beat. This time allotment is called the *value* of the note. Note values are listed in Appendix C.

Meter

Although beats in music are evenly spaced, some receive special emphasis. This occurrence reflects a natural human tendency. A clock may sound out identical "ticks," but the brain tends to superimpose a pattern on them and organize them in twos as "tick-tock." Carl Seashore, a music psychologist, describes the phenomenon in his book *Psychology of Music*.[2] He experienced it while riding on a train and listening to the click of the wheels. Although all the clicks were nearly alike, he could not make himself hear them as being of identical strength for any length of time. He could, however, easily group the clicks into a pattern.

The tendency for grouping can be further understood by considering how human beings speak. They do not say every word exactly like every other word, with identical stress and spacing. Words and syllables are grouped together, some being stressed while others are minimized. It is a human characteristic to group words, because such patterns aid comprehension and produce a more pleasant and more interesting sound.

In music, some beats receive more emphasis than others. That is, they appear with more intensity, more volume, and are called "accented beats." If one beat in every two is accented, the listener feels the rhythm thus: "*beat* beat, *beat* beat." If the accent occurs once in every *three* beats, the listener feels "*beat* beat beat, *beat* beat beat." The beats occur evenly in each case, but now they exhibit a pattern, and this pattern is called *meter*.

Metrical patterns in music hark back to the metrical patterns used in poetry—iambic, trochaic, and others. At one time in music history the terms were identical in each medium. Here is a portion of "Annabel Lee" by Edgar Allan Poe:

---

[2] New York: McGraw-Hill Book Company, Inc., 1938, p. 138.

It was many and many a year ago,
   In a kingdom by the sea,
That a maiden there lived whom you may know
   By the name of Annabel Lee;—
And this maiden she lived with no other thought
   Than to love and be loved by me.

When the poet wrote these lines, he achieved a metrical pattern that could be notated in music. The throbbing quality of Poe's lines gives them a vibrant appeal as well as metric organization. Much the same thing occurs in music.

Meter in music is the way in which beats are grouped and measured. For example, the pattern *"beat* beat beat" suggests *"one* two three," or a three-beat meter. The heavy beat is always regarded as the first beat of each group. In music notation, each group of beats is marked off into a separate unit called a *measure*. Measures are set apart by vertical bar lines on the staff, and each measure contains all the notes to be sounded over the span of time ticked off by two beats, three beats, or whatever number of beats the meter indicates.

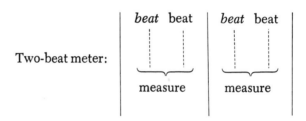

Two-beat meter:

At the beginning of almost every piece, and sometimes within it, you will see two numbers, one on top of the other. This is known as the *meter signature,* or *time signature,* and it tells the musician how the beats are going to be grouped and how they will be indicated in the notation. Generally the top number tells how many beats are in each measure, and the bottom number tells which note value represents the duration of one beat.

Tempo

The word *tempo* in music refers to the rate of speed at which the beats recur. It is the pace of the beat. Tempo can be indicated with considerable accuracy by use of the metronome, commonly seen as a pyramid-shaped object whose inverted pendulum can be set to tick at varying speeds. (Electric models are rapidly replacing their odd-shaped predecessors.) Some pieces of music display a marking like this at the beginning:

$\flat$ = M.M. 120. The initials M.M. stand for Maelzel's Metronome; Maelzel patented the work of another man and had the device named for himself. The number refers to the number of ticks that are to be produced per minute. The quarter note means that in this particular piece each quarter note should last for one "tick," with other note values in direct proportion to this norm.

Since the metronome was an invention of the early nineteenth century, composers of earlier eras were not able to indicate the desired tempo so exactly. They indicated the tempo in a general way by the use of a word, such as "fast" or "slow." Even today, though a metronome marking may be written in the music, it is still customary to include word descriptions of the desired tempo. These words give the performer some leeway in establishing the speed of the piece, and this freedom tends to make for more inspired and imaginative performances. For this reason, even with the metronome available, many composers prefer not to indicate tempo so exactly.

The words indicating tempo are generally written in Italian, although in the last one hundred years some composers with strong feelings of nationalism have chosen to use their native tongue. These words are significant for the student of music because they are often listed in concert programs to identify the movements of a longer work. Here are some of the more commonly used terms.

ITALIAN TERM	MEANING
Largo	Very slow, broad
Grave	Very slow, heavy
Adagio	Slow, leisurely
Andante	"Walking," moderate tempo, unhurried
Moderato	Moderate speed
Allegretto	"Little allegro," moving easily
Allegro	Moderately fast, moving briskly
Allegro molto	"Much allegro," very brisk
Vivace	Lively
Presto	Very fast
Prestissimo	As fast as possible

Composers often couple other directives with the tempo marking. Usually the additions have more to do with style than with speed (such as *con fuoco*, "with fire or force"; *sostenuto*, "smooth, sustained"). Within the broad framework of a specific tempo there may be indications of lesser tempo changes: *meno*, "less" (as in *meno allegro*); *piu*, "more"; *poco*, "a little"; *rit.* or *ritard*, "gradually slower"; *accel.* or *accelerando*, "gradually faster."

DYNAMICS

A fifth means of manipulating sound is to alter its strength. In music the word *dynamics* refers to the amount, strength, or volume of sound. It is perhaps the most easily understood dimension of music. Good composers and performers make skillful use of shadings of volume, so that the music reveals an almost constant interplay between loud and soft sound. The extent of this interplay, and its subtlety, may surprise you when you first listen for it.

While the concept of dynamic level is easily understood intellectually, the aural perception of volume is often deceiving. Many times the ear confuses pitch level with volume, the higher pitches tending to sound louder. Or the difference between tone quality and volume becomes less distinguishable, so that a nasal, piercing sound seems louder than a mellow sound reaching the ear with the same force. These experiences demonstrate the inter-relatedness of the various dimensions of music.

Dynamic change is one of the most common and most effective means of musical expression. In interpreting a piece of music, a performer speaks of *phrasing*, which refers to the way musical segments, called *phrases*, are presented by the performer. Phrases in music are somewhat comparable to phrases and clauses found in language. The performer studies a musical phrase and decides which notes should be emphasized. He performs these notes with more stress, more volume; he "leans" on them, so to speak. He may also alter the rhythm and tone color slightly, according to the demands of the phrase. All of these refinements cause the phrase to take shape and become meaningful. Minute but skillful gradations of dynamic level can make the difference between a sensitive performance and one that is matter-of-fact.

The relationship between rhythmic meter and dynamics was pointed out previously in this chapter. Without dynamic change it would be difficult to sense a meter.

The method of indicating volume in the music is rather simple. Two Italian words are basic: *p* or *piano*, "soft"; and *f* or *forte*, "loud." (The instrument known today as the piano was originally called the "pianoforte" because it was able to make gradual changes from loud to soft, something its predecessor, the harpsichord, could not do.) The words can be made more extreme: *ff* or *fortissimo*, "very loud"; *pp* or *pianissimo*, "very soft." Or they may be made more moderate by adding the prefix *mezzo* (pronounced *met*-zo), meaning "medium": *mf* or *mezzo forte*, "moderately loud"; *mp* or *mezzo piano*, "moderately soft."

Gradual changes of volume are indicated by *cresc.* or *crescendo*, "get louder," and *decresc.* or *decrescendo*, "get softer." The latter term can be indicated equally well by *dim.* or *diminuendo.* Frequently the *crescendo* is represented by the sign ‹ and the *decrescendo* by the sign ›.

TONE COLOR

Yet another way to change a sound is to alter its quality or "color." Many instruments can play middle C (violin, clarinet, flute, trumpet, trombone, cello, and others), and most people can sing that note. Yet each instrument mentioned and each person will sound the same pitch with a different quality, a different color. The technical word for tone quality is *timbre* (*tam*-ber).

Differences of quality can also be achieved on a single instrument. A phrase played at one pitch level may sound very different if played at another level on the same instrument. For example, the low notes on the clarinet have a resonant but mellow quality, while the high notes are shrill and piercing.

A good composer uses the colors of voices and instruments to achieve the effect he wants. If he wants a stirring, strong sound in an instrumental work, he may call for a trombone; when he wants a lyric, high sound, he may specify the flute or violin.

Not only does a composer use the colors of voices and instruments individually; he also combines different qualities to achieve new colors. French horns and cellos playing together produce a certain quality; add clarinets and the quality is changed slightly; add bassoons and it is changed again. The possibilities available to the composer are almost without limit, if he knows instruments and voices and how to write for them. It is especially well demonstrated in *The Roman Carnival Overture,* presented in Chapter 4.

The standard orchestral instruments referred to in the foregoing paragraphs are pictured and briefly described in Appendix B.

If dynamics is the most easily understood phase of music, tone color is possibly the most underrated or overlooked. As is mentioned in Chapter 4, there is much sensuous appeal in an attractive quality of sound. Every sound has a distinctive tone color, which can contribute to the effectiveness of a melody, for example. Combinations of sounds, too, often have a characteristic quality.

In recent years composers have become even more intrigued with tone color. They are exploring sounds other than those made on conventional musical instruments, which already offer the composer myriad possibilities. It is possible to tape-record any sound and then to re-record, splice, and in other ways manipulate the tape so that any desired sound effect can be created. Different qualities of sound can form the basis of entire pieces of music that contain little else except tone colors produced in a planned order and space of time. Although such pieces usually strike you as strange the first time you hear them, they demonstrate the inventiveness of the human mind and the vast possibilities available through the use of tone color. But more on this in Chapters 15 and 17.

COMBINING THE ELEMENTS: MUSIC

Music is more than the random changing of pitch, rhythmic patterns, and tone colors. Music is created when the elements are organized and combined in such a way that the hearer finds the listening experience rewarding and meaningful. The resulting combination is greater than the sum of its parts because each element is reinforced and enhanced by another. Thus the work of manipulating the elements, of composing, is crucial in the art of music and warrants closer study.

How the Composer Works

Where does the composer begin? How does he start? In some respects he goes about writing music in the same way you go about writing an essay for English class. Before the composer can begin, he needs to have sufficient technical skill in writing music, just as you need to have familiarity with spelling, punctuation, and grammar in order to write clearly. He has at least a general idea of something he wants to put into sound, just as you have an idea about what you want to say in words. Copland says he begins with a musical idea—a melody, an accompanying figure, or a rhythmic pattern. He takes this idea and begins to develop it into a musical composition.

Composers vary in their methods, just as students in English vary in the manner by which they work out their compositions. Some spend much time thinking before putting anything on paper; others make trial runs with ideas; still others work up an outline. Quite early in the process, most composers are thinking of the medium for which they are writing: a song, a symphony, a piano sonata. The end result of this effort can be sophisticated or simple, depending on the composer's inclination and ability.

One thing the composer does *not* do is languish about, waiting to be "inspired." Creative ideas, unlike rain, do not fall from the sky. Creative efforts involve false starts, revisions, and hard work. One need only look at manuscripts of Beethoven, for example, to see in the anguished scrawls and messy erasures the struggles that he went through in order to create. It seems inappropriate, therefore, to credit composers with superhuman and mysterious powers. True, most composers are creative artists who possess much natural talent. But to them, writing music is a logical and expected activity; it is their work. If there is a mystery in composing, it is in the marvelous ability of the human mind to create. As the sociologist John H. Mueller wrote, "There is much mysticism in creativity; but no more than in the test tube."[3]

---

[3] John H. Mueller, *The American Symphony Orchestra: A Social History of Musical Taste* (Bloomington, Ind.: Indiana University Press, 1951), p. 392.

The creative and planning mind of man, then, is the most important factor in the process of forming music. Without it there is no way to unite the parts into a convincing whole.

Form

The word *form* in music refers to the overall design that can be observed in relatively long segments of a composition. It can also describe the nature of complete works—symphony, oratorio, concerto—or the pattern of shorter sections and lines of music. Although the term "form" can be used in three different ways, each use of the term still refers to the organization of sounds as revealed through planned patterns in music.

A knowledge of the conventional forms is not a sure road to the understanding of music, although it helps. (To this end, ensuing chapters will familiarize you with the most common forms as the actual music is studied.) You may be able to sense the presence of form even though you cannot identify it by name. The fact that you sense it indicates that you are recognizing, to some degree, the organization of musical elements. This is a step toward understanding. You need not be able to say, upon hearing a Mozart symphony, "Why, that's in sonata form, and right now the second theme of the exposition is being played." If you *can* recognize the form to that extent, however, you are far more likely to understand the music than is the person who cannot. You probably have a much better idea of what you are listening for, and consequently you will enjoy it more.

You may have written rhyme schemes for poetry. The procedure is much the same for analyzing small segments of music. The familiar carol "Deck the Halls" will serve to illustrate a short, common form. The first line of music is:

Deck the halls with boughs of hol-ly, Fa la la la la, la la la la.

It is common practice in form analysis to label a line or phrase with a letter so that the lines that follow can be adjudged identical to it, similar, or dissimilar. The first line, therefore, is usually called *a*. For more lengthy sections of a work, capital letters are used. In any case, these letters have nothing to do with names of pitches. They merely denote the order of appearance of phrases or sections.

As you can tell, the second line of the song is exactly like the first, so this line may also be indicated by an *a*:

'Tis the sea-son to be jol-ly, Fa la la la la, la la la la.

The third line is conspicuously different, so it is indicated with the letter *b:*

Don   we now   our   gay   ap - par - el,   Fa___   la,   la___   la,   la   la   la,

The first half of the last line is identical to the first two lines, and the last half is similar:

Troll   the an - cient   Yule - tide   car - ol,   Fa la la la la,   la   la la la.

This fourth line is enough like the first so that it can be indicated as *a'*. The prime mark (*'*) denotes a slight alteration but not enough to warrant a completely different label.

The form of "Deck the Halls," therefore, is *a a b a'*, or more basically *a b a* with the first *a* repeated. It contains the seeds of contrast and unity necessary for attractive musical composition. The *a* line is heard twice, so that its second appearance provides an element of familiarity and unity; the *b* part provides the unfamiliar, the contrast.

The coalescence of musical elements is crucial to the composer, the performer, and the listener. Here is the advice given to his colleagues by Chopin, an outstanding pianist and composer of the Romantic period: "An artist should never lose sight of the thing as a whole. He who goes too much into details will find that the thread which holds the whole thing together will break, and instead of a necklace, single pearls will remain in his stupid hands."

Ethnic and Functional Music

2

Each year people all over the world spend countless hours making music or listening to it, and they spend vast amounts of money for instruments, records, and record-playing equipment. It is impossible to find out exactly how much time and money is invested in music, but it must be a tremendous amount. At weddings, coronations, and religious events, music is present. People dance and sing lullabies in just about every country in the world.

Why? Why is all that time, money, and attention centered on organized sounds? There are two basic reasons. One reason is that music can be *functional*—it can be used to achieve non-musical goals. It serves as an outlet for feelings of love, tension, or happiness; it provides something to dance to; it contributes to the atmosphere of worship or heightens the impact of a drama; it develops solidarity in a group; it provides a background of sound in restaurants and supermarkets; and it promotes many other non-musical goals. In the broad category of functional music, musical sounds are intended to achieve something outside the music itself.

The other reason for music is an artistic one. In art music, sounds are organized for the fascination and satisfaction they provide the person who listens to them. This type of music is the subject of the next chapter.

There is not always a clear-cut distinction between functional music and art music. Depending on the circumstances in which it is heard, a piece might be studied for its artistic interest or promoted for its functional value. Furthermore, depending on the inclinations of the individual, the same piece of music may be treated functionally or artistically. Occasionally portions of symphonies or concertos are worked into the sound tracks of films, and sometimes a functional piece is adapted by a composer to create a more artistic composition. The Baroque dance suite presented in Chapter 8 is an example of this. Some musical works lead a "double life," but that does not undo the basic validity of the distinction; a person who creates a piece of music generally slants it toward one purpose or the other. In general usage, most musical works can be classified as either artistic or functional with little disagreement.

Both the functional and artistic reasons for music are valid and proper. But the particular reason for the creation of music can affect its character. Dance numbers need a steady beat, for example, and music written to provide fascinating listening shouldn't sound dull or routine. But more on this point in the next chapter.

SOME USES OF MUSIC

Some of the areas in which music functions have briefly been mentioned. Let's examine them more closely. Music is frequently used to promote economic, religious, and social outcomes. For example, the motion-picture maker realizes that the dramatic impact of a scene can be enhanced by the addition of appropriate music. So he has someone write music to augment the mood of the picture at various points. For most movies, the composer of the music is told what the scene is about and how long it is; the music must be exactly the right length. The dramatic and financial success of the movie is most important to the film-maker; he doesn't really care how the music sounds as long as it adds to the effect of the picture.

Music has an important, functional role in nearly every religious ritual in all cultures. As with the motion picture, the purpose of the music is to promote something other than music. In Western civilization (generally Europe and North America), religious music is designed to encourage an attitude of devotion and commitment to religious beliefs.

The proper use of music in religious observances has often caused problems between musicians and clergymen. The musicians want to use the most interesting and worthwhile music that's available. The clergy and church officials want the emphasis to be on the act of worship. They want music that contributes to the service but does not overpower it. In a way, both are right. Good music is desirable, and yet a religious service should not be a concert. For this reason, some fine works of religious music (Beethoven's *Missa Solemnis* and Mozart's *Requiem,* for example) quite properly are seldom performed in their entirety as part of a religious service.

Recently another conflict has emerged, this time between currently popular music and traditional religious music. Some argue that the organ should be replaced by the guitar and that religious music should sound like the other music of the culture.

Those who would like religious music to sound like everyday popular music argue that religion must be *here* and *now.* Traditional music is, to them, only of historical interest; it isn't relevant to today's problems and issues. Their influence can be seen in jazz masses, folk masses, and other attempts to break away from traditional church music.

Others wish to retain a distinct body of church music. Their feeling is that religious music should put the worshiper into the mainstream of belief and practice extending back over the centuries; music thus helps to emphasize the eternal qualities of religious beliefs. A sense of history and heritage comes from singing music that has been sung by members of a faith for 1500 years. Besides, they argue, if you dance to a popular song on Saturday night and then hear the same tune in church on Sunday morning, what will you think about—religious thoughts or memories of the night before? A good question.

Perhaps no resolution to the different points of view is possible. Each, however, is valid; and both affect the creation of music for worship.

Music has a more defined function in non-Western religions. In India, the physical vibrations of musical sound are believed to be involved with the spiritual world. The correct singing of a religious hymn is considered essential not only to the ritual but also to the stability of the universe. In African and American Indian cultures, music is sung to beg for the help of the gods in winning a battle or curing the illness of a chief, as well as on many other occasions.

Music is often used to promote social causes or to aid in social situations. Popular music in the United States has traditionally played a role in the dating process. Sociologists have described and analyzed how the popular songs of the 1950s provided, in a roundabout way, communication and guidance to teenagers in the matter of dating.[1] Not only does the popular song allow the adolescent to play an imaginary role in many possible dating situations; it also offers cues as to what to expect and how to act. Even the teenage "idol" has a role as communicator and object of fancied relationships.

---

[1] Horton, Donald, "The Dialogue of Courtship in Popular Songs," *The American Journal of Sociology* (May 1957), Vol. LXII, No. 6, p. 569. See also James T. Carey, "Changing Courtship Patterns in the Popular Song," *The American Journal of Sociology* (May 1969), Vol. LXXIV, No. 6.

Other examples of socially oriented music are the "protest" and "unity" songs associated with the civil rights movement, labor union meetings, and political movements.[2] Songs are important to these causes in establishing an emotional tone and giving the participants a sense of oneness in the effort.

Recent years have witnessed another development with regard to the popular song—the greatly increased use of music as a means of group identification. Social psychologists have long pointed out the need for young people to have their own clothing styles, hair styles, dances, and music. Such music and dress can be a way of saying, "Look at me—I've grown up!" and "I'm one of you" to other teenagers.

Music has a valuable function in relieving emotions and feelings. About 1000 B.C., David played on a lyre to lift King Saul's depressed spirits (I Samuel 16:23). For many centuries mankind has realized the ability of music to affect people psychologically. The profession of music therapy, which uses music to aid the mentally ill, has developed in recognition of this fact.

What is mentioned here is not just the reaction that normally occurs when music is listened to attentively, but the seeking from music of deeply felt emotional release. It's a matter of why you listen to the music. For example, two persons can watch the same motion picture; one is fascinated and impressed by the drama, and the other has a "good cry." The second person has used the film to unload pent-up feelings.

Some songs are largely for recreation and diversion. Nonsense and humorous songs can be found in many cultures. Sometimes such songs are employed in social events such as square dances in America, or the singing games of children throughout the world. Most camp songs, Broadway musicals, and marching band shows are also largely recreational.

And music is called upon to promote some very non-musical activities. Music is sometimes used in factories to increase production. Even dairy cows give more milk when music is played in the dairy barns. Many supermarkets and banks have music sounding continuously to give their establishments a more leisurely, comfortable atmosphere. The same is true of restaurants and airports.

Religious ritual, emotional well-being, social commentary, recreation—music has an important function in each of these areas.

FOLK AND ETHNIC MUSIC

There is a logical reason for considering ethnic music and functional music together. Generally speaking, folk-ethnic music is functional

---

[2] Denisoff, R. Serge, "Songs of Persuasion: A Sociological Analysis of Urban Propaganda Songs," *Journal of American Folklore,* LXXIX (October 1966), p. 581.

music.[3,4] Usually it is judged not according to musical factors, but rather according to how well it fulfills its task of persuading spirits, accompanying the telling of a historical event, or providing a sense of group solidarity. The music may have considerable beauty in itself, but its effectiveness largely depends on the degree of its success in promoting non-musical situations.

The words "folk" and "ethnic" are not synonymous. "Ethnic" refers to music identified with a particular race or group of people. "Folk" refers only to music actually created or adopted by the common people. A Hungarian peasant song about harvesting hay is a folk song. And because it is characteristic of that country, it is also ethnic music. The *raga* of India is not folk music; it is not the music of the common people but rather of a highly trained musical elite. It is characteristic of India, though, so it is ethnic music. Therefore all folk music is ethnic, but not all ethnic music is folk music.

Characteristics of Ethnic Music

Creation. Contrary to popular belief, there is little "community composition"—music created by a group of people sitting around a campfire or marching into battle. Individuals create ethnic music, just as individuals compose art music. But there the similarity ends. The ethnic music creator is almost always unknown. In fact, the individual might not admit to his accomplishment even if he could be located. In many areas of the world, songs are supposed to be gifts from the gods revealed in dreams or visions or created on "orders" from a supernatural being. Besides, in most cultures people neither care nor remember who was first responsible for providing a song.

Oral tradition. Once created, the music is perpetuated through *oral tradition,* whereby individuals hear the music, remember it, and perform it for others. If no one except the originator likes the song, it passes into oblivion. This tradition insures the survival of only those songs that are liked by the particular culture. Oral tradition also means that the music is subject to many changes. Suppose that three people hear a song and that one of them is very musical. He remembers it clearly, but decides to make a few small "improvements" in it. The second person also remembers the song clearly. But he belongs to another culture, so he adapts the song for use in his culture by setting new words to it and altering its rhythm and melody to sound more like the music he knows. The third person isn't so musical. He forgets half of the song, and inaccurately sings the portion he

---

[3] Nettl, Bruno, *Folk and Traditional Music of Western Continents.* Englewood Cliffs, N.J.: Prentice-Hall, Inc., 1965, p. 12.

[4] Collaer, Paul, and Albert Vander Linden, *Historical Atlas of Music.* trans, Allan Miller. Cleveland: World Publishing Company, 1968, p. 3.

does recall. The result is that what started out as one song is now three songs. And each of these versions will in turn be subjected to the same process of revision and alteration.

Non-literate societies have no system of musical notation. Even in the advanced societies of ancient India and China, only a system of visual cues was developed. Without a system of notation or recordings, music cannot be preserved accurately. For this reason, folk music is ever changing, which may be one of its strengths. It is both old and contemporary; it represents the heritage of the people and also their current tastes.

Relationship with culture. The thorough study of ethnic and folk music is an enormously involved undertaking. The musical aspects are only the beginning. Also, the total culture must be included—language, customs, thought forms, and so on. Ethnic music cannot be separated from the culture in which it exists. For example, among the Yoruba tribe in Africa, each type of drum represents one or several deities, and each deity has its own distinctive rhythm. The rituals can be understood only by a person who knows the particular drums, rhythms, and the appropriate god. Some Indian scholars object to attempts to illustrate *ragas* in musical notation and to discuss their musical aspects. To do so, they maintain, is to leave out the vital spiritual aspects of the music.

Complexity. It's not just a play on words to say that the question of complexity is complex. Complexity involves the number of things that happen in the music. Imagine a series of quarter notes, all on the same pitch, all sounded on the piano, and all played in the same style. Not much happens in this music. If a few different pitches are sounded, the level of complexity is increased. If several different pitches are sounded in unfamiliar patterns, the complexity level is increased further. One could go on and alter the rhythm, change the style of playing the notes, vary the timbre of the notes, and add harmonizing parts—all the ways of manipulating sound that were presented in Chapter 1. With each change that increases the number of happenings in the music, there is a corresponding increase in the level of complexity. More sophistication is required to perform and understand such music.

Most of the folk-ethnic music of the world is less complex than art music. Why? First, most of it is confined to short works, usually songs. True, some African rituals last for hours, but the same music tends to be repeated over and over, with only slight variations. The Indian *raga* is also long, but it is an exceptional kind of music. Without a system of notation, musical works are usually rather shortwinded. The short length allows for little formal or thematic development, something that is important to art music.

When ethnic music does display complexity, such as the rhythm of African music, it tends to do so with only one aspect of the music, leaving the other aspects relatively undeveloped. By contrast, art music, especially in the twentieth century, has involved combinations of pitch, harmony, rhythm, timbre, dynamics, and form.

Characteristics of Non-Western Music

What makes much of the ethnic music found throughout the world different from most of the music familiar to us? Let's start with the rhythm.

Rhythm. As was pointed out in Chapter 1, most of the rhythms in the music of Western civilization have regular patterns of accented and unaccented beats. Measure after measure are linked, something like beads on a string. But much of the world's music exhibits unequal rhythmic patterns. Sometimes the rhythm is very free, especially in epic songs, funeral lamentations, and religious ritual. Much of the rhythm conforms to natural speech patterns, so that the words are not adapted to a given metrical pattern, as is usually true of the music we know. When no regular pattern is necessary, it is easy to make the musical accents match the syllables of the words.

Here is a simple children's playsong from the Ewe tribe in Ghana in West Africa. The accenting of the word "gbasasrã" breaks the regularity of the pattern. This change does not bother the African, because he doesn't think *1 – 2, 1 – 2* as a Western-trained musician does. In the example, single bar lines have been added to show where the stress occurs.

Ewe Children's Song*

Ta-me-lo le, Ee, Go-ta-lo le, Ee, Su ku vi̱wo̱ mi-fa du, gba - sa - srã, gba-sa - srã!

Translation: The Water-crocodile, oh!
The Land-crocodile, oh!
School children ran away!
Swiftly, swiftly.

---

* From A. M. Jones, *Studies in African Music*. London: Oxford University Press, Vol. II, 1959, p. 1. Used by permission.

Melodic structure. Two important differences exist between most Western music and other types of music. One concerns the exact tuning of pitches. The interval of an octave has a solid basis in the physical laws of sound, and it appears throughout the world. The higher of the two pitches is produced by twice as many vibrations as the pitch an octave lower. All other intervals are tampered with in the present system of keyboard tuning, so the splitting of the octave into twelve equal parts was an arbitrary decision by Western musicians. Non-Western music generally does not divide the octave into twelve equal half steps. *Microtones,* which are pitches less than a half step apart, are found in the Near East and Far East and to some extent in Africa. The octave is divided into 22 parts in India; in the Moslem world it has been variously divided into 25, 17, and 15 parts. To a listener unaccustomed to them, microtones can sound hauntingly expressive or just plain out of tune.

The other difference is the type of scale on which the music is based. A *scale* is a series of ascending and descending tones that follow a specific pattern of intervals. Usually the top and bottom notes are one octave apart. A scale with all its pitches sounded in order for an octave or more seldom appears in a piece of music; instead, it is the underlying "formula" for the pitches appearing in a particular section of music. The *major* and *minor* scale patterns are predominant in Western music today, although other seven-note scales called *modes* are favored in folk and popular songs. The most common scale in folk music is the *pentatonic* scale, a five-note pattern that duplicates the pitches of the black keys on the piano keyboard. ("Penta" means "five.") This is the basic scale of Mongolia, Tibet, China, parts of Japan, Indochina, Indonesia, the Philippines, Malaysia, and the Polynesian Islands. It is also heard in the music of the American Indians, the Bantus in central Africa, and those Celts who live along the Atlantic coast. Many other scales are found throughout the world.

Add to the variable tuning of notes and the wide diversity of scales the fact that in some musical systems certain notes can be altered or ornamented by the performer. You can see why genuine ethnic music sounds different to our ears.

Harmony. Most of the world's music contains very little harmony. Some melodies are never intended to have other sounds occurring with them. If harmony is found, it is in one of two forms. One is a *drone,* a single continuous sound lasting throughout a piece. The Scottish bagpipe produces one of the few examples of a drone in Western music. The other type of harmony is produced by adding a duplicate melodic line which moves along strictly parallel to the original melody. This harmony part is often a fourth or fifth below the melody. Sometimes it is a third lower, which is the usual interval in Western harmony.

Form. As was pointed out earlier, most ethnic songs are too brief to allow for much formal development. However, short sections are often

An old man in Java (Indonesia) playing a rebab, *a two-stringed instrument that is often used in native instrumental groups called* gamelan.

arranged in various patterns. One type is the leader-response found in African music. The result is a game of "musical tennis" in which lines of music alternate between a soloist and group. In many parts of the world the music is subjected to a simple variation treatment in which the basic melody is varied slightly and repeated many times.

Improvisation. Almost all art music is written out. The performer's main task is to recreate the notes on the page and adhere to the composer's intent. Not so with most ethnic music. No accurate system for notating music exists outside the West, and most composers of ethnic music are unknown, so the performer is encouraged to create new music of his own as he plays or sings. This art of performing music spontaneously, without the aid of notes, is called *improvisation.* The performer does not often improvise "out of thin air"—that is, without any guidelines at all. Usually he has melodic or rhythmic patterns and performance customs to guide him.

Most ethnic music is geared to the performer, in contrast to art music, in which the ideas of the composer prevail. Improvised performances are never quite the same twice. They reflect the inspiration of the moment, and they tend to sound fresh and vital each time.

Instruments. The thousands of different types of instruments in the world can be grouped into four large categories. One is composed of instruments that are played with the breath. The most common instruments of this type are flutes. Some flutes are played sideways; others are played straight out from the player's mouth and are held like a recorder. A type of flute played by the natives of Oceania and Hawaii is literally blown with the nose. Double reed instruments similar to the oboe and single reed instruments similar to the clarinet are also found. The *pungi* played by the snake charmers in India also belongs in the reed category. A few simple brass instruments are also found in non-literate cultures.

A second classification of instruments involves percussion instruments other than drums. Included in it are bells, chimes, xylophones, rattles, and the Jew's harp.

A third group includes all kinds of drums, which involve a stretched membrane of some kind. Drums are constructed from many materials, including wood, metal, coconut, and gourd, and they come in shapes ranging from the hourglass drums of the Cameroons to friction drums, on which sound is made when a piece of hide is rubbed across the drum skin.

The fourth classification includes all the string instruments. Most of these are plucked—zithers, lyres, and harps, for example—but some are struck with mallets and a few are bowed like a violin.

The instruments of a culture are usually constructed of materials readily available in that culture's area—animal horns or bones, skins, wood, gourds, etc. The availability and complexity of instruments also depends on the knowledge of such crafts as smelting metals and shaping wood. Some folk instruments, such as the *rebab* pictured in this chapter, are not particularly reliable and have a weak tone.

Some Significant Types of Ethnic Music

At this point the discussion moves from a general description of non-Western folk and ethnic music to a specific examination of a few notable types. To keep the chapter within reasonable limits, it is necessary to leave out music from many areas of the world. The topic of ethnic music is so vast that it could occupy many volumes.

Europe. As might be expected, the folk music of Europe resembles Western art music more closely than does other ethnic music, although wide differences can be found within the European continent, especially in isolated rural areas.

One characteristic of European folk music is the singing of different lines of words, each time to the same melody. Such songs are called *strophic*. Some pentatonic scales are encountered, especially in Hungary and eastern Europe, but major and minor scales and modes predominate. The rhythm is metrical, with somewhat more freedom of meter in eastern European music.

The topics found in European folksongs include a greater percentage of epic-narrative tales and love sentiments than do the songs of other cultures. There are some folk hymns and songs revolving around turning points in a person's life such as birth or marriage. The French have songs to urge a child to eat and teach him to count. Songs about agriculture are common, especially in eastern Europe. Dance music is prevalent too. Some of these dances represent events, feelings, or animals.

India. Probably the most sophisticated music outside of Western civilization is found in India. Folk music is not being described here; rather an ethnic music that requires much training for both performer and listener.

Indian music is very much intertwined with religious belief and practice. It began at least a thousand years B.C., and it continues today. Despite pressures from the Near East, the invasions by the Mohammedans a thousand years ago, and the British occupation in the nineteenth and twentieth centuries, it is believed that the music has not changed much since its inception.

At the heart of Indian music is the *raga*. It is a melodic formula somewhat resembling a scale. But it also embraces important Indian religious concepts. They believe its vibrations must be in tune with the universe, and that other arts such as poetry and painting must fit with music into the great cosmic scheme. For example, there are *ragas* that should be performed only in the morning, others only in the evening, others only in the rainy season, and so on. Theoretically, thousands of *ragas* exist, but only about 50 are used frequently. *Ragas* vary in length; the average is about 20 to 25 notes. Two tones tend to stand out in each *raga*, one being a fourth or fifth higher than the other. Here is a *raga* from North India, notated as accurately as possible. The rhythmic values of the notes indicate importance, not length. The very small note heads indicate slides or zigzag figures, and the brackets over the line mark off the phrases.

Raga Miyan-ki-Mallar*

---

* From Kaufmann, Walter. *The Ragas of North India*. Bloomington, Ind.: Indiana University Press, 1968, p. 3. Used by permission.

The next significant element in Indian music is its rhythm, which is built around the *tala*. Each *tala* is a rhythmic cycle of from 3 to 128 beats; most are from 5 to 8 beats long. Each *tala* is divided into smaller groups. A *tala* is not a measure, as was described in the first chapter; it is a pattern. For example, a seven-beat *tala* might be made up of 3 beats + 2 beats + 2 beats. If an Indian musician taps his foot as he plays, it is not a steady tapping but an indication of the unequal divisions of the *tala*. Furthermore, the first beat in a *tala* should not be accented more heavily than the other beats. Like each *raga*, each *tala* is named.

Using the *raga* and *tala* as his guides, the singer-performer improvises as he sings a religious poem from one of the holy books. Because the musical system is so complicated, he has a dazzling array of melodic and rhythmic possibilities—enough to last him for a lifetime. The pleasure for the listener lies in hearing the performer create his own music within the guidelines of the system.

The *raga-tala* improvisations follow a loose form in which the *raga* is introduced, followed by sections that feature the *raga* in different ranges of the voice and instruments. A simple bass pattern of three notes sounds throughout to provide the listener with a constant reminder of the tonal centers of the *raga*. The *tala* pattern is played on a small drum. If several players participate, a flute or oboe or *sitar* can be included. The *sitar* is a complicated string instrument with five melodic strings, two drones, and thirteen more strings that sound in sympathy with the melodic strings. It looks like a large guitar with pegs along the neck of the instrument. It is played on the floor, as are all Indian instruments.

Today in India a prospective musician studies either Western or Indian music. Few musicians know both types. Indian music is often learned from a religious teacher who knows music, a *guru*, who traditionally receives no pay for his lessons. His purpose is to guide the disciple spiritually through the study and performance of the music.

Indian music is one of the very few types that have been able to remain intact despite the influence of Western music. In fact, some of the effects of Indian music have appeared in Western popular music in recent years, making it better known than other types from the Orient. Still, it requires some getting used to for persons raised on Western music. Whatever one's reaction, it certainly cannot be considered a primitive or inferior type of music.

China. China's musical heritage is as old as India's. Because China had a system of writing words (not music), accurate accounts are available about its music throughout its history. Like Indian music, Chinese music was closely related to philosophy and religion. In fact, one early emperor ordered musicians and astrologers to work together in calculating the length of the pipe that was to determine the standard pitch for all music; he wanted his reign to be in harmony with the universe and the supernatural.

Through such investigations the Chinese developed a theoretical system that provided the twelve pitches that appear within the octave in Western music. Although they had more than five pitches, their basic melodic tool was the pentatonic scale, the five-tone pattern described earlier in this chapter.

In addition to an intricate theoretical system, the Chinese developed several exotic instruments. One was a model of a crouching tiger with a serrated ridge or set of wooden slats along its backbone. It was sounded by dragging a bamboo stick across the bumps or slats. Another instrument was a mouth organ with 17 bamboo pipes.

In some periods of China's history, music thrived; in other eras it hardly survived. Much of the music was created for the official court, often for banquets. As with Indian music, folk music is not being described here. A few large orchestras existed in China—a situation rare outside of the West. Many theatrical, opera-like productions were presented also.

Over the years, Chinese opera has developed to include preludes of crashing cymbals, acrobats, female impersonators, and solo songs. Hero roles are sung with a rasping sound, and heroines sing in a high, thin voice. Mastery of Chinese opera style requires years of rigorous training and practice. The lines of music consist of rather short phrases separated by instrumental interludes. A drum maintains a steady rhythm and sections of the music are concluded with a cymbal crash.

In 1911 the last Chinese dynasty fell and the country was declared a republic. The ensuing years have been hard ones for music, largely because of internal strife and repression. Since 1949 the Communist party has controlled the mainland and sophisticated music has been discouraged. More in favor is the unison singing of politically oriented songs such as "Socialism Is Good" and "I'm So Happy on the Collective Farm"—actual titles observed in record catalogs and music collections of about 1962. Some of the Chinese musical tradition is being preserved on Formosa, but the influence of Western music is strongly felt there.

Arabian music. The Arabian world extends 4000 miles from the north coast of Africa (just across the Strait of Gibraltar from Spain) to the borders of Pakistan. Although most Arabs share the same religious faith —Islam—their culture and music have never been well unified. Four main groupings of Arabian music can be identified. One is Persian, which centers in Iran. A second is Arab, centering in Egypt. A third is Andalusian; it exists mostly in North Africa. The fourth is Turkish. To further complicate matters, Arabian music has complicated and confusing music theories that vary from country to country. And when performed, the music often differs from the stated musical theories.

Much music from the Arabian world is vocal and is characterized by a tense, nasal quality. Some call and response between chorus and soloist is found. Accompaniment often consists of hand claps or tambourines— small hoops with a hide stretched over one side and metal jingles in the hoop. Mohammed, the prophet of Islam, did not approve of music in the mosque, so it is restricted in orthodox Islamic worship. A few restrained prayers and chants are "sung" in the mosque, but they are not officially considered to be music, so they are acceptable. The dervish and a few other sects incorporate ecstatic chants into their worship.

In Iran a *gushe,* which is similar to the Indian *raga,* is played. Usually playing a flute, the performer improvises a highly decorated line based on the *gushe.* The rhythm is free and allows him time in which to follow his musical inclinations.

Important Arabian instruments include the *tombak*—a drum in the shape of an hourglass, played with the hand and fingers; the *ud*—a string instrument with a pear-shaped body; and the *rebab*—a direct ancestor of the violin.

Although there are some professional musicians in the Arabian countries, there are few concerts in the Western sense of the word. Cafés are the usual setting for music performances, and one may listen or sip a drink as he wishes. As an added attraction, the more thoughtful numbers may be interspersed with the gyrating female dancers for which the Arabian world is noted. Artistic musical standards are difficult to maintain against such competition, and they seem often to be largely abandoned.

Jewish music in Israel. Because the Jews were for so long separated into minorities throughout the world, their non-religious music has assimilated many regional characteristics. And even the pre-Christian music of the Jews was influenced by both the East and the West. Jerusalem was a crossroads for caravans traveling between the two worlds. It is not unusual for a German Jew to sing a German or Yiddish song, or for an Armenian-Russian Jew to sing a song of his former homeland. The Arabian world, which nearly surrounds Israel, has also had its influence. Many Jews, however, sing Arabian songs in a different style from the one they use for Jewish music.

Jewish religious music has remained rather well unified. Judaism was not so evangelistic as Christianity; it tended to keep its faith within the group, and it seldom incorporated local music into its worship. Its religious music is mostly for prayers and invocations, not anthems such as are found in many Protestant churches. The use and type of music varies somewhat according to the degree of orthodoxy. The more orthodox congregations permit only unaccompanied chanting by cantors, while more liberal congregations often employ non-Jewish instrumentalists and singers to perform some adaptations of music written for Christian worship. The orthodox style is chanting, with a free rhythm and some decorative notes. Some Jewish religious music is similar to Arabian music. A few Jewish melodies have been adapted as hymns in Protestant churches, and Judaic music and worship were very influential in early Christian music.

Since modern Israel was established in 1948, attempts are being made to create new folk traditions to help unify a multi-ethnic nation whose bonds are largely religious and political. New popular songs have been composed about economic and political topics. Arabian tambourines and hourglass drums accompany them, as well as guitars and accordions. Arabian-like scales are often harmonized with Western chords. Like its people, Israel's music is highly cosmopolitan.

Spanish-American music. The term "Spanish-American" includes a wide variety of music. To begin with, the music of Spain itself is immensely varied. It includes the music of the Spanish gypsies and of the Basque people of northern Spain; Arabian influence results from 600 years of occupation by the Moors; and Provençal music has been heavily influenced by France. With the Spanish conquests in the New World, elements of its music were transplanted to the Americas. Here Spanish music became mixed with native Indian music and the music of the blacks, especially in Cuba, Brazil, and the West Indies.

A Peruvian Indian of the Hauncarjo Valley playing an instrument made from animal horns.

In the centuries since the Spanish entered Latin America, their music has been adapted so extensively that it has become impossible in many cases to tell where a particular song came from. Some Spanish dances have been adapted, also. For example, the *bolero* was originally Spanish, but in Cuba its rhythm became more complex. Elements of Spanish-American rhythms appear in jazz. Among other features to carry over from Spanish music into Latin American music are the frequent use of meters having three notes to the beat, the presence of a line moving in parallel thirds with the melody, and melodies with a rather narrow range.

Mexican music is largely Spanish in character, more so than most other Latin American music. Some Mexican Indians have retained their own music, but the Indian influence is not significant in Mexico's music. The Mexicans have a narrative type of song called a *corrido*. Like the English broadside ballad, it relates a happening or tells a story. Instruments play an important role in Mexican music and are sometimes featured in instrumental interludes. The often-heard *mariachi* band consists of from three to twelve players playing violins, guitars, brasses, and other instruments. Some of the band music has a complex rhythmic structure. The name *mariachi* comes from the French word *mariage*, because these musicians once played mainly for weddings.

Spanish-American music enjoys considerable favor in the United States. Much of it, however, is "commercial" music created for nightclubs and cocktail lounges. It is not authentic, and to a musician it is less interesting than the legitimate music of the Spanish-American peoples. Fortunately, some Spanish-American folk songs have been incorporated into the musical heritage of the United States, and Spanish-American people, especially in New York City and the Southwest, have preserved many of their distinctive songs.

Africa South of the Sahara. The areas north of the vast Sahara desert are largely Arabian in character. To the south are the provinces of the Negro peoples, and it is their music that will be discussed here. For the sake of brevity, the term will be shortened to "Africa" for the remainder of this book.

Music for the African is more important, more an integral part of his life, than it is for many of the peoples of the world. Music is called upon to cure illness, appease gods, and celebrate the birth of a baby. It inspires the person who is singing praises to cattle, telling about an elephant hunt, or paddling a canoe either against the current or with it—there is a song for each direction. Some music is sheerly for entertainment and is performed by men whose livelihood comes from their music making. In some tribes there is a small musical elite, usually drummers, who practice their trade from youth. They spend most of their childhood learning how to drum, and they do not perform "publicly" until they are young adults.

An African drummer in Mumbasa.

The Western idea of a performer and a passive group of listeners is unusual in African thought. A musical performance is truly a participatory event in which everyone sings, claps, or dances. Furthermore, the African musician wants his music to have an impact on the listeners. He doesn't particularly care whether they consider his music "beautiful," but he does want them to share his feelings. Objective contemplation, no; involvement, yes!

Music is even used for signaling. Sometimes the drum rhythms resemble a simplified Morse code, but the signals are also related to the pitch structure of the language. Many African languages are tonal. A sound, *ba* for example, takes on a different meaning depending on the pitch level at which it is spoken. As many as four pitch levels are found in some languages. A drummer then approximates the pitch of the word he is signaling by using different-sized drums or hitting a log drum at different places. Again, the signaling is done by specialists, and the signals are usually rather brief and to the point, such as "Help! Our village is being attacked!"

The form found in African music was mentioned briefly earlier in this chapter. It is a short unit of music that is repeated, varied slightly, or alternated with group response. The "call-and-response" technique between leader and group is central to African music. It assures the participation of which Africans are so fond. The music continues for as long as the ritual requires, or in the case of non-ritualistic music, as long as the performer and audience wish.

Improvisation is common in African styles. The variations of the short musical unit are improvised. Not only does the leader improvise; in some tribes, the group members improvise simultaneously among themselves, so that a variety of music is being sounded at the same time. More on the significance of this shortly.

Melodically, African music is not far different from Western music. The underlying scale contains seven different notes—the same patterns described in Chapter 1. But more use is made of microtones and the pentatonic scale. Glides and other ornaments are incorporated into the singing, and this sometimes disguises the true pitch of a note.

The main feature of African music is its rhythm. The fact that it does not follow a regular pattern has already been mentioned. The Ewe children's song provided a simple example of the rhythmic freedom of African music. A feature of West African music is the musician's ability to maintain a steady tempo for minutes or even hours. Western musicians keep a generally steady tempo, but they make slight fluctuations in it. The exactness of the tempo in African music makes it easier to emphasize accents and rhythmic patterns.

A more spectacular feature of African rhythm is the sounding of two or more rhythms at the same time. The term for this is *polyrhythm*. If one person taps the rhythm of a waltz while another taps the rhythm of a march, they are producing polyrhythm. In African music the sounding of different rhythms at the same time occurs most often in drumming, but it appears in other types of music, too. Some works contain as many as six different rhythmic parts sounding simultaneously. The effect is truly exciting. It would be interesting to know how the African performer conceives of his polyrhythmic music. Perhaps he regards each part as being independent but played at the same time as the other parts, or maybe he thinks of each part as fitting into an overall structure. When the music is improvised, however, the player probably cannot spend much time thinking about an overall composition.

African music has some simple types of harmony and counterpoint. One type is the parallel movement created by a melodic line and its duplicate. There are also some two-part rounds. These rounds may have developed from instances in which either the leader or chorus was overly anxious and began its part before the other had finished. Accompaniment is evident in African music. Instruments such as the xylophone or harp sometimes accompany a melody by persistently repeating a short melodic phrase that contrasts with the melody.

African music is interesting not only in itself, but also because of the influence it has had on American music. American art music is presented in Chapter 16, and American folk and popular music are discussed in the next section of this chapter.

American Folk Music

The English heritage. Since English is the language of the United States, it is not surprising that the main source of its folk music is the British Isles. Many songs were imported intact from Britain, and many other songs have been patterned after British types.

The most significant type of British folk song is the ballad. It is a narrative song of 5 to 20 or more stanzas. Traditionally the ballad had a common iambic meter and stanzas of four lines, in which a four-foot-line alternates with a three-foot line:

> There lived a wife at Usher's Well,
>   And a wealthy wife was she;
> She had three stout and stalwart sons,
>   And sent them o'er the sea.

Ballad stories are often tragic. In "The Wife at Usher's Well," the sons die at sea. Their mother wishes to see them again, so they return one night as ghosts, only to leave in the morning as soon as the rooster crows. Some ballads have happy endings, and some are humorous. In "The Farmer's Crust Wife," the wife is taken to hell by the devil, but she is so ornery that the devil returns her to her husband.

In a ballad the narrator-singer is a third person relating a tale, so he is not involved. The music often reflects this by a calm and detached attitude.

In older ballads the music often reveals a seven-note modal scale, not the major-minor system of today. The rhythm largely depends on the text, which means that a regular pattern is followed. Much of the ballad singing in the United States is unaccompanied, although in Kentucky an accompaniment is taken for granted and is provided by a banjo, guitar, or dulcimer. The dulcimer looks like a long, flat violin with three strings. It is laid on the player's lap and plucked with a quill. Two of its strings produce a drone, which was a common feature of ballad singing.

An interesting type of ballad is called a *"broadside."* The name comes from the old English practice of printing ballads on large sheets of paper called "broadsides," which were then sold in the streets. Broadsides were often about current events and famous personalities. About 200 broadsides were circulated in the United States. They dealt with war, love, crime, and a few are humorous. The poetry is not always the best, and sometimes the situations are rather cliché, but broadsides did reflect the feeling of the people.

The ballad style is evident in many American folk songs associated with occupations—sailors, cowboys, lumberjacks, miners, farmers, and so on. The ballad's influence can also be observed in American religious hymns. It has been estimated that most songs in the English heritage descended from about 55 tunes or "tune families."[5]

Much English folk music from the Elizabethan period is better preserved in the United States than in England. In the Appalachian mountains of Tennessee, Kentucky, and the Carolinas, some people for generations have been largely isolated from contemporary American influences. Their speech patterns, for example, are authentically old English. John Jacob Niles and others have uncovered a wealth of early English music, retained and preserved intact by these descendents of early English settlers in America.

Non-British music also came to the United States with various immigrant groups. In a few cases it was incorporated into the culture and stands along with the British style music: *Du, du liegst mir im Herzen* is a German song which has been adopted into the culture; *Alouette* is a French-Canadian example; and *Chiapanecas* (sometimes called "The Mexican Clapping Song") is a Spanish-American contribution that is clapped and stomped at many major league ballparks. Some of these songs have had new words put to the music. The Pennsylvania German song "Marjets wann ich uffschteh" became "Go Tell Aunt Rhody the Old Grey Goose Is Dead."[6] Unfortunately, much non-British music was lost in the New World.

American Indian music. The functional nature of American Indian music is apparent in the names given to the ritual procedures. As the titles imply, a sun dance or rabbit dance is created for a specific purpose. Indian love songs and lullabies are also functional, of course.

Traditionally, Indian instruments consisted of a variety of drums, usually played with sticks. Sometimes kettledrums were filled with water before playing or the drum head was moistened to achieve the pitch desired by the performer—a practice that indicates some musical sophistication. Many types of rattles were developed. Several types of flutes were played, especially by the males, who performed love music on them to impress their chosen young women.

The Indian population was never large (not more than one or two million in all of North America), and it was spread over a vast land area. As a result, musical styles differed widely among the various tribes, a

---

[5] Bayard, Samuel P., "Prolegomena to a Study of the Principal Melodic Families of British-American Folk Songs," *Journal of American Folklore*, LXIII (1950), pp. 1–44.

[6] *Pennsylvania Songs and Legends*. George Korson, ed., Philadelphia, 1949.

fact that is also true in Africa. The Indians of the Pacific Northwest and the Eskimo area developed music characterized by non-strophic forms, complex rhythms, and small melodic intervals. The Indians of California and the extreme southwest sing with a harsh vocal sound. The songs consist of two or more separate sections that are repeated, alternated, and interwoven. A third general area includes Utah, Nevada, and the interior of northern California. In this region the singing is more relaxed in style, and songs are made up of paired phrases, with each phrase repeated. The fourth type of Indian culture is distinguished more by language than geography. It consists of the Navaho, Apache, and some western Canadian tribes. Their melodies have a wide range, and male singers freely perform in the high "false" voice. The Pueblo and plains Indians display more tension in singing and use a two-part song form. The Indians in the eastern and southern parts of the United States feature responsorial singing—shouts tossed back and forth between leader and group. Elaborate forms are evident, and phrases recur in the music.

Indian music has not had a significant effect on other American music for two reasons. One: most Indians do not live in close proximity to non-Indians. They have lived apart on reservations, and their music tends to remain there. Two: Indian music is quite different from Western music. In some respects it is more oriental than Western. When one culture incorporates music from another, the two styles are likely to be somewhat similar. Some change, but not too much, is accepted in music. In the few instances in which Indian music has been incorporated into American compositions, it has been changed and "westernized" freely.

Occupational songs. An important contribution to America's folk music heritage can be heard in songs about various occupations. In many cowboy songs, the text and music are often tinged with loneliness and melancholy, reflecting the fact that life on the frontier was not an easy or particularly happy existence. Some of the cowboy tunes originally had other words before being adapted by the cowboy. Such adaptations are not unusual in folk music.

The development of the railroad provided another source for occupational songs. Some of these songs are about the men who worked the railroads ("Drill Ye Tarriers, Drill"), some describe famous personalities ("John Henry" and "Casey Jones"), and others tell about trains themselves ("The Wabash Cannonball"). Sailors have provided their share of occupational songs, as well. But today's computers and assembly lines don't encourage the development of song literature. One doesn't sing to a computer, and the assembly line noise drowns out all other sounds. So the occupational song may become a thing of the past.

Afro-American music. It is difficult to determine which aspects of Afro-American music were transplanted from Africa and which were developed in America. In a complex and pluralistic society, the causes of a cultural amalgamation are hard to assess. In any case, some of the African's rhythmic ideas, his call-and-response patterns, love of instruments, and improvisation are now a part of American music. The African brought with him something perhaps more important than any technical features: his great use of and interest in music, and his musical attitudes, especially the desire to achieve an impact and involve the listener in his efforts.

Haiti in the Caribbean, the Guianas on the north coast of South America, and northern Brazil have large Negro populations. Because of the isolation of these people from the mainstream of society, their music has remained strongly African. The mutual adaptation that can be noted between African and Western music has occurred to the greatest extent in the United States. Cuba, Jamaica, and Trinidad are next in the amount of musical interaction observable between African styles and their own styles.

The African influence has been felt most in the area of performance. The spiritual is a good example of this fact. Actually, the spiritual, which is so widely associated with the American black, is largely borrowed from southern rural whites.[7] The text and melodic ideas are identical with the "white spirituals." The difference between the two kinds of spirituals is in the way they are sung. The black spiritual is more rhythmic and stresses call-and-response, with some improvisation; the white version is more lyric and polished. The performance differences are also apparent in other types of Negro folk songs: work songs, love songs, ballads, and lullabies. Some were originated by blacks, but many were simply taken from the American culture. The songs may look similar on paper, but in performance the Afro-American qualities become evident.

Another performance area in which the influence of African music is evident is in the greater variety of singing style. African singers produce more varied sounds when singing. Some tones are purposely harsh and raucous in order to imitate animals; some are tense and some are throaty, but generally the style is relaxed and warm.

The song used to accompany work is definitely the property of the Negro. Songs sung while working are not common in Western music, except in sea chanties. The text of some of these songs is not related directly to the job at hand; often the words only supply a pleasant accompaniment to labor.

As in Africa, instruments play an important role in Afro-American folk music. Some of the instruments are derived from Europe, while others are intended to duplicate sound effects. Included in the latter category are washboards, pans, cowbells, bottles, various clappers, and the gutbucket (an inverted washtub with a rope pulled through it and connected to a stick; the pitch is varied according to the tension of the rope).

---

[7] Wilgus, D. K., *Anglo-American Folksong Scholarship Since 1888.* Brunswick, N.J.: Rutgers University Press, 1959, pp. 344–364.

JAZZ

The roots of jazz reach back to the Negro's African heritage. But other elements also influenced the course of this new style: minstrel-show music, work songs, field hollers, funeral marching bands, blues, French-Creole and Spanish-American music, and more recently, West Indian music. Jazz did not develop as a musical form until about the turn of the twentieth century. Basin Street in New Orleans is traditionally considered its birthplace, and it was brought to public attention by the funeral procession. On the way back from the cemetery the band played its tunes in a way quite different from when they marched to the gravesite. They shifted the emphasis from the strong to the weak beat, and the players launched into a decorated version of the melody. When Storyville, New Orleans' red-light district, was closed down in 1917, many jazz musicians lost their jobs and sought work in other cities. Jazz moved up the Mississippi River through Memphis and St. Louis to Chicago and the rest of the United States.

Two types of Afro-American folk music existed with early jazz and later merged with it. One of these was *ragtime.* It featured the piano, but other instruments sometimes appeared with it. The music sounds like a lively march with a decorated right-hand part. Early musicians associated with ragtime are Scott Joplin in Sedalia, Missouri, and Ben Harvey, who published his *Ragtime Instructor* in 1897.

The other folk type involved with early jazz was the folk *blues.* Its musical characteristics will be discussed shortly. Some of the most famous names associated with blues are Lead Belly, a Texas convict whose real name was Huddie Ledbetter, W. C. Handy, who was known for his "Memphis Blues" and "St. Louis Blues," and Ferdinand "Jelly Roll" Morton, whose first published blues appeared in 1905—the "Jelly Roll Blues."

Like folk music, jazz was created by mostly untutored musicians who could not have written down what they played and sang even if they'd wanted to. But jazz is different in two respects. It has sprung from the cities rather than the fields and forests; it is an urban form of music. And for most people, it is a spectator experience. Usually only a few people perform, although listeners may contribute a little hand clapping and foot stomping.

But what is jazz? It has several elements.

Melody. The most significant feature of jazz melodies is the *blue note.* These notes are derived from an altered version of the regular major scale. The blues scale merely lowers the third, fifth, and seventh steps. Many times the performer shifts around between the regular note and its lower counterpart as if he were searching for a sound. And in truth, he may be. The blue-note interval is an approximation of a microtone, roughly half of a half step in this case. The African heritage is the influence behind its use in jazz. Blue notes are a source of unique and subtle color. Their effect in jazz is further enhanced by the fact that the chord in the harmony usually contains the particular note at its conventional pitch while the lowered blue note appears simultaneously in the melody. This combination creates an interesting and characteristic dissonance.

Harmony. Early jazz harmony was as conservative as any church hymn. The typical chords were the same three that form the backbone of traditional tonal harmony: tonic, dominant, and subdominant. More recently, modernistic versions of jazz have employed the advanced harmonic idioms of Debussy, Bartók, and Stravinsky. The appeal of jazz, however, does not lie primarily in its harmony.

Rhythm. Here is one of the most unique features of jazz. Although its meter is nearly always two beats per measure, with irregular meters occurring only rarely, the jazz musician employs an endless variety of syncopated patterns and rhythmic figures over this regular pulse. *Syncopation*—the redistribution of accents so that the rhythmic patterns do not conform to the meter as the listener expects—is the lifeblood of jazz.

Jazz rhythms do not fit well into the traditional divisions of time according to sixteenths, eighths, and quarters. The jazz musician performs rhythm with small deviations of timing and accent that cannot be adequately conveyed through notation. He even makes slight alterations of the patterns of conventional notation when he reads them. In some styles of jazz, the accent pattern is almost the reverse of that found in traditional music. These deviations in rhythm are one reason that explains why well-trained serious musicians often do not achieve an authentic jazz sound.

Timbre. The basic tone color sought by jazz instrumentalists is an imitation of the Negro singing voice: a bit breathy with a little *vibrato* (rapid and slight variance of pitch on a tone). Certain instruments, therefore, have become associated with this idiom. The saxophone was invented by a Frenchman named Adolphe Sax. It was intended to be a concert instrument, but it was taken up by the jazz musician because it can produce the slightly breathy quality desired. Besides, it is not difficult to play, and it has a big tone. Mutes—metal or fiber devices inserted in or over the bell to change the tone quality—are often used on brass instruments, and their names are as distinctive as the sounds they produce: "cup," "wah-wah," and "plunger," the latter of which can be duplicated by the end of a rubber sink plunger. Many jazz trumpeters use a particular type of mouthpiece that gives them a shriller sound and makes it easier to play high notes. In jazz style the clarinet is played in a manner that produces a saxophone-like quality. Thus a jazz clarinet's tone differs from the orchestral clarinet's tone. The tone qualities of other instruments also vary according to their use in orchestral or jazz playing.

Some jazz timbres, like the bongo and conga drums and the Cuban cowbell, are from Afro-Cuban sources, while others, such as the Chinese woodblock, cymbals, and vibraphone, have an oriental flavor.

Form. Jazz has no form that is applicable to all its styles. Generally it is a series of stanzas based on the chords to a popular tune. The form of the blues is more definite. A line is sung and immediately repeated, and then a third line concludes the stanza, making an *a a b* structure. Sometimes the singer does not sing all the way through a section, and an instrumentalist will fill in with a short *break*.

Text. The metrical scheme of the text is often one of the standard poetic meters. It is not uncommon to find iambic pentameter in verses of the blues. The texts are seldom of literary significance, but some are quite moving.

Improvisation. Improvisation is a fundamental component of jazz. Traditionally, jazz is not written down; it is made up on the spot. This improvisation is what gives it its ever-fresh quality. Sometimes people confuse a "torchy" or "hot" popular song with jazz. A popular song does not become jazz until it is improvised upon.

What happens is this. The musicians agree that they will play a certain popular song in a certain key. They also agree generally on the order of each player's featured section. Then the first player, while keeping in mind the harmonies and melody of the song, improvises a part that reflects the rhythmic and melodic characteristics of jazz. This procedure is followed as each player takes his turn. On the final chorus, all play together in simultaneous, semi-accidental counterpoint. It is like an improvised musical conversation. Throughout the number, no player knows exactly what the others will do, but he follows his musical instinct and fits in with whatever happens. Nor is he entirely certain what he himself will do, because each time he takes a "ride" on the number, he will play it somewhat differently.

Sometimes there seems to be so much improvisation that the piece is no longer identifiable. Why does that happen? Because the player improvises on the basic harmony as well as the melody. For example, if the song starts on the tonic chord, as it usually does, and if the piece is in the key of C, then the notes of the tonic chord will be C E G. The improviser may play any or all of these three notes. But he can also play tones that are nonharmonic in relation to that chord. In other words, he can weave other tones around the notes of the chord. That is why the melody of the popular song may no longer be recognizable in the new embroidery of sound.

The particular song may get lost for another reason. Most popular songs have such simple chord patterns that there is little difference between the chords of one popular song and another. When the melody is being improvised upon, the harmony is often not distinguishable from that of other songs. And the rhapsodic nature of jazz improvisation also leads to a sameness of mood that makes it more difficult to distinguish the basic song.

Several jazz features are illustrated in the example on page 48. It is a trumpet solo by Bubber Miley, recorded in 1927 while he was playing with Duke Ellington's band. In it you can see blue notes (called minor third, flat fifth, and minor seventh on the coded chart), growls (indicated by the lines through the note stems), and slides (indicated by "gliss," or a waving line). The underlying chords are identified in large letters above the melody. Syncopation occurs in measures 5, 7, 8, 10, 12, 13, 14, 15, 19, 20, 22, and 23.

Black and Tan Fantasy*

Blue Notes: a = minor third
              b = flat fifth
              c = minor seventh
              d = minor ninth
              e is a bent tone which goes from a flat octave through the minor seventh to the sixth degree, anticipating the return to B flat.

The Development of Jazz

The 1920s saw the real emergence of jazz, which was given impetus in 1918 by Joe "King" Oliver's famous Creole Jazz Band in Chicago. Other musicians soon became prominent: Paul Whiteman, whose band presented the first jazz concert in 1924, featuring the premier of George Gershwin's *Rhapsody in Blue;* Bessie Smith, the famous blues singer; Fletcher Henderson and his band; Bix Beiderbecke, who started "white"

---

* Schuller, Gunther, *Early Jazz.* New York: Oxford University Press, 1968, p. 331. Used by permission of Belwin-Mills Music, Inc.

King Oliver's Creole Jazz Band, 1923. Standing, L. to R.: Baby Dodds, Honoré Dutrey, Bill Johnson, Louis Armstrong, Johnny Dodds, Lil Hardin. Seated: Joe King Oliver. (The Record Changer)

Benny Goodman's orchestra at the height of its fame, 1937, seen here in one of its Hollywood motion picture appearances. The rhythm section comprises Harry Goodman, bass; Jess Stacy, piano; Allan Reuss, guitar; and Gene Krupa, drums. Trumpets are, L. to R.: Harry James, Ziggy Elman, Chris Griffin; trombones: Murray McEachern, Red Ballard; saxophones: Vido Musso, Hymie Schertzer, Arthur Rollini, George Koenig. (Metronome)

Louis Armstrong in about 1940.

jazz with his cornet and the band called the "Wolverines"; and the notable Louis Armstrong, who began his music making as a boy in a New Orleans waif band. Through his trumpet playing and vocal renditions, Armstrong has had considerable influence on the basic sound and style of jazz.

The prevailing style in the 1920s was *dixieland.* It is characterized by a strong upbeat, a meter of two beats to the measure, and certain tonal and stylistic qualities that are impossible to notate. It has a "busy" sound, since there is simultaneous improvisation by perhaps 4 to 7 players. The result is a type of "accidental" counterpoint that is held together only by the song's basic harmony and the musical instincts of the players. The presence of simultaneous improvisation in both African music and jazz can hardly be a coincidence. Dixieland style is often described as "hot"; it's fast, furious, and usually loud.

During the depression of the 1930s the hiring of bands became prohibitively expensive. So pianists enjoyed increasing popularity, especially as they developed a jazz piano style called *boogie-woogie.* It features a persistently repeated melodic figure in the bass. The musical term for such repeating figures is *ostinato,* a word that comes from the Italian word for "obstinate" or "stubborn." Usually the boogie-woogie ostinato consists of eight notes per measure, which explains why this type of music is sometimes called "eight to the bar." Over the continuous bass the pianist plays trills, octave tremolos, and other melodic figures.

The *swing era* in jazz lasted from 1935 to about 1950. It featured intricate arrangements and big bands of about 17 players, under the leadership of such musicians as Benny Goodman, Count Basie, and Duke Ellington. It was also the era of the featured soloist—Gene Krupa, Fats Waller, and Tommy Dorsey, to name a few. Other notable figures from the period include Artie Shaw, Harry James, Glenn Miller, Coleman Hawkins, and Fletcher Henderson. Musically, swing has four beats to the measure and rhythms with a "bounce." The swing era was one in which the audience danced. Its "concert halls" were such places as the Roseland Ballroom in New York and California's Hollywood Palladium.

Following World War II there emerged a style called *bebop*, or more commonly, *bop*. It was developed chiefly by Charlie "Bird" Parker and Dizzy Gillespie, who once defined the term by saying that in bop you go *Ba*-oo *Ba*-oo *Ba*-oo instead of *Oo*-ba *Oo*-ba *Oo*-ba. What he was describing was the nearly continuous syncopation that occurs in bop. It also features dissonant chords and freely developed melodies. Often the performers play in unison at the octave instead of presenting the traditional improvised counterpoint. In bop, the fifth degree of the scale is lowered, which is a carry-over of the blue notes discussed earlier. The bass drum does not sound all the time—a change from earlier styles. Instead, the string bass is given the responsibility for keeping the beat. Bop bands were much smaller than the bands of the swing era.

Duke Ellington in 1943.

Stan Kenton was the leader of *progressive* jazz, which is characterized by big bands and highly dissonant chords. In a sense, the progressive style is an updated, intellectual version of the swing style that prevailed about fifteen years earlier. With Miles Davis jazz turned toward a "cool" style, still intellectual and well-ordered, but performed by much smaller groups. Charlie Mingus, Ornette Coleman, and John Coltrane led a movement toward *free form* jazz. No longer was improvisation held together by the harmony; all restraints were removed.

Over the years jazz has become more of a "listener's" type of music, in contrast to its early history. Gone is much of jazz's image as a "music of the people." It has "grown up" in the sense that it is not always played just for fun, at least not by many jazz musicians. It is now serious business, performed by musicians who have studied Stravinsky and Bartók. Jazz represents the rediscovery of the art of improvising, which was largely neglected after the time of Bach and Mozart. Perhaps it was a better counterbalance to the deadly seriousness of nineteenth-century music than were the arty, chic attempts at ridicule propounded by Satie and his followers, which will be described in Chapter 15. Jazz has greatly enriched the world of music.

THE CURRENT SCENE

Writing about current developments in popular music is somewhat risky. One is so close in time to what is going on that a sense of perspective is impossible. And even the necessary terminology suffers from a lack of clear definition. The terms "rock" or "soul music" vary in meaning from person to person, city to city, and social group to social group. But the subject is too important to ignore.

One of the most striking features of the current musical scene is the diversity, what sociologists call "pluralism." No single type of music predominates. Rock has been in the headlines for about 15 years, but during many of those years non-rock groups and music styles enjoyed greater record sales (if that can be considered a measure of public popularity). For example, Herb Alpert's Tijuana Brass and Simon and Garfunkel have often surpassed the more newsy Beatles and Rolling Stones. Nor should the country-western music centered in Nashville be overlooked; its share of attention in the popular music world is significant. Existing with the many types of rock and country-western music is the more staid popular music of Lawrence Welk; during his long tenure on television, many a more-talked-about performer has come and gone. To the types of music already mentioned, add the soul music of the black people; the folk styles revived by groups such as the New Christy Minstrels (who deliberately adopted the name of a nineteenth-century folk group); the protest songs of Bob Dylan,

Joan Baez and others; the big band style of Buddy Rich; and the rather sophisticated songs of Burt Bacharach—you can see why the word "pluralism" applies to popular music today.

As if the many styles were not enough, they overlap and influence one another. For example, rock is the offspring of country-western and rhythm and blues. In turn, rock has inspired the creation of further varieties such as "rockabilly" (rock + hillbilly) and soul music. Delineations of style are further complicated by performance customs. For example, a rock tune may be recorded by a performing star of the more traditional pop type, and his version is hardly rock at all. The result of this overlapping is a kind of musical "chop suey"—pluralistic chop suey.

A second point that is noteworthy about the current musical scene is the importance of music in the lives of people, especially young persons. Increasing numbers of people are using music as a means of expressing themselves. Sometimes this expression takes the form of singing while accompanying oneself on a guitar, no matter how simply. Sometimes it consists of singing along in an audience. Sometimes it means just listening to certain songs because they say something the person feels. Simple instruments such as the mandolin, ukulele, accordion, and guitar have a long history of acceptance among college students, and their popularity has never seemed to be higher. People seem increasingly impelled to sing about their frustrations, their hopes, and their beliefs.

A thorough analysis of the causes for and uses of rock and popular music would take us out of the field of music and into the areas of sociology and psychology, for the subject is as complex as American society itself. Because music is such a vital part of people's lives, it is inevitable that the current music reveals concern over matters as diverse and serious as war, race relations, drugs, sex, religion, love, and the search for personal identity.

A third significant aspect of popular music is the sheer economic size of it. The amount of money spent for recordings and record playing equipment, musical instruments, radio and television shows, and printed music is immense. The fact that big money is involved encourages heated competition and some dishonesty in the business. Some of the songs are prurient or anti-social. Sometimes drug use or sex acts are sung about explicitly, or in *double entendres* or in words that only the "in" crowd knows. Some performers put on a show for their audiences, complete with denunciations of materialism, after which they toss aside their wigs and garish clothes, get into their expensive automobiles, and drive to their luxurious homes. Even the sounds that come from many of the recordings are not genuine. Mistakes are spliced out, resonance is increased by the addition of reverberation, and the voices of unknown performers are sometimes dubbed in as substitutes for "name" performers. The singer and the accompanying performers often don't record together; the sound engineers combine the music from two different days' recordings. Payola (paying discs jockeys to push certain recordings) is not as open as it was in the early 1960s, but it still occurs in some situations.[8] Weekend vacations, expensive liquor, and pretty girls have largely replaced cash. It's a business without any consumer safeguards.

A fourth feature of the current popular music scene is some fascinating music. True, much of today's popular music will enjoy only a brief life and soon pass into oblivion, a fact that is also true of much of the art music being created today. But some of the music that is currently popular will be picked up by composers ten, forty, or a hundred years from now and be rewritten or stylized into art music. Bach did this with the bourrée and Stravinsky has done it with ragtime, so there is no reason to think that it won't happen again. Some of today's pop music is interesting and worthwhile, and can stand on its own merits without hard-sell promotion. Groups such as the New York Rock and Roll Ensemble, and Blood, Sweat and Tears have achieved sounds that are different and have musical quality. No longer is it possible to talk about a "stock" tune or a "stock" arrangement, as was possible for the past several decades.

Today's popular music is world-conscious to a degree that no one could have imagined a decade ago. Although raga rock isn't authentic Indian music, it certainly isn't standard popular music either. Influences from Africa, Asia, South America, or traditional Western European art and folk music can be found in a number of popular songs. The possibilities offered by electronic instruments are being explored also. Although some current popular pieces are trite and commercial, more of them are fresh and interesting than has been true in a long, long time.

---

[8] Syndicated article. Bell-McClure Syndicate, January, 1970. Based on interview with Jerry Fonarow, recording musician and author of *Coming of a God.*

Music as a
Fine Art

3

In one sense, music is music. It is all some type of organized sound, and it has rhythm, timbre, dynamics, form, and usually pitch. To this extent, there is no difference between functional music and art music. However, differences appear in the complexities of the rhythm, timbre, and other factors. The increased level of sophistication with which sounds are organized in art music is the result of fundamental differences in the very reason for the existence of the music. Therefore, some basic philosophical and psychological matters need to be explored. A logical place to start is with the word "aesthetics" and some of its ramifications.

MUSIC AND AESTHETICS

As a branch of philosophy dealing with beauty, aesthetics can be intellectually demanding. But aesthetics can be understood in a practical sense, too, and in a way that will be helpful to someone who wishes to understand music better. In fact, aesthetic experiences are common. What is a person doing when he stands and looks at the graceful shapes of clouds glowing in the sunset? He is stopping to enjoy the view and to contemplate its meaning *for the pleasure, satisfaction, and enjoyment of doing so.* He does not gaze at this beauty in order to ensure his survival, to earn money, to improve himself physically, or to solve a problem. In terms of mere existence, viewing a sunset is a senseless and unnecessary action. Contemplating the sunset, however, is an *aesthetic* experience—that is, something experienced and valued for its own sake. The shapes of the clouds, the reddish hues, the silhouettes of objects against the darkening sky are studied for no other reason than the experience of seeing them and the enjoyment and meaning they give the viewer.

Aesthetic experiences seem to rise above ordinary, everyday events. They touch the imagination and lift the spirit, if one is but sensitive to them. Take as an example this passage from the book of Isaiah.

> For you shall go out in joy,
>   and be led forth in peace;
> the mountains and the hills before you
>   shall break forth into singing,
> and all the trees of the field
>   shall clap their hands.

Certainly these lines are not meant literally. Rather the poet is telling the people how they will feel when God delivers them from Babylon. The poet could have said "You will leave feeling very happy"; the message is there, in even more clear and concise form than in the book of Isaiah. But how much more stirring it is, and how much more effective, to invoke some poetic imagination! The Biblical version has rhythm, beauty, and color that attract and please. It is a joy to read.

One quick, easy definition of aesthetics is that it is the study of beauty. This definition is only partially true, depending upon how the word "beauty" is understood. Frequently it is used superficially to mean "pretty," a word that connotes something pleasing to the eye or ear but without much substance. If this were all that beauty meant, then the best music would be that which contained the prettiest and least offensive sounds. Instead of the exciting, powerful works of Beethoven and Brahms, there would be only sweet, flimsy, and innocuous little tunes. Fortunately, Beethoven and Brahms wrote music of such significance that it has captivated generations of listeners.

Aesthetic, artistic experiences call for thought, contemplation, cognition, reflection. That is why a recreational experience such as riding a roller coaster or a sheerly physical one such as standing under a cold shower is not aesthetic. The aesthetic experience involves getting outside oneself and contemplating the object.

What's the difference between art music and functional music?

Aesthetic music exists for the contemplative value it offers the listener; functional music exists to achieve a wide variety of non-musical goals. Notice the distinction that Carl Belz draws between "rock and roll" and art music in his book *The Story of Rock*.

> In the early days of the *American Bandstand* television show, for instance, a panel of three or four teenagers periodically reviewed newly released records. The record was played, the audience danced, and a discussion of the song's merits followed. This discussion invariably contained remarks such as, "It's got a great beat . . . I'll give it an 80," or, "You can really dance to it . . . I'll give it an 85." The panelists never talked about the artistic properties of the record: the way the song was structured, the relation between its structure and meaning, its manipulations of the medium, the implications of its content, or any of the kinds of issues that are central to a meaningful statement about a work of fine art.[1]

There is another important difference between art music and functional music. Most of us do not consider them in the same way, and we shouldn't. There are types we don't think about deeply or listen to carefully, just as there is reading matter that we don't read seriously. The comic strips in the daily newspaper and the paperback murder mysteries bought at the drugstore are not read as thoughtfully as a Faulkner novel or a Shakespeare play. Sometimes, even the person who admires and likes Faulkner's and Shakespeare's works wants to relax and read something simple and undemanding. There's nothing wrong with that, and there's nothing inconsistent about liking both art and popular music—for different reasons.

The fact that music is used for a variety of purposes can be seen in the different situations in which music is heard. Mozart piano concertos are miserably out of place at school dances, and most popular dance music (ballet excepted) is out of its element in a symphony concert. One doesn't listen analytically to the thematic development of the latest hit song, anymore than one sips a drink and converses during a concert. The panelists on *American Bandstand* did an adequate job of assessing the type of music they were evaluating.

The third important difference between the two types of music is probably a result of the one just mentioned. There is a correlation between the type of music and its worth in terms of listening for aesthetic reasons. Generally (but by no means always), "music for listening" is more worthwhile to listen to than "music for social dancing" or "music for protesting." Why? Because "music for listening" must make it on its own; it has to be interesting and satisfying without being able to "ride along" on its social message or danceable beat. The musical quality of the protest

---

[1] New York: Oxford University Press, 1969. Page 7.

song or dance number is not the main consideration. The situation is very different with a sonata or art song. Seldom is there a social message in such music, and almost never does anyone attempt to dance to it. It is not unusual for a composer to pore over a symphony or opera for months or even years in order to make it just what he wants. By contrast, hundreds of popular songs are turned out each year; and in jazz and several of its offspring, the music is largely made up on the spot.

Because art music generally offers greater aesthetic rewards, it is the type that receives the greater share of attention in music courses. That is why most of this book is devoted to art music. It is the music that merits close attention on its own, a point that's brought out in an exchange between Lucy and Schroeder in this "Peanuts" cartoon.

There is another reason for studying art music: it is the type of music people usually know the least about. Even if there were no instruction in music in the schools and colleges, most people would become familiar with the popular music of the day. As in the case of learning to ride a bicycle, most popular music (there are, of course, some exceptions) is simple enough so that little instruction is needed. Also, it is ever-present on the radio and in other places. But just as one needs instruction in something as complex as flying an airplane, one needs training in understanding sophisticated works of music. Mere exposure to art music is not enough, even if there were many opportunities for hearing it.

THE IMPORTANCE OF AESTHETIC EXPERIENCES

Why are the fine arts important? Discarded is the notion that the arts are a means of helping man *exist*. But remaining is a greater reason: they are a means of helping man *live*, to be more than an animal grubbing his way through this world, to be a creature, in the words from Genesis, formed "in the image of God." *Aesthetic experiences are a part of what makes human beings human.* The cow and the kangaroo both have ears, eyes, and a central nervous system, but their reaction to a symphony or a fine painting is so small that it amounts to not noticing. What animal is it that derives enjoyment and meaning from the artistic use of color, shape, and sound? Only *Homo sapiens*, "the thinking man," as the words are translated.

The prominent place of the arts in man's humanity is the bedrock foundation upon which the importance and worthiness of the arts rest. It is a point of the first magnitude and one that is not generally realized in our society. There is abundant evidence to support the claim. The following is but a sampling.

From a scientist: In discussing the evolution of man, Lecomte du Noüy in his book *Human Destiny*[2] says that when the Cro-Magnon man began artistically adorning his caves and tools, this marked "the most important date in all the history of mankind," and became "proof of the progress of the human spirit in the direction of evolution, that is, in the direction leading away from the animal."

From a philosopher: In seeking to prove the existence of the entity of the human spirit, William Ernest Hocking of Harvard University cites as evidence man's creativity in the arts, specifically as exemplified by the music of Bach.[3]

From educators: Starting with Plato, who urged music in the education of every citizen, and continuing through the universities of the middle ages, which included music in the quadrivium of subjects required for the master's degree, to present-day educators and organizations like the Educational Policies Commission, music has been deemed an essential part of a good education.

From theologians: Every religion in the world incorporates music in one form or another in its worship. Throughout history, music has been regarded as a worthy offering, a fitting expression of man's relationship to a higher being. In the crucial moments of interhuman relationships, also, music seems necessary and right. Seldom is a person married or buried in a religious service without music's expressive power being called upon.

---

[2] Pierre Lecomte du Noüy, *Human Destiny* (New York: David McKay Company, Inc., 1947), pp. 125–126. Used by permission of David McKay Company, Inc.
[3] William Ernest Hocking, *The Meaning of Immortality in Human Experience* (New York: Harper & Row, Publishers, 1957), pp. 62–63.

"The Black Bull," a cave painting from Lascaux, France. This picture was painted by a Cro-Magnon man about 15,000 years ago.

From the common man: Since the Cro-Magnon man over 15,000 years ago, people have been looking at beauty in the world about them. They have been fascinated by the shifting color of a sunset, the shape of a flower, the rhythm of the rolling surf. What's more, they have created beauty and artistic objects. They have built parks and museums. They have valued paintings, symphonies, and poetry. And they seek artistic quality in their everyday surroundings—in their clothing, homes, furniture, automobiles. A cardboard carton could serve as a lamp table; it would even have the virtue of being far cheaper than a fine piece of furniture. But human beings simply do not want to live that way. Fundamentally they want to do more than exist.

Since it is evident that the arts, including music, have so much significance in human life, a logical question is: why? To answer this, one must delve into the areas of aesthetics, philosophy, and psychology. Several explanations can be found. One group of philosophers holds that in music and other arts man re-experiences in a symbolic way the events of his life. The theory proposes that in the recurrent rise and fall of intensity in music, the listener relives the feelings associated with personal peaks and depressions. Other philosophers claim that music is "transfigured Nature," transcending the world and revealing the realm of the ultimate Will (God).

These two examples illustrate the differing ways in which aesthetic experiences are explained. There is no final answer. Fortunately, for the purposes of studying music there does not need to be an ultimate answer. As long as there is a recognition of aesthetic experience, it is enough to know that the fine arts are significant in human life. The differing theories concerning their origin and purpose should not be allowed to obscure this significance.

LEARNING ABOUT MUSIC

Since music and the fine arts involve aesthetic experiences, the nature of the course work will differ from that found in other classes. This circumstance can cause misunderstanding and confusion, particularly in regard to the role of *factual learning*. In a foreign-language class, one learns to speak and write the language being studied. In science, one learns a mass of facts covering such diverse topics as the periodic table and the number of light years to a distant star. In understanding music, however, the nature of the content to be studied is not obvious, nor is the place of factual learning clear. It is a fact that the pitch A above middle C is generally 440 vibrations per second. That fact is of little value in helping you understand a Bach fugue, however.

The learning of facts does have a place in a course on understanding music, because facts can contribute to a greater comprehension of what is heard. It is good to know that Beethoven was born in 1770, died in 1827, lived in Vienna, met Mozart, played the piano brilliantly, composed nine symphonies, went deaf in his later years, and was a nonconformist. But it is more important that his works do not strike you as a jumble of sound when you hear them. If you hear a jumble, you have failed to understand Beethoven's *music*. Facts about music are helpful, but in and of themselves, they do not replace organized sound.

There is something else you should learn in a music course: a sense of musical organization and pattern, or *syntax*. Musical syntax is similar to syntax in language. We find the words "arms her the girl lifted delicate beautiful" hard to understand, not because they are difficult words but because they don't fall into a logical pattern. When the words are arranged into "The beautiful girl lifted her delicate arms," they are easy to comprehend.

Since you were a child you have heard music, so you already have some sense of musical syntax. However, that sense may not include all the types of music presented in this book. When the music is unfamiliar, more careful listening is required to build up your sense of pattern for that particular type of music.

Closely related to a syntactical sense is skill in listening to music. Without this ability to hear what is happening in a piece, you are as helpless as a man with poor vision in an art gallery. Listening skill is so important that an entire chapter is devoted just to it. Also, three albums of

recordings have been prepared to make the music you study more available
and to give you a chance to gain listening skills on your own.*

There is one more area of learning in music. It is a mode of
thought, a *way of thinking*. To understand music, you need to consider
sounds with somewhat the same outlook as a musician. This statement does
not mean that you must perform music, although that helps. Rather, it
means that sounds are to be contemplated and valued for their own sake.
Musician-like thinking does not regard music as something to have in the
background as you study or socialize with friends. A musician is interested
in the sounds and how they have been handled by a composer or performer.
In this comic strip, the company's intellectual may not be an artist, but he
thinks like one.

What about music reading? It is useful and valuable, but not
absolutely necessary. You can get by without it, but if you can comprehend
musical notation, you will be able to learn more about music. The musical
examples in the book will be more meaningful, which in turn will improve
your listening ability. Following a simple score of the music as you listen
can help focus your attention while listening. As a supplement to this book,
a book of simplified scores has been prepared for non-musicians to follow.**

So you are studying a subject that is in some inexplicable way
important to humanity, and the content of which consists of organized intangible sounds. Now you can begin to see why the study of music will be
challenging, why at times it may be frustrating, and why the accustomed
mode of thought used in most courses will not be successful in music. To
illustrate the different thinking needed, let us consider the word "meaning"
as it applies to music.

---

*Between them, *Scored for The Understanding of Music Record Album* and *The Understanding of Music Enrichment Record Album* contain all the works discussed in this book. Also,
both albums contain self-instructional booklets entitled "Learning to Listen," which provide
a program of study using the recordings to develop greater listening skill. *The Understanding
of Music Record Album* offers a balanced choice of selections. All three albums are produced
by Columbia Records.

**Hoffer, Charles, and Marjorie Latham Hoffer, *Scored for the Understanding of Music—
Supplemented Edition.* Belmont, Calif.: Wadsworth Publishing Company, Inc., 1969, 1971.

MUSIC AND CULTURE

How do you determine whether a particular organization of sounds has meaning? Of course, you can decide that *for you* one set of sounds makes music and one does not. But would your judgment hold true for your father, an *avant-garde* composer, or a person from India? It's very unlikely that everyone would agree with you on what sounds are meaningful. What is significant about this fact? It means that a person's understanding of music depends on his cultural background and intelligence.

Music is created by people. The patterns of sound called "music" were not preordained in the dim past, with man's task being the discovery of those patterns. A search for the perfect melody and the lost chord is about as likely to succeed as a search for the pot of gold at the end of the rainbow. Man does not look for music; he creates it.

Since music is a creation of man, it too is a part of culture. Thus, understanding a culture requires at least a limited understanding of that culture's music, and vice versa. Similarly, a composer is influenced by his culture, just as he in turn influences it. The interrelationship between music and culture is so basic and significant that it is influential in the organization of this book; music is presented according to the musical styles prevailing in various cultural periods. More about this subject will be discussed in Chapter 6.

The importance of culture and society in making a human personality was dramatically illustrated by two feral or "wolf" children who were found by missionaries in New Guinea in the 1920s. The two girls were human only in body. They never learned to utter more than one or two sounds, showed almost no emotions, and when given food they scampered with it into a dark corner to eat it. In short, they existed only on an animal level.

Of course, not knowing some aspects of your culture, music for example, does not mean you are existing as an animal. But to the extent that a person is ignorant of his culture, he is not in the mainstream of its life and feels alien and out of place. Suppose that you move to India. Like most Westerners, you would probably find Indian music difficult to understand; the complexities described in Chapter 2 are not quickly comprehended. But if you are going to live there, you should learn something about its music. If you don't, you will to a degree be an outsider in that society. Furthermore, you will miss out on the enjoyment and enrichment the music can give your life. You would find your Indian life a little duller, shallower, and less satisfying. So it is to your advantage to learn at least the music of your own culture. And in a day of jet airplanes and instant communication, it is desirable to learn a little about the music of other cultures as well—the reason for the inclusion of some material on ethnic music in this book.

MEANING IN MUSIC

     In everyday usage, "meaning" indicates that a word or symbol represents something specific. "Strasse" in German means "street," and a gold ring worn on the third finger of the left hand indicates a married state; both stand for something. In music and the fine arts the term is used somewhat differently. Sounds, lines, and colors are organized so that they have meaning, make sense, are satisfying entities worthy of contemplation and capable of eliciting feelings from the observer or listener. When music occurs alone, without the addition of words as in song, it is unable to provide meaning in the usual specific sense.

     Here is a melody from the fourth movement of Brahms' *Symphony No. 4.*

Can you tell what it means, what it is saying? It may suggest a mood or remind you of a place or event, but a melody cannot tell you anything specific. Words do this, not music. Thus you can see why it is not accurate to describe music as a "language," at least in the conventional use of the word.

     Music does, however, have *musical* meaning. Brahms' melody means much musically; it is a logical, sensible arrangement of sounds that are worth listening to. The row of pitches sounds eminently *musical* to most people. Therefore, when the word "meaning" is used in connection with music, it implies that the sounds in their unique way make musical sense.

     Does music have meaning? Yes. Can that meaning be stated in words? No. The point is imaginatively put by Leonard Bernstein in *The Joy of Music.*[4] In the playlet, L.B. represents Leonard Bernstein, L.P. is Lyric Poet, a poet's poet from Britain, and Y.B. is Younger Brother, a sixteen-year-old. The three are driving across New Mexico, searching for a place to stay and discussing music.

        L.B.: . . . If I react similarly to two different stimuli, then my two reactions are the same; but that doesn't mean that both stimuli possess the same meaning. If a person catches cold (1) from rainy weather and (2) from cats, those facts certainly don't establish any similarity of meaning between rain and cats, do they?

        L.P.: No, if we can head off a joke from Y.B. about raining cats and

---

[4] From *The Joy of Music.* Copyright © 1954, 1955, 1956, 1957, 1958, 1959 by Leonard Bernstein. Reprinted by permission of Simon and Schuster, Inc.

dogs. . . . But let's talk more simply. You will admit that there is a definite relation between the meanings of a sunset and of a Chopin prelude, between the Mona Lisa and the Book of Ruth, between—

L.B.: Relation, yes, in a comprehensive critical sense. But that is not to say that they *mean* the same thing.

L.P.: Of course it is to say *just* that! Take the sunset and the prelude, for example. We can break their meanings down into certain abstract terms, like calm, spaciousness, *sostenuto*, gentle motion, color, imperceptible changes of color, and so on. All these terms apply to both, don't they?

L.B.: But the prelude doesn't *mean* calm, color and the rest. It suggests them, perhaps. What it means is purely musical.

L.P.: And what does *that* mean?

L.B.: If it could be told in words, then why could Chopin have found it necessary to tell it through notes in the first place? Of course, I could try to articulate the musical meaning of a prelude in words, but what a bore it would be! Let me show you, if you have the strength:[*] a prolonged upbeat in the middle register (like the A-string of the cello), yearning upwards in an octave stretch, its meaning suddenly clarified by the entrance of the accompaniment, which is a series of repeated insistent E-minor triads that pulse under the sustained chromatic longing of the melodic line (which vacillates tearfully between B and C), while a tenor voice in the accompaniment adds to the general sense of languishing dolor through suspension and *appoggiatura*—

L.P.: "Thanks, they cry, 'tis thrilling!
Take, O take this shilling!
Let us have no more!"

L.B.: See? I told you it would be a bore. And that may give you perhaps a fraction of the meaning of some three bars. That, as I said, is just the point about music. It stands in a special lonely region, unlit—

Y.B.: Hey, look! *Kozy Kabins!*

The graphic arts have in this century sought to change their orientation from the artistic rendition of specific objects to one of aesthetic expression, much to the confusion and consternation of the general public. Until the twentieth century, painters were called upon to play the role that the camera does today. That is, they were to paint a scene or person so that the subject could be recognized and admired. The better painters did more than that. They designed and interpreted as they made reproductions faithful to the original subject. Then came the camera, and faithful pictorial representation became an unimportant function of the painter. Now he was freed from the limitation of painting a picture that "looked like something."

---

[*] The music for this Prelude appears on page 277.

Now he could concentrate solely on shape, line, texture, color, and design. In short, his painting could be valued for its purely aesthetic qualities, without regard to its pictorial accuracy. When painting reached this stage of development, it approximated visually what music had done aurally for hundreds of years. A work such as Piet Mondrian's "Composition" (plate 12) has value purely for its aesthetic quality, and not because it is an accurate reproduction of a scene. Wassily Kandinsky's "Improvisation No. 30" (plate 10) is also an example of this type of art.

THE EVALUATION OF MUSIC

The matter of evaluation, of assessing artistic works as "better" or "poorer," is often confusing. It might appear that the label "poorer" or "bad" on a work indicates something defective about it. That is almost never true. A poor piece of music is seldom a clashing, hashlike mess of sound. Instead, it usually is one that is dull, trite, ineffective, or lacking in a sense of direction and quality of elegance. In any case, it is judged to be poor to the extent that it lacks qualities of craftsmanship and fails to offer enough imaginative musical happenings to hold interest.

The differences in the quality of artistic works are not obvious. It is not easy to tell that a sincere but third-rate try at musical composition is of poor quality. Accurate evaluation of music requires a wide range of experience to serve as a basis for comparison. A superficial evaluation of a ball team is easy, because it either wins or loses games. But only an observer well-versed in the game can evaluate a team solely by observing the quality of its playing, without reference to the score. There is no won-lost record for an opera or concerto, so the knowledge and experience of the listener is essential to any valid assessment.

The knowledgeability of the listener points to the central problem of the composer in relating to an audience. The composer treads a delicate line between offering the listener something new and something old. He must write in a way that is known and recognizable; he must follow convention somewhat. But he also needs to have in his work something of interest, something new. If a composer strays too far to the side of novelty and variety, his work becomes a senseless array of sounds. If he sticks too closely to the expected pattern, the piece becomes boring and trite. In the days of the silent motion picture, a favorite comedy device was for one character to pick up a custard pie and throw it in the face of another actor. Pie-in-the-face humor is funny—the first time it is seen. But after a while the routine becomes ineffective; it seems too obvious to be funny. Just how much pie in the face can be appreciated and in what setting depends, of course, on the sensitivity and maturity of the viewer. The same is true of the listener's reaction to what he hears in a piece of music.

Sometimes works of art music seem too long and complex. Often there is a relationship between the level of sophistication and length, although this is by no means always true. Back in elementary school days when we learned how to read, we started with simple sentences like "See Dick run" and brief stories that required only one page to relate. This level of reading was fine for us as first graders. But as adults we are bored with "See-Dick-run" sentences and one-incident stories. Now we appreciate an interesting and varied use of words. Furthermore, the relating of a simple incident no longer satisfies us; we want an intriguing plot and character development, often with subtle insights and symbolisms woven in. An author needs space in which to provide these complexities—hence a novel or drama. To express profound feelings and demonstrate skill at organizing sounds, a composer usually needs works longer than a minute or two and a more complex structure than a pretty melody. A musical work that merits aesthetic attention needs to have more than an attractive rhythmic pattern or a catchy tune, just as a literary masterpiece must be more than a few simple phrases describing an incident.

Effort, thought, and undivided attention will be required if you wish to probe the profound and complex nature of music; it cannot be grasped through hasty or superficial study. Fortunately, the effort is well worth making. Music as one of the hallmarks of man's humanity yields a wealth of meaning and enjoyment to every person who is experienced and sensitive enough to understand it.

Listening
to Music

4

Would you visit an art gallery with your sunglasses on? Or worse, would you go with a blindfold over your eyes? Unfortunately many people do much the same thing when they listen to music. Of course they do not physically put on ear muffs or insert ear plugs. Rather, they don't listen carefully enough, or they don't know what to listen for, or they don't know how to listen. So they unintentionally miss much of what the composer and performer intended for them to hear. Like the person wearing dark glasses in the art gallery, the hampered listener finds music drab and uninteresting.

Psychologists and physiologists use the word "threshold" to indicate the point at which an effect can be noticed. A lighted match held one yard away from the skin probably will not be felt because the amount of heat reaching the skin is not great enough for persons to notice. A sensitive measuring device, however, would have no trouble registering the heat. But if the match is held just an inch from the skin, it is decidedly above the human threshold. A composer may slightly alter a note or rhythmic pattern. Some listeners notice and enjoy the subtle change of sounds; their threshold of aural sensitivity is low enough to permit them to perceive the subtlety. Other listeners miss the alteration, since their threshold is too high. They become bored and cannot understand why anyone spends time listening to the piece.

Why do some persons have more sensitivity (lower thresholds) than others? Among the several reasons are factors such as attitude, previous knowledge and experience, intelligence, and skill and training in listening. (Only rarely are inherent limitations in the hearing capability of the ear a factor.) Can something be done to make a person more sensitive to music, and therefore more able to understand it? The answer is "yes," provided that the right kind of effort is made. Attitudes can change, and experience and knowledge can be gained.

ATTITUDE

It may seem strange to make "attitude" a prime requisite for appreciation of an art. But it is essential. As was pointed out in Chapter 3, the limits of musical understanding depend on you as an individual. The same is true of learning music. You are the only person who can make yourself pay attention, who can center your listening on one part of the music or another, who can make yourself remember a musical pattern. All a book can do is (1) suggest ways to better your listening comprehension, (2) provide information that aids you in listening to a particular work, and (3) give you more understanding of what you hear.

What makes up the attitude necessary for increased understanding? One part of it is the willingness to make an effort. And the word "effort" is used advisedly here. Courses in music appreciation have sometimes been regarded as snap courses. Perhaps they did not stress significant musical learnings, or perhaps the students who thought them a snap remained unaware that there was more to music than mere superficial acquaintance. The effort may not be in library research and writing lengthy term papers, but it does require diligence in concentrating while listening.

A second aspect of attitude is the acknowledgment that you are dealing with something profound, subtle, and complex. If music were too simple, too obvious, it would fail in artistic expression. Certainly an art that reaches to the very roots of man's psychological being is not going to be understood all at once. Every attempt will be made to present the subject simply and clearly, but if it all seems very easy, chances are you're not realizing the full significance of what the music has to offer.

Another feature of proper attitude is tolerance toward all music. Some of the music discussed in this book will probably be new to you. Some of it may seem strange or undecipherable. But if you are open-minded—if you assume the integrity of the creative artist and give yourself a chance to understand his work—you will hear the work as the composer intended you to hear it. And in the process your chances of growing to like it are greatly increased.

The point about assuming the integrity of the artist may seem surprising. But some persons, when they have difficulty understanding a work, rationalize their position by thinking "Since I don't understand the work and don't like it, something must be wrong with it." Even though a musical work may seem unusual and extreme, it should be regarded as the best and most honest effort of the composer, and not the work of a charlatan or mentally deranged person. The listener should assume in the case of established, recognized works that it is he who has failed to hear the significance of the music, and that with more careful study and listening he will come to understand it.

Further, an attitude of tolerance gives you a chance to learn. If your energies are devoted to deciding whether you like a work or not, your capacity for learning will be reduced. Do *not* at first ask yourself "Do I like it?" Rather, ask "What melody is being played now? How does it fit in with what I heard earlier?" and similar questions.

A feature of attitude that bears repeating is the basic concern with hearing and understanding what the composer does with sound. If music is organized sound, then how is it organized? Factual knowledge may help you in answering this question, but it cannot replace hearing.

The first question is more properly "Do you want to understand music?" than "How do you learn to understand music?"

INTELLECT AND EMOTION IN MUSIC

Listening to music is a complex activity. Don't listen exclusively for emotional thrills or only for intellectual stimulation, as though music were a form of brain food. It is nearly impossible for anyone to separate intellect and emotion when listening to music, because human beings display both qualities when responding to their environment or experience. Man in real life never operates completely by reason. He has feelings about what he knows and experiences, except perhaps in purely abstract calculations such as $8 \times 7 = 56$. Neither is civilized man completely emotional. He may feel like punching the football referee in the nose, but for good *reasons* he doesn't. Just as both emotion and intellect are factors in man's behavior, so they are found in every piece of music, and so they are perceived to some degree by the listener.

The relationship between emotion and music requires clarification. Inevitably, people react emotionally to musical stimuli. A soft, low minor chord on the piano gives the listener a particular feeling, while the shrill sound of a piccolo gives him another. If the music moves from one note to the next higher note, a slight rising or expanding effect is created. If the movement upward from the original note extended for a distance of six notes, the effect would be one of considerably greater stretch, reach, tension, or whatever words might best describe it. This process of musical stimuli and listener reaction goes on continually in music. In fact, a principle from physics might be paraphrased for music: for every musical action, there will be a corresponding listener reaction. Every tone color, level of volume, combination of pitches, interval between notes in a melody, and rhythm will give you a slightly different feeling if you are but sensitive to the changes of sound.

To notice your own reactions to sounds, try this experiment. Listen intently (in a quiet place) to a series of rather different sounds, with about 5 seconds of silence inserted between sounds to allow you to contemplate. You probably won't be able to describe exactly what you feel about each sound, but you will have some response. The experiencing of the reactions when you listen to music is one of its main fascinations. In musical compositions, of course, the sounds come at you rapidly, with few silent spots in which to analyze your reactions. Single sounds heard in a gapped series could soon become boring.

PLANES OF LISTENING

Aaron Copland, the esteemed American composer, has spelled out three emphases or "planes" of listening.[1] The planes are discussed here as though they were independent entities, but of course they are not. As mentioned earlier, it is impossible to separate intellect and emotion. But certain aspects of listening can be more important than others at particular moments. An awareness of these planes will enable you to increase your understanding of the music and your response to it.

The Sensuous Plane

The first plane is termed "sensuous." This delicious word means "of or appealing to the senses." In music it refers to the purely physical effect that music has on its listeners. When the orchestra works its way to a climactic point and a chill runs up your spine, the effect is primarily a sensuous one. The same is true when you react to a stirring march by tapping your foot, or when a virtuoso performer dazzles you with his breathtaking performance of a technical passage. Most of the time, however, sensuous qualities in music are not appreciated in so obvious a way. A

---

[1] Aaron Copland, *What to Listen for in Music* (New York: McGraw-Hill Book Company, Inc., 1957), pp. 9–19.

lush chord in the music may cause you to feel a certain response, but you don't break into tears or cheers. The feeling is not that strong; and besides, as you grew up you were taught to control your emotions.

Hearing is an action involving a sense organ. Sounds are physical in nature. So the sensuous pleasures of music are not intellectually profound. They should not be downgraded, however. There is real pleasure to be gained by listening to even a single long tone on a violin or French horn, just as there is pleasure in looking at a beautiful blue color in a picture. The majestic sounds that an orchestra or large choral group can achieve have a certain inherent excitement about them, just as does the view from the top of a mountain. Such pleasures are good. In fact, you might well try concentrating your attention at first on the pure quality of a flute tone or the pulsating rhythm of a Latin American work. By doing so you will become more aware of the sensuous qualities in music.

Don't make the mistake of thinking that sensuous effects are the main thing in music. An emphasis solely on sensuous qualities eliminates from consideration many musical works of exceptional merit. What is worse, dependence on sheer sensuous effects leads down a musical blind alley. The listener grows accustomed to the effects of one musical work, so he searches for another with even greater physical impact. This cycle leads finally to music that is simply orgiastic. When music reaches this point, it has lost most of its aesthetic validity. Music cannot stand artistically if it is merely an aural roller-coaster ride or cold shower. An example of too much attention to sensuousness is the hi-fi enthusiast who adjusts his set to the maximum volume, bass, and reverberation.

Not only is sensuous impact brought about by great amounts of sound (volume) and the appeal of various tone qualities; it also utilizes the elements of time and rhythm. Music, because it is perceived in a context of time, is relived with each hearing. It unfolds as the listener follows. A composer can take the musical resources available and space them out to achieve the maximum effect. Thus music has the power to make a sudden thunderous chord or the delicate tone of a flute occur at just the right moment as the listener follows the undulations of the music. It is the timing of such effects that gives music much of its sensuous impact.

The Expressive Plane

The second plane of listening is termed by Copland "expressive." Music can convey a feeling or mood, but most pieces of music were composed without deliberate attempt to create an association with a story. The music that was written with deliberate associations in mind was one of the types composed during the Romantic era, which encompassed most of the nineteenth century.

There can be little doubt that music has expressive power. Music frequently can relate to something the listener thinks or feels. A particular phrase may evoke a psychological reaction that is nearly identical to the reaction to some event in life. But music is limited in its ability to designate specific thoughts that can be interpreted in words. For example, music may give an impression of sadness, but it cannot describe what is causing this feeling. Nor can it define objects. For most people, one sound does not represent "clouds," another "bread," and another "wheel." Music can provide general moods, but not specific thoughts.

If you wish to prove this point to yourself, try a little experiment: get a recording of a work that is associated with a specific scene, perhaps Respighi's "The Pines of the Appian Way," from *The Pines of Rome*, or Mussorgsky's *Pictures at an Exhibition*. Find some friends who are unfamiliar with the music. Without divulging the title, play the music for them and ask them to describe the scene they envisage. The chances are that their responses will correspond in general but vary in specifics.

The indefiniteness of music is to its advantage. One musical work may be heard by a thousand people, but each will hear it in a slightly different way, depending on his individual inclinations. More importantly, music can break through the barrier of words. Words are too brittle, too inflexible, too conventional to allow for full expression. Between the words "anger" and "rage," for instance, there are infinite shades of meaning. Also, anger is usually coupled with frustration, or sadness, or both. As a feeling becomes more complex, it is harder to express. When a loved one dies, a person feels emptiness, grief, remorse, and powerlessness. But these feelings cannot be fully communicated to someone else, no matter how many words are used or how carefully the words are chosen. Music conveys mood; each listener can fill in the meanings for himself from his personal resources.

A piece of music, then, has expressive power. When this is coupled with music's sensuous and intellectual appeal, the impact of the music is heightened. The sensing of music's expressive content adds much to the listener's understanding of music.

The Sheerly Musical Plane

The third plane of music listening is the one that nonmusicians tend to ignore. Copland calls it the "sheerly musical" plane. The term refers to concentration on what happens in the music—what notes are being played, at what speed, in combination with what other notes, on what instrument, in what range, and so on. It is on this plane that the listener can realize the real musical values of music. It is here that he reaches the most sophisticated stage of aesthetic experience, a stage in which he appreciates the sounds and their manipulation unhampered by physical response or a search for expressive meanings. Achievement of this type of listening requires more education, but it offers greater rewards. And so the attention of this book is concentrated primarily on this plane of listening.

LISTENING TECHNIQUES

When a trained musician uses the word "listen," he does not mean merely hearing, being aware of the sounds. He refers to an activity involving keen concentration. If you were majoring in music, you would be subjected to something called "ear training," which isn't exactly what the words seem to imply. In such training the student listens to melodies, rhythms, and chords, usually played on the piano, notating what he hears. Often the music majors discover an important fact: until they needed to listen in order to pass ear-training tests, they hadn't really listened carefully. They had heard, but had not genuinely listened. And as the training continued, they began to hear things in the music they had never heard before.

It is too bad that many day-to-day hearing experiences encourage people not to listen. The mind has a faculty for "tuning out" sounds it does not want or need to hear. Thus the ticking of a clock goes unnoticed, as does the noise of traffic and the sound of the refrigerator turning on and off. People become adept at ignoring music, too. Since supermarkets, banks, and eating places offer a continual stream of music, and since transistor radios appear in many social situations with sufficient volume to hold a captive audience, it becomes necessary to learn to ignore its presence. But as this is happening, sensitivity to sound is being dulled. A course in understanding music, therefore, is going to require a reversal of many ingrained listening habits. Many sounds can and should be ignored, but not music. It should be listened to intently.

Is there one right way to listen to music? Since there is wide variation among musical compositions and the people who listen to them, the answer is "no." There are suggestions, however, that will help.

1. *Improve your memory for music.* Memory is absolutely necessary for the comprehension of music. At any particular instant, all that can be heard is one sound. This may be a single tone or several tones occurring simultaneously—a chord. In any event, it can be perceived only briefly, for time moves on and other sounds are heard in succeeding moments. The only way to make sense out of these brief and apparently isolated aural experiences is to utilize the phenomena of memory and anticipation. Even anticipation is a memory activity in that it involves a prediction of what will happen in the future based on what has happened in the past. In any human experience involving the dimension of time, meaningfulness occurs only to the extent that the person sees the relationship between past, pres-. ent, and future.

Visual experiences do not rely basically on the element of time. The graphic arts, for example, are not involved in time. They exist in space. An entire picture can be seen in a moment. (Closer analysis and full appreciation will require a longer period of viewing, true.) But suppose that memory and anticipation are made an integral part of the viewing experience. It might be done as follows. Assume you are to see an unfamiliar picture which is entirely covered except for a thin slit running vertically. Then the slit is drawn slowly across the picture. Your knowledge of the picture will have to be derived solely from (1) your memory of what you have seen, (2) the slit-sized portion you are presently viewing, and (3) your guess as to what might yet be revealed in succeeding moments. Difficult? Yes. But that's the way music is perceived. This is why memory is so necessary in understanding it.

As a general rule, the more frequently you engage in an activity involving memory, the better your skill at recall will become. Think again of the picture analogy. The fifth time the slit is drawn across the picture, you will have a much clearer idea of what the picture is like; your memory of it will be better, and consequently the experience will make more sense to you. The same is true of music. The more you hear a piece, the better you will remember it and the more fully you will understand it. Repeated hearing of a musical work is about the surest way to gain greater understanding of it. In fact, with many aesthetically worthy works, repeated hearings are necessary in order to reach a satisfactory degree of understanding.

Memory can be developed in several other ways. Actual participation helps you to learn more thoroughly and remember more accurately, so sing, play, and whistle themes yourself when possible.

Following the notated music while listening will help you remember the work better. Even though you may not read music well, you can gain some impression of it from the contour of the lines and the time values of the notes. For example, look at the melody from *The Roman Carnival Overture* by Hector Berlioz (*Bear*-lee-ohz). It is a work that will be mentioned often in this chapter. Try singing it to yourself, or playing it on an instrument.

Another way to improve musical memory is to listen to music, lots of it. The greater your familiarity with various styles, the easier it will be for you to recognize and remember patterns of melody, harmony, or rhythm, and the more accurately you will be able to predict the course of unfamiliar musical passages.

2. *Concentrate on main themes and the important musical ideas.* When listening to a work that is new to you, especially if you are not particularly experienced at listening to serious music, don't try to comprehend everything the first time. Learning to listen is like learning to drive a car. When you first learn to drive, your total attention is directed toward executing a few basic actions; your primary goal is to keep the car on the road and avoid hitting other cars or pedestrians. With increased experience, however, you find you can safely do other things—notice the scenery or carry on a conversation with a passenger. Had you tried to do all this too early in your training, a catastrophe might have occurred! The same principle applies to music; instead of a collision, however, the end result would be confusion and disillusionment.

How can you distinguish the important features of a piece before hearing it? In this book and in *Scored for the Understanding of Music,* the main themes and sections are indicated for you. A "roadmap" or "guided tour" of the composition is provided. If you are listening at a concert or to a recording of a work not covered in these books, you can read the notes on the concert program or record jacket. Such commentary can be extremely helpful if well written. There are several books available, such as *The Listener's Guide to Music,*[2] that contain information about specific works and are well worth consulting. If no written information is available, then try to keep your attention on the materials of music: melodies, harmonies, and rhythms. They are not all present in equal amounts, but if you can follow them when they do appear, you will have taken an important step toward understanding the music.

Develop the ability to listen selectively. That is, learn to focus your attention on the one aspect of the music that seems most significant in a particular passage or piece. Perhaps you will try to follow the melody, or the recurrence of a rhythmic pattern, or the distinctive tone quality of a particular instrument. On subsequent hearings you may choose to concentrate on another important aspect. Whatever it is, give undivided attention to this feature of the music.

[2] Percy A. Scholes (New York: Oxford University Press, 1948).

Before you listen to *The Roman Carnival Overture,* have the previously cited theme in mind, and concentrate on it while listening. It appears several times in the slow beginning section, and the first portion of it is used in the fast second section. This theme gives unity to the piece. To comprehend the music adequately, you must remember and recognize the theme with each hearing.

Selective listening has further application to study of this theme. Toward the end of the slow beginning section, the theme is played in both the high-pitched instruments (violins, etc.) and the low-pitched instruments (cellos, etc.). In this segment of the music, however, the low instruments stay consistently one beat ahead, creating a follow-the-leader effect, which in music is termed *canon* or *strict imitation.* If you focus your attention on the high instruments the first time you listen and on the low instruments the next, you will gain a clearer understanding of this music.

3. *Hear as much detail as possible.* Although following single aspects of the music is helpful, you should not stop there. Serious works— those written for aesthetic purposes—have many inflections, many subtleties. And as in other phases of life, it is the little things that make the difference. A slightly changed chord, a brief interruption of the rhythmic pattern, a new combination of instruments, the sounding of a tiny fragment of the theme—such apparently insignificant techniques can spell the difference between an ordinary piece and an exceptional one. In fact, it is sometimes a "little thing" that excites the listener. He may even grow accustomed to waiting for a particular nuance while dismissing the rest of the music—a listening habit that is *not* recommended!

Here is a subtle passage in *The Roman Carnival Overture.* The cellos reach for one of their higher tones, hold it, and then glide out of it. It is only a fragment in the complex, overall sound of the orchestra, but what a beautiful little passage! Listen for it.

(original in tenor clef)

Sometimes music courses place much stress on the listener's ability to identify instruments by sound. How important is this skill in the understanding of music? It is helpful, but it certainly is not necessary. If a beautiful melody is being played, the important thing is to hear and appreciate the melody for its own sake. Which instrument is playing the melody is secondary. Actually, it is rather easy to learn to identify instruments aurally. Descriptions of musical instruments are presented in Appendix B.

The overriding reason for hearing as much as possible in a musical work is that the composer intends for *everything* to be heard; he regards every note as important to the musical effect. And he is right. The infinite variety of music comes about because of the unlimited combinations of pitch, tone color, rhythm, and volume.

4. *Do not attempt to visualize specific scenes*. Sometimes students in elementary school are given listening lessons dealing almost exclusively with "program" music—music in which the composer consciously attempts to associate his work with a particular story or scene. This type of music is in many ways well suited to the requirements of guided listening experiences in the early grades. Unfortunately, however, students sometimes begin to assume that for every piece there must be a picture. They conclude that music is incomplete or inadequate if it exists alone. This misconception hampers true understanding of music, because it presupposes that music cannot exist for its own sake.

As was observed earlier, the best music is that which is most fascinating in terms of sheer sound. Trying to conjure a tender love scene or the image of a ship plowing through the waves only distracts the listener's attention from the sound of the music itself. Instead of listening, his mind is engaged in creating fantasies. Pictorial association can easily become an invitation to daydream. Only keen concentration on the music itself will lead to understanding of it.

5. *Apply knowledge to your listening*. It has been said that knowledge begets understanding. If a section of a work is in sonata form, knowing the characteristics of this form will better enable you to follow its design and thereby grasp more of its meaning. Remember the theme from *The Roman Carnival Overture?* Berlioz does some interesting things with it. Near the end of the piece he takes the first part of the melody and brings it in, first in the bassoon, then the trombones, then the flute and oboes in the manner referred to earlier as imitation. The use of the melody later in the piece gives unity to the work.

By knowing this melody and by understanding that its function is to provide greater unity, you increase your understanding of Berlioz' work.

6. *Practice listening skills*. A modest effort in improving your listening ability can be a great help to you in terms of enjoying music. How can you practice listening skills? First, the accompanying record albums and their booklets offer many specific exercises in listening.

Second, work with a classmate to develop listening acuity by pinpointing changes in short rhythmic or melodic figures. For example, play a four-note pattern on the piano. Then repeat the pattern, but change one note. Ask your friend to say whether the first, second, third, or fourth note was altered. Or tap out two rhythmic patterns, with the second pat-

containing a change. The length of the melodic or rhythmic patterns can be increased as your skill improves.

Third, when listening to a recording by yourself, select short portions for repeated listening. This practice is especially useful in places that sound like a jumble of sound to you. Between playings, attempt to run through it in your mind. Shut your eyes and try to rehear in your own mind what you previously heard. Repeat this process of actual and imagined hearings, several times if necessary, until your mental rendition of the place is quite accurate.

Fourth, if you need practice identifying instruments, listen to *A Young Person's Guide to the Orchestra* by Benjamin Britten. (Don't let the title fool you; it's worthwhile listening for adults.) Besides being educational, it is interesting music. If you are weak on identifying voice types, select a recording of an oratorio or excerpts from an opera and listen to the solos for the various types of voices. Usually the record label or jacket will identify the voice type for each band of the record—"tenor aria," "soprano recitative," and so on.

7. *Encourage your reactions to music.* This suggestion should *not* be taken to mean that you should emote or talk to yourself when hearing a piece. Rather, be aware of your feelings about what you hear and let them be active. Listen and consciously notice your response. This is vital to your enjoyment of music.

No one can or should attempt to tell you what to feel. Feelings are very private and are impossible to communicate fully. Because feelings are so difficult to describe, and because no one can be sure what another's feelings are, music cannot be accurately expressed using highly subjective adjectives. "Sad" music to one may be "devout" music to another. In no case should someone tell you that "This music should make you feel sad." While a person may correctly say "It makes *me* feel sad," such a statement can apply only to him. Some aspects of music are more objective and "public," and therefore helpful. "The music is loud" is a far more useful and defensible statement than "The music is sad." What happens in the music can be discussed in terms of facts and definitive statements; how you react to the music cannot.

TESTS OF GOOD LISTENING

Sometimes thoughtful students in music classes ask: "I understand all about music's being the sensible and aesthetically effective arrangement of sounds. I even agree that this is a valuable means of human expression. What I want to know is whether or not I'm really hearing and understanding the music as fully as I should. How can I tell when I've really heard it?" There is no easy answer. No litmus-paper test can be applied. But you *can* ask yourself these practical questions:

Does the music in its own way seem sensible?

Does it move along without seeming dead and stagnant?

Am I hearing specific details of form, rhythm, and melody?

Have I kept my attention focused on the music throughout its entirety?

Do I get some reactions or feelings from the music as I hear it?

Do I like to listen to the music? Do I enjoy it? Does it seem interesting?

Do I want to hear the work again?

If your answer to all these questions is "yes," there can be little doubt that you are apprehending the essence of the music. The composer intends for his music to be enjoyed, to be found interesting and meaningful. He means for his skill at handling music to be appreciated, and he wants to produce something that will have lasting attraction. In most cases he realizes that the music will engender reactions in the listener. When you hear the music fully and with feeling, you are understanding most of what is intended.

KNOWING WHAT TO LISTEN FOR

Information about music is useful in helping you know what to listen for and, maybe even more important, what not to listen for. It's a little like learning the game of football. If you know the game, you won't stand up and cheer when a lineman of the opposing team scoops up a fumble and races unmolested across your goal line for a touchdown. The more you know about football, the more you enjoy the game. So it is with music.

People are often disappointed in a piece or composer because they expect to hear something in the music that is not there. For example, Mozart wrote music that is tasteful, well designed, and beautiful. He lived in an age that esteemed the tasteful, the well designed, and the beautiful. In his day, flamboyant emotional display was not in style. So if you listen to his music expecting to be overwhelmed by lush harmonies and sensuous melody, you will surely be disappointed. The music may be superb, but if it does not meet your expectations, you will probably find it unsatisfying. A little knowledge can prevent this.

What information might increase your understanding of Berlioz' *Roman Carnival Overture?* An overture is often written to precede a musical drama, but sometimes it is simply a name for a piece of music, which is true of this overture. The "Roman Carnival" portion of the title may come from the carnival-like quality of the music. In any case, it represents a product of the times and of a man. It was written in 1844, in the Roman-

Hector Berlioz.

tic period. The word "romantic" as used in the fine arts refers to the tendency toward a reliance on personal feelings that characterizes many artistic works of the nineteenth century. The Romantic composer or artist rebelled against the restraints and rules of the previous period. He believed that his feelings about something were more important and more valid than his objective appraisal of it. Therefore he was interested in mood and color and, at times, fervent excitement. Berlioz displayed these traits. This is perhaps to be expected from an erratic and impulsive Frenchman. Berlioz was especially interested in manipulating the vast array of tone colors offered by the orchestra. He even wrote a book on the subject of writing effectively for instruments, one that was a recognized treatise on the subject for nearly one hundred years.

As you listen to the *Overture,* you will probably find that its variety and richness of tone color directs the music's appeal first to your senses. Perhaps this appeal was Berlioz' intention when he gave the melody to the English horn, that oversized oboe with its dark plaintive sounds. This use of the instrument was quite unusual at the time the music was written. Knowing that Berlioz was an emotional man living in an age that believed in expressing emotions, you can understand why his music has a loose formal structure and why his music is exciting and at times even slightly zany. Finally, you can see that this piece, viewed in the context of its time and its composer's intentions, is a valid artistic expression.

Musical
Performance

5

There is one aspect of music that sets it apart from several of its sister disciplines in the fine arts. When you look at a painting, a piece of sculpture, or a building, you experience the artistic impact of the object without the involvement of an intervening person. You see the actual work of the creative artist. But in the realm of music (and drama and dance), you do not directly experience the product of the creator. When you hear a symphony or opera, it is being performed by an intermediary; someone is bringing to life the notational symbols and directions put on the page by the composer. An exception is the use of the tape recorder as a musical instrument. No intermediary is involved in this new and experimental music. But the vast preponderance of music in our culture does require a human agent to fulfill the composer's intent.

Suppose a painting had to be recreated for each viewing. Instead of looking at a masterpiece for yourself, you would have to watch a contemporary "performing painter" repaint the picture from technical directions left by the original artist. Once completed, the painting would fade away—impermanent, but indispensible to the viewer trying to appreciate the intent

83

of the original artist. Furthermore, the impression of the quality of the original masterpiece would depend largely on the quality of the "performing painter's" rendition. Music is like this. Performance is the necessary link between composer and listener, and the performer thus has a crucial role in the musical process. He can enhance the composer's work through a good performance or deform it through a bad one.

When music is being performed, it is to some degree being re-created. There is an aura of immediacy and aliveness surrounding such a process. It is an experience that covers a definite span of time during which things happen, and the listener feels directly involved in the unfolding of these "musical events." He participates in the development of a musical idea, and in the buildup to a climactic moment. This is a phase of artistic experience that is not shared in the relationship between painter and viewer, for example.

FACTORS AFFECTING PERFORMANCE

Since performance is vital to the art of music, students of music should be informed about elements that affect the re-creation of musical works. These factors are many and varied, and include artistic problems such as a performer's ability and mundane matters such as money needed to hire musicians to perform.

The Performer's Skill

Foremost among the factors affecting musical performance is the skill of the performer rendering the music. Any amateur can read the lines of a play and follow stage directions. But his attempts cannot compare with the performance of a first-rate actor, who knows how to make every inflection and every movement convey the intent of the playwright. The same is true with music. Two performances of the same piece can vary to such an extent that what is exciting and moving when performed by one group can be dull and bland when performed by another.

For reasons that will be presented shortly, performances by well-trained musicians normally do not vary radically. You need to listen closely in order to notice the differences at all. Listen sometime to two recordings of the same work by different professional performers. The differences between the two are probably slight, but they can affect your overall impression of the music.

The Live Performance

Other factors besides the ability of the performer contribute to your impression of the music. It makes a difference whether you hear a "live" performance of the work or listen to a recording of it. As a rule, live performance is superior because it involves you, the listener, more directly. This sense of presence is especially helpful in establishing the proper environment for chamber music (small-group performance). Live performance also enables you to hear better the sounds coming from one portion or another of a large group.

There is also advantage in seeing the performer. His stage presence and physical motions augment the effect of the sounds he makes. This is particularly true in opera, in which the singer-actor must move about and create a visual as well as aural impression. But it is also a factor in instrumental playing. Whether the bow strokes of a violinist are vigorous and fast or slow-moving and delicate, the listener's awareness of how the music being played is heightened by watching the performer at work.

More important, however, is the fact that a live performance is usually heard without distortion. It is heard as the composer and performer intend it to be. Recordings often do not reproduce the full sound as it really existed. The tone of the instruments or voices is not quite as rich, and the sounds produced by a group covering many square feet are compressed and amplified through a few inches of speakers. To compensate for this, recording manufacturers sometimes exaggerate the echo or reverberation, emphasize the bass tones, or in other ways tamper with the original sound. This can create a distorted idea of how the music should really sound, as in the case of the sound engineer who walked out of a performance by the New York Philharmonic muttering "Not enough bass." A symphony may occasionally seem more dazzling when its sounds have been artificially altered, but the musical content is no longer genuine.

The fact that a piece is being performed live by a competent artist does not guarantee that the music is being heard properly. The acoustical environment in which the music is heard has a significant effect on what the listener experiences. The room or concert hall can be too large or small, have too much or not enough reverberation, or have "dead" spots where the sound is only weakly heard. The one characteristic that all good concert halls have is "presence," giving the listener a sense of being close and involved with what is going on. Large halls, having perhaps three thousand or more seats, seem unable to do this. But smaller halls can fail too, for reasons of poor acoustical design. The most publicized instance of efforts to achieve correct acoustical conditions involved Philharmonic Hall at Lincoln Center in New York City. It required much money and two interior designs to achieve only satisfactory sound conditions.

If the hall is too hot or one's seat is so high in a balcony that only the tops of the performers' heads are seen, the enjoyment of the music is reduced. Sometimes the atmosphere is not conducive to careful listening. At outdoor concerts there are so many distractions, in addition to poor acoustical conditions, that complex and subtle works are ineffective.

Night view of Philharmonic Hall for the Performing Arts in Lincoln Center, New York. Philharmonic Hall was the first building completed in Lincoln Center.

The Inadequacy of Music Notation

A playwright can indicate the words he wants the actor to say and can give general directions about how the words should be spoken, but he cannot *by means of writing* tell the actor the exact voice inflection and timing for speaking them. The situation is much the same in music. Music notation tells the performer what pitch is to be produced and when, and it supplements this information with a few general directions regarding dynamics and expression. The performer must then determine the musical inflections that seem most logical to him as a re-creation of the music. The incompleteness of any system of music notation places more importance on the ability of the performer.

Even if notation could indicate fully how the music should be performed, it might not be desirable from the standpoint of both the listener and performer. All performances of a work would be identical, which would reduce the freshness caused by slightly different interpretations. Even more serious would be the absence of the many subtle shadings and nuances that make music a human rather than a mechanical means of expression. For instance, even the most capable concert performers do not play the rhythms and pitches exactly as written. (The pianist is an exception: pitches on a keyboard instrument cannot be varied at will.) If these performances were subjected to scientific scrutiny, many slight deviations of pitch and rhythm would be found. But the playing sounds better for these deviations, because a split-second's hesitation at one spot, or a slight raising of pitch at another, makes the music more effective.

Part of a musician's training consists of learning the traditions of performance that are not written down. He learns, for example, that a particular rhythmic figure is performed in a number of slightly different ways, depending on the period in history or the country from which the music came. Singers and instrumentalists learn that slightly different tone qualities are called for in different kinds of music. Markings for dynamics and note lengths vary to some degree in their meaning according to the composer and period. There is nothing in music to demand that a performer slavishly follow the practices of the past, but it behooves him to know and consider them if he wishes to be a good performer.

Further efforts have been made to bring about more uniform performances. There is an unwritten international agreement, followed in most countries, to tune all instruments to a standard pitch, identified by its number of vibrations per second. Another area in which there is some consensus is the instrumentation and size of the symphony orchestra. Most professional symphony orchestras throughout the world vary in size by not more than thirty players (eighty to one hundred and ten), and the players are distributed in about the same proportion among the various instrumental parts. So a composer can write for the cello section of an orchestra and be fairly certain of the number of cellos that will perform the part.

The situation with regard to the concert band is not well standardized. European and American bands do not even use entirely the same types of instruments. Even within the United States, the size of a group can vary from fifty to over one hundred players. Associations of band directors have been attempting to develop more standardization in the instrumentation of bands. To date, these efforts have had limited success.

Preparation before the Performance

Seldom are performances by good musicians presented without benefit of careful preparation. Difficult works cannot be given the best performance when the notation is read at first sight, even by very able musicians. The correct notes and rhythms need to be worked out, and the performer must decide upon the dynamic shadings, the proper tempos, and the many subtleties involved with performance. This is the *interpretation* of music.

Professional musicians speak more often about "rehearsing" music than "practicing." The distinction between the two words is not great. When a youngster begins lessons on an instrument, there is much talk, chiefly from his parents, about practicing. Practice connotes learning the technical skills necessary for performance. It suggests individual work. Rehearsal, on the other hand, implies group effort—the relating of various parts to one another and the perfecting of the whole—under simulated performance conditions. Each performer in a group needs to know what the others are doing; he needs to become familiar with all that goes into the piece. A unified interpretation has to be established so that the group performs with consistency of phrasing and style. Some works require intricate interlacings of musical lines among the various parts, and these have to be perfected.

The task of coordinating a group is especially difficult in the case of instrumental music. To begin with, an instrumental group has many instruments requiring different parts, often more than twenty. A choral group usually has four parts, almost never more than eight. Instrumentalists are usually called upon to perform longer pieces, requiring much faster execution of notes, than are the singers in a choral organization. Another difference lies in the manner in which vocal and instrumental music is printed. In a choral group, all the singers look at complete copies of the music. Each performer can see how his part fits with the others, and he can anticipate the overall effect of the combined sounds. An instrumentalist, however, sees only his own part, be it second clarinet, first violin, or tuba. He has no clear idea of what anyone else is doing, so he must become familiar with the piece through repeated hearing.

In music for many instruments, the only person who knows everyone's part is the conductor, who has before him a master copy of all parts, called a *score*. The size and complexity of the score explains why instrumentalists are given only their own parts to read. Scores are bulky and expensive to print. Following a score while the music is in progress requires technical knowledge and frequent turning of pages. On page 89 is the first page from the score to *Don Juan* by Richard Strauss. This work is presented in more detail in Chapter 13.

Not only does Strauss' score present twenty-three lines to follow simultaneously; it also demonstrates the common phenomenon called *transposition*. That is, the player reacts to a printed pitch, but mechanical characteristics of the instrument cause the actual sound to be heard at a different pitch level. When the French horn plays C, the listener hears F, five notes lower; when the clarinetist plays C on the most common type of clarinet, the listener hears B-flat, one note lower. Many instruments do not transpose, however. The origins of transposition are rooted in a tradition that allowed players to change easily between instruments with identical fingering systems. Transposition also enables more of an instruments' notes to be written *within* a staff, rather than extended far above or below it. So much is now invested in methods books and printed music that it would scarcely be feasible to replace transposition just so that every instrument could sound the same pitch that is read.

Traditions have grown up regarding memorization of music for performance. Because of the number of parts in the music, works for orchestra, band, and chamber groups are seldom memorized; neither are long choral works. Soloists almost always memorize, and so do most choral

groups when singing short selections. Conductors frequently conduct a performance without a score before them, but this does not mean they have memorized every single note. They know the work in considerable detail, and they know the interpretation they want. These resources are sufficient for conducting a performance, particularly if the performing musicians are skilled and well-rehearsed.

The Conductor

A performing group of any size invariably has a conductor. Many people, however, misunderstand his function. A good professional orchestra can start with a nod from one of the players and proceed to play a symphony acceptably. So why a conductor? The conductor's position is comparable to that of a baseball or football coach. A good team can play quite well without a manager—for a while. But problems inevitably arise, and decisions have to be made. In a musical organization as well as a ball team, the situations requiring decisions do not usually lend themselves to resolution by group debate or vote. A knowledgeable and respected leader must be in charge, to instruct, to be the guiding spirit for the team's efforts, and to galvanize the group into action.

A conductor's most important job, however, is to decide on and implement the interpretation of the music. Prior to directing a piece, therefore, he spends hours studying the score to determine in advance the tempos, styles, and nuances. It is his role in rehearsal to tell and show the performers how they are to perform the piece.

The conductor keeps the performance together by starting the group concisely, maintaining the tempo, and giving cues—visual indications that an important passage is to begin at that moment. In the early days of orchestras, all a conductor did was set the beat and start the group. He was not required to do more, because the performers were few and music was relatively simple. He used a minimum of motions, stood literally in the center of the orchestra, and in general assumed a less important place than the performers. As the need for more concise direction became apparent, the conductor took increasing responsibility for interpretation and leadership. Only in the last hundred years has the conductor risen to his present prominent position as undisputed leader and artist in his own right.

Gestures are used in conducting because they are silent and do not interfere with the sound of the music. With his right hand the conductor sets the beat. The basic patterns are simple:

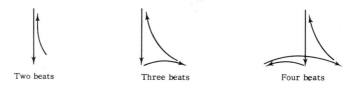

Two beats   Three beats   Four beats

These pictures of Leonard Bernstein show the forcefulness and expressiveness of his conducting.

Most music falls into one of these three patterns, although sometimes only one beat per measure is conducted, just as sometimes more than four beats are found. With his left hand the conductor indicates dynamics and cues the various parts. If you watch a professional conductor, you may not be able to recognize the beat patterns outlined above. Why? Because he wants his motions to be more expressive and less mechanical. Students of conducting are often admonished to "look like the music," meaning that their facial expressions and bodily motions should project the proper feeling for the music. When the music is quiet and serene, the conductor should not be wildly thrashing his arms about. The professional director is able to concentrate on expression because his performers are able to count the rhythm accurately and come in at the right moment. With nonprofessional groups, time-beating and cueing are more necessary.

Unfortunately the conductor does not operate in a vacuum. He is seldom free of matters pertaining to the public's reaction to the performance and to himself. Too often the public's acceptance is not based on valid musical considerations. Some people recall that a conductor's hair flopped about or that he conducted from memory or that he did not use a baton (the small stick used to help clarify the beats of the right hand). These and similar observations are of course irrelevant to the sound of the music itself.

In earlier years, when orchestras depended more on the support of a few wealthy patrons, the conductor's flair for public relations was scrutinized almost as closely as his musicianship. It was the handsome, middle-aged conductor who kissed the ladies' hands and offered flattering remarks who sometimes got and kept the desirable conducting posts.

Occasionally, a conductor has seemed overly concerned that the public remember him, and so he has engaged in displays that detract from the music: excessive arm waving and erratic actions, or novel and extreme interpretations seldom faithful to the composer's intentions. Fortunately, such idiosyncrasies are not the rule. The majority of conductors pursue their art with dedication and conscientious hard work.

Orchestras and opera companies usually have a permanent conductor who is given the title "Musical Director." Besides conducting most performances, he is responsible for the selection of music and soloists. He also makes recommendations on the hiring and firing of players and other matters pertaining to the business of the musical organization.

Time and Money

Time is a critical issue in putting together a performance. For instance, the professional orchestra today can seldom spend a week preparing for a single concert. Frequently there are other performances, such as educational concerts, recording sessions, and out-of-town performances, that cut into rehearsal time. If a weekend concert features a concerto with a soloist, rehearsal time with the soloist is needed for purposes of coordination and unity of interpretation. (In general, the soloist's views on interpretation prevail.) The other numbers on the program, perhaps a symphony and a long overture, can be given only cursory attention, sometimes as little as one run-through of the music.

The reason for limited rehearsal time is economic. The hours of employment are carefully spelled out in a contract between the musicians' union and the symphony's board of directors. Extra rehearsal time can be had, but for an orchestra the cost is several hundred dollars per hour, a figure that financially hard-pressed symphony orchestras can seldom afford.

The same situation exists in opera, except that the problem is worse. Stage productions involve the employment of many craft-union men such as electricians, carpenters, and stage hands. These men usually earn more than most of the performers, so the financial implications are far-reaching. These economic realities require the professional musician to perform well with little or no rehearsal, and they occasionally cause the public to hear a performance that has not been adequately prepared.

FINANCIAL SUPPORT OF MUSICAL GROUPS

Since music must be brought to life through the efforts of a performer, the quality of musical performances and their availability to the listener are crucial factors in shaping the art of music. For example, after Bach died in 1750, his music was virtually forgotten until 1829, when Felix Mendelssohn organized a performance of the *St. Matthew Passion*. It was only then, seventy-nine years after his death, that the interest in Bach's music began to grow. The music of the eighteenth-century Bach lives in the twentieth century only as it is played and sung. Without performance, his music is just so many books on a library shelf.

The United States differs from other modern societies in the way it provides for the performance of music. In Europe, most professional opera companies and orchestras operate under some direct subsidy from the government, both local and national. In America, the arts have traditionally been supported entirely through private donations and ticket sales. Only in recent years has public money been made available to the arts, and the amounts have been small. Most governmental support has been for specific projects: performances in remote or less affluent communities, performances of new musical compositions, concerts for school students. Almost never have general subsidy grants been made available.

When a person buys a ticket to the symphony or opera, he is likely to assume that the amount he paid covers the actual cost of the program according to the number of seats in the concert hall. Unfortunately this is not the case. Of every dollar received for the operation of a symphony orchestra, about thirty cents comes from the sale of tickets. The total operation of the musical organization could be met through ticket sales only if the admission price were about triple its present level. There is a reluctance to increase the admission charge, because people of moderate or lower income would be "priced out" of musical events, and such a result is inconsistent with a tenet of democracy which affirms that equal access to the arts is a human right.

Traditionally the difference between income and expenditures has been made up by subscription drives and other forms of donation. Today it is rarely possible for a few wealthy patrons to provide sole support for an orchestra or opera company, although monied people are still necessary for the continuance of musical organizations. Since about 1960 a new form of arts support has emerged: the arts council and its fund drive. The arts fund drive operates in a manner similar to the united health and welfare drives. The various arts organizations pool their efforts into one united campaign. Such united drives have the advantage of receiving support from a broad section of the public. The arts council helps coordinate and promote artistic events as well as articulate the goals and needs of the arts to the community. When governmental assistance has been made available, it is often channeled through arts councils.

The American method of private support for musical performances has disadvantages. It tends to devote too much of the musical organization's efforts to pleasing a small, well-to-do minority of the community. Also, sufficient operational funds have usually been hard to come by. The advantage of the American system is its obvious freedom from governmental interference. In fairness, however, it should be mentioned that in the democratic countries of Western Europe, governmental interference has not been a problem. The creative artist has been allowed to work freely. So governmental support in democratic countries need not mean governmental dictation of the arts.

Results of Limited Financial Support

The shortage of funds for the arts in America has been an inhibiting factor in the cultural life of the nation. Many musical works have never been performed publicly, and the number of performances of music in general has been limited. Like everyone else, musicians must eat. The limitation of funds has been especially detrimental to the performances of new compositions. Because the music is unfamiliar, the musicians may need more time for rehearsal. Furthermore, the public is not so quick to respond to a new work as it is to a familiar one. So the odds are against the untried contemporary composer.

The pattern of support for music in America has produced some curious inconsistencies. One is the position of the professional musician. He was one of the first to suffer from technological unemployment. First, many theater musicians were put out of work when sound films were introduced at the end of the twenties. The situation was further aggravated by the depression of the thirties. Then, after World War II, came the vastly improved techniques of sound recording. People could hear excellent performances in their living rooms, so the need to attend a live concert was reduced. As a final blow to the performers' livelihood, television replaced the few remaining radio orchestras. By the mid-fifties only a small minority of the membership of the American Federation of Musicians was made up of people who earned the major share of their livelihood as performing musicians. The pay of most symphony musicians was below the minimum subsistence level as spelled out by the U.S. Department of Labor.

The situation has improved only slightly since that low point. The greater attention given the arts, beginning in the early 1960s, has brought a significant improvement in the circumstances of some musicians. In the five or six best-known symphony orchestras, players' wages have reached over $250 per week for fifty-two weeks, plus income from recording sessions and special concerts. But the improvement has been uneven, so that the players of a few orchestras are well rewarded while their nearly-as-able colleagues earn substandard wages, if they can find work as musicians.

The composer is in a similar curious position. The present situation presents him with the best and worst of times. It is possible for him *as a composer* to earn a good living, something even Bach, Mozart, and Liszt could not do. Private foundations offer him grants and help him find avenues of performance for his works. An organization called the American Society of Composers, Authors, and Publishers (ASCAP) helps protect his legal rights to his work and gives him access to a complex system of profit sharing. In addition, there are more and better positions at universities as the demand increases for teachers of composition and related subjects. Never has the composer had more freedom to write exactly what he feels like writing. Such freedom was unknown to Haydn, Bach, and others. Today's composer, however, sometimes finds that his efforts are greeted coolly by the public and occasionally even by the performers themselves. Where there isn't antipathy, there seems to be apathy. In Beethoven's day, the performance of a new symphony was an event of considerable interest. Today a new symphony attracts about as much attention as another cloud in the sky.

THE ROLE OF MUSIC EDUCATION

An encouraging aspect of music in contemporary America is the strong evidence that Americans are interested in quality music. Americans spend more money on quality music than on spectator sports;[1] the sales of recordings and record-playing equipment have become a significant factor in the economy; new arts centers and concert halls have been built in many major cities. Equally gratifying is the virile state of amateur music. There are about twelve hundred amateur orchestras in the United States. Such extensive interest indicates that the art of music is alive and that people are finding various degrees of fulfillment through it—the mark of a quality civilization.

---

[1] *The Facts of American Life,* ed. M. B. Schnapper. Washington, D.C.: Public Affairs Press, 1960, p. 270.

Partial credit for the current interest in music should go to the great American experiment in universal education and its inclusion of music in that education. Music is now too complex a creation to be passed along informally from one generation to another, as is done in primitive societies. In a culture such as ours, dependent on a system of formal education to teach the younger generation, it is not surprising that the curriculum incorporates many aspects of our heritage, artistic as well as scientific.

The purpose of music in the school curriculum has not always been made clear to the public. Simply stated, schools offer music for the same reason that they offer languages and science: all are areas of knowledge, of human endeavor that students should know. Music classes exist primarily to instruct students in music, and not to provide free entertainment for the community. Children learn songs because in so doing they are gaining an understanding of the organization and arrangement of musical sounds. Students learn to play clarinet and violin because the experience teaches them to appreciate good instrumental performance and familiarizes them with the wealth of music that has enriched our culture.

One aspect of American music education has perhaps been overemphasized. Because wind instruments are more easily learned and have stronger tones, and because much attention has been focused on bands and marching activities, many schools offer no instruction on string instruments. This trend has restricted the type of music that many teenagers study, and has made it difficult for professional orchestras to build adequate string sections. In the past, good string players were "imported" from Europe, but this source is now limited.

Music education, because its benefits are intangible, has too often been justified on nonmusical grounds. It is said to improve character, teach teamwork, build healthy bodies, and establish good public relations for the school. Such reasons are spurious and serve only to obscure the true purpose of music education.

REVIEWS OF MUSICAL EVENTS

Many daily publications hire critics to write reviews of musical events. In New York City the would-be concert artist presents his recital, then anxiously waits for several hours to find out what judgment the newspaper critics have passed on his career. (The fact that the newspaper critics frequently do not agree with one another has not discouraged this custom.) In other cities the review is not taken so seriously, although it can affect the morale of a local amateur group.

Traditionally the main purpose of the review was to guard artistic standards. For example, if an opera was produced poorly, then the public was so advised by the expert reviewer. The question may arise: Why review a performance that is presented only once? After all, there is no opportunity in such cases for the performers to improve their presentation or for the audience to attend ensuing performances on the basis of the reviewer's recommendations. Probably the answer lies in the fact that some readers like to read and talk about musical events, just as some enjoy discussing football games. What a critic said makes a topic for conversation, even if you disagree with his opinion. In addition, for people who don't know what is current in the musical world, the review is an easy way to become "informed."

Not all reviews appearing in print are necessarily authoritative. Few people are expert in all phases of music, from opera to organ, from medieval to modern. Sometimes in small cities the music critic also reviews plays, books, and art shows and is responsible for evaluation in such learned fields as philosophy and education. Expertise in all these areas seems more than can be expected from any mortal. Furthermore, the critic usually has little time to write his review, and it is often subject to cuts or last-minute alterations because of space limitations.

In spite of the pitfalls inherent in artistic criticism, newspaper and magazine reviews are usually a positive force. They do stress artistic quality, and they help to keep music alive by acknowledging the essential place of performance in the realm of music.

The abilities of performing musicians, the circumstances of their performances, the interest of society, and trends in music education and musical criticism—all have a direct bearing on the music you hear. Understanding these factors enables you to appreciate their importance to the art of music and makes you aware of the many problems involved in the presentation of musical works.

Early and Renaissance Music

6

No one knows how or where music began, but it seems to be universal. In every culture, primitive or sophisticated, man sings, chants, dances, and creates instruments. Pictures on the walls of pyramids and on Mesopotamian vases show people making music. In early Greek civilization, bards like Homer sang their tales as they accompanied themselves on simple string instruments. Even the lonely Tibetans sound a tremendous trumpet that can be heard for great distances.

The intellectual Greeks considered music an important part of a citizen's education, although their use of the word "music" included rhythmic activities more suitable for physical education. They even ascribed to music certain moral qualities and effects. Their dramas included a chorus that chanted and sang its lines. The Greeks developed several instruments, including the lyre, which is seen on many music emblems today. Most impressive, however, were the acoustical discoveries of Pythagoras (about 550 B.C.), the same man for whom the geometrical theorem is named. Pythagoras (or some of his assistants) discovered that intervals—the distance from one pitch to another—can be represented by mathematical ratios,

In this painting from an ancient Etruscan tomb, several musical instruments can be seen.

and that there is a correlation between these ratios and the degree of consonance or dissonance suggested by any particular interval.

Our understanding of Greek music suffers from the same unfortunate circumstance that affects our knowledge of most music until about the twelfth century: it is impossible to determine how such music sounded. No accurate system was devised for writing music; or if one existed, it has been lost. Only a few scraps of music notation have been found, and attempts to reconstruct these fragments have been mostly guesswork. The Greeks talked about music a great deal, believed (falsely) that it influenced man's moral character, theorized about music and acoustics, but made no provision for the preservation of its sounds. The continuance of their music depended on oral tradition.

The Romans had music, too. Probably most of it, along with much of Roman culture, was taken over from Hellenic civilization. The Romans, naturally, emphasized military music more than did the Greeks.

With the fall of the Roman empire in 476 A.D., the Christian church deliberately attempted to root out of society everything that had been associated with pagan Rome. One object of this reform was Roman music, which had so often been used for festivals (and orgies). Again, almost all remnants of Roman music have been lost or destroyed.

Because Christianity began in the context of Judaism, early church music assumed much of the heritage of the Jewish temple. Daily prayer hours were adopted, along with the responsive singing of psalms between a soloist and congregation. As the church spread through Asia Minor into Europe and Africa, it accumulated other musical elements. The fact that the early church incorporated singing into its worship activities is recorded in Matthew (26:30) and Mark (14:26) and in non-Biblical writings. It is probable that during the first three centuries of the Christian era, before Christianity became the official religion of the Roman Empire, there were no uniform musical customs. Individual improvisation was a feature of early church music. *Improvisation* means to make up on the spot, without prior planning. Usually melodic formulas were used to provide some basis for the music being improvised, rather like Indian *raga*.

GREGORIAN CHANT

From the fourth to the sixth centuries A.D., church music became more uniform and evolved along Western lines. Trained singers were increasingly given more responsibility for the music. Late in the sixth century, as a part of the organization of the total church, Pope Gregory I directed a recodification and compilation of the chants (the actual work was probably done by his assistants). He assigned particular chants to certain services throughout the year. Gregory's work was so highly esteemed that even today this entire body of church music is called *Gregorian chant*. (It is also known as *plainsong* or *plainchant*.) When Gregory's work was done, the church had a liturgy, a body of rites prescribed for public worship.

The music that evolved from the centuries of modification and adaptation by the early church and under Gregory's direction is one of the finest monuments of Western civilization. It is valuable in its own right as a part of our cultural heritage, and it is important to the understanding of the music that follows it.

When you studied Berlioz' *The Roman Carnival Overture* in Chapter 4, and Sibelius' *Symphony No. 2* and Bach's chorus in Chapter 1, you were hearing music that was in the same musical idiom or "language" as most of the music with which you are familiar. Its purpose and degree of complexity may have been different, but at least it was not foreign. For many readers, however, Gregorian chant will be new and different.

In chant, only one line of music is heard, without the enriching sounds of harmony. And even that one melodic line is strangely unlike the characteristic patterns of familiar melodies. For one thing, in place of beats and regular rhythmic patterns there is a flexible rhythm. Furthermore, the major-minor scale system, common to most music in Western civilization, is not used. No attempt is made to appeal to the senses or to involve the listener's emotions. Only men's voices are used, and they sing in a restrained, other-worldly way.

St. Gregory receiving the Chant melodies from the Holy Spirit, represented by the dove, and dictating them to his scribe, who has stuck his pen through the curtain to watch. (Actually, Gregory probably did very little of the work himself.) From a Trier manuscript dated about 983.

To appreciate Gregorian chant, you need to realize the extent to which it was interwoven with religious practice. Removed from this context, it would have little value. After all, it was created for one purpose only: to embody the spirit of worship. Heard as concert music, Gregorian chant seems rather ineffective. When sung by the religious in a seminary or monastery, however, it is strangely moving. Undoubtedly the impression is created partially by the setting and the obvious religious devotion of the participants, and by the knowledge that the music helps to put modern man in the procession of the faithful stretching back nearly two thousand years. But much of the effect is due to qualities of the music itself.

Traditionally, the Roman Catholic Church specified the order and content of every service, depending on the type of service and its place in the church year. Since Vatican Council II (1964–67) much of the former practice has changed greatly, and much freedom is permitted in the amount and type of music to be used in the service. The most significant change has been the use of *vernacular* languages (non-Latin). Unfortunately, most chants lose much of their meaning when translated, so chant is being used less widely now than in the past.

The musical example shows an *Ave Maria*. Until a few years ago, the words of the service were specified, and the same words have been set to music by many composers. Certainly the *Ave Maria* has been so favored; the versions by Schubert and Bach-Gounod are extremely well-known. The text is translated: "Hail Mary, full of grace, the Lord is with thee; thou art blessed among women, and blessed is the fruit of thy womb." The music is shown here in two versions. One is the traditional four-line staff and square notes; the second is a rendition in modern notation. By marking the pitches that are to be stressed, the traditional Roman notation helps to indicate the performance style of the music.

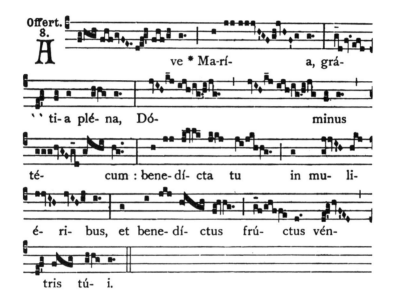

té - - cum: be-ne - dí - cta tu

in mu - li - é - ri - bus, et be-ne - dí - ctus

frú - ctus vén - - tris tú - i.

Even in modern notation, the music looks somewhat unusual. It has no time or meter signature. Almost all notes have the same rhythmic value, but the last note of each phrase is consistently longer. The grouping of notes is irregular; sometimes there are two in a group, sometimes three, sometimes more. The melody seldom jumps very far from one note to another; its contour is smooth. The entire melody covers a range of about one octave, and it centers around the note G.[1] The piece is quite short, taking only about two and a half minutes to perform.

The unfamiliar sound of Gregorian chant can be partly attributed to an unusual organization of tones. Today we are accustomed to music that usually reflects one of two patterns: *major* or *minor*. These patterns are called *keys* or *modes*. Originally, however, the term "mode" was the only one used, and it encompassed several other patterns, as well as major and minor. The notes of any mode, when lined up in order, resulted in a scale with its own characteristic pattern. In medieval times, musicians seemed to prefer the *non*-major/minor modes, and these are the sounds experienced in Gregorian chant. The same modal characteristics are sometimes found in folk music, and they are common in popular songs of today. It is easy to duplicate the sounds of these modes. At the piano, play scales *on the white keys only* from D to D, E to E, F to F, and G to G.

As you listen to a recording of the *Ave Maria* or other examples of Gregorian chant, remind yourself that this is not concert-hall music. It is not going to command your attention through mighty sounds or dramatic changes. Rather it seeks to convey a spirit, an attitude. Like the devout and pious monks who sing it, the music strives for a purity and reverence worthy

---

[1] The pitch is only approximate. The notes of Gregorian chant are not absolute pitches, such as are found today.

A page of manuscript written in 1290 showing the old system of notation and beautiful decorations (illuminations). The picture in the decoration shows an early organ.

of acceptance by God. Although such an ideal may seem remote from the busy pace of modern American life, seldom has an ideal come closer to fulfillment in an artistic medium.

Unlike other early music, Gregorian chant was carefully preserved in the monasteries by oral tradition and written manuscripts. This music has been painstakingly researched by musicologists from within the Church and from outside it. The recognized authorities on chant are the Benedictine monks of the Abbey of Solesmes (So-*lem*). They have recorded several albums of Gregorian chant.

SECULAR MUSIC

Because of the dominant role of the church, Gregorian chant dominated the music of the times. But music of a *secular* (worldly or non-sacred) nature also existed. Again, most of the nonreligious music was not written down, so less is known about it. Most of the secular music was in the language of a particular country—French, German, English, Italian, Spanish—rather than in the ecclesiastical Latin that was prescribed for worship. At first such music was largely the contribution of wandering musicians who traveled from place to place singing songs, reciting poems, and even exhibiting trained animals. Later, about the twelfth and thirteenth centuries, troubadours and trouvères dominated secular music in France. They were noblemen who were poets and composers but usually not performers, since they often hired minstrels to sing their songs. The music was for solo voice, and was often sung with instrumental accompaniment. Most of the poems and songs were about an idealized type of chivalric love, with a passion more of the spirit than of the flesh. About 4600 such poems and 1660 such melodies have been preserved. Unlike Gregorian chant, they are clear-cut in their display of regular rhythmic patterns and sound quite a bit like the folk melodies heard today.

During this time there existed a close relationship between secular vocal music and instrumental music. A song could be played or sung, or both. Many of the songs appeared in conjunction with dancing. The rhythm for the dances and other secular pieces followed any of six *rhythmic modes* —patterns that are identical or similar to those used in classifying poetry meters today. The short-long pattern corresponds to today's iambic meter, while the long-short pattern corresponds to the trochaic.

POLYPHONY

Until about 1000 A.D., music consisted largely of single melodic lines with an occasional improvised accompaniment. Although examples of the simultaneous sounding of tones are found in early Western music, as well as in the music of other civilizations to a limited extent, these examples account for only a small amount of the total body of music. In the eleventh century, Western music began to depart from its past. It began to indicate in notation the simultaneous sounding of musical tones.

Medieval musicians, many of whom were anonymous monks, accomplished the simultaneous sounding of pitches in the simplest possible way. They merely took the lines of Gregorian chant they already had and *added to* them. The process was one of adding another layer of sound to the original. At first the added line ran exactly parallel to the original line and four or five notes below it, similar to the harmony often found in African music. Since this did not allow for much musical freedom, the added line was permitted to break out of its strictly parallel pattern and little by little to assume a more independent character. When independent lines of melody were written for simultaneous performance, counterpoint was accomplished. As was pointed out in Chapter 1, counterpoint represents one of two ways in which simultaneous sounds can be formed. The general term for this type of writing is *polyphony.*

Polyphony is an important concept in music. It is the combining of lines of nearly equal melodic interest; no particular line is superior. Listening to polyphony might be compared to watching a three-ring circus. Each act is equally interesting. Although it is not easy to look at all the acts at once, there are no dull moments during which little is happening.

An interesting fact can be observed in this early manipulation of music: notes of the same pitch, those an octave apart, and those four and five tones apart were considered to be consonant. (These intervals are the same ones Pythagoras had regarded as most consonant.) In other words, the interval of a third, the interval upon which our system of chords is based (Appendix C), was regarded as a dissonance. It was, however, found in the folk music of that time, especially in England. It would be nearly five hundred years before chords containing thirds would be considered consonant enough to appear as the all-important final chord of a piece.

MUSICAL STYLES AND PERIODS

The concept of style in music, and the need for references to stylistic periods, should be clarified at this point. A term such as "Renaissance," when applied to music, describes primarily a style of music rather than a period of time. Even after a style has passed the peak of its use, composers occasionally return to it, sometimes centuries later. Entire works in old styles such as Renaissance and Baroque are still being written occasionally today. And certain elements of these styles appear in other pieces that are primarily in a contemporary idiom. Although a style of music is not confined to a particular time and place, it is named for the historical period in which it was most conspicuously developed and brought to prominence.

The designation of periods can be made only after the actual years have passed, because such categorizing requires historical perspective. No one awoke on New Year's Day in 1100 and said, "Well, the Gothic period has arrived." After all, the people of earlier eras considered themselves modern, just as we do today. It makes one wonder what scholars a hundred years from now will call our age. Only this can be said for certain: it will *not* be called "modern." And the dates of its beginning and ending will never be known precisely. As in every age, the dates of historic and artistic trends must always be approximate.

Literature, art, and music are generally identified in relation to the same stylistic periods. And the fine arts of a particular period do contain similarities of outlook and artistic goals. A word of caution: much that appears in Gothic or modern art cannot be related to Gothic or modern music. Each art is influenced by technical matters peculiar to it, and each is affected by conditions that are not present in other fine arts. Until about the last one hundred years, art and literature tended to be "ahead" of music. Several factors may have contributed to the developmental lag of music: the inadequacy of its notation, problems of instrumental construction, the uncertainty of various tuning systems, and the lack of recording devices with which to preserve musical performance. Close parallels of style, therefore, cannot be drawn among the arts in the various style periods. Nor are the approximate dates for a period the same in the various arts. During past centuries, cultural developments could not spread uniformly, largely because of limited communication and travel between countries. A highly popular movement in Italy could be unheard of in Germany. In fact, a new style of music in Venice might not have caught on for many years in cities as close as Rome or Florence.

In spite of its drawbacks, the concept of style in music can be a useful aid to you as a student of music. It enables you to organize your thinking about music and recognize the way musical material is treated. Not only are styles useful, they are valid. When you understand what constitutes musical style, you are learning the very stuff of music. An understanding of style helps you listen for the right things in music. Knowing that the Renaissance ideal was purity and restraint of sound, you should not be surprised or disappointed by the lack of volume and flashing brilliance in Renaissance music. You will be able to listen to the music of that or any other period with more realistic expectations and greater reward. Hence the organization of this book according to musical styles. If you want to review the various periods, check the end pages inside the front and back covers of this book.

1

Jan Van Eyck: *Angels Playing,* right panel from altarpiece in St. Bavo's, Ghent, Belgium. (Giradoun, Paris. Courtesy of Art Reference Bureau, Inc.)

2 Botticelli: *The Adoration of the Magi.* (Andrew Mellon Collection, National Gallery of Art, Washington, D.C.)

THE GOTHIC PERIOD AND THE MOTET

The late medieval period from about 1100 to 1450 has come to be known as the Gothic period. This was the era of the building of great cathedrals, the founding of universities and the high point of scholasticism, the Magna Charta, Dante's *The Divine Comedy* (from which Delacroix centuries later drew his subject matter for "The Bark of Dante," plate 7), the Crusades, and the Hundred Years' War. The painting "Angels Playing" (plate 1) is from Jan Van Eyck's altarpiece in St. Bavo's, Ghent, Belgium. It is a late Gothic–early Renaissance work, completed in 1432. Aided somewhat by his brother Hubert, Jan Van Eyck painted with meticulous precision. For example, the organist is fingering a chord: C E G. The spiritual expression on the angels' faces and the rather flat perspective are characteristic of the painting of the time. The music that developed during this time is termed "Gothic," and it was characterized, among other things, by a more sophisticated type of polyphony. One type had the chant melody sung or played in a very slow tempo, while the added part sounded several shorter notes within the same duration. Later the chant melody and extra part were treated rhythmically through the use of the rhythmic modes. Sometimes as many as four lines were combined in the music. When words were added to the non-chant lines, the piece became known as a *motet,* from the French *mot,* meaning "word."

The motet was a curious musical animal. First, it often combined various languages as well as sacred and secular texts. For example, one motet has two different sets of words for the top part, one in Latin, praising the Virgin Mary, and another in French, which reads: "When I see the summer season returning and all the little birds make the woods resound, then I weep and sigh for the great desire I have for fair Marion, who holds my heart imprisoned." The Latin text reads: "Virgin of virgins, Light of lights, restorer of men, who didst bear the Lord: through Thee, O Mary, let grace be given as the angel announced: Thou art Virgin before and after." The lower line typically utilizes a phrase of Gregorian chant: "This is the day which the Lord hath made." The length of the motet was determined by the length of the text, so you can see that this one is not long. Its brevity is typical of the form. Second, the composers tended to concentrate on working out each line, relatively unconcerned about how it might sound with the other lines. Some harsh dissonances were the result. Third, composers became fascinated, especially in the fourteenth century, by mystical relationships and concealed meanings in the music. They took great delight in concealing a chant phrase in the upper lines. Or they set up a complicated scheme of rhythmic and melodic patterns, so that a rhythmic pattern might appear three times for every two times the melodic pattern was repeated. Such intellectual complexities pleased the medieval musician, but

The facade and towers of the cathedral at Chartres, one of the finest examples of Gothic architecture. The right spire (351 feet) dates from the 12th century, while the left spire (377 feet) was not completed until the 16th century.

they were generally lost on the listener, since he could comprehend it only by looking at the music, not by hearing it. Such music was a form of intellectual puzzle. The fascination with intricate patterns and tricks (such as going through a melody backward) is revived periodically. An especially active interest in such complexities has reappeared in the twentieth century.

In summary, the Gothic motet featured rhythmic patterns adapted from secular music, but it was based on and developed from Gregorian chant. Often highly complex techniques of composition were employed. Various lines were added one upon another in layers. Although the motet did not branch out into the major-minor patterns, it represented, for its time, a sophisticated form of polyphony.

While the Gothic motet was reaching its acme with the compositions of Machaut (Mah-*sho*), the pendulum was already beginning to swing away from this complex and intellectually oriented type of music. Actually, it had been largely a French development; composers in other countries were evidently indifferent to the style or not advanced enough to attempt composing in it. In Italy a blind musician named Landini (Lahn-*dee*-nee) and in England a remarkable composer named John Dunstable were writing music that was simpler and more listenable. Both men and their followers used the same text for all parts. Their music enabled the words to be sung more or less simultaneously so that the text could be understood by the listener, something that was impossible with the Gothic motet. They avoided jarring dissonances. A special contribution of Dunstable and other English composers was the placement of simultaneously sounded pitches three and six notes apart, the pattern that is still the most common in Western music. To the listener today, these intervals give the music a richer sound than the fourths and fifths of previous music. In fact, the works of Landini and Dunstable are a pleasure to hear today, six centuries later.

As the 1450s approached, the Gothic motet was rapidly disappearing, although vestiges of its style remain even today. Gregorian chant was continuing to influence other musical forms. Drawing to a close, however, was that long stretch of human history called "the Middle Ages." This period had not been dark, as it is sometimes described. Development had taken place in music and other fields. In fact, the years leading up to 1450 had laid the foundation for a new era: the Renaissance.

THE RENAISSANCE ERA

The word "Renaissance" literally means "rebirth." Historically it meant a revival of interest in the philosophy and arts of ancient Greece and Rome. Music, however, had no ancient Greek roots to which to return. So the concept of rebirth in regard to music has little direct significance. The term "Renaissance" as applied to this field simply refers to the style of music that predominated from about 1450 until 1600.

The Renaissance reflected an intense interest in ancient Greek civilization. This interest led to a curious amalgamation of Greek and Christian belief. Michelangelo gave expression to this union of the pagan and Christian by decorating the ceiling of the Sistine Chapel with alternating figures of prophets and sibyls. Erasmus, the great philosopher, regarded Socrates as a pre-Christian saint, and once wrote, "St. Socrates, pray for us."

Closely allied with the renewal of interest in ancient Greek ideals was the "humanistic" view of man. This ideal, still very much alive today, affirmed that human dignity consists of moral and intellectual freedom. One outgrowth of this philosophy was an emphasis on man and his life on earth. People began to take delight in the natural world and man's place in it.

The results of humanism are well illustrated by the two treatments of the human body shown on page 113. One is a piece of Gothic sculpture found on the cathedral at Chartres. Notice that this figure has a spiritual, other-worldly quality about it. The attitude of the head and eyes is serene, and the position of the body is formal. The proportions of the figure are distorted through exaggerated length, thus giving the body an emaciated look. The feet seem to dangle from the robes as though they were merely attached. Michelangelo's *David*, on the other hand, looks like a magnificent Greek god. (The figure of David stands over thirteen and a half feet in height.) The impression is one of confidence in and admiration of man. David looks natural, almost casual, and free. The human body emerges from the withered state given it by medieval beliefs to the idealized status accorded it by Renaissance attitudes.

With the increasing interest in the value of worldly life, there was a corresponding interest in the fine arts. A beautiful painting or piece of music began to have value for its own sake, and not merely as a means to religious devotion. As a result of this fortunate change of outlook, the list of great Renaissance sculptors and painters is long—Botticelli, da Vinci, Michelangelo, Dürer, Raphael, Titian, Bruegel, Tintoretto. Botticelli's "The Adoration of the Magi" (plate 2) shows the Renaissance fondness for order and balance. A group of figures at the left of the painting is balanced by a group on the right. The infant Jesus is in the center. The converging lines of the Greek and Roman ruins add perspective to the painting and show the renewed interest in these ancient civilizations. Notice also the brightly colored clothing on the figures.

Not only were works of art being enjoyed in a new climate of acceptance. The increasing level of the economy, especially in the cities of northern Italy and the Netherlands, meant that money was available with which to hire artists and musicians. The Church sought rich adornment for its buildings, one of several practices that led to the reform movement started by Martin Luther in 1517. The effect of the Reformation on the

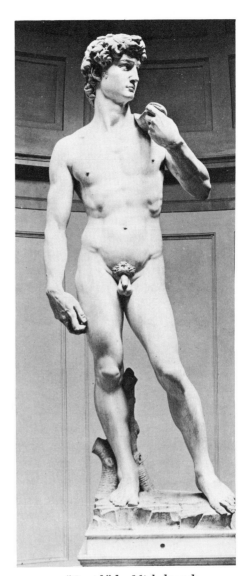

Sculptured figure of Christ on the cathedral at Chartres.

"David," by Michelangelo.

world of music did not show its full impact until after 1600. But the seeds of change were planted.

An event that reached into every area of human endeavor—education, religion, commerce—was Gutenberg's invention of printing from movable type. Printing made possible the wide dissemination of music, beginning with the appearance of the first printed music books in 1501.

The spirit of the times was one of optimism and discovery. The voyages of Columbus, Cabot, Balboa, and Magellan took place during the

Renaissance. Copernicus was announcing his new discoveries about the universe. Rabelais, Machiavelli, Boccaccio, Montaigne, Thomas More, Francis Bacon, and Erasmus were exploring new ideas in literature and philosophy. The world was changing.

RENAISSANCE MUSIC

The musical Renaissance started in the Netherlands, which then included Holland, northern Belgium, and part of northern France. The composers of the area had reached a level of proficiency that was the envy of Europe. Composers from the Netherlands were lured away from their homeland to better-paying jobs in Spain, Bohemia, Austria, Germany, and especially the cities of northern Italy. The style and technique of the Netherlanders became internationally known and imitated. So cosmopolitan did composers become that they thought of themselves as musicians first and as citizens of a particular country second. This outlook is well illustrated by Orlando di Lasso (the name he used in Italy), alias Roland de Lassus (the name he used in Germany), who wrote music in the German, French, and Italian idioms, as well as in the Netherlands style. Versatility was further evidenced by the scope of a musician's duties. He was employed not just to compose. He was expected to perform himself, train a choir (often of boys), and teach.

The most esteemed composer of the early Renaissance was Josquin des Prez (Zhoss-can day *Pray*), who lived from about 1440 to 1521. Born in Flanders, Josquin was a choir singer in Milan, a musician in the service of the Sforza family, a member of the Papal Chapel, a choirmaster, and a musician in the service of Louis XII of France. In his compositions, Josquin continued some of the techniques developed in the Gothic period. His religious music was derived from various sources: chant, secular music, themes from other composers. Like composers before him, he used the device of imitation, in which one line of melody appears in another part a measure or two later, somewhat like a round. But whereas his predecessors had obscured the imitative effect by requiring all parts to be performed continuously, Josquin emphasized the beginning of each imitative passage by having voices "enter" one after the other. By drawing attention to each successive voice in this manner, he made the words sung by each entering part more easily understood by the listener. Thus the music itself took on more clarity. It assumed a phrase-by-phrase form, which proved to be more appealing than the previous technique of continuous sound at the same level of volume.

Josquin, more than any previous composer, wrote with an awareness of a consistent organization of harmonies. This aspect of his music coincided with a trend that was then becoming apparent. Closely related to an improved harmonic quality was the development at the beginning of the Renaissance of a bass line in the music. When composers started adding melodies to chant, they placed the chant around middle C (on a piano, this pitch is near the middle of the keyboard) and placed the additional melodies above it. This level of pitch is generally too high to provide a convincing sense of chord movement. So about 1450, composers began to add another line *below* the chant to give the music a more solid foundation. The arrangement of voices that resulted from this change remains to this day the standard division of a choral group. In Josquin's time, the sections were called "superius," "altus," "tenor," and "bassus"; today they are the familiar soprano, alto, tenor, and bass. The change was significant because it indicated the growing importance of music's vertical dimension—harmony.

The most esteemed composer of the sixteenth century was Giovanni Pierluigi da Palestrina (c.1525–1594). Palestrina was the name of the small town in which he was born. Many of the practices of Josquin des Prez reached their highest development in Palestrina's music. Unlike Josquin, who changed jobs frequently, Palestrina largely confined his career to Rome, where he held several positions, the most notable being that of choirmaster at St. Peter's. Undoubtedly Palestrina was thoroughly familiar with the music of Josquin and other Netherlands composers. He utilized many of their devices, such as canon, with taste and skill.

Historical circumstances encouraged Palestrina to be a conservative reformer instead of an innovator. One such event was the Council of Trent, held intermittently between 1545 and 1563. The Church felt threatened by the impact of the Reformation, so the Council met to respond to this situation and to acknowledge the need for some reform within the Church. One phase of the Church's life that came under attack was the music, which over the centuries had departed far from the Gregorian ideal. Complaints were registered about the incorporation of secular tunes in music for the Mass, the complicated polyphony that made the words unintelligible, the use of noisy instruments, and the carelessness and irreverent attitude of the church singers. The Council directed by order that the chants be purged of "barbarisms, obscurities, contrarieties, and superfluities" so that "the House of God might rightly be called a house of prayer." Palestrina, therefore, composed for a Church that wanted to return to the simplicity and purity of its earlier music. To his credit, he achieved this ideal *without* discarding the highly developed style of his predecessors. It is against this background that his music must be heard and understood. His music is the embodiment in spirit if not in fact of the worshipful ideal of Gregorian chant.

The Renaissance Motet

As you will recall, during the Gothic period a motet was a composition using a line of Gregorian chant to which were added other melodies

I. Hodgson. Sculp.

In this old woodcut, Palestrina is handing Pope Marcellus his new Mass. Notice the style of notation on the pages of music.

containing other words, often in various languages. The motet of the Renaissance is quite different. It is a unified piece with all voices singing the same text. The Gothic motet was always based on Gregorian chant, but it could contain conspicuous secular elements too. The Renaissance motet, on the other hand, did not necessarily borrow from chant, but it conveyed that spirit and was suitable for use in worship. The Renaissance motet was serious, restrained, and appropriate to the worship service.

Palestrina's "Sanctus" from the Mass *Aeterna Christi Munera* (pages 118–20) reveals many characteristics of his writing style. The title of the Mass comes not from its words, but from the phrase of chant on which portions of this particular mass are based.

What are the significant features of "Sanctus" and other Renaissance motets?

1. The text is in ecclesiastical Latin. It is:

Sanctus, Sanctus, Sanctus,	Holy, Holy, Holy,
Dominus Deus Sabaoth.	Lord God of hosts.
Pleni sunt coeli et terra	Heaven and earth are full
gloria tua.	of thy glory.
Hosanna in Excelsis	Hosanna in the highest.

2. The music is polyphonic. All of the lines are given equal attention and each has distinct melodic character. Concentrate especially on the top line as you listen to a recording of the motet or hear it played. Then do the same for each of the other lines: the alto, then the tenor and bass.

3. Each voice usually enters in imitation of another. Look closely at the notes for the words "Sanctus." First the soprano starts, followed by the alto two beats later, the tenor halfway through measure 3, and finally the bass in measure 7. All voices sing the first eight or nine notes in imitation. But as the music progresses, the voices tend to move on to melodies of their own. At each addition of a new phrase of the text ("Dominus Deus," "Pleni sunt coeli," and so on), the process of imitation is repeated. It was through the use of such imitative entrances, sometimes called "staggered entrances," that Palestrina enabled the text to be understood. He realized that if the listener knows the words, not every phrase of text needs to be heard to its conclusion. If in a piece you can hear "O say can you see by . . . ," you know that "the dawn's early light" will follow, even though your attention may be drawn at that moment to another aspect of the music.

SANCTUS

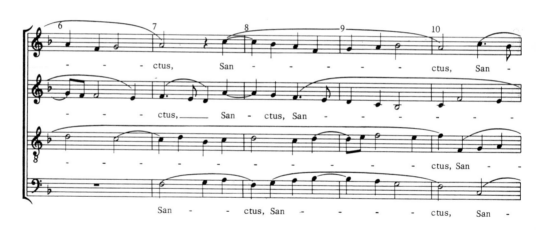

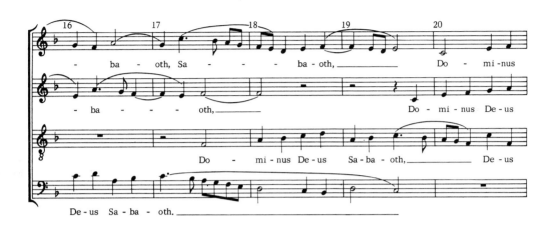

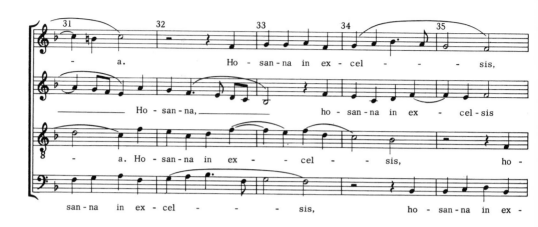

4. It does not have a strong feeling of harmonic movement. The sound is pleasing and smooth, but the chords lack the harmonic "drive" found in later styles. This lack is due largely to the polyphonic nature of the music, with its emphasis on the horizontal line. The absence of strong harmonic organization can also be viewed as a carry-over from the use of modes in Gregorian chant.

5. The music does not have a strong feeling of meter or beat. The "Sanctus" certainly does not encourage you to tap your foot. Again, this is similar to Gregorian chant, which had no meter. Even though present-day notation for "Sanctus" has measure or bar lines, the original probably did not. The bar lines have been added by editors for the convenience of modern-day singers so that they can more easily keep their place. Most of the chord changes in Palestrina's music occur at moments of subtle stress,

giving the music a gentle rhythmic regularity. Absent, however, is a feeling of definite rhythmic patterns.

6. The motet has no written accompaniment, but the voice parts were in fact doubled by a few instruments in the Renaissance. The performance ideal was *a cappella* (meaning literally "for the chapel") without accompaniments.

7. A small choir is used for the motet. Probably not more than two singers were assigned to each part. Boys, or men singing in falsetto voice, sang the high voice parts, since women were not allowed to participate in the Mass.

8. The melodies are very singable. The range of notes in any one part generally does not exceed an octave. Furthermore, the singers do not have to move far from one pitch to the next. In musical terms, there are few wide "leaps," although the bass part characteristically contains more leaps than do the other lines.

9. The form of this motet is derived from the structure of the Psalm. Each verse is usually treated to its own polyphonic setting and then moves on to new music in the next verse. The form is a succession of verses, each with music that is not repeated in other verses. (The return of the opening melody on the word "Hosanna" makes this "Sanctus" an exception.)

10. The music has a restrained, unemotional quality. Bombast and emotionalism were considered insincere and not in keeping with the attitude of respect and awe that should prevail in the worship of God. Even though the text speaks of "Hosanna in the highest," the music does not suggest a triumphal procession or a fanfare. When Palestrina does emphasize particular words, he does it so subtly that the modern listener, who has grown accustomed to the grandiose moods of Romantic music, may overlook them.

11. The melodic lines are fitted together with unexcelled craftsmanship. That is why Palestrina stands out among the composers of his age. Craftsmanship is often not fully appreciated by the nonmusician, since it is apparent only insofar as the listener can judge the composer's handling of musical materials. Knowledgeable assessment of a composer's skill can be developed, however, through familiarity with his style and comparison of his works with those of his contemporaries. It is on this basis that the excellence of Palestrina's music has been determined.

Part of the problem in understanding polyphony is inherent in the music. In homophonic music, a listener can concentrate on the melody and merely sense the effect of the enriching accompaniment. But in polyphonic music, attention can be centered on any line with equal reward. For this reason, repeated hearings of "Sanctus" are strongly urged. On hearing the piece for the fourth or fifth time (not in succession but on at least two different days), see if you can sense the skill with which Palestrina manipulates sounds to achieve the goal of sacred music in the Renaissance.

The Madrigal

Not only was the Renaissance a period of religious idealism. It also had a distinctly earthy side. There were many kinds of secular compositions, several of them national in character. The main type of secular music was the *madrigal*.[3] It has sometimes been described as a secular version of the motet, but there are significant differences between the two forms. The madrigal was in the vernacular rather than ecclesiastical Latin. Its text dealt with sentimental and sometimes erotic love. The texts used for madrigals written early in the Renaissance generally had little literary merit, but later texts, especially the poems of Petrarch, revealed exceptional quality. Instead of being sung in church, madrigals were sung at courtly social gatherings and at meetings of learned and artistic societies. Madrigals were very popular, and an enormous number were composed. In England, madrigal singing—with its requirement of music reading—was expected of an educated person. Since madrigals were prominent in situations not bound by religious custom, they contained greater freedom of expression than the motet, and they offered the composer more opportunity for experimentation. For instance, if the word "cuckoo" appeared in a madrigal, it was not uncommon for a composer to write an imitation of the actual sound of the cuckoo.

Instruments were often used to accompany the singing of secular music. The madrigal, therefore, was often heard in conjunction with a lute or harpsichord. The instrumentalist simplified the written parts, reducing the complicated polyphony to chords, which resulted in homophony. The lute, by the way, was the most popular instrument of the Renaissance. It had a pear-shaped body and varying numbers of strings. Its pegbox was slanted back sharply away from the rest of the instrument. The fingerboard had "frets"—upraised strips placed crosswise, as on a guitar. The lute was played by strumming, and rather intricate music could be executed on it.

The madrigal was largely an Italian development, associated with composers such as da Rore and Marenzio. By the mid-1500s, madrigals had spread to other countries. Interest in the madrigal reached England late in the sixteenth century. When the first madrigals with English translation were printed in 1588, the response was a brief but brilliant period of original English secular music. The English madrigal is especially enjoyable for three reasons: (1) its text is in English and therefore no translation is necessary for American audiences, (2) its composers had a knack for making the lines of music tuneful and singable, and (3) the English had the delightful trait of not taking themselves seriously. No matter how sad the song may be, the listener senses a tongue-in-cheek quality.

---

[3] There were also religious madrigals called *madrigali spirituali*, which were nonliturgical pieces on religious topics, oftentimes songs to the Virgin Mary.

A copper engraving by Hendrik Goltzius (1558-1616) showing the lute being played.

One well-known English madrigal is "April Is In My Mistress' Face" by Thomas Morley (1557–1602). About half of the music appears on 124 and 125. The text is a wistful comment on life. In this work, "Mistress" does not mean "paramour," as it does today; "fiancée" is closer to the original intent.

The madrigal is similar to the motet in several respects. There are imitative entrances at the beginning of word phrases, and the texture is basically polyphonic. The vocal lines are smooth and singable. The harmony is not firmly established in one particular key. The use of instruments was optional during the Renaissance, but today both madrigal and motet are sung without accompaniment. The form is a phrase-by-phrase setting of the text.

But there are also some differences. The madrigal's rhythm is more metrical; the moments of rhythmic stress fall in a more regular pattern. The tempo is faster. There is some tendency to set the women's parts in contrast to the men's, which may or may not be an attempt to relate to the text. And in overall spirit, Morley's madrigal is vastly different from Palestrina's motet.

As charming as Morley's madrigal is, it is only one of his many

April is in my Mistress' face

Thomas Morley (1557—1603)

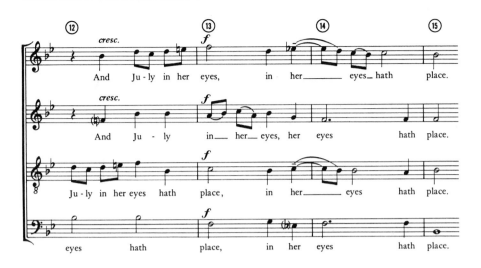

compositions. And Morley is only one of the many fine English composers of his time, who in turn represent only a small proportion of the creative musicians at work during the Renaissance. Partly to do justice to other fine composers, but more important, to acquaint you with additional sources for music well worth hearing, the following annotated list is included as a reference for your independent listening.

ENGLISH COMPOSERS

William Byrd	(1543–1623)	probably the best English composer of the Renaissance; madrigals, church music, and keyboard music
William Cornyshe	(c.1465–1523)	songs
John Dowland	(1562–1626)	madrigals
Robert Fayrfax	(1464–1521)	church music
Thomas Tallis	(c.1505–1585)	church music
John Taverner	(c.1495–1545)	church music
Thomas Weelkes	(c.1575–1623)	madrigals
John Wilbye	(1574–1638)	madrigals

NETHERLANDS COMPOSERS

Jacob Arcadelt	(c.1505–c.1567)	*chansons* (songs), madrigals; influential teacher in Rome
Jacobus Clemens	(c.1510–c.1556)	church music
Heinrich Isaac	(c.1450–1517)	church and secular music; international in use of texts

Jacob Obrecht	(c.1452–1505)	church music; used many technical devices
Johannes Ockeghem	(c.1430–1495)	church music; used many technical devices
Jan Sweelinck	(1562–1621)	*chansons* in old style
Adrian Willaert	(c.1480–1562)	influential composer and teacher at St. Mark's in Venice

FRENCH COMPOSERS

Clément Jannequin	(c.1475–c.1560)	*chansons;* fond of imitative sounds in music
Claude Le Jeune	(1528–1600)	madrigals, *chansons*
Claudin de Sermisy	(c.1490–1562)	French *chansons* (rhythmic, simple, four-part songs)

GERMAN COMPOSERS

| Hans Leo Hassler | (1564–1612) | *lieder* (German version of the madrigal), church music |
| Orlando di Lasso (Roland de Lassus) | (1532–1594) | *lieder* (also wrote in French and Italian styles) |

ITALIAN COMPOSERS

Costanzo Festa	(c.1490–1545)	early madrigals
Carlo Gesualdo	(c.1560–1613)	madrigals with experimental harmonies
Luca Marenzio	(1553–1599)	madrigals
Philippe de Monte	(1521–1603)	madrigals
Claudio Monteverdi	(1567–1643)	madrigals written when a young man; important Baroque composer later
Giovanni Mario Nanino	(c.1545–1607)	Palestrina's successor at Papal Chapel
Cipriano da Rore	(1516–1565)	probably the best composer of madrigals

SPANISH COMPOSERS

Antonio de Cabezón	(1510–1566)	keyboard music
Francisco Guerrero	(1527–1599)	church music
Cristóbal de Morales	(c.1500–1553)	church music
Tomás Luis de Victoria	(c.1549–1611)	church music in style of Palestrina

Renaissance Music in Perspective

The length of the preceding list of composers should put to rest any thought that little good music was written before 1600. If the music was plentiful and of a high caliber, why is it still largely unknown to the general public? How does Renaissance music compare in quality with the music of the centuries that followed? The two questions can be answered together.

Renaissance music is not intended for the concert stage; its charm and subtle nuances are lost in a large auditorium—the main place for musical performances today. It is not big or flashy like much of the music to which we are accustomed. Furthermore, specialized skills are required to perform it well. A chorus may sing cantatas and hymns beautifully and yet be unable to execute in proper style the polyphonic music of the Renaissance. Also, many types of music familiar today were unheard of before 1600; no concertos, symphonies, operas, or oratorios were composed before that time. Except for lute and keyboard music, instrumental music received little attention. Intervening centuries, then, have seen the development of new forms and media. As our musical heritage has expanded, our ability and desire to emphasize any one aspect of it has diminished.

These explanations for the lack of widespread acclaim do not by any means indicate that Renaissance music is inferior. On the contrary: in certain concentrated areas—madrigal, motet, and other vocal ensemble music—Renaissance composers achieved a quality that has still not been exceeded. In this regard Renaissance motets and madrigals are like Greek sculpture: different pieces in different styles have been created since, but the newer efforts have at best only equaled their predecessors. Renaissance composers gave the world of music not a vast number of forms but a standard of excellence that has seldom been matched.

Baroque Vocal Music

7

Even before 1600, the approximate beginning of the Baroque period, a new style and spirit was slowly emerging. It could be seen to some extent in Michelangelo's twisted statue "The Bound Slave" (page 130), in contrast to the objective quality of his "David" (p. 113). And it could be heard in Giovanni Gabrieli's massive works for brass instruments and double chorus. The Renaissance ideals of restraint and proportion began to lose their appeal. The initial attitude toward the new style is indicated by the term *baroque,* which was probably derived from a Portuguese word that meant "irregular." The Renaissance was being replaced, not necessarily by better artistic works but by creations in a different style. The result was a vast enrichment of the art of music.

Sometimes in everyday usage "baroque" means "extravagant," "grotesque," and "in bad taste," perhaps a carry-over from its original meaning. In discussions of the fine arts, however, "baroque" refers only to the style of artistic expression prevalent roughly from 1600 to 1750. And this expression was by no means grotesque or in bad taste.

"The Bound Slave,"
by Michelangelo.

The years from 1600 to 1750 saw such turbulence and change that it is impossible in a few lines to characterize the period fully. The following comments, however, may provide at least some indication of the temper of the times.

CHARACTERISTICS OF THE BAROQUE STYLE

One of the most striking features of the Baroque was its fondness for the large, the grandiose. In music this fact is exemplified by the prominent role of the pipe organ. In architecture, grandeur is illustrated in Lorenzo Bernini's monumental colonnades enclosing the vast piazza in front of St. Peter's Cathedral in Rome. The huge columns reach out before St. Peter's like giant pincers seeking to draw everyone into the building. There are four rows of columns running parallel to one another. When standing in the center of the piazza, however, you can see only a single row of columns, since the other three rows are perfectly blocked from view.

Aerial view of St. Peter's in Rome, showing Lorenzo Bernini's huge colonnades. Their size and grandeur are typical of the Baroque period.

Measured across, the piazza itself exceeds the length of two football fields, and the colonnades are made up of 284 different columns. Statues of 140 saints sit on top of the columns. Baroque painters, architects, and composers seemed at times to want to overwhelm the viewer or listener.

A second notable characteristic of the Baroque was its interest in the dramatic. In music, three major dramatic forms were developed: opera, oratorio, and cantata. Drama can also be seen in the twisted lines and struggling subjects in art works. Rembrandt van Rijn's "The Descent from the Cross" (plate 3), painted about 1650, features the play of light on the faces of the people to achieve a sense of drama. The light actually seems to be coming from the candle shielded by a man's hand, and it gives the scene an eerie pall. The cross is not in the center, as were Botticelli's Madonna and Child (plate 2), but is off center. Jesus' body is twisted, another popular Baroque effect. The emotions of tenderness and grief are evident in the faces.

A third significant trait of the Baroque was its intensity of religious feeling, which tended to take two forms: Protestant and Catholic. The Protestant churches established themselves generally in northern Europe and on the British Isles. Protestant worship was devout, unvarnished, and very serious. John Milton's *Paradise Lost* and John Bunyan's *Pilgrim's Progress* were two monumental writings that expressed the Protestant spirit.

The other form of religious intensity was Catholic and was generally found in southern Europe. The Catholic Counter-Reformation developed in response to the Protestant Reformation, and a series of tragic religious wars between Protestants and Catholics ensued. A happier result, however, was the encouragement of some outstanding religious art. Two examples demonstrate the Counter-Reformation. One is El Greco's "The Holy Family" (plate 4), which was painted in 1610. In some ways it is almost Gothic. The bodies have a stretched out, almost spiritual appearance. But the flickering light marks its true Baroque character. Although it depicts a peaceful scene, the picture is more charged with emotion than is Botticelli's "The Adoration of the Magi" (plate 2). Notice the differences in the two skies. Bernini's statue "Saint Theresa in Ecstasy" (p 133) represents a dream, described by the saint in her writings, in which an angel appeared before her holding a dart, symbolic of divine love, with which he pierced her heart. Even though the material is stone, Bernini achieves an astounding sense of movement. Notice again the corkscrew twist in the figures.

Although it was marked by religious fervor, the Baroque era was also a time of significant advance in science. Among the famous scientists of the period were Sir Isaac Newton, who developed the theory of gravity; Kepler and Galileo, who developed Copernicus' theories about the movement of planets; William Gilbert, who introduced the word "electricity" into the language; Robert Boyle, who helped make chemistry a pure science;

3
Rembrandt van Ryn: *The Descent from the Cross.* (Widener Collection, National Gallery of Art, Washington, D.C.)

4
El Greco: *The Holy Family.* (Samuel H. Kress Collection, National Gallery of Art, Washington, D.C.)

"St. Theresa in Ecstasy," by Bernini.

Robert Hooke, who first described the cellular structure of plants; Sir William Harvey, who described the circulation of the blood; Gottfried Wilhelm von Leibniz, who with Newton developed infinitesimal calculus; and René Descartes, who founded analytical geometry.

The Baroque saw the rise of a sizable middle class, which was breaking away from the traditional society based on inherited land, title, and wealth. One result of this change was the inclusion of everyday scenes in paintings, prose novels, and comic operas.

Governmentally the Baroque was a heterogeneous mixture of petty principalities and absolute monarchies, which were ever quarreling with one another. The church still patronized the arts, but its role was less important than it had been in the Renaissance. The middle class, made up of merchants and financiers, ran the cities of northern Europe, while the Hapsburg and Bourbon dynasties ruled to the south.

In short, the Baroque era was a time of contrasts. Religious fervor existed side by side with scientific advances, drama, and grandeur. This quality of dualism, at times bordering on cultural schizophrenia, is also evident in Baroque music.

BAROQUE MUSIC

A period such as the Baroque, which saw burgeoning activity in many fields, could hardly pass without significant changes occurring in music, too. And music did change—greatly. It would be an oversimplification to say that Baroque music was unified in style. Some scholars have divided the Baroque into three periods: early, middle, and mature. Music in the early years tended to be experimental, while the middle and mature periods represent the style usually associated with the term "Baroque." The mature Baroque brought forth more sophisticated works, which culminated in the music of Bach and Handel. It is through their compositions that Baroque music will be studied. Handel is given concentrated attention in this chapter and Bach in the next.

GEORGE FRIDERIC HANDEL

George Frideric Handel (1685–1759) was a German by birth, the son of a well-to-do barber-surgeon in the city of Halle in Saxony. His father did not think music a suitable livelihood and only grudgingly allowed his son to take music lessons. The boy showed proficiency in composition and theory, organ and harpsichord. His study also encompassed the oboe and violin. His father's early death permitted George to pursue his interest in music. After one year of college he went to Hamburg, where he took a position playing second violin in the orchestra. Italian opera was in vogue in Hamburg, as it was throughout much of Europe, and Handel became absorbed in the operatic style. By the age of twenty he had written his first opera.

Since Italy was the musical center during the Baroque, it was the logical place for Handel to go. For three years he studied with the leading Italian composers and cultivated his friendship with patrons of music. He was well on the road to fame as a composer by the time he left Italy at the age of twenty-five. In fact, before leaving he had an opera presented in Venice, and the work was received with much cheering and applause.

In 1710 he returned to Germany to be musical director of the Electoral Court at Hanover. In his two years at Hanover he managed to take two leaves of absence to go to London, where his operas in Italian language and musical style were sensations. Although his second visit was made on

George Frideric Handel.
Painting by Philip Mercier,
formerly in Halle.

the condition that he return to Hanover "within a reasonable time," he was still in London two years later when his master, the Elector of Hanover, was proclaimed King George I of England. Just how Handel took care of the embarrassing situation is not known. One story has it that he composed a suite of pieces to be played while the King sailed in his barge on the Thames. Thus the title for his familiar instrumental work *Water Music.*

For eight years, from 1720 to 1728, Handel occupied a key position in the musical life of England as a musical director of the Royal Academy of Music. The enterprise, founded for the purpose of presenting Italian opera, had a stormy life. Cliques of musicians and temperamental singers squabbled, a situation that was not helped by Handel's overbearing and stubborn personality. At one point the two leading sopranos actually got into a hair-pulling, name-calling match on stage during a performance at which Princess Caroline was in attendance. Despite the turmoil of the Academy, Handel composed some of his best operas during this time. His life was crowded with activity, a far cry from the quiet and solitude usually deemed necessary for composing.

In 1728 John Gay's *The Beggar's Opera* became popular. This ballad opera, more nearly a play with inserted songs than a true opera, was an outgrowth of French *vaudevilles.* It was an entertaining English satire on political subjects. While Italian opera continued for a while after the initial success of *The Beggar's Opera,* the popularity of the latter cut into the support given Handel's Italian works. Obstinate and unrelenting, Handel would not accept the waning interest in Italian opera. For another nine years he furiously wrote more operas, investing and losing money in them. At the age of fifty-two he could maintain the pace no longer. Victim of a paralytic stroke and heavily in debt, he acknowledged defeat and went abroad to recover his health.

And recover he did. After five more expensive operatic failures, he finally decided to turn away from opera. In the process he ensured his immortality. Some years before, he had written one or two works in Italian operatic style, but with this difference: they were in English and were performed without actions, costumes, or scenery. This type of unstaged "opera," usually on a religious topic, is called *oratorio.* It was this form to which Handel turned, and within a few years he was again at the top of the English musical world. During the 1740s and early '50s there flowed from his pen a remarkable series of such works: *Messiah, Samson, Semele, Joseph and His Brethren, Hercules, Belshazzar, Judas Maccabaeus, Joshua, Susanna, Solomon, Jephtha*—over twenty-six in all.

By 1750, his sixty-fifth year, he was acknowledged to be the grand old man of English music. During the last nine years of his life, although blindness overcame him, he maintained a vigorous schedule of conducting and performing. On such programs, as a special added attraction, he would improvise at the organ between sections of the music.

In 1759 Handel collapsed following a performance that he had conducted. A few days later he died. He was buried with state honors in Westminster Abbey. The German, who was an English citizen for the last forty years of his life, had earned a rightful place among England's national heroes.

THE ORATORIO

The oratorio is one of the significant contributions of the Baroque period to music. It was not an outgrowth of Renaissance forms but rather a new entity in the world of music. The roots of the oratorio go back to a popular type of Renaissance worship service. In style, it closely resembled opera, which was a creation of the Baroque (see Chapter 10). In fact, the first works called "oratorios" were religious operas, complete with costumes and staging. By Handel's time, the scenery, costumes, and actions had been abandoned, but the idea of drama, that fundamental characteristic of the Baroque, was retained. Each soloist represented a specific character. Like opera, an oratorio was a work of considerable scope, requiring two or more hours to perform. It featured an accompanying orchestra and a chorus in addition to the soloists. Most of Handel's oratorios were drawn from religious sources, with Old Testament subjects being especially favored.

Handel's Messiah

The oratorio *Messiah* is musically rather typical. It differs from other oratorios chiefly in that its text is entirely scriptural and it has no part for a narrator, who through singing describes the events of a story. *Messiah* is primarily a contemplation on Christian belief, starting with a section on prophecy and Christ's birth, followed by His suffering and death, and concluding with the resurrection and redemption. Handel wrote its nearly three hours of music in the unbelievably short time of twenty-four days. As he wrote he was aware that he was creating a great work. Afraid that if he stopped he might lose his momentum, he hardly slept, ate, or left his house for the three weeks. At the end of his labor he is reported to have said, "I think God has visited me."

Messiah was well received by critics and public at its first performance in Dublin. At the first performance in London on March 23, 1743, King George II was so awed by the "Hallelujah Chorus" that he rose and stood at his seat. And in those days, when the King stood, everyone stood. So the King's spontaneous action became a tradition that is still followed today.

Like other oratorios, *Messiah* contains many individual musical numbers—fifty-three in all. Each number is one of three types: recitative, aria, or chorus. Each type represents features of Baroque vocal music.

Recitative. *Recitative* (*Reh*-sit-a-*teev*) refers both to a section of music in an opera or oratorio and to a style of singing. A good clue to this type of singing can be found in the first five letters of "recitative"; the word "recite" rather well describes it. Although recitative does denote singing, it nevertheless approaches the style of the spoken word.

Look closely at this recitative from *Messiah,* and listen to it several times.

Lord,   make   straight in the des-ert   a   high-way   for our   God.

Most of its features are typical. There is a part for only one singer, and there are only a few chords in the entire accompaniment. Just this much observation can tell you something about recitative. First, it is music that has a single melodic line, although other pitches are sounded with it to enhance its quality. This type of music is called *homophony* and was mentioned in Chapter 1.

Homophony—music made up of one melodic line plus a chordal accompaniment—had existed long before the Baroque. Composers had given it little attention in serious musical works, however, and consequently it never developed very far. By 1600 the polyphonic style of Palestrina had reached its optimum development. Composers began to feel that something new and fresh was needed. The process of change is clearly evident in the books of madrigals by the outstanding innovative composer Claudio Monteverdi (1567–1643). Between 1587 and 1603 Monteverdi published four books of madrigals in Renaissance style. In 1605 he published a book of pieces that were truly homophonic. They were no longer madrigals but rather songs—solos, duets, trios—with accompaniment. By the eighth book (1638), Monteverdi's music called for chorus, soloists, and orchestra. Another result of this change was the development of opera, which began about the same time as the Baroque. The subject of opera will be presented in Chapter 10.

Not only did vocal style evolve from polyphony in the Renaissance to homophony in the Baroque; the entire outlook toward such music had changed. Essentially, the change involved the relationship between words and music. The Renaissance composer wrote so that several melodies would fit well with one another. Since the words did not often occur at the same time among the various lines, they could not be easily understood and their dramatic impact was lessened.

But a group of early Baroque composers wanted to reactivate the ancient Greek practice of having musical declarations in dramas. They reasoned that a single line of melody would be freer to express the thought behind the words. Thus recitative was created. In early attempts at recitative, the singers went so far as to grimace, act, and imitate the inflections of crying and gasping. Whatever the merits of early recitative, it did open up for the composer a new dimension in vocal music. The single melody could have a wider range, more chromatic notes, and freer rhythm than a line in a motet of the previous period. Listen again to the way Handel treats the word "crieth." The music supports the feeling evoked by the word. Certainly Handel would not have given similar musical treatment to the words "peaceful" or "silence." He combined text and music in such a way that each was enhanced by the other.

The effort at achieving expression had another consequence: the idea of regular rhythm was discarded. Early Baroque composers seemed to reason that feelings should not be regulated or shaped by time. Their idea was to follow the inflections of the speaking voice. Thus the singer was given the liberty of speeding up and slowing down, holding certain notes, and generally singing the words as he felt them. The few chords that the accompanying orchestra or instrument did play were sounded at whatever moment was indicated by the singer's performance. The Renaissance idea of an even flow of music was replaced by the new freedom of rhythmic interpretation granted to the performer.

The recitative also demonstrates the Baroque concept of harmony. In Chapter 1 the topic of key and tonality was mentioned briefly. Tonality was one of the Baroque's most significant contributions to music. Prior to that period, music was characterized by non-major/minor modal patterns. Such patterns were not built around particular chords. Any harmony was felt to be adequate as long as the sonority at any given moment was satisfying. There was little sense of harmonic *progression*—movement implied by the chords themselves. The tonality of the Baroque style, on the other hand, is a system of chord relationships based on the attraction or "magnetic pull" of a tonal center, which was demonstrated in Chapter 1. Listen to the chords of the recitative; notice that they tend to move in a logical and interesting way. The chord progression is convincingly ended by the final two chords. These particular chords give a feeling of finality or conclusion, which is just what Handel wanted. Knowing the gravitational tendencies of chords, a composer can almost "punctuate" his music by inserting musical commas and periods to suggest varying degrees of finality.

This same recitative demonstrates another musical fact: the tonal center can be changed. This process of changing from one key or tonal center to another is called *modulation*. It imparts variety and freshness to the music. Today we are so accustomed to hearing pieces modulate that we do not realize how monotonous they would sound without it. Music that does not modulate is comparable to a room with beige carpeting, beige draperies, beige walls and ceiling, and beige upholstered furniture; there would be no contrast, only uniformity and dullness. Even a simple, short song like "Deck the Halls" (page 21) suggests a new key briefly in the last two measures of the third line. It could be rewritten so that it would stay in the same key, but it would be a less interesting piece. In the beginning of the *Messiah* recitative, the music centers around E, but it ends in A major. The modulation gives Handel greater freedom in the melodic line and permits a more interesting progression of chords.

Because recitative is closely related to dramatic speaking, the quality of its melodic line is not tuneful in the usual sense of the word. The emphasis is on the proper dramatic rendition of the words rather than the contour of the melody. The reciting style is also an outgrowth of the desire to cover a text as economically as possible. Notice that each note of the recitative is coupled with one syllable of a word. This technique enables several lines of text to be covered in about thirty seconds.

Variety within the recitative style can be achieved in several ways. Later in *Messiah* the soprano sings the recitative "There were shepherds abiding in the field, keeping watch over their flocks by night" to an extremely simple accompaniment. This is followed by "And lo! the angel of the Lord came upon them, and the glory of the Lord shone round about them, and they were sore afraid." These lines are sung to a bright-sounding orchestral accompaniment. The pattern played by the violins is still chordal, but the notes are sounded in succession rather than simultaneously. The next recitative, which begins "And the angel said unto them, Fear not," again uses a minimum of chords. It gives the impression of steadfastness and calm. The fourth recitative in the series, which begins "And suddenly," projects the idea of excitement. The strings are playing a lively melodic pattern that is again made up of the notes found in the chords. The five verses (from Luke 2:8–13) are set forth with much freedom and sensitivity to convey the meaning of the words. Such expressive rendition of this text was not a part of the Renaissance outlook on music and would have been difficult to achieve in the polyphonic style of Palestrina.

Aria. A second type of homophonic vocal music developed in the Baroque period was the *aria* (*ar*-eeah). One of these is "Every valley shall be exalted," from *Messiah*. When you hear the music, you can tell that the aria differs radically from the recitatives just discussed, and a glance at the musical notation confirms this fact.

shall be ex-alt - - - - - - ed, and ev-'ry moun - tain and hill_____ made low;

the crook - ed____ straight, and the rough plac-es

plain,_____ the crook - ed

straight,   the crook - ed straight,__ and rough plac-es plain,__

__ and the rough plac-es plain.

First, the aria is much longer than the recitative. Only about half of it is included here. In fact, "Every valley" requires about four minutes to perform, whereas the recitative that precedes it takes only about thirty seconds. Its greater length is characteristic of an aria.

The part for the orchestra or accompanying instrument also differs. No longer is it plunking out chords or outlining them. In an aria the accompaniment plays portions of the music by itself and adds character to the overall effect. It may reiterate a figure that the soloist has sung or play its own melody.

A third difference between recitative and aria can easily be observed. The soloist often has to sing rapidly moving notes, or perform long phrases on a single word or syllable. The long runs of sixteenth notes (♫♫♫♫), such as appear on the word "exalted," illustrate one of the musical practices of the Baroque: virtuoso singing.

The word "virtuoso" refers to someone who has unusual technical skill in the performing arts. Early in the Baroque period, much attention was given the solo singer. Vocalists began to compete with one another for the favor ot the audience by adding flashy runs and trills to the music. The custom snowballed until the composer's music became merely a skeletal frame that the singer dressed up as he wished. Astonishing technical accomplishments in singing resulted, often to the neglect of musical quality. Reform movements had taken hold by Handel's time, but elements of the beloved virtuoso style carried over from opera into the oratorio. Audiences expected to hear vocal technical display in the music.

In "Every valley," the runs do more than show off the singer's skill. Handel cleverly integrates them into the entire musical fabric so that they enhance the effect of the piece. For example, it is easy to imagine that the singer's runs are an instrument adding a countermelody or variations on the melody. Handel in the best of Baroque tradition uses the virtuoso runs to bring out the idea of the words. In this aria the word "exalted" is treated to the long runs. "Exalted," meaning "raised, lifted up" in a spiritual sense, is the word that most appropriately expresses the main thought of the text. The low places will be raised up spiritually, says the poet in Isaiah 40:4. Not only does "exalted" have a crucial meaning within the text; it has an especially good vowel on which to sustain the singing: the "awe" or dark, broad "a."

The virtuoso passages in Baroque singing are sometimes baffling and disturbing to nonmusicians today. They cannot understand why a part of a word is stretched out over forty or more notes. Of course, "exalted" can be sung with just three notes, and these can even occur on a single pitch level. But the musical interest would thereby be diminished. It is impressive to hear a skilled singer execute the long runs, and it is even more rewarding to hear the line fit into the music and to sense the emphasis that is given certain words. In everyday practical terms it is silly to use forty notes to sing one word, but in aesthetic, musical terms it makes much sense.

The relationship between length of text and length of music in the recitative and aria is worth noting. The recitative "The voice of him" and the aria "Every valley" have texts of almost identical length. The aria takes about eight times as long to perform, however, because its text is spread out by repetition, by runs on some of the words, and by passages for the accompaniment alone.

Another difference between recitative and aria is the presence of form in the aria. Sections of an aria are usually repeated. The most frequent aria form is *A B A*. This design is often referred to as *da Capo*, meaning that the second hearing of the *A* section is really a return to the beginning or the head of the piece. (The term *da Capo* literally means "to the head.") "Every valley" has a form of *A B A B; A* is the melody for the words "every valley," and *B* is "the crooked straight." Although the printed musical example is incomplete, the form is apparent when this aria is heard in its entirety.

The aria and recitative have a different type of rhythm. The recitative allows for much rhythmic freedom, but the aria and other types of Baroque music represent rhythmic regularity. Except for unmetered recitatives and a few other free passages, Baroque music followed both a set tempo and consistency of meter. (This Baroque characteristic remained intact until the twentieth century.) Changes were permitted only at the ends of sections in a long work, although holds were sometimes inserted, as heard near the end of "Every valley." So regular was Baroque music that it could be and usually was performed without a conductor, such as his role is known today. The custom was for the keyboard player to give the starting signal and set the tempo. Curiously, even though recitatives were performed without a regular beat, composers wrote them with meter signatures just as if they were to be performed strictly.

The aria is intended to stand on its musical merit to a greater extent than is the recitative, which so often serves as a bridge between other numbers. Therefore the composer gives the aria more distinguished melodic qualities.

The Chorus. The word "chorus" has a double meaning in music. It can refer to a group that sings choral music or to the choral sections of an oratorio or opera. Thus a chorus sings a chorus.

In many ways, the chorus portion of the music is similar to the aria. It is a rather lengthy section. It uses about the same amount of text and has frequent repetition of words. Metrical rhythmic patterns are followed strictly, and lines of music calling for considerable singing ability are found. The accompaniment has a similar amount of character.

There is one fundamental difference between chorus and aria, however. If you study the music for the chorus "For unto us a child is born," you will observe, especially in the four measures before letter B, that while the tenors sing "For unto us," the sopranos are executing a run. The same thing can be found again in the third through fifth measures after letter B. Two lines of approximately equal interest performed together—this is what was found in Gothic and Renaissance music! Sure enough, polyphony is present in the chorus. Again the Baroque is true to its nature in the presentation of extremes. While developing homophony—the expressive melodic line and its accompaniment—Baroque composers still retained the polyphonic style of the Renaissance and consciously wrote in both styles.

The polyphony of the Baroque does not sound much like the polyphony of the Renaissance, however. Baroque polyphony is built around tonality, around the major/minor key system. The simultaneous melodies of Baroque polyphony are influenced by the same gravitational pull toward a tonal center that affects chords. Baroque polyphony can

modulate, too. Then there is the unflagging pattern of beats in its rhythm. So the same substance (polyphony) has been poured into two quite different molds. In fact, Baroque polyphony is often called "counterpoint" instead of "polyphony."

The chorus "For unto us" offers the listener three different moods, each of which fits the text (from Isaiah 9:6). The first feeling is tender, to suit the thought about an infant. It suggests the happiness felt at the birth of a child. The second section has a more rugged, martial character. The words describe what lies in store for this infant: "And the government shall be upon His shoulder." As these words are finished, the orchestra breaks into an excited, joyful melodic pattern. What are the words that call for such a reaction? "And His name shall be called Wonderful, Counselor, the mighty God, the everlasting Father, the Prince of Peace."

Handel then takes the three passages and goes through them four times. The repetitions are never exact. The first time, for instance, the sopranos start the melody of "For unto us"; the second time the altos start it, and the third time it returns to the sopranos. The fourth time the basses start, and the sound is made even heavier and stronger when another section of the chorus is added to the line. In this way the piece has a sense of building toward a climactic finish.

Handel's unerring judgment in the placement of text and music is particularly evident in this chorus, especially on the phrase that begins "Wonderful, Counselor." First he sets an excited figure in the accompaniment. Next he emphasizes the words, not by making them louder but by allowing them to stand alone with rests on either side. In this way he builds on the listener's expectations. Normally, the phrase would proceed, "And His name shall be called Wonderful, Counselor." But Handel wrote it this way: "And His name shall be called (*rest*) Wonderful, (*rest rest*) Counselor." The beat or two of silence circumscribing the proper words can make the difference between something average and something outstanding in the world of music.

The same passage also demonstrates the importance of rhythmic patterns and word accents. The word "wonderful" is sung with three-fourths of a beat on "won" and only one-fourth on "der." The final syllable receives the second beat of the measure. This rhythmic pattern approximates the spoken accents of the word, so Handel utilizes this pattern to make the word more natural and effective. He causes the important words and syllables to fall on the beat so that they can be as properly emphasized when sung as when they are spoken. One such phrase is "the EV-er-LAST-ing FA-ther (*rest*), the PRINCE of PEACE." To appreciate the importance of the placement of words in music, say the phrase to yourself in this way: "THE ev-ER-last-ING fa-THER." Handel understood rhythm and speech patterns, and he applied this knowledge to a language that he never learned to speak very well in his forty plus years in England.

Often Handel's choruses project a feeling of grandeur; somehow they seem to belong in a large hall like Westminster Abbey or St. Paul's Cathedral. The purity of Renaissance choral music had been exchanged for the power of Baroque choral music. More singers were required for Baroque works. Handel gave the chorus a more important place in the oratorio. He also gave it a style that became the norm for the oratorio in England and America.

THE CHORALE

Just as Gregorian chant was an outgrowth of the belief and practice of the Roman Catholic Church, the chorale was an outgrowth of Protestant belief and practice. In the sixteenth century, when Martin Luther's break with the Roman Church had become final, Luther and some of his colleagues set about to provide music suitable for worship in the newly developed services. They wanted the members of the congregation to be participants in the service, not just observers as they had tended to be in the past. One way to involve them was to have them sing. But what should they sing? Chant was too reminiscent of the rejected Roman Church. Also, its flexible style is difficult for untrained singers to perform well. The answer was to create a new body of religious music. So from German religious songs, adaptations of chant and secular tunes, and from the pen of Luther and others came the chorale.

Luther believed not only that worshipers should sing but that their music should contribute to the proper religious attitude. The purpose of the chorale, therefore, was to state belief and to contribute to the spirit of worship. The Protestant religious attitudes of that time are graphically expressed in "A Mighty Fortress Is Our God," which Luther himself wrote. Part of the words for this chorale are:

> Though devils all the world should fill,
> All eager to devour us;
> We tremble not, we fear no ill,
> They shall not overpower us.

In his analogy for God, Luther chose the German word *Burg*, a medieval stone fortress, a symbol of austere strength. The chorale reflects, then, the deadly serious and unadorned religious attitudes of the early Protestants. Each note in its melody stands like a block of stone in a medieval castle.

At first hearing, a chorale, like Gregorian chant, may seem like dull music. It is true that the chorale and chant are lacking in novelty and flashiness. But to be valid, religious music must give expression to what the believer feels to be the ultimate and eternal. Music of a trivial and flamboyant nature is inappropriate to a God greater and more lasting than all the universe. So it is inconceivable that a chorale melody should sound like "De Camptown Races" or an operatic aria. The music and the idea of God must be congruent; they must fit together. In both chant and chorale, the sincerity and reverence of belief is expressed effectively and beautifully.

Both chant and chorale today have the stamp of tradition upon them. They have become the prototypes of religious music. A deliberate association between a certain type of music and religious attitude has therefore been established. Whether or not it is desirable, it does affect the response of the listener and participant. The issue has been brought to a head by the use of jazz and popular idioms in worship services held in churches. Listeners who like rock and jazz often find that they enjoy the church service but that it has no religious impact for them. In other words, jazz and popular music as might be expected, do not conjure religious associations. Traditional religious music seems better able to link the modern worshiper with the faithful who have gone before and to give him some concept of the timeless nature of his belief.

THE CANTATA

Because of their simple, strong qualities, chorale melodies are well suited for use as themes for other musical works. Several types of pieces for organ, which will be discussed in the next chapter, have chorale melodies as their basis. Probably the most frequent use of chorale melodies was in the *cantata*. Originally the word "cantata" meant any sizable work that was sung, either sacred or secular. But by the time of Bach, the cantata had become a miniature oratorio, with an instrumental accompaniment, arias, recitatives, and choruses. The cantata was much shorter, however. Furthermore, it generally incorporated a chorale melody into some of its sections and was presented as a part of the worship service.

And there was plenty of time in the service for a twenty-minute cantata in Bach's church in Leipzig. The principal Sunday service began at seven in the morning and lasted until about noon! In addition, there were three other short services on Sunday as well as daily services in all churches and special religious celebrations. Altogether Leipzig churches required fifty-eight cantatas each year, plus other types of music for special occasions. Bach composed many cantatas for these services. During most of his career he averaged one cantata per month. About two hundred have been preserved of the three hundred he wrote.

Bach's Cantata No. 140

One of Bach's better-known cantatas has been mentioned on two earlier occasions in this book: *Cantata No. 140*, *"Wachet auf, ruft uns die*

Stimme" ("Wake Up, Call the Voices"). The text, based on Matthew
25:1–13, tells the parable of the five wise and the five foolish virgins. The
chorale melody appears at the beginning, middle, and end of the cantata.
The opening chorus consists of variations on the chorale melody. Its text is:

Wachet auf, ruft uns die Stimme	Wake up, call to us the voices
Der Wächter sehr hoch auf der Zinne,	Of watchmen high up on the tower,
Wach' auf, du Stadt Jerusalem!	Wake up, thou town Jerusalem!
Mitternacht heisst diese Stunde;	It is now the hour of midnight;
Sie rufen uns mit hellem Munde:	They call to us with shining faces:
Wo seid ihr klugen Jungfrauen?	Where are you now, O virgins wise?
Wohl auf, der Bräutgam kommt,	Cheer up, the Bridegroom comes,*
Steht auf, die Lampen nehmt! Alleluja!	Get up, and take your lamps! Alleluia!
Macht euch bereit zu de Hochzeit,	Prepare yourselves, the wedding nears,
Ihr müsset ihm entsprungen gehn.	You must go forth to welcome him.

This chorus is the longest and most complex portion of the cantata. There is
a driving uneven rhythmic figure, contrasted with a countermelody played
by the violins. The chorale melody itself appears in long notes in the
soprano. As these notes are sung, the alto, tenor, and bass sing contrasting
musical lines in good polyphonic style. Again, the orchestra plays a significant part.

   This chorus illustrates the belief of Baroque composers in pro-
jecting ideas in the text through patterns of sound. This outlook, called the
doctrine of affects or *doctrine of affections,* is evident in many Baroque
works. Because the type of music associated with particular moods or
ideas is not so well known by listeners today, the doctrine is mainly of
historical interest. Examples in Bach's cantata of the doctrine of affections
include words such as *wach' auf* (wake up), *wohl auf* (cheer up), and
steht auf (arise or get up). As they are sung, the music usually leaps upward. In another great Bach work, the *St. Matthew Passion,* the words of
Christ are sung with an airy, halo-like accompaniment in the strings. These
musical efforts are further evidence of Baroque composers' concern for the
proper setting of the words.

---

* In many cantatas Jesus is referred to symbolically as the bridegroom, and the church as his
bride.

CANTATA NO. 140

First Section

Johann Sebastian Bach

The second part of the cantata is a recitative for tenor. It tells about the coming of the bridegroom and sets forth the image of Christ as the Heavenly Bridegroom.

The third section is a duet for soprano and bass. It is in dialogue form, with an important part for violin solo.

The fourth section was cited on pages 8–9. A gentle melody occurs in the strings while the tenors sing the chorale melody.

After a recitative by the bass, another duet is heard. Again it is a dialogue between bass and soprano. The form is the typical *A B A* found so often in Baroque arias. In this duet the oboe has several important solos.

The final section of the cantata is a harmonization of the chorale melody. The music was cited on page 13. It was customary for the congregation to join in the singing of this section. The chorales were thoroughly familiar to the congregation. Furthermore, the music was sung in the native tongue of the participants, which increased its impact.

The concept of chorale singing was also influenced by the educational level of the worshipers. A large proportion of the population in the Baroque era could not read or write. Nor did they receive information via mass communications media. Therefore pictures, statues, and music in churches were intended to be educational as well as beautiful. The text of a choral work was chosen for purposes of instruction as well as praise.

The cantata and oratorio are but two of many types of vocal music written for Protestant worship services in the Baroque. Another type of religious music is the *Passion,* which is like an oratorio except that its topic is the suffering of Christ on the cross. The work that earned posthumous recognition for all of Bach's music is the *St. Matthew Passion.* Like the cantatas, this work gives a prominent place to a chorale: "O Sacred Head Now Wounded."

There was a Baroque motet, too. It resembled the Renaissance motet in that it was unaccompanied, religious, and contrapuntal. In the Baroque style, however, it had a strict rhythmic meter and major/minor tonality. Its text was in the vernacular language.

What have you learned about Baroque vocal music? There was a new interest in variety, first of all, with a marked desire for expressiveness. This tendency led to the recitative and to the aria, with its virtuoso passages. The aria also revealed a new interest in form; the *A B A* structure, reflecting the principles of contrast and repetition, was characteristic of the aria. The chorus was valued for its ability to provide solid sound and intricate polyphony. Composers wrote almost exclusively in major/minor tonalities and in strict metrical rhythm. Although these changes were monumental in importance, they did not by any means represent all that happened to music in the Baroque period. The next chapter examines those changes associated more closely with instrumental music.

SUGGESTIONS FOR FURTHER LISTENING

BACH:
Cantata No. 4, "Christ Lay in the Bonds of Death" (*"Christ Lag in Todesbanden"*)
Cantata No. 80, "A Mighty Fortress Is Our God" (*"Ein' Feste Burg ist Unser Gott"*)
St. Matthew Passion
Mass in B Minor, "Kyrie"
Magnificat

BUXTEHUDE:
Cantatas
Magnificat

GABRIELI:
Processional and Ceremonial Music, "In Ecclesiis"

HANDEL:
Oratorios cited on page 136.

MONTEVERDI:
Vespro della Beata Virgine

PURCELL:
Anthems

SCHÜTZ:
The Seven Last Words

Baroque Instrumental Music

8

There are noticeable differences between the instrumental and vocal music of the Baroque period. This fact makes the Baroque different from previous stylistic periods. Until the Baroque, a composition was not written particularly as a vocal or instrumental work. Except for a few keyboard and lute compositions, the same piece of music could be performed entirely by voices, by instruments, or by a combination of the two. The Baroque composer, however, wrote specifically for chorus, organ, violin, or other instrument. The nature of the instrument or voice figured prominently in his artistic decisions in creating the piece. Thus the composition could be recognized as being in an instrumental style or a vocal style.

The eventual distinction between the two styles was probably inevitable. Instruments and voices do not make music in the same way, and so each sounds best in different types of music. For instance, a violin or flute can easily produce sounds that are higher than the upper limits of the human voice; other instruments are capable of sounding below the range of the voice. Performers on most instruments can also play notes with a speed and clarity impossible for a singer to achieve. (A singer tends to blur the sound of notes that move very fast.) An instrument is more agile than the voice; it can bound from high to low with ease.

In spite of the characteristic styles that emerged, the Baroque saw considerable interchange between them. After an aria was written, for example, it was not uncommon for the composer to make a transcription of that aria for harpsichord or violin. Making a *transcription* in music means adapting a piece written for an instrument or voice to another instrument or voice, or to a group of either. As you can imagine, the musical success of a transcription depends on the composer: he must choose an appropriate piece for adaptation and then exercise skill in making the necessary changes to fit the new medium.

In general, Baroque instrumental music tended to be more polyphonic than homophonic, while the opposite seemed to be true for vocal music. There is a logical explanation for this tendency. Remember that vocal music was valued for its ability to project a message. Recitative and aria were developed as a means of giving expression to the ideas contained in the text. Instrumental music, of course, was not affected by the interest in verbal expression.[1] Therefore, the development of a single melody was more attractive in the vocal than in the instrumental idiom. Also, because instruments can execute sounds with greater clarity and rapidity, the more complex music was better suited for them.

The Baroque era was a time of considerable development of instruments. Although organs had existed since the days of the Romans, the Baroque saw them perfected. The violin, a descendant of an Arabian instrument, was developed during this time. Trumpets and kettledrums (timpani) began to be used in serious music. In fact, the first composition that specified instruments other than keyboard was a work for brasses. The flute was much improved during this period. Originally it had been played by being held in front of the performer; during the Baroque the flute held in the transverse or sideways position gained equal favor. The harpsichord, which will be discussed later in this chapter, was also largely a Baroque development and was played with almost all instrumental combinations.

It was during the Baroque era that a significant technical breakthrough was made. Remember Pythagoras? His discovery of certain basic intervals did not solve the problem of exactly where the intervening notes were to be placed. The situation was complicated by a caprice of nature. Theoretically, if one plays intervals of a fifth one after another, he should on the thirteenth note reach the original pitch (in a different octave, of course). But if the Pythagorean ratio for a perfect fifth is used, and if the

---

[1] Some composers did attempt, unsuccessfully, to write instrumental pieces expressing specific ideas. One of these attempts is Biber's *Christ Prayed on the Mountain*. In this piece the sounds of the violin are supposed to tell specifically of Christ's actions.

fifths are computed upward, the thirteenth note is noticeably higher than the original! This gap did not bother singers, because they could easily make slight pitch adjustments. But the problem plagued keyboard-instrument makers. In order to get perfect tuning in some keys, they had to sacrifice the accuracy of pitch in other keys. Especially serious were the discrepancies existing in keys where several sharps or flats were involved, because keys with the fewest number of sharps or flats were favored both in frequency of use and in tuning. Opportunities for modulation and transposition were quite limited by the pitch problem.

The resolution of the problem came when the size of the perfect fifth was reduced slightly, so that the distance between all pitches was equal, even if slightly imperfect. The Baroque saw increasing use of the idea of *equal temperament,* the system of tuning still used today. To promote such a system, and to encourage a player's facility in all keys, a few composers, including Bach, wrote a series of pieces in all twenty-four major and minor keys. Bach's *Well-Tempered Clavier* was music of such high quality that it is frequently performed at recitals today.[2]

JOHANN SEBASTIAN BACH

The name of Johann Sebastian Bach seems to crop up in nearly every discussion of Baroque music. And well it should! Certainly this man ranks as one of the musical giants of all time.

Bach lived an uneventful life, one not very different from that of many successful musicians of his time. The most notable feature about him was his lineage—he was one of a gifted musical family. Over a period of about six generations, from 1580 to 1845, more than sixty Bachs were musicians of some sort, and at least thirty-eight of these attained eminence as musicians. Included among the latter were Johann Christoph (1642–1703), who was a cousin of J. S. Bach's father, and several of J. S. Bach's own sons: Wilhelm Friedemann (1710–1784), Carl Philipp Emanuel (1714–1788), Johann Christoph Friedrich (1732–1795), and Johann Christian (1735–1782).

Johann Sebastian Bach was born in Eisenach in 1685, the son of a town musician. When the boy was ten, his father died. Johann's musical training was taken over by his elder brother, Johann Christoph, who was an organist. During his early career Bach was known more as an organ virtuoso than as a composer. After two short-lived positions as organist, Bach at the age of twenty-three was appointed to his first significant post, that of court organist and chamber musician to the Duke of Weimar (*Vy*-mar). He

---

[2] The word *clavier* referred to a keyboard instrument of the harpsichord type.

stayed nine years. It was during his Weimar years that he concentrated on organ, as both performer and composer.

When the Duke failed to advance him, Bach accepted another position at Cöthen (*Keh*-ten). The prince at Cöthen was interested in chamber music, so the versatile Bach turned from writing church and organ music to composing primarily for instruments other than the organ. It was during this time that he wrote the famous Brandenburg concertos, one of which is discussed later in this chapter. After the sudden death of his wife, Maria Barbara, he remarried and immortalized his second wife, Anna Magdalena, by writing a book of keyboard music for her.

The third and last portion of Bach's life began with his appointment in 1723 as organist-teacher of St. Thomas Church in Leipzig. It was one of the more important musical posts in Germany, but it demanded that Bach teach the choir boys both musical and nonmusical subjects (and "in case they do not wish to obey," his contract stated, "chastise them with moderation"). He was required to "so manage the music that it shall not last too long, and shall be of such a nature as not to make an operatic impression, but rather incite the listeners to devotion."

Bach was not the first choice for the position. A member of the town council is reported to have said, "Since the best man could not be obtained, lesser ones will have to be accepted." The Leipzig position required the writing and direction of church music, so Bach again complied by changing the emphasis of his musical work. Not only were the Leipzig city fathers unaware of Bach's genius; they were stingy. They paid him only about $3,000 a year, and provided him with a choir of about thirty singers, few of whom were competent musicians.

In spite of the annoyances of the position at Leipzig and tragedy in his personal life (six of his first eight children born in Leipzig died), Bach continued his endless stream of great music. Late in life he suffered a stroke and became blind. In 1750 he died, with his true stature still unrecognized. Bach and his music went largely unnoticed until 1829, when young Felix Mendelssohn rediscovered the *St. Matthew Passion*.

Bach was a prolific composer who was capable of writing in any medium, vocal or instrumental. Nearly one hundred years after his death, the Bach Gesellschaft (Society) was organized to collect his music. The manuscripts printed in the completed collection are in bound volumes. The fact that about sixty-five inches of shelf space is required to hold them attests to the magnitude of Bach's output. And even this is not a complete catalog of his works, since a sizable amount of his music has been lost.

Except for a few brief journeys in Germany, Bach knew little of the world outside his immediate environment. He was neither well read nor well educated. He was religious almost to the point of superstition. (He believed in numerology, ascribing occult meaning to coincidences of numbers such as the four letters in his last name, and he saw unusual sig-

Johann Sebastian Bach. Detail from the Bach monument in Leipzig.

nificance in the number fourteen, which is derived when these letters are totaled according to their position in the alphabet.) He created no new musical forms and instituted no new compositional techniques. His music was seldom heard outside of Leipzig during his lifetime, and even there it was probably not performed well.

Why is it that Bach is so dominating a figure in music? The answer lies in the simple fact that Bach wrote with such skill and effectiveness. Especially remarkable was his ability to write counterpoint. Words are inadequate to describe Bach's genius. Perhaps the late Dag Hammarskjold, Secretary General of the United Nations, expressed it best. In speaking of Bach and Vivaldi, another Baroque composer, he said, "Both have a beautiful way of creating order in the brain."[3]

Lithograph of St. Thomas Churchyard in Leipzig.

THE ORGAN

Before listening to Bach's music, you should know something about his instrument, the organ. The organ is both a simple and a complex instrument. The sound of the organ is made when air is blown into a variety of pipes. Even a small change in the design of a pipe will cause a change of tone quality. Each timbre must have its own set or rank of pipes, one for each pitch in the rank. It is not unusual for a large organ to have as many as one hundred ranks; medium-sized organs have forty to sixty. Each rank is brought into play by pulling a knob; various knob combinations can be activated by pushing a button with the hand or foot. In the accompanying picture, the knobs are on both sides of the keyboards; the buttons are below the keys and on both sides of the center pedals. So even when the organist depresses only one key, fifty or more pipes can be sounded, depending on the knobs activated.

---

[3] Joseph P. Lash, *Dag Hammarskjold: Custodian of the Brushfire Peace* (New York: Doubleday & Company, Inc., 1961), p. 198.

The console of a pipe organ.

As you can see in the picture, there are several keyboards. On an organ they are called *manuals*. Each manual has 61 keys, which is less than the piano's 88. The different manuals facilitate the use of different ranks of pipes. There isn't time during the playing of a piece for the organist to adjust many of the knobs. This process must be done ahead of time. So for one manual he may set up brassy qualities; for another, light flute qualities; and for yet another, heavy or dark qualities. When playing the piece, the organist can produce the different timbres by simply moving from one manual to another. Actually it is more complicated than that, because there are buttons that permit the sounds of one manual to be coupled to another. Also, merely by pulling the knobs the organist can add sounds that are higher or lower by one or two octaves.

It is the performer who decides which ranks of pipes will be used. The composer cannot dictate his choice because organs are seldom exactly alike in the quality produced by any given rank. If an organist is to play publicly on an instrument unfamiliar to him, he will probably spend one or more practice sessions deciding which timbres on that particular organ are most appropriate for the music he has selected. Usually he pencils reminders on the side of his music.

The ranks are occasionally given the names of orchestral instruments. Only the name is the same, however. An organ "trumpet" is different in sound from a real trumpet. In fact, organs seem at their worst when they attempt to copy the sounds of other instruments.

The organist's feet are nearly as important as his hands. As you can see in the picture, on the floor are black and blond wooden slats. The slats form another keyboard, the pedal board, which is played with the feet. Most tones sounded by the pedals are low in pitch. Playing music with the feet is not easy, as you can imagine, but good organists can perform remarkably fast passages on the pedals.

The organist also uses his feet to push the expression pedals. These pedals, which look like the accelerator pedal on an automobile, increase and decrease the level of dynamics. The organist does not need to keep his feet on them, since they remain in place unless moved and do not spring back to any given position. Expression pedals are a more recent invention and were not available in Bach's time.

There are several basic types of pipes. Some are made of wood, but most are of metal. Some have a metal reed that is activated against a pipe, while others are constructed on the bottle principle with one end closed. The proper manufacture of pipes is an art in itself, because a slight deviation in the opening of the pipe can cause a different tone color or pitch to be heard.

The twentieth century has brought forth many inventions, among them the electric organ. Most pipe organists strenuously object to the electric version. Their objection is based on the fact that the synthetic tones simply do not sound like an organ as it is traditionally conceived. It is generally conceded, however, that a *good* electric organ has a better sound than a *poor* pipe organ, and the price is about equal. In any event, the tone quality of most electric models is a far cry from the instrument of Bach. The organ of Bach's time is considered the standard for organs built today. Modern, quality pipe organs have copied the Baroque organ in nearly every detail. They are custom-made and extremely expensive. The electric blower is the only modern feature on most of these instruments. The Baroque organ, then, is "the" organ for the serious composer and musician.

THE FUGUE

This remarkable music-maker, the organ, can play in a wide variety of tone colors, with tremendous power and range. What possibilities it offers the composer! No wonder, then, that Baroque composers began to write music specifically for the organ. They developed several forms of organ composition, of which the most prominent is the *fugue* (fewg).

The fugue, like most musical forms, did not appear full-blown. It evolved from less complex types of keyboard music. The fugue and its predecessors have one thing in common: they are conceived polyphonically (contrapuntally), with the lines of music imitating one another frequently. Imitation has been found in musical examples cited already in this book: Berlioz' *The Roman Carnival Overture* and Palestrina's imitative entrances in the "Sanctus." The fugue is a form that extends this idea into a complete musical composition.

Bach's *Fugue in G Minor* ("The Little") is so called to differentiate it from a longer and more complicated fugue in the same key. The first twenty-four measures are reproduced here.

Looking at the music, you will notice that it utilizes three staves simultaneously: one in treble clef and two in bass clef. Generally, the organist plays the treble clef part with his right hand, the upper bass clef part with his left hand, and the lowest line with his feet on the pedals.

As you listen to the music and follow the notation, you will observe that for five measures only one melody is played. It is a solid-sounding melody that serves as the basis for the remainder of the composition. The essential theme of a fugue is called the *subject*. At measure six, the subject enters in another line. In a fugue these lines are called *voices*, even though they are to be played, not sung. If you read music you may have noticed that although the first voice began with the notes G D B-flat, the second voice begins with the notes D A F. This change indicates that the music has modulated, in this case to the key whose center is five notes above the original. This is known as the *dominant* key, because it is built around step five of the original key. (Step five is called "dominant" because in any given key it is felt to be almost as significant as the key center itself.)

While the second voice sounds the subject, the first continues with a line of counterpoint. This line is not as easily remembered as the subject, but it does have melodic character. It is called the *countersubject*.

The third voice then enters in the original key, while the second voice has the countermelody. The first voice begins free contrapuntal material.

At measure 17 the fourth voice enters in the pedal part. Its notes are D A F, indicating a modulation to the dominant key again. The first and second voices continue in free counterpoint, while the third voice has the countersubject.

The fourth voice completes the subject at the beginning of measure 22, marking the end of the *exposition*—the rather standard beginning section of a fugue. From measure 22 until its end at measure 68, the fugue presents the subject in different keys and voices, and it makes use of free counterpoint, which often reveals fragments from the subject. In this particular fugue Bach brings in the subject with unusual frequency. And at each appearance, most if not all of the countersubject appears with it. The fugue closes with a final playing of the subject.

The basic design of the *Fugue in G Minor* can be diagrammed in this way·

EXPOSITION				DEVELOPMENT	
Voice I	S	CS	FM		Return	Close
Voice II		S	CS	FM	and	with
Voice III			S	CS	development	subject
Voice IV				S	of	
					subject	
					and countersubject	

S = subject   CS = countersubject   FM = free contrapuntal material

The fugue has four voices. It could have had two, three, or five; more than five is not common. The order in which the voices enter is a matter of choice for the composer. Composers often vary the structure slightly to suit their desires for the piece. For instance, in this fugue Bach extends the first and second voices one and a half measures just before the entrance of the third voice.

What is necessary for the understanding of a fugue? Certainly knowing the plan of the exposition helps, but it doesn't guarantee that you will understand the music. More valuable is the ability to listen and think in linear, contrapuntal terms. During one hearing, try to center your attention on the effect of the subject and countersubject when played together. The interplay among the lines is interesting to listen to.

Next, remember that the subject is the unifying element of the fugue. The plan of the exposition makes it likely that you will recognize the subject when you hear it again. The interlacing of counterpoint around a central subject (with its contrasting countersubject added for interest) reminds one of a complicated mathematical formula working itself out to a beautifully correct conclusion. It was this quality that Hammarskjold was referring to in the quotation cited earlier.

A procedure generally typical of Baroque music is well illustrated in the measures from the *Fugue in G Minor* shown in the next example.

Circles have been drawn to mark off a figure that is repeated several times in succession, each time at a different pitch level. This technique is called *sequence*. Notice, too, that the sixteenth notes above each circle form a

sequence in themselves. Most of the sequence moves down at each measure
to suggest a new key, thus giving the effect of rapid modulation.

Another sequence occurs in the next musical excerpt. The
pitches outline specific chords, but instead of being sounded simultaneously
they are played one after the other. As in the previous example, the pitch
level of the sequence moves downward with each repetition. Because most
sequential patterns are short and thus easily remembered by the listener,
they present the organist with an opportunity to use some of the varied tone
colors of the organ. Sometimes in performance the figure is played the
second time in a contrasting color.

The last chord of this particular fugue displays a rather common
Baroque technique. The fugue is in the key of G minor. Although it modulates during the course of the music, the piece typically returns to its
original key. But here Bach changes the last chord so that it is G major
instead of the expected G minor. The effect is a sudden brightening of the
music, as well as an especially strong feeling of finality.

OTHER ORGAN FORMS

The fugue is not the only form that is particularly well suited to
the organ, although it is perhaps the most important. Two others are based
on the chorale; one is called *chorale variations;* the other, the *chorale*

prelude. Variation form will be discussed later in this book; for the present, it can be described as the treatment of a theme that is repeated several times in succession but with modifications each time. The chorale prelude is a contrapuntal piece built around a chorale melody.

A third type of music well adapted to organ is the *passacaglia* (pah-sah-*cahl*-yah). It begins with a statement of the theme, usually in the bass and without accompaniment. This melody, in triple meter, is repeated over and over in its original form, but new variations are added in other voices each time. The melody is likely to stay in the bass throughout. (The pedals are ideal for maintaining the rather slow-moving melody, leaving the hands free to play the faster, higher-pitched lines of music.) The continuous repetition, combined with continuous variation, can build to a mighty climax. One of Bach's finest organ works is his *Passacaglia in C Minor.*

Some types of pieces that were common for the harpsichord were also written for organ. One such type was the *toccata,* a flashy work with many rapid scale passages. The *prelude* was another such type. In the Baroque, it simply meant a short piece of instrumental music.

THE SUITE

The organ is inevitably associated with church music. Although a fugue is not sacred music (instrumental music has no words to convey specific meanings), it is usually serious and complex. There was another kind of music written and played during the Baroque: secular music written not for the organ but for orchestral instruments and for the harpsichord. This non-organ music took two forms—suite and sonata.

First, the *suite* (sweet). The word simply means a collection or group of items that belong together. Thus we speak of a suite of rooms or a suite of furniture. In the Baroque period, "suite" referred to a collection of dances that were intended for performance as a group.

These dances were *stylized;* that is, they were "dressed up" to make them attractive pieces for listening. The composer wrote his own music for them, but in meter, tempo, and other characteristics, their similarity to known dance types was apparent. A modern-day composer might do the same thing by taking a popular dance of a generation ago, say the fox trot or Charleston, and writing similar music with more interesting melodies and harmonies while retaining the essential rhythm and style of the original dance. This is what Bach and other Baroque composers did. They took several contrasting dances that were no longer in vogue, then applied their compositional skills at stylizing them. The resultant music was for listening, not dancing.

Many different dances were incorporated into suites. The four most commonly found were the allemande, sarabande, courante, and gigue. The *allemande* (*ahla*-mahnd), which means "German" in French, probably came from Germany. It has a moderate tempo and a rather continuous movement of eighth or sixteenth notes. The *courante* (koo-*rahnt*) was French in origin. It moves a little more rapidly than the allemande. The *sarabande* (*sara*-bahnd) is a slow dance. It was probably imported by the Spaniards from Mexico. The *gigue* (zheeg) originated in Britain, where it was called "jig." It is lively and is appropriately placed as the final dance in a suite. It also tends to be more contrapuntal in character than most dance types. With elements drawn from many countries, the Baroque suite was thus an international musical form.

Other dances less frequently encountered in the suite were the bourrée, minuet, gavotte, loure, polonaise, and passapied. Often a composer wrote a *double*—a variation of the dance preceding it. Many times a suite was prefaced by a prelude or overture. It was customary for all the dances in a suite to be written in the same key. The composer achieved variety by arranging the movements in a suite so that the faster dances contrasted with slower ones. Most dances were in two-part form, with each part repeated. In the system described in Chapter 1 the form is *A A B B*.

Suites originally were composed for keyboard instruments, but later they were written also for orchestra.

Bach's Suite No. 3

One of the best-known suites for orchestra is *Suite No. 3* by Bach.[4] The orchestra consists of strings (violin I, violin II, viola, and cello, with string bass duplicating the cello part), keyboard, two oboes, three trumpets, and timpani. The addition of trumpets and timpani gave rise to the term "festival" orchestra. The keyboard player was the leader of the orchestra and normally the other musicians sat on each side of him.

By the time of Bach, the overture was more than a short introductory section; it could and often did stand as an independent composition. The overture for Bach's *Suite No. 3* is typical of the form. It is the longest part of the work. It begins in a slow tempo and has a massive, throbbing quality. The middle portion is contrapuntal and in a quick-moving tempo. The overture closes with a portion of the music that was used at the beginning of the piece.

The middle portion of the overture illustrates a concept of string playing that was prevalent in the Baroque era. The violin bow during that period still retained its original shape: the wood of the stick curved slightly *away* from the taut hair. In this respect it resembled an archer's bow, which

---

[4] Designations were not consistent during the Baroque. Bach often called suites "overtures," and this work was originally so titled. In the present discussion, the term "overture" will refer only to the opening movement of the composition, and the word "suite" will characterize the entire work.

is why it came to be called a "bow" in the first place. (Eventually the curvature of the violin stick was inverted, and the bow was lengthened for greater flexibility of handling.) The Baroque bow was held somewhat differently than are bows today. The traditional style of playing in the early development of the violin was a rapid back-and-forth rubbing motion of the bow on the strings. Smooth, sustained playing was a later development. Partly because of tradition and partly because of the type of bow used, Bach and other composers wrote string parts with many repeated notes and measure after measure of continuous eighth and sixteenth notes. This style of playing adds a certain charm to Baroque music.

The second section of the suite is an *air*. Like an aria, an air is melodious. This one contains some of Bach's most beautiful writing. The movement is widely known as *Air for the G String*, an arrangement for violin solo. The arrangement was done not by Bach but by a nineteenth-century violinist; hence it is sometimes performed in a manner better suited to the Romantic period, with occasional sliding sounds that convey a sentimentality not intended by Bach. The music is at its best when performed in a simple, straightforward manner.

In the original version of the Air, the first violins play a gently floating melody:

The third measure in the example begins on A. Its motion swings down and back up again, like a pendulum. The interest of the melody is increased through the repetition of a brief falling pattern occurring at successively higher pitch levels. To emphasize the pattern further, rhythmic stress is felt on the circled notes.

The aesthetic success of the Air may lie more in the other parts than it does in the melody itself. Listen closely to the effects achieved by the weaving together of the violin II and viola lines with the melody. Notice that there is a tendency for the motion of one to answer the motion of another. When the melody sustains a long tone, another part usually has a moving figure. The cello and bass outline the chords in simple eighth notes. The line sounds almost as though it were walking gently, first moving down the scale and then easing its way back to where it started: D C-sharp B A G G-sharp A G D. Rather than repeat each pitch at the same level, Bach writes the second note to sound either an octave higher or lower, a subtle technique that adds just the right amount of interest. Toward the end of the piece the bass line helps build to a point of interest by moving up almost entirely by half steps: F-sharp G G-sharp A A-sharp B C-sharp D.

Having done this, it turns right around and walks back down: D C-natural B A G-sharp E D.

The whole work is simple, so superbly simple. Bach creates a mood of serenity and yet adds enough action to hold the listener's interest. This musical jewel illustrates the manner in which a great composer uses conventional patterns of chords and notes and adds to them the proper proportion of change, unexpectedness, and imagination.

The Air is followed by two *gavottes,* each with the typical two beats per measure that characterize this dance type. The gavottes are followed by a *bourrée* (boo-*ray*). The bourrée also has two beats to the measure, but it moves more quickly than the gavotte. The suite concludes with a gigue, which was favored as the last movement because of its gaiety.

THE HARPSICHORD

In some respects Bach's *Suite No. 3* is not a typical Baroque suite. Only one of its dances, the gigue, was a standard component in the average suite. Furthermore, the work was written for orchestra instead of for a keyboard instrument. Composers in Baroque times did not always specify which keyboard instrument they wanted. In Bach's famous *Well-Tempered Clavier,* the word "clavier" does not refer to a special kind of piano; rather it means simply "keyboard." The pieces in that collection might have been played originally on a now defunct instrument called the clavichord, or on the harpsichord or piano. The piano was not developed until about 1710, and early models were far inferior to those of today. The prominent keyboard instrument of the time, aside from the organ, was the harpsichord.

The harpsichord looks somewhat like the grand piano. The case or body is much the same, there are black and white keys in the same arrangement, and both instruments have a few pedals. But there the similarity ends. Unlike the piano, in which the strings are struck by a hammer, the harpsichord's strings are *plucked* by a quill, which looks something like the point of a tack. When a key is depressed, a wooden jack with a quill in it moves up by the string, catches it, and makes the typical brittle sound as it is released.

The mechanism of the harpsichord does not allow the player to alter the volume by the finger pressure he applies to the keys. He can make changes in dynamic level only by playing on a second manual (which is available on many harpsichords) or, on some harpsichords, by pushing a pedal to engage the strings an octave higher or lower. In either case the change is necessarily abrupt, because no gradual dynamic shadings are possible on the instrument. This fact encouraged the Baroque technique called *terraced dynamics,* in which each dynamic level is distinct from those that precede or follow it Often in harpsichord suites you hear a statement-echo effect created by the terraced loud-soft dynamic levels.

Harpsichord by Johannes Daniel Dulcken, Antwerp, 1745.

      The lighter sound of the harpsichord and the mechanism of its action are especially conducive to the playing of rapid decorative notes. Since the harpsichord figured so prominently in the Baroque period, decorative notes became an integral part of Baroque keyboard music. These ornaments were called *agréments* and were indicated by an elaborate set of stenographic symbols. Some of the decoration was written out by the composer. The circled measures in the excerpts are examples of such writing. Sometimes composers wrote a second, ornamented version of a stylized dance. Bach did this with the sarabande from *Suite No. 2* of the *English Suites.* Here is an excerpt from the unadorned sarabande:

Now look at the ornamented version of the same passage. It contains many more fast-moving notes:

The piano and harpsichord both have the same characteristic: as soon as a sound is produced, it begins to fade away. It is impossible, therefore, to increase the volume of a tone after it is first sounded. Even the use of a sustaining pedal cannot maintain the tone at a constant dynamic level. The voice, organ, and wind and string instruments do not have this innate restriction. A composer often writes many notes in pieces for the harpsichord and piano, partly because of the instruments' inability to sustain sound, and partly because of the ease with which the fingers can produce many notes. In the Bach sarabande cited earlier, seldom does a beat pass without the appearance of a second note, sounded shortly after the first.

An even clearer example of this practice is the first bourrée from the same suite:

equals

Here Bach uses the notes that are found in a particular chord, but instead of having them sound together (and then fade together), he strings them out, one after another, thereby using a technique called "broken" chords. One such chord has been circled and is also shown in its normal form. In this way continuous sound is maintained. The sounding of many notes to compensate for the limited sustaining ability of the harpsichord and piano is a factor not only in Baroque music but also in works that are being written today.

In the *Suite No. 3* by Bach and in most Baroque music, the dynamic levels were indicated only occasionally. During this time, the performer was given considerable freedom in deciding how the music was to be performed. In fact, the performer was often the composer himself, so he felt no need to write out interpretative signs in detail.

There is another factor to account for the lack of detail in the composer's directions. It is hard for us today to appreciate the constant demand for new music during the eighteenth century. There were no established "classics" from which performers could draw. The result was a prodigious output from many composers. Since they were under pressure to turn out large amounts of music, which like magazine articles would soon outlive their usefulness, composers did not fret over each detail. No one, not even the composer, expected a work to survive more than a few years. Furthermore, since it seemed unlikely that a music manuscript would be disseminated widely, it was assumed that any question regarding details could be resolved by consulting the composer himself.

The harpsichord slowly passed from the musical scene after Bach's death. It was replaced by the piano, with its more flexible dynamic levels and its more solid and forceful tone. The twentieth century has seen a revival of interest in the harpsichord, and it can even be heard in some recordings of popular songs.

THE BAROQUE SONATA

In the Baroque period, the word *sonata* referred to an instrumental piece. This definition is admittedly broad, but it is about the only one that can be stated without qualification. Early Baroque sonatas involved several instruments and tended to evolve into two types: one developed along the lines of the suite, and the other came to be known as the sonata. The sonata included several subtypes. One had three parts played by four performers. (The logic of this statement is explained later in the chapter.) Another subtype involved one instrument plus accompaniment. A third type figured prominently in the works of Bach: a sonata for one unaccompanied instrument.

Not only was the sonata an instrumental form; it was generally made up of movements that alternated between slow and fast tempos. A three-movement sonata revealed a fast-slow-fast format, while a four-movement sonata was likely to be arranged into slow-fast-slow-fast segments The Baroque sonata, then, was an instrumental work of several movements, performed by one, two, or more players. The term "sonata" assumed a more definite meaning later in music history.

THE CONCERTO GROSSO

A favorite musical effect during the Baroque was the contrast between groups of instruments. This idea of group contrast was known as *concerted* style, and it took two forms. One of these stressed the contrast between types of instruments, such as woodwinds versus strings. The other, and more common, technique was the juxtaposition of a large group against a small group or an individual player. This form later developed into the *concerto:* a large group, representing weight and volume, is contrasted with a single player or small group, whose parts suggest lightness.

The more common type of concerto during the Baroque period was the *concerto grosso* ("grand concerto"), in which a small group was pitted against a large group. Of the many concerti grossi written, perhaps the best known today are Bach's six Brandenburg concertos, written for the Margrave of Brandenburg. The Margrave, who collected concerto manuscripts with which he graced the table of the vestibule of his residence, in 1720 commissioned Bach to write some works for him. It is not known whether the Margrave liked them or whether Bach ever heard the concertos performed. They are generally typical of Baroque concerti grossi, except for the unusual instruments used in the small group. For example, *Brandenburg Concerto No. 5* calls for a flute, violin, and keyboard against a string orchestra. Normally the small group would have involved only strings and possibly a keyboard instrument.

Bach's Brandenburg Concerto No. 5

First Movement. The *Brandenburg Concerto No. 5* opens with a sprightly tempo. The first four pitches of the melody outline the main chord in the key of the piece, D major:

The Baroque technique of short, fast bow strokes is evident in the melody played by the strings. The two sixteenths could have been replaced by one eighth note, but that would have reduced the impression of energy. The melody also reveals a quality that is often found in Baroque instrumental music. This quality might best be described as "comfortable," for lack of a better word. The melody isn't exciting; it doesn't tax the listener. It is pleasant, enjoyable, and comfortable, like putting on an old pair of shoes. It is this quality that perhaps accounts for the staying ability of Baroque music through the years.

The "comfortable" nature of Bach's melody can be partly attributed to a Baroque characteristic that was another aspect of the "doctrine of affections" referred to in Chapter 7. It is this: a single emotional quality is usually retained throughout a movement. The first moments of a Baroque work, then, are a reliable indication of the emotional tone, the "feel," to be found in the remainder of the movement. The twentieth-century listener is accustomed to more dramatic or more frequent changes of mood, such as are heard in the music of later periods. Therefore, as one of the conditions for appreciating Baroque music to the fullest extent, the listener today should realize that it will not seize his attention with startling changes of mood. Baroque music is predictable. But what satisfying listening this predictable music makes!

As you can hear in the first movement of Bach's *Brandenburg Concerto No. 5*, the flute, violin, and harpsichord or piano alternate sections with the string orchestra. Notice that the music played by the three solo instruments is contrapuntal and is characterized by a conversational give-and-take among the three.

As the movement goes past the half-way point, about eight minutes after it began, all instruments except the keyboard drop out. The keyboard instrument continues alone with a long dazzling section—a somewhat unusual occurrence in Baroque instrumental music. The basic rhythm of the section is maintained. Bach wrote it with bar lines and gave no indication that the regularity of the beat was to be broken. Nor is the music improvised, as Baroque music often was. Every note is indicated for the performer. Nevertheless, the aural impression of the passage is one of freedom of expression.

As this solo section closes, the orchestra returns with its original theme. Although the return of the original theme gives the impression of following an established formal pattern, such is not the case. The movement does have unity, and it sounds organized. But this unity is not achieved by adherence to a conventional form, as was found in the exposition of a fugue. It is accomplished rather by Bach's intuitive sense of composition. He is free to choose his theme and treat it according to his own musical judgment. The feeling of "rightness" of his music, as sensed by the listener, attests to the high caliber of that judgment.

Second Movement. The first-movement Allegro is followed by a slow tempo in the second movement. Not only is there a contrast of tempo, but there also occurs a change in instrumentation. In this movement Bach writes nothing for the violins and violas in the orchestra. He specifies again the three instruments of the solo group: the flute, violin, and cembalo (*cembalo* being the Italian name for harpsichord). The harpsichord is cast in a dual role, serving either as a soloist along with the other two solo instruments or as accompaniment.

The small notes in the musical example were added by an editor for the benefit of modern-day keyboard players who may not be so adept at reading the symbols as were their Baroque predecessors. In this edition, the small-note passages are those in which the harpsichord is functioning in the role of continuo; the passages written in regular-sized notation are those that feature the instrument as part of the solo group. In the latter situation, the placement of the notes is considered too vital to be left to the discretion of the player.

The notation in the foregoing musical example offers a clue to an important performance custom during the Baroque. Notice that the keyboard part has regular-sized notes in the bass clef, while the treble-clef notes are smaller. Furthermore, beneath the bass clef there are several numbers and an occasional sharp sign. The single note in the bass-clef part and the numbers below it are evidence of a common Baroque practice: *basso continuo* (also known as *thorough bass* or *through bass*). The low notes with their "shorthand" symbols—the numbers and accidentals—are called *figured bass*.

Basso continuo means literally "continuous bass" and refers to the function of the keyboard part. That function was to maintain the harmonic background, no matter how many or how few instruments or voices might be performing at the moment. Traditionally, the basso continuo (or merely *continuo*) was played on a keyboard instrument and the bass line was doubled by another instrument, usually a cello or the cello's predecessor, the viola da gamba. This is why you can sometimes hear other instruments (low strings) playing along with the harpsichord, even though they are not specifically called for in the music. The keyboard player was expected to complete the proper chords above this bass line, according to the symbols supplied by the composer. Obviously, then, keyboard players of continuo needed an understanding of basic chord structures and the ability to read and perform from the limited notation given them.

The Renaissance concept of equally important lines had indeed changed. The continuo emphasized the bass line, while other instruments were responsible for the principal melody or melodies. The remaining musical material was considered to be of so much less significance that its completion was left to the keyboard player. He was not free to *choose* the chords, but he was free to arrange the placement of tones within the prescribed harmonies. Different players, therefore, performed the same continuo in slightly different ways. In fact, an individual player might well decide to vary the placement of notes in his own playing of the part from one performance to the next. The differences are hardly noticeable, however, and do not affect the music to any degree.

The continuo was usually present in Baroque music. Its use gave rise to an apparent contradiction of terms: a *trio* sonata had four players—the two solo performers, plus the continuo with its customary keyboard and cello players. The continuo itself is aptly named—it sounds continuous, just as its name implies. The steady notes of the continuo contribute to the unflagging quality that is characteristic of Baroque music.

The slow movement of this Brandenburg concerto is in many ways a melodious, contrapuntal trio. The three solo instruments all play the same melody but not usually at the same time. The flute follows the violin with the melody. Much of the time there is a conversation-like exchange between the instruments.

The movement is a masterpiece in its effective use of a few musical ideas. The first and main theme appears in the violin, then the flute, and then the harpsichord. The various combinations of the theme, as well as a few embellishments, take up much of the movement. The next example (which contains only the flute and violin parts) shows how Bach develops a musical idea in addition to the main melody. In the example the idea appears three times and has a bracket over it. One way in which it is treated can be predicted merely from knowing that the music is Baroque: the pattern appears sequentially. In addition to sequence, most of the three phrases are canonic. The violin plays exactly what the flute played, except one beat later.

Another way to develop the melodic idea is to invert it. *Inversion* means turning the theme upside down. For example, if the original line moved up by step, the inversion moves down by step; a leap upward becomes a leap downward. In the next example, the inverted figure in the harpsichord answers the original melody in the flute and violin. To the listener, the inversion sounds similar to the original, although it may not be recognized as being the same melody with inverted contour. The result is a sense of both unity and variety. Inversion is a common compositional device in contrapuntal music.

Even though this movement is essentially homophonic, with the chordal accompaniment of continuo, the various lines contain a considerable amount of counterpoint. Polyphony and homophony are not mutually exclusive.

Third Movement. The third and final movement sounds much like a gigue from a suite:

Most of the movement centers on one theme. Again, it is treated conversationally among the instruments. Sometimes the theme is broken apart, and only the first few notes are developed. The harpsichord is given further opportunity to show off its scale-playing capabilities.

The principal contrasting idea consists of a short figure that is treated sequentially. Bach especially liked this sort of figure because it is musically malleable and he could handle it in many ways.

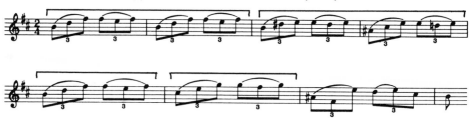

Several times in the movement Bach uses another compositional technique often heard in Baroque music. The device is to hold a consonant note over into another beat on which the chord changes, so that the once consonant note is now dissonant. The dissonance then resolves downward to a consonance. This technique is called *suspension,* and it illustrates one of the techniques for creating and handling dissonance.

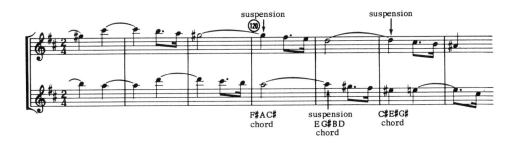

Dissonant effects are not derived by chance. They are based on a simple principle of harmony stipulating that the notes in a chord be set up according to an every-other-note pattern. That is, instead of containing the consecutive notes A B C, a chord constructed on A must contain some form of A C E (alternate letters of the alphabet, perhaps modified by sharps or flats). The remaining notes (B D F G, with any modifying accidentals) will tend to be dissonant when sounded with the A C E harmony. In the fourth measure of the Bach example above, the first beat pits G-sharp played by the flute against A played by the violin. The G-sharp is a hold-over from the preceding measure. After one beat it moves down to F-sharp, a consonant note in the F-sharp A C-sharp chord. In several such instances, the suspensions in the flute and violin parts demonstrate the fluctuation of consonance-dissonance-consonance. The musical interest generated by this one device is apparent when the music is played without the suspensions. Bach realized the value of this technique, but he did not overuse it. To do so would dull the element of the unexpected experienced by the listener, and the dissonance would lose its impact. Again Bach displayed keen judgment and rendered musical decisions that have made his music worthy of longevity.

OTHER BAROQUE COMPOSERS

The Baroque era brought forth fine composers other than Handel and Bach, of course. No discussion of the period should conclude without at least a brief mention of some of them.

Arcangelo Corelli (1653–1713) was an excellent composer of sonatas and concerti grossi. He was one of the first composers to write with a
full realization of major/minor tonality.

Giuseppe Torelli (1658–1709) was another important composer
of sonatas and concerti grossi.

Antonio Vivaldi (1678–1741) was a priest who, because of ill
health, devoted himself entirely to music. An excellent composer of vocal
music, he wrote many concertos, including *The Four Seasons,* for violin solo
and orchestra, in which each movement depicts the scenes and activities of
a particular season of the year. Vivaldi was the first to give equal importance to the slow movement of the concerto.

Jean Philippe Rameau (1683–1764) was a successful composer of
opera. He wrote a highly regarded treatise on harmony, one that influenced
Bach.

Girolamo Frescobaldi (1583–1643) was one of the earliest composers for organ.

Germany produced many fine organ composers during the Baroque. They included *Georg Böhm* (1661–1733), *Dietrich Buxtehude*
(c.1637–1707), and *Johann Pachelbel* (1653–1706). Both Buxtehude and
Pachelbel wrote choral music as well as works for organ.

Early hints of the Baroque style appeared with *Giovanni Gabrieli* (c.1557–1612) in Venice.

Jean Baptiste Lully (1632–1687) brought ballet into the opera
and influenced French music. He developed the instrumental overture into
a distinctive form.

Alessandro Scarlatti (1660–1725) is remembered for his more
than five hundred cantatas, his contributions to the Italian overture, and
his influence on Neopolitan opera.

Domenico Scarlatti (1685–1757), the son of Alessandro, was an
outstanding keyboard performer and composer of numerous keyboard
works bearing the name "sonata."

Georg Philipp Telemann (1681–1767) was a highly prolific composer. His output numbers over 3,000 pieces: forty operas, cycles of cantatas and motets, forty-four Passions, and hundreds of orchestral and chamber works. Telemann was one of the men offered the job at Leipzig before
Bach.

Henry Purcell (c.1659–1695) was perhaps the greatest English
composer. Although chiefly interested in opera, he was also skilled at composing for instruments.

The developments that occurred in music during the Baroque
were vast and significant. Among the musical accomplishments were the
development of homophony with its expressiveness and accompanying

chords; the establishment of tonality and its major/minor keys; the functional use of chords; the introduction of a better system of tuning; the differentiation between vocal and instrumental music; the development of the harpsichord, organ, and other instruments; the creation of several new forms, such as the fugue, suite, and oratorio; and the use of rhythm in both a strict, metrical way and a free manner. The Baroque period also produced Bach, Handel, and many other fine composers. The years from 1600 to 1750 were indeed significant in the art of music.

SUGGESTIONS FOR FURTHER LISTENING

BACH:
Concerto in D Minor for Two Violins and Orchestra
Brandenburg Concertos, Nos. 1–6
Suites for Orchestra, Nos. 1–4
Flute and harpsichord sonatas
Goldberg Variations
Well-Tempered Clavier
Toccata and Fugue in D Minor
Passacaglia and Fugue in C Minor

BUXTEHUDE:
Organ music

CORELLI:
La Follia (violin)
Sonatas and concerti grossi

COUPERIN:
Clavecin (harpsichord) suites

HANDEL:
Concerti Grossi, Nos. 1–12
Water Music
Royal Fireworks Music
Harmonious Blacksmith, Variations

PURCELL:
Keyboard music

VIVALDI:
Concerti grossi
The Four Seasons
Solo concertos for violin and flute

The Classical
Period

9

By the time of Bach's death in 1750, the elements in art and music that are distinguished as being Baroque in style had largely fallen into disuse. In fact, Bach's own sons thought of their father as something of an out-of-date old man, a not unknown attitude of sons toward their fathers. But the world *was* changing. Passing was the intensity of religious feeling and the domination of the churches. Gone was the old order, the love of the dramatic and grandiose. A new age had been born, one that would see significant changes in the style of art and music.

THE ROCOCO SUBPERIOD

As with all the stylistic periods in music, the Classical period did not have a clearly marked beginning. An early vestige of the gradual departure from the heavy, complex Baroque style was the *Rococo* or *galant style*, which began early in the eighteenth century in the courts of Europe, especially France. It was the art of the aristocracy, of the people of the

189

lavish courts of Versailles and similar places. Like the aristocracy they served, Rococo music and art were light, elegant, and frivolous. In painting, the Rococo was represented by Fragonard, Watteau, and Boucher. Their subject matter was often amoral love, and their pictures were laced with figures of cupids and thinly clad nymphs. Boucher's "Venus Consoling Love" (plate 5) is typical. Rococo furniture and clothing were highly decorated; the lace cuff and the powdered wig were in vogue. Elegant manners were cultivated.

Francois Couperin (1668–1733) is probably most representative of Rococo composers. He wrote a large amount of music, mostly suites, for the clavecin, the French version of the harpsichord. Bach used some of Couperin's music as models when he wrote his *French* and *English Suites*. Couperin's music was highly embellished, with many ornaments added to the happy, short melodies.

Although music and art in the Rococo style were not profound, they served as a pleasant diversion for the aristocracy during much of the eighteenth century. More important, the Rococo represented a break away from the complex counterpoint of the Baroque, and it ushered in a new type of music. The Classical period had arrived.

THE CLASSICAL ATTITUDE

During the Classical period, which scholars consider to be roughly from 1750 to 1825, several conditions in society influenced the artist and composer. The first of these was a new philosophical outlook of such scope that the period came to be called the Age of Enlightenment or the Age of Reason. The trend was strongly influenced by Descartes, Diderot, Moses Mendelssohn (grandfather of Felix Mendelssohn, an important composer of the Romantic period), Spinoza, and others who revived and added to the idealistic, idea-centered philosophy of ancient Greece. In fact, the word "classical" traditionally refers to the reason and restraint found in the life of the ancient Athenians.

Briefly, the philosophy of the eighteenth-century thinkers was this: First, truth can be realized only by the process of reason; thus the utmost emphasis must be placed on learning and intellectual pursuits. Second, the universe is a machine governed by inflexible laws that man cannot override. Therefore, what is true is true throughout the world; it is universal. Third, man's emotions as a guide to truth are false, so his rational intellect should control his behavior. The Classical man was not impressed by the unknown, since he believed that in time he would come to know it through thought and knowledge. He rejected the past, especially the Middle Ages, because he felt mysticism had stifled man's natural capacities. Reason, not faith, was to be man's new beacon.

5
Boucher: *Venus Consoling Love*. (Chester Dale Collection, National Gallery of Art, Washington, D.C.)

6

David: *Oath of the Horatii.* (Louvre, Paris. Courtesy of Art Reference Bureau, Inc.)

The Classical Man

Thomas Jefferson (1743–1826) is perhaps the epitome of the Classical, enlightened man. He was well educated. He founded the University of Virginia and gave the last years of his life to it. He was fluent in six languages and was a first-rate scholar in the classics, once requesting a copy of Ossian in the original Gaelic so that he might make an accurate translation of it. He had a talent for mathematics and natural science, including its application to agriculture. He believed in God, but passionately opposed any connection between church and state. It is through him that the principle of separation of church and state became incorporated into the Constitution and life of the United States. He was a cultured man, a fine violinist who loved to play in string quartets. He was also a good singer and dancer. He was the architect for his own home, Monticello, the design of which is evident also in the Jefferson Memorial in Washington, D.C. His talents were so rich and diverse that President John F. Kennedy was prompted to say to a White House reception for 125 distinguished scholars, including 42 Nobel Prize winners, "This is probably the greatest concentration of talent in this house except for perhaps those times Thomas Jefferson ate alone."[1]

Jefferson is probably best remembered for his accomplishments as a statesman—as ambassador to France, Secretary of State, Vice-President and President of the United States, formulator of the Louisiana Purchase, and author of the Declaration of Independence.

The Declaration itself is a thoroughly Classical document. It is difficult for us, who tend to think of revolutionaries as bomb-throwing zealots, to consider Jefferson, Washington, Adams, and the others as revolutionaries. But revolutionaries they were, even though their demands and statements of purpose were shaped in the language of reason and Classical thought. These individuals were cultured, intelligent, reasonable men, and their Declaration shows it. Although at its conclusion they pledge "our Lives, our Fortunes, and our Sacred Honor," the Declaration is essentially a legal brief, a list of the colonists' grievances against the King of England. Instead of screaming "Death to the tyrant!" Jefferson begins "When in the course of human events, it becomes necessary for one people to dissolve the political bands which have connected them with another. . . ." At a moment that would seem to require overt displays of passion—the declaring of national independence and the pledging of one's life to a cause—the man of the Classical period is dispassionate, restrained, sensible, logical.

---

[1] *New York Times*, April 30, 1962.

*Monticello, Thomas Jefferson's home at Charlottesville, Virginia.
Designed by Jefferson himself, the building shows the symmetry
and balance typical of the Classical period.*

Another example of the Classical spirit comes from the world of painting: Jacques Louis David's "The Oath of the Horatii" (plate 4). The painting depicts the three sons of Horatius swearing to their father that they will come home either with their shields or upon them (in other words, dead). Notice how frozen are the figures, like characters on the frieze of a Greek temple. They bear a striking resemblance to the figures from the ancient tomb on page 100. Notice the symmetry and balance of design in the painting—the staged and planned appearance, the focus of interest (the swords) in the center, the group of figures to the left of Horatius (his sons) and to the right (the weeping women). Notice too that the composition of the painting causes one line to lead to another with which it is balanced—the spear on the far left with the legs of the sons, the lines of the two women on the far right, and so on. The colors are not vibrant. The sum of the work is the formal, restrained quality that is classicism in the arts.

Again, like the signers of the Declaration of Independence, the sons of Horatius are pledging their lives to a cause. But instead of a violent or emotional display, the effect is surprisingly cool and detached. Emotions do not become involved, and the goal is objectivity for both writer and reader, artist and viewer. In an age that believed man should above all be rational, is this not to be expected?

Patronage

Although it was beginning to wane, patronage was very much a part of the Classical era. Briefly, the patronage system was one in which a composer accepted exclusive employment under the auspices of a patron. Patrons were either the wealthy (and sometimes decadent) aristocracy or the Church. The more frivolous taste of the aristocracy gave impetus to the movement away from the heaviness of Baroque counterpoint and toward the more fanciful style of the Classical period.

When a composer found a good patron, he was assured a stable life and a cultivated audience for his compositions. The writing of new works was expected. At its best, patronage was a good incubator for creative talent.

There were liabilities, however. Most serious among these was the fact that the composer had to please his patron, lest he find himself helping in the stables or looking for a new patron. The result was much trivial music written according to standard formulas. Too, the patronage system regarded the composer not as a unique creative artist but as the source of a product for the privileged classes to use and enjoy. Since the relationship between a composer and his work was taken lightly, it was common practice for composers to borrow themes and ideas from one another. In fact, plagiarism was understood to be a form of flattery and commendation. Legal niceties such as copyrights with resultant royalties were unheard of. Not until the advent of the Romantic philosophy of the nineteenth century did composers feel compelled to create in a way that was uniquely individual.

WOLFGANG AMADEUS MOZART

Of all the names in the Classical period, Wolfgang Amadeus Mozart stands out. Not only was he probably the best composer of his era; his music has about it a clearness, delicacy, and simplicity that seem to defy analysis. His music is so—musical! But first a look at the man.

Mozart was born in 1756 in Salzburg, Austria. His father, Leopold, was a recognized violinist and composer in the court of the Archbishop. The elder Mozart was quick to realize and capitalize on his son's extraordinary talents. Under his father's tutelage, young Mozart showed remarkable mastery of the piano and to a lesser extent the violin. By the time he was five he had composed his first pieces, and at six he performed at the court of the Empress Maria Theresa. When he was seven Mozart and his sister, who was four years his elder, went on a grand tour of Europe that included Paris, London, and Munich. By the age of thirteen he had written concertos, symphonies, and a comic opera; at fourteen he was knighted by the Pope.

The most phenomenal aspect of Mozart's musical talent was his memory for music and his ability to work out whole pieces in his mind. He once wrote, "Though it be long, the work is complete and finished in my mind. I take out of the bag of my memory what has previously been collected into it. For this reason the committing to paper is done quickly enough. For everything is already finished, and it rarely differs on paper from what it was in my imagination."

Mozart never enjoyed the stability of a good appointment as a composer to a patron. For a while he worked for the Prince-Archbishop of Salzburg. The Archbishop was a difficult man, and the high-spirited Mozart resented the restrictions of the patronage system. (He wrote his father, "The two valets sit at the head of the table. I at least have the honor of sitting above the cooks.") He quarreled with the Archbishop and was dismissed. At the age of twenty-five he left Salzburg to pursue a career as a free artist in Vienna.

A year later he married Constanze Weber, an undistinguished woman who during his lifetime was not aware of the true stature of her husband. Since Mozart did not fare well under the patronage system, he spent the next, and last, ten years of his life, as he put it, "Hovering between hope and anxiety." Due in part to his impractical and overgenerous nature in financial affairs, his only recourse was to eke out an existence by teaching, giving concerts, composing, and borrowing from friends.

In 1791, at the age of thirty-five, Mozart died of uremic poisoning. Because he was so deeply in debt, he was given the cheapest funeral and buried in a pauper's grave.

Despite his short life and the disappointments that plagued him, Mozart composed over 600 complete works: 22 operas, 25 piano concertos, 12 violin concertos, 14 concertos for other instruments, 24 string quartets, 60 solo works for piano, 27 choral works, and 52 symphonies. Mozart never used opus numbers, although some were added later by publishers.[2] His

---

[2] The word "opus," meaning "work," is put on compositions by the composer (or publisher) to indicate the general order in which works were written. The practice began early in the seventeenth century, but only since the mid-nineteenth century have opus numbers been applied consistently to new compositions.

Wolfgang Amadeus Mozart. An unfinished painting by Joseph Lange, his brother-in-law.

works were catalogued by a Viennese botanist and amateur musician named Köchel (*Keh*-shul), who assigned each composition a number on a generally chronological basis. Hence today every Mozart work is identified by a number (up to 626), preceded by the initial K. for Köchel. A few Köchel numbers have been corrected on the basis of later musicological research, notably by Alfred Einstein.

THE SYMPHONY

Probably the most significant change in music from the Baroque to the Classical periods was the establishment of the orchestra and the development of musical forms to go with it. Until the Classical period, and to some extent in it, there was little difference between music written for large groups and music intended for small ensembles. Furthermore, a composer often did not specify precisely what instruments he wanted. Being a craftsman-artisan in a patronage system, he had to accept whatever instrumentation was available. He might have two, four, or six violins on a part; maybe an oboe, maybe some flutes. At any rate, the woodwinds could substitute for one another, and if none were available, a violin could play the missing part.

But this was soon to change. About the middle of the eighteenth century an orchestra began at Mannheim, supported by a patron, that was to influence the course of musical history. The Mannheim orchestra was noted for its excellence and its experimentation with new effects, such as the gradual *crescendo* and *decrescendo,* which are standard techniques today. Inevitably, Mannheim attracted composers who wrote music for the orchestra. The pieces they developed through trial and error were called "symphonies." Although these works seem pale and immature when compared to the full-fledged symphonies of Haydn and Mozart, they were nevertheless influential.

The word *symphony* has since the Classical period come to mean a work of several movements, written for full orchestra. Bach wrote instrumental works that he called "sinfonias," but these were more on the order of overtures for cantatas. So the symphony stands as one of the important contributions of the Classical period.

The composers of the Classical period did more than merely refine the symphony. They also developed forms for the individual movements. The most important of these was the *first-movement,* also known as *sonata-allegro* or, more commonly, *sonata form.* This form proved so satisfactory that it served for practically all the first movements of Classical symphonies, concertos, sonatas, and string quartets, for many fourth movements, and even for some second movements. With modifications, it has served composers to the twentieth century, and it is still used occasionally today. Of all the forms in music, sonata form has proved to be the one most commonly used in serious musical works. Its widespread acceptance has come about without deliberate promotion; no convention of composers was called at which time it was decided that the musical plan called "sonata form" was to be the prescribed form for first movements. Rather, composers have written in patterns that seem musically satisfying to them, and the result is a frequent use of the pattern known as sonata form.

Sonata form should not be confused with the term "sonata" meaning an entire piece (discussed in the preceding chapter). Sonata form involves only *one* movement. A sonata usually has several movements. Although Classical and Romantic sonatas usually have at least one movement in sonata form, the form is not limited to compositions called sonatas.

Mozart's Symphony No. 40

The *Symphony No. 40 in G Minor, K.550,* is an excellent work through which to examine the symphony and the sonata form as well as to become familiar with the music of Mozart. The symphony was written in the summer of 1788 along with two other symphonies, *Symphony No. 39* and *Symphony No. 41,* the "Jupiter." The year was probably the most disappointing one of his personal life. Little is known about the circumstances that precipitated the writing of these symphonies, but it is probable that Mozart never heard them performed. The instruments called for in *Sympony No. 40* are violins, violas, cellos and string basses (different parts were not yet written for the latter two instruments), a flute, two oboes, two bassoons, and two French horns. Mozart himself later added parts for two clarinets. The orchestra is noticeably smaller than the modern symphony orchestra. Not only are fewer kinds of instruments used; the string sections are also smaller. When playing Mozart symphonies today, most professional orchestras do not use all of their regular string players.

First Movement—Sonata Form. The first movement of *Symphony No. 40* is in sonata form—of course. With no introduction, it opens in a moderately fast tempo with this first theme:

There are several interesting things to be heard in these nine measures:

    1. The theme is broken into two equal parts, the second being nearly identical to the first but one note lower. Each half is further divided in half, the first being on the order of a melodic statement and the second a sort of musical answer. Thus the melody is symmetrical in both its larger and smaller sections.

    2. With its many fast notes, the theme would not be well suited to singing, but it is well suited to the violins that play it. It is not a strong, independent melody, but it has qualities that enable it to be developed—a prerequisite for a theme in sonata form.

    3. The theme is disarmingly simple. This rhythmic pattern appears in each of the four phrases:

Nothing very exciting about that. The rhythmic pattern does have a cumulative effect that leads up to the next-to-last note. But even though this is a musically sensible and satisfying effect, similar rhythmic patterns can easily be found in other musical works. If you look at the quarter notes, you will notice that they merely suggest basic chords: D D D B-flat (G minor), G E-flat C C (C minor), and so on. To this simple structure Mozart adds some musical "pepper"—a little dissonance. The eighth notes marked with an X in the example at the top of this page are not in the harmony of the chord. Since they are short and do not occur on the beat, the effect is not one of harshness. It is rather like a quick nudge.

4. The three-note groups in the melody create a sense of forward movement, a quality that is necessary for interesting music. This sense of motion is achieved partly through the cumulative effect of the rhythm and partly by the manner in which each phrase is ended. Two of the first four phrases end by soaring up six notes, and in none of the four cases does the phrase end on the beat. The effect is one of needing to move onward, without stopping.

5. The melody is in a minor key, which tends to transmit its own particular mood to the piece. Many composers of the Romantic period used the sound of minor to achieve self-pitying, "heart-on-sleeve" melodies, but not Mozart. He uses it to add only a tinge of color; never does it become sticky and sentimental. This is especially noteworthy in view of the fact that the symphony was written during a time of serious financial difficulties for Mozart. The other symphonies he wrote that summer were in major. Even when he is writing in the context of minor, however, Mozart's personal feelings are not apparent.

6. The melody is in a sense a collection of many melodic fragments. It is not a sweeping, flowing, over-arching array of tones. It is neat, precise, dainty. Not only does this type of melody fit well with the Classical attitude; it also subjects itself well to development.

After a few closing chords, the theme begins to be repeated, but this time, halfway through, the music shifts to some firm chords and rapid, running scales—a *transition* of fifteen measures. The transition acts as a bridge to the second theme and a new key. It might seem that a transition does not need to have much musical interest in itself, if its function is merely to join one theme to another. However, a fine composer like Mozart can make a transition musically quite interesting. Later, composers in the Romantic era became much more subtle in their use of transitions, but Mozart wrote his in such a way that the parts of the sonata form are clearly delineated. In fact, the end of the transition is easily identified by its two closing chords followed by a measure of rest.

"Why have any transition at all?" you may ask. "Why not just present the themes?" One reason is that in the Classical symphony the second theme is almost always presented in a different key, so a smooth modulation must be effected somehow. The first theme is in the *tonic* key, the key that predominates in a movement. If the tonic key (and hence the first theme) is a major key, the second theme will almost always be in the key that is centered five notes higher (the dominant key). If the original key is minor, as in the case of this *Symphony No. 40*, the second theme is usually in the relative major, the major key that uses the same key signature but whose center is one and a half steps higher.

There is another reason for the existence of a transition. Composers found that presenting a new theme on the heels of the first one was not satisfactory, musically speaking. It didn't allow the listener enough time to absorb the first melody. Furthermore, turning out one theme after another is too obvious and crude to be aesthetically desirable.

The second theme of this particular movement is played between the violins and the woodwinds:

Even if you don't read music fluently you can see that the second theme doesn't look like the first. The second has longer note values. It doesn't have the repeated rhythmic pattern, either. There are few skips up or down to other notes. The theme is more difficult to remember than the first. In fact, it comes dangerously near being innocuous. But the two themes in sonata form are seldom similar in mood or style; one must contrast with the other.

In this second theme, there are many sharp, natural, and flat signs, indicating motion by half steps. Such movement is called *chromatic*, and it involves the frequent use of *accidentals* (sharps, flats, and naturals not indicated in the key signature). Chromaticism was not emphasized in the Classical period; it is an individual trait of Mozart. Although he uses it in this particular theme, and in much of his other music, it usually appears in the melody on notes not on the beat, and therefore it does not affect the basically simple chord structure.

Upon completion of the second theme of this movement, a transition-like passage appears. Interspersed in it are fragments of the first theme, which are sounded alternately between the clarinet and bassoon. At this place in sonata form, composers have some options. Sometimes they introduce a third theme, at other times they engage in an extended transition, and occasionally they use a fragment of one of the preceding themes, which is what Mozart does here.

The transitional section following the second theme concludes with a *codetta*. The term is derived from the word "coda," meaning "tail." The suffix is a diminutive ending suggesting brevity, and so the codetta is simply a short wrap-up section, a concluding series of scales and chords. Often it has a brief melody associated with it.

Exposition. So far only a third of the movement has been accounted for. In it the musical ideas Mozart uses in this movement have been presented, exposed. The section to this point, therefore, is called the *exposition*. It might help to diagram the manner in which the movement has progressed thus far:

EXPOSITION

First theme (in tonic key)	Transition	Second theme (in dominant key or relative major)	Transition	Codetta (in dominant key)

Normally a composer writing in this form indicated a repeat of the entire exposition. In performances today this sign is frequently ignored, and the music moves right into the next section, the development.

Development. In music, *development* means the manipulation of the themes. It is a demonstration of the composer's ability to present the themes in different and musically satisfying ways. Development means more than variation of a theme, however. Variation is a limited concept, suggesting that a theme is merely recast in a new light. Development is a restructuring of the theme, as you will observe from Mozart's development section.

What does Mozart do in the development section of the first movement of his *Symphony No. 40?* Basically, he subjects the first theme to three kinds of treatment.

1. He has the first half of the theme played three times, each time in a new key. Musical interest is thus achieved by theme abridgment and by frequent modulation.

2. He employs counterpoint. While the lower strings play the first theme in yet another key, the violins begin a countermelody of rapidly moving notes:

When the lower strings finish the first half of the first theme, they pick up the countermelody, while the violins play the theme in yet another key. A similar exchange occurs two more times, with each key center a note lower than its predecessor. The result is an example of sequence, a technique discussed in Chapter 8.

3. He further fragments the theme. The first few notes are tossed back and forth between the flute, clarinet, and violins. Again new keys are utilized, but the section is quiet as compared with the busy, vigorous exchange that preceded it. Soon the answer in the woodwinds is shortened further, to include only the first three notes of the first theme. Several times the direction of the first two notes is inverted, so that they ascend in pitch rather than descend as in the original theme:

Theme fragmentation is so pervasive throughout this section that the first two descending eighth notes appear, at various pitches and in various instruments, in *all but the first two measures* of the development section. Fragmentation is also apparent in the transition leading from the development into the next main section of the sonata form.

In this particular development section, Mozart works with only the first theme. He fragments it, uses frequent modulation, adds counter-melodies, and reverses the direction of melodic intervals. These devices are typical of development sections in sonata form. He could have done more. He could have developed the second theme, or he could have introduced an entirely new one. He might have altered the rhythm of the original theme, written different chords to harmonize it, or combined the two themes in a contrapuntal manner. The means of development are endlessly varied.

Now you can see why sonata form is so well suited to music written for aesthetic purposes. In this form the composer is challenged to show what he can do, not only in writing melodies but, equally important, in manipulating and developing them. The form allows for a most sophisticated type of creative effort. And it is the evidence of creativity that makes people want to hear certain works of music again and again. Therefore development is probably the most important feature of sonata form.

Recapitulation. The term for the third section of sonata form, *recapitulation,* means literally "return to the top." And sure enough, Mozart comes back to the same theme that began the movement. It is played by exactly the same instruments, with exactly the same accompaniment, and it involves exactly the same notes. The literal repetition is quite short. At first, the changes are small; the bassoon adds a few notes in contrast to the theme. But as the music moves into the transition heading toward the second theme, more changes occur. The transition is longer than it was in the exposition. In fact, for a short time it sounds as though another development section is going on. While the second violins play rapidly moving notes, the short fragment heard just briefly in the exposition is exchanged between the first violins and low strings:

Another difference is observed: the second theme is not in a new key. It stays in the tonic. If the second theme were in a different key, the composer would find himself caught off base, away from the home key and near the end of the movement. He would need to get back to the tonic in a hurry and make the key change sound convincing—a difficult thing to do. So the second theme stays in the same key as the first in the recapitulation. Following the second theme the transitional music is similar to that found at a comparable place in the exposition.

The movement ends with a *coda*. The coda is like the codetta except that it is longer, thereby providing the movement with a convincing conclusion. In the coda to this movement, Mozart again utilizes a fragment from the first theme, passing it to the violins, then to the violas, and finally to the woodwinds. Concluding chords alternate between dominant and tonic. Thus ends one movement of one symphony.

No two movements in sonata form are exactly alike. Each example contains some small deviations from the form. In general, however, the Classical sonata form can be diagrammed as follows:

EXPOSITION					DEVELOPMENT	RECAPITULATION				
First theme (tonic)	Trans.	Second theme (dominant ....) (or relative major)	Trans.	Codetta	Working over of musical ideas. Rarely are new melodies introduced	First theme (tonic	Trans.	Second theme	Trans. ....)	Coda

Although this symphony does not have a slow introduction before the exposition, many first movements in sonata form do have this optional feature.

Two more points need to be mentioned with regard to sonata form. One deals with key. The Classical composers were quite circumspect in their use of keys. Mozart's *Symphony No. 40* is planned around the key of G minor. Not only is the first movement expected to begin, end, and center around the tonic key; the other movements are schemed accordingly. The second movement is in E-flat major, a closely related key by virtue of the fact that it has only one flat more than the original key of G minor. The third and fourth movements are in G minor. This careful attention to key may have had considerable effect on the eighteenth-century listener; it is hard to say how people heard things almost two hundred years ago. Today we are used to music that modulates frequently, so the impact of key change in the Classical symphony is greatly reduced for us. Our ears have also become more accustomed to combinations of keys that are remote, or distantly related. (A *remote* key is one that differs from another by at least two sharps or two flats.) The loosening of relationships among keys and within a given key has led inevitably to music that is *atonal*—that is, having no key center whatsoever. To the listener today, the significance of key in Classical forms lies not in the particular key scheme but rather in the musical effectiveness of the modulations.

The other point that needs emphasis is the unity of all that is incorporated in the form. Themes are created by the composer for the purpose of being developed. It is easy to assume, then, that only the themes are worthy of attention, while transitions and development are merely "fillers" and of little musical merit. But a transition does far more than connect themes and provide modulations; it has musical interest in itself, and it contributes to the total impact of the music. A coda has a necessary place in providing a satisfactory musical conclusion, which gives the movement a feeling of finality and completeness. So knowing the themes is only the first step in understanding a movement in sonata form.

Second Movement. The second movement of the *Symphony No. 40* is also in sonata form, and this in itself is somewhat unusual. Traditionally, this movement is slow and melodious, and a theme is difficult to develop in such music. The slow tempo creates a time problem for the composer: the time relationships are stretched out, which means that everything, including development, is slowed down. Furthermore, the graceful melody usually does not adapt well to fragmentation or other devices of development. Thus in this symphony the development section of the second movement is shorter and less important than it was in the first movement. It consists primarily of a first theme and a pattern of coupled quick notes being exchanged between the woodwinds and the strings, concluding with a new short phrase repeated four times. The codetta and coda are not long.

The first theme starts with six equal soundings of the same pitch—hardly a melodious beginning.

But Mozart achieves beauty by having the theme re-enter in another instrument. To balance the evenly spaced unison notes, he concludes the theme with a gentle rocking melody that could easily remind one of a gentleman's graceful eighteenth-century bow. The notes altered by sharps and flats are typical of Mozart's style:

The quick couplet of notes 𝅘𝅥𝅮𝅘𝅥𝅮 is most interesting. Essentially Mozart is suggesting a melodic contour that goes:

There is nothing wrong with the two alternate examples. But Mozart's version is much more appealing. The quickness of the notes in contrast to the others around them, the short rest that helps the listener to anticipate the important note with its *sforzando* (sudden attack)—all these features transform what would have been ordinary into something worth noticing. A subtle change, yes. But it is such subtleties that have made Mozart's music live.

The two quick notes have another function in this movement. Mozart works them into the transitions and the development. In fact, this pattern of notes becomes a *motive* that acts as a unifying thread throughout the entire movement. In music the word "motive" means a very brief fragment (sometimes consisting of only two notes), that is intelligible and self-contained.

The second theme, in good sonata-form tradition, contrasts with the first:

Notice how symmetrical the theme is. Each short phrase in the first two measures is played twice; then the entire theme is played again. The second time the theme appears, the third measure is more embellished, but this version is easily heard as being related to the first. The key of the second theme, typically, is centered around the dominant, five notes higher than the key center of the first theme. Again the two quick notes appear between the playings of the theme.

The codetta is only nine measures long. It features the throbbing qualities of the first theme in the low strings while moving through chromatically altered chords.

Twice in the codetta Mozart presents this melodic figure:

It is called a five-note turn. In this case Mozart has written out an ornament that was found in both the Baroque and Classical periods.

The codetta of the exposition includes an example typical of Mozart's writing:

There are two chords in the last measure. The notes in the first are A-natural B-flat C E-flat. The second has only two notes, B-flat (which appears twice) and D. As explained in Chapter 8 and Appendix C, a chord normally consists of alternate scale steps. But the first chord here does not, so it has tension, dissonance in it. By contrast, the second chord has little tension and is consonant. The motion from the first to the second chord gives a strong feeling of conclusion, a clearly defined ending to this section of the music.

The aural impression gained from these two chords proves again that a composer creates a constant state of motion by manipulating sounds in pitch and time, and he involves the listener's memory and anticipation while so doing. Normally, the music would have resolved to the tonic chord in the concluding measure, and normal motion would have been quite acceptable here. But if only the expected happened in music, it would be quite dull. In this instance, Mozart decided to add some interest, to create musical tension by delaying the normal progression of the music. Of course, there are limits to the number of surprises that a listener can accept. Too much of the new and unexpected creates not interest but confusion and frustration. So Mozart handles the *unexpected* (a delay in chord resolution among some sections of the orchestra) in the *expected* way (resolution to the tonic chord). Thus he achieves a blend of something old and something new.

As a concluding observation on these two chords, it would be well to notice the length of the dissonant chord, for the composer's choice here is as crucial to the musical effect as is his original decision to do the unexpected. The music has six beats to the measure. The normal accenting of beats in this meter is *1* 2 3 *4* 5 6. Mozart begins the dissonance on the heavy first beat and resolves it on the fourth, another strong beat. If he had sustained the dissonance for only one or two beats, it would have been too short to be effective. It would probably have seemed rushed and out of character with the rest of the music, and it would have resolved on a weak beat in the rhythmic pattern. If he had held the dissonance for four beats, it would probably have been too long, and the final tonic chord would have been too short to convey the proper feeling of finality and repose.

Third Movement—Minuet and Trio. For the third movement of this work, Mozart composed the traditional *minuet and trio.* Stylized dances, of which the minuet is one, were discussed in Chapter 7. Although Classical composers were not so fond of writing music based on stylized dances as were their Baroque predecessors, the minuet had enough appeal so that it came to be accepted as the third movement of works containing four movements.

The movement begins at a moderately fast speed with this melody, in the minor key of the symphony:

It contains an unusual rhythmic pattern for the minuet of the Classical period. Normally the first beat in each measure is the strongest, and Classical composers wrote accordingly. But instead of following the normal *1* 2 3, *1* 2 3 pattern, Mozart in this theme accents almost every other beat in the first five measures: 3, *1* 2 *3*, 1 *2* 3, *1* 2 3, *1* 2 *3*, 1 *2* 3. Today we are accustomed to rhythmic freedom, so a change such as this is not as impressive as it must have been to the symphony's first hearers. The short fourteen-measure section containing the theme is then repeated exactly.

Next there occurs a thirteen-measure section that is quite similar to the first, but it is in the relative major key, B-flat. The low strings and woodwinds play a two-measure segment much like the first, with this addition: the violins and bassoon play a downward pattern outlining the tonic chord, B-flat major:

On its reappearance, the theme is treated somewhat in strict imitation, something encountered in Berlioz's *Roman Carnival Overture*. The melodic lines are very similar to the original and to each other, but some liberties are taken with them. When listening to music of this type, try to hear the entrance of each part playing the theme. In this case one violin section enters, then the other. The use of a contrapuntal device such as canon is not so common in the Classical period as in the Baroque. Its presence here, however, demonstrates the fact that some contrapuntal writing is present in all historical periods, even though homophonic music may at the time be predominant.

The trio section derives its name from the fact that traditionally it contained only three instrumental parts: the continuo plus two other instruments. As a result, the sound was lighter and quieter than the preceding minuet. By the time Mozart wrote his symphony, custom no longer required such sparse instrumentation for the trio, but the distinct change to a quieter mood, with fewer players, was retained. The trio contrasts with the minuet not only in style and instrumentation but also in key. For example, minuets in minor keys are followed by trios in major keys. In the *Symphony No. 40,* the minuet is in G minor, the trio in the parallel major key, G major. (Major and minor keys are called "parallel" when they have different key signatures but the same starting note.) The first theme of the trio is simple:

The section is repeated. The second melody of the trio is also simple, merely outlining basic chords. In fact, it is so common a pattern that it is hardly distinguishable as a melody. Then the first theme is heard again, with one change: two French horns are added for contrast.

This second section of the trio is repeated. The minuet is then played through again exactly, but without repeats.

A survey of the entire third movement discloses that it is based on a strict formal structure:

Minuet	Trio	Minuet
A	B	A
a a *b a'* *b a'*	*a a* *b a'* *b a'*	*a b a'*

Of all the forms in the Classical period, the minuet-and-trio structure was the most strict and formal. It presented the composer with the challenge of following convention and yet writing interesting music, a challenge that Mozart met admirably in this symphony.

Fourth Movement. As is typical of symphonies in the Classical era, the last movement of Mozart's *Symphony No. 40* is lively and brilliant. It moves at a rapid rate and provides an exhilarating finish to the work. In fact, Mozart marked the movement with the word *"finale"* (fee-*nahl*-ee) in addition to a tempo marking. When a composer wants a dashing conclusion to a symphony, he does not pour into it his most profound musical efforts. Instead, he tends to fall back on simpler ideas, common patterns, and technical brilliance. That is what Mozart did in this movement.

Final movements come in several forms, some of which will be presented later. Mozart on this occasion chooses—you guessed it—sonata form. The first theme is based on the notes of the G minor chord. The theme itself was not completely original with Mozart. Many other Classical composers also used a similar pattern, so many in fact that the theme has acquired a nickname, "the Mannheim rocket." Like the first theme in the first movement, the melody again follows a symmetrical statement-answer scheme:

The transition that follows is longer and of more interest than the transitions found in the other movements of the symphony. Again, the end of the transition is easily heard because of the clearly marked phrase ending followed by a rest.

The second theme, again like that of the first movement, contains many chromatic notes and makes more use of the woodwinds. It is in the relative-major key, B flat:

A melodic fragment from the first theme occurs frequently in the codetta that concludes the exposition.

The development is built around the first theme. It begins with harmonies that sound unsettled. Soon the "rocket" is passed back and forth between the violins and bassoon. Then the strings treat the theme canonically, in a manner that resembles a round. The appearances of the theme are not identical as they appear in the various string parts. They are similar enough, however, to suggest the theme strongly. Throughout the development, especially during the imitative parts, the music modulates many times. The development concludes with the woodwinds and strings trading the theme back and forth, followed by an abrupt stop.

The recapitulation is conventional and faithful to the requisites of the form. The development and recapitulation are marked to be repeated—a direction that is quite usual. The coda is almost identical to the codetta except for being slightly expanded.

This symphony, like others, is both typical and unique. In general, however, it serves well as an example of the style and a standard by which you can better evaluate and understand all symphonies of this period.

THE CONCERTO

The Classical period saw the development of the solo concerto as well as the symphony. Although the solo concerto existed in the Baroque era, the concerto grosso was the more common type. The Classical period, however, saw a complete reversal in the relative popularity of the two forms. The concerto grosso with its small group disappeared almost entirely, not to be resurrected until the twentieth century. The predominant concerto form became the solo concerto, in which one player was featured. Since the concerto grosso was no longer popular, it was not necessary to retain the word "solo" in designating the other form. Hence, from the Classical period to the present, the word "concerto" refers to the solo type.

The concerto of the Classical period instituted another change. No longer did it rely as heavily on the contrast between a large group and a small group or solo instrument. The music for the soloist became more elaborate and more difficult than the music for the large accompanying group. The exact nature of the soloist's part will be discussed shortly.

In many ways the concerto is like the symphony. It is a work of some length and importance. It makes use of the same forms as the symphony. It is divided into movements that are arranged in the same order of tempo and style. There is one difference, however. Usually concertos contain three movements instead of four. The movement dropped from the four-movement scheme is the third, the minuet and trio.

Mozart wrote many concertos, the majority of them for the usual concerto instruments such as piano and violin. But an often overlooked aspect of his genius are the concertos he wrote for unusual solo instruments: the French horn, flute, clarinet, and bassoon. Particularly noteworthy about these concertos is the fact that after nearly two hundred years they are still considered among the best for those instruments. Today if a bassoonist or clarinetist plays a concerto with orchestra, chances are that it will be a concerto by Mozart. Equally impressive is the fact that when Mozart wrote these works, instruments such as clarinet, French horn, and bassoon were in a technically primitive state compared to today's models. The clarinet had only five keys compared to today's seventeen, and the horn had no valves, which limited the number of notes it could play well. Fortunately, Mozart managed to write around these obstacles.

Mozart's Concerto for Violin and Orchestra (K. 219)

Mozart wrote his *Violin Concerto No. 5 in A Major* in nine months in 1775, when he was 19 years old. The reason for its composition is not known. Probably he composed it for himself to perform as first violinist in the orchestra at Salzburg.

First Movement. Since the focus of our attention is on the techniques involved in writing for a soloist and orchestra, the features of this particular sonata form need not receive detailed attention.

Before the soloist plays a note in this concerto, the orchestra presents a shortened version of the exposition, complete with its two themes. The first theme does little except outline the notes of the home or tonic chord and the dominant chord.

The second theme bubbles along.

When the solo violin enters, there is a bit of a surprise. A slow expressive interlude is inserted prior to the beginning of the second pres-

entation of the exposition. The concerto features a *double exposition,* one for the orchestra and one for the soloist. When the exposition begins, the soloist plays a countermelody to the first theme. Mozart sometimes employs this technique to add interest to the music. Notice that the soloist receives a more technically demanding, interesting part to play.

Except for the double exposition, which is typical of Classical concertos, the movement proceeds through the normal sonata form. The development section is shorter and simpler than was its counterpart in the G Minor Symphony. The concerto was written when neither Mozart nor sonata form had reached full maturity. The development section is more like the addition of different musical ideas than a true development.

There is another feature of the concerto that is not found in symphonies. Shortly before the end of the movement the orchestra comes to a stop, and the soloist begins playing by himself a freely constructed and technically difficult paraphrase of the preceding musical material. Many stops and starts are made, holds and altered tempos appear freely, and the rhythm is entirely flexible. This portion of a concerto is called a *cadenza.* During the Classical period it came to be expected in at least one movement of the concerto, and frequently in more than one movement. The cadenza was conceived as an unabashed opportunity for the performer to show off his skills, both in playing the instrument and in improvising.

Improvisation was a far more common practice among concert performers in Mozart's time than it is today. As a part of their piano recitals, both Mozart and Beethoven frequently made up variations on the spot, and were even known to take a theme supplied by someone else and improvise on it immediately. In those days, the cadenzas a performer played were supposed to be his own, and theoretically were to be improvised, although one suspects that the performer must have thought out well in advance what he would play for his cadenza. Therefore, Mozart indicated only where the cadenzas were to be inserted in his music; he seldom wrote them out for the performer. By the time of the Romantic period, however, composers wrote out everything, including the cadenzas.

Second Movement. The theme of the second movement of the G Minor Symphony may not have been very melodic, but the theme of the second movement of the Violin Concerto more than makes up for that. The theme is lyric, and in many ways it is similar to an operatic aria. Concealed

in its expressive melodies is an abbreviated sonata form. Its second theme is:

Again, a cadenza appears just before the close of the movement.

Some of the notes in the musical example of the first theme have been circled. Although these notes occur on the beat, they really don't fit with the underlying harmony at that point in the music. They are significant because of the interest they give the music. Suppose that Mozart had stuck to just nice, common harmonic notes. Would the music have been as worthy of attention? Probably not. The temporary delay in getting to the harmonic tone causes us to enjoy the nonharmonic tone because (1) it is interesting and imaginative, (2) we have a sense of mastery since we anticipate, correctly, that the harmonic tone will follow promptly, and (3) its resolution to a harmonic note causes the music to be logical, satisfying, and meaningful. A good performer will take advantage of the musical possibilities here. For the sake of emphasis, he will probably stay just a fraction longer on the circled notes. In this way he avoids the mechanical effect that would result if the notes were of identical length.

Third Movement—Rondo Form. For the final movement of the concerto, Mozart chose *rondo* form. The basis of the rondo idea is a melody that returns several times, with other melodies interspersed among its various appearances. Symbolically it can be represented *A B A C A D A*, and so on. Theoretically there is no limit to the number of sections possible in rondo form, but a minimum of five sections (*A B A C A*) is customary.

In this Violin Concerto, Mozart utilizes some of the spirit of the omitted minuet by prescribing the meter and tempo of the minuet for the final movement. The main theme of the movement is a straightforward melody of eight measures:

The *A* section has a short concluding phrase, and then moves on to contrasting material, the *B* section. Normally the contrasting sections in a rondo do not have melodies that are so easily remembered, although contrasts in type of melody are characteristic.

The *A* theme returns, but in a somewhat shorter version than the initial presentation. There is further contrast in the *C* section that follows.

Once more the *A* returns, this time with a real change. The meter switches from the 3/4 of the minuet to 2/4 music that sounds vaguely oriental. All oriental-sounding music, regardless of its true origin, was called "Turkish" by the eighteenth-century Viennese. The style enjoyed some popularity in Mozart's time, but the section is not Turkish at all, and it is probably the least musical portion of this concerto.

The *A* theme appears again. After another cadenza, a final variation of the *A* theme concludes the movement.

As you can see (or better yet, hear), the rondo form contains one musical theme to which it returns alternately between new musical ideas. Its sections are not lengthy, and there is little attempt to develop melodies or deal in profound musical ideas. Since the final movement was traditionally supposed to be light and cheerful, encouraging the listeners to leave in a happy frame of mind, you can see why rondo form was so often used for a final movement and why it is largely limited to that movement. The form reached its widest popularity in the Classical era. By the time of the Romantic period, its appeal had dropped drastically, although it is still used occasionally today.

What has been gained by your study of the G Minor Symphony and the Violin Concerto No. 5? First, these works have served as models of music in the Classical style, models that can help you understand similar musical works. Second, they have demonstrated several forms of the era— sonata, rondo, minuet and trio. And it was through these forms that the Classical composer expressed the reason of his age and developed his musical ideas. Finally, these creations have introduced you to one of the great musical minds of all time—Wolfgang Amadeus Mozart. He is the embodiment of music in the Classical period, and there is perhaps no one about whose music we more often use the word "perfection."

SUGGESTIONS FOR FURTHER LISTENING

MOZART:
Concerto No. 20 in D Minor for Piano, K. 466
Concerto No. 21 in C Major for Piano, K. 467
Concerto No. 23 in A Major for Piano, K. 488
Concerto No. 24 in C Minor for Piano, K. 491
Concerto No. 4 in D Major for Violin, K. 218
Concerto No. 5 in A Major for Violin, K. 219
Concerto in E-Flat Major for French Horn, K. 495
Concerto in A Major for Clarinet, K. 622
Concertos for Flute, K. 313, 314
Sinfonia Concertante in E-Flat Major for Violin and Viola, K. 364
Sinfonia Concertante in E-Flat Major for Winds, K. 297b
Symphony No. 34 in C Major, K. 338
Symphony No. 35 in D Major, K. 385, "Haffner"
Symphony No. 36 in C Major, K. 425, "Linz" ·
Symphony No. 38 in D Major, K. 504, "Prague"
Symphony No. 39 in E-Flat Major, K. 543
Symphony No. 41 in C Major, K. 551, "Jupiter"

HAYDN:
Symphony No. 94, "Surprise"
Symphony No. 100, "Military"
Symphony No. 101, "Clock"
Symphony No. 102
Symphony No. 103, "Drum Roll"
Symphony No. 104, "London"

COMPARING STYLISTIC PERIODS

Before proceeding further in your study of music, you will find it helpful to review the three musical styles presented thus far: Renaissance, Baroque, and Classical. This review can be done in two ways. First, you can refer to the various ways of manipulating sound (listed in Chapter 1) and make a list of how each was used in the particular period. For instance, Renaissance rhythm was usually unmetered but had a gentle, regular motion. Baroque had the extremes of strict meter and, in the recitative, rhythmic freedom. After you have prepared your list, compare it with the chart of such characteristics on the inside back cover of this book. No chart can adequately describe what happened musically during a period, but it can point to significant trends.

A second way to review is to listen to recordings of music from the three periods. Listen again to the examples in this book, or select music from the works of other composers, in order to establish in your ear and mind the characteristic sound of each style. Each reveals a quality of sound that cannot be put into words. Words can help, but in the end you must learn to recognize the "aural flavor" of the various styles of music.

Classical Opera
and Chamber
Music

10

So far in this book only Mozart's instrumental music has been examined. Certainly no study of his music is complete without a discussion of his operas. During his lifetime they were his primary interest and source of income.

Because opera is less well known than symphonic music in America (not Europe), it is often not as well liked or understood. Perhaps it evokes disparate feelings more than any other musical medium. Among a small group of devotees, it is considered the summit of musical and artistic expression. To other persons, it smacks of excessive showmanship and exaggerated emotional appeal. They regard it as an unfortunate hybrid, lacking both the dramatic power of the stage or motion picture and the musical appeal of a symphony or concerto. In fairness it should be pointed out that opera does have a loyal following among a portion of the general public. But it deserves a wider acceptance.

How can a listener approach opera in order to achieve the fullest possible understanding of the medium? Let us begin by looking at what opera aspires to be.

THE ELEMENTS OF OPERA

Opera includes several artistic elements in addition to music. Opera takes place on a stage; therefore, it is a form of theater, requiring eye appeal and action. Thus the success of opera depends to some extent on its staging—the scenery, costumes, and actors' movements. As drama, it must present a story, delineate the various characters, and project their feelings. Frequently dancing is integrated into the production. Opera, then, involves many things: literature, drama, vocal and instrumental music, staging, and dancing. It is the great union of the arts. And for that very reason, opera is an extremely difficult medium in which to achieve convincing performance.

Believability is hard to achieve because, although the stage action attempts to duplicate the realism of human affairs, the verbal communication of the participants takes place through singing rather than normal speech. In the morning we say "Please pass the toast." If we sang it, people would rightly begin to wonder! But there is more to it than that. Suppose this everyday breakfast scene is being enacted in an operatic context. If, for the sake of realism, a character sings the words "Please pass the toast" with a minimum of musical expressiveness, then the music will surely be uninteresting. The drama may have been saved, but at the expense of the music. On the other hand, if a composer writes a beautiful melody to these words, complete with an aesthetically satisfying *A B A* form, then realism and credibility have been sacrificed.

The element of time is a factor, also. Stage action can proceed normally if "Please pass the toast" is spoken in the routine manner of real life. But if an aria is developed from these words, the forward motion of the plot will have to be suspended for its duration. If interesting music is to be included, therefore, the drama will have to be abbreviated to accommodate the pressures of time, and it will have to be interrupted occasionally to allow for artistic balance between drama and music.

Audiences realize that no theater production can be wholly realistic, and so they accept certain conventions and restrictions of stagecraft. In conventional theater, for example, interior scenes are designed to suggest four-walled rooms, even though one wall must be missing to permit audience viewing. The audience also accepts the fact that time in a drama is not measured in absolute terms. Months or years are presumed to have elapsed during a ten-minute intermission. Such concessions of space and time are necessary and are not disturbing to the viewer.

Frequently more distracting in opera is the problem of understanding the words. Even when sung in English, the words are not easily comprehended. But the problem is compounded by the large number of operas in foreign languages. The question is often asked: "Why can't the words be sung in English so I can understand what's going on?" There is no easy answer, but translation poses more hazards than are generally supposed. Some of these will be discussed in Chapter 12: the differing number of syllables, the altered accents, and the varying shades of meaning incurred. Furthermore, the lines are often in the form of poetry with a rhyme scheme, and this imposes further limitations. Fortunately, better translations of operas are slowly becoming available, and these in turn encourage opera companies to sing more operas in English. Change is slow, however, and tradition is strong. Some veteran singers are reluctant to relearn a role in English. After all, *they* understand the old language, and the regular opera-going public knows what is going on, so why change? The answer "To create a larger audience" doesn't appear to convince them.

The impression of realism has been further hampered by the style of singing that has evolved, of necessity, within the operatic tradition. This style was developed in the centuries before recordings and mechanical amplification were available. Above all, a singer had to be heard—clearly— all the way to the last row of the balcony. If the style was somewhat unnatural, it was at least powerful. Nuances and shadings were sometimes sacrificed to the need for sheer projection of the voice, and the style that resulted has not always encouraged ready acceptance by the inexperienced listener.

The drama-music dilemma has a bearing on the appearance and acting ability of the opera singer. Some outstanding singers of the past were either not talented or not interested in acting. Because of the great vocal demands of opera, it is difficult to find persons who can both sing and act with skill. And these roles were lengthy and difficult to learn, so that years of experience were required to do them justice. It is hard to imagine an aging, matronly woman as a tempting young seductress. Fortunately, opera companies today are very much aware of the need for a little more natural vocal sound and an appropriate visual image.

It must also be admitted that some opera plots will hardly win the praise of thoughtful drama critics. Many of the stories make no attempt to be believable, or they try to be seriously realistic and fail. Others are dated and quaint.

The public that has followed opera through the years is to be commended for its interest, but it has sometimes shown a lack of understanding of opera's purpose. Some of these observers apparently knew or cared little about music. They attended the opera for its spectacle. They cheered the singers' virtuoso efforts and applauded the pomp and color of the staging. Others wanted to associate with the "right" people and be numbered among the elite. So the opening night of an opera season was often a social event, and the music was only incidental.

The repertoire of most opera companies caters to the audience, which means that certain favorite operas are performed year after year, to the exclusion of works in the modern style. Financial considerations, as well as audience preference, tend to work against the performance of a new opera. As was mentioned in Chapter 5, the cost of producing an opera is appalling, and therefore few opera-company managers wish to undertake the risk and expense of trying a new work. When they have done so in the past, the public has generally not indicated enough interest to make the venture seem worthwhile.

APPRECIATING OPERA

After this discourse on the problems of opera's acceptance, you may wonder whether there is any chance at all for you to understand and like the form. The answer is an emphatic "Yes!" Where do you start? By accepting, as you do in watching a drama, some limitations on realism. Accept the fact that commonplace statements will be sung and that the stage action will differ from the routine of ordinary events. An opera is not intended to be a slice of life.

Realize also that the drama will have to be abbreviated. A good story helps make a better opera, but the plot in itself does not guarantee a successful opera. So don't judge the finished product solely on its literary merit. Accept the fact that the characterizations will not receive the subtle development found in good drama. It just isn't possible to dwell on such niceties and still devote proper attention to the music.

What is there to appreciate in an opera? First and foremost, there is music. Because it is associated with specific events in a story, operatic music is singularly expressive. The drama provides the composer with situations that are ripe for musical expression. The emotional impact of the right music at the right place in the drama accounts for much of opera's appeal, especially nineteenth- and twentieth-century operas. Some operatic "I-love-yous" cause in some listeners a sensuous reaction best described as "goosepimply."

Opera also has nonmusical appeal. The pageantry of the staging can be quite impressive. The combination of the visual and the aural has an impact that neither can achieve alone. A person who hears opera without seeing the action on stage is missing a vital part of the opera experience. It is like listening to a radio broadcast of a basketball game—the sense of involvement is lessened. Opera really must be seen to be appreciated.

As with any type of music, the more you know about opera, the better will be your understanding and appreciation of it.

EARLY OPERA

Opera began in Italy shortly before 1600 as an attempt to revive the authentic form of the ancient Greek dramas, which were combined with music. The founders of opera were known as the Camerata, a group of musical amateurs in Florence. They rightly felt that the prevalent pol-

*Gorgeous Baroque decorations and staging adorn the presentation
of the opera* La Contesa dei Numi, *presented at the Polignac
palace in Rome in 1729. The painting is by Panini.*

yphonic style was incapable of being expressive. And so they came up with
a drama that was sung entirely in recitative. Because recitative is such a
flexible and expressive vocal style (described in Chapter 7), it was a logical
choice. Jacopo Peri's *Euridice*, generally considered to be the first opera,
was one long recitative with a few melodious portions that might qualify as
arias or choruses. Initially, opera performances were for a small aristocratic
audience. Although *Euridice* sounds thin and rather vapid to us, it must
have made quite an impression on its audience in 1600, because the idea
quickly caught on.

Soon this form of dramatic homophonic music began to appear
elsewhere. Claudio Monteverdi wrote an opera in 1607 and another in 1608,
giving impetus to the trend that was moving to Rome and other Italian
cities. In 1637 Venice opened the first public opera house. By this time,
however, the artistic ideals of the Camerata had been rather badly muti-
lated. The stories were burdened by the addition of irrelevant incidents,
spectacular scenes, and incongruous comedy episodes. But other changes
were more constructive. The tradition of using recitative almost exculsively

was abandoned. Arias, duets, and ensembles evolved, and the orchestra took on more prominence.

As opera spread throughout Europe, its dramatic element became less and less important. The singer reigned supreme. In their desire to hold the center of the stage, soloists added all kinds of embellishments to the melody to show off their virtuosity. The situation deteriorated so markedly that Christoph Willibald von Gluck (1714–1787) felt compelled to lead a reform movement. Gluck had written many operas himself, so he knew the field and was undeniably right when he said that opera was in need of correction. He tried to bring back its dramatic integrity by making music serve the text. Everything in the opera, including ballet, was to be an integral part of the drama. Gluck wrote several operas that demonstrated his reforms.

In the decades following the opening of the opera house in Venice, opera evolved into two rather distinct styles. One was *opera seria*, which was of a serious nature more akin to the original dramatic purpose of the first operas; the other was *opera buffa* (*boo*-fa) which was lighter opera of a comic nature. Mozart wrote both kinds of opera, but his greatest public successes were of the *buffa* type.

Mozart's The Marriage of Figaro

The original title of the work is *Le Nozze di Figaro*, revealing its language to be Italian. The Austrian Mozart, then, wrote an opera in a language other than his native German. But he had made several journeys to Italy and knew the language. The *libretto* (the text of an opera) was written in this case by the Italian Lorenzo da Ponte, the best librettist of his day. The selection of an Italian text was a happy choice for the further reason that opera was a thoroughly Italian product and audiences in Vienna were more accustomed to hearing opera in Italian than in their own tongue.

Mozart's *The Marriage of Figaro* should not be confused with Rossini's *The Barber of Seville*, which was written some thirty years later. Both are based on plays from a trilogy by Beaumarchais. The principal characters appear in both operas, but some differences are apparent. For example, Figaro is a valet in Mozart's opera, and not a barber.

Because of the opera's length, the discussion here is limited to only the first of its four acts. The plot is complex, with each character trying to do the others in, so you should listen to the music with libretto in hand.

The overture is full of gaiety and devilishness. It sets the appropriate mood for the action that follows. As the curtain rises, Susanna (fiancée of Figaro and maid to Countess Almaviva) and Figaro (valet to Count Almaviva) are in Figaro's unfurnished apartment. Susanna is trying on a hat before a mirror, while Figaro is measuring the room in order to plan its furnishings.

In the recitative that follows (often spoken instead of sung in modern-day performances), Figaro explains that the room will accommodate the bed the Count has given them for a wedding gift. Susanna objects to using the room as their bedroom. In the duet that follows, Figaro points out that the room is convenient to the Count's apartment on one side and the Countess' on the other. Should their employers ring in the night, it would be only two steps to their doors. Notice again how the music fits Figaro's description of the ringing bell. *But,* Susanna replies, what would happen if Figaro had to be absent for a few days? She then reveals that the Count has been trying to woo her and take advantage of his feudal rights (the right to court a maid in his service before she is wed). Susanna leaves to answer the Countess' ring.

Now Figaro knows why he and Susanna have been asked to accompany the Count to London! "If that is the way Sir Count wishes to dance," sings Figaro in an aria, "I'll be glad to play the tune." Figaro has a few tricks of his own in mind.[1]

The plot thickens as Dr. Bartolo and Marcellina enter, discussing a contract Figaro has signed. The contract stipulates that he will repay the money he has borrowed from Marcellina or else marry her. Bartolo sings of his determination to do away with Figaro. (In Italian the aria is appropriately named "La vendetta!") Susanna returns. She and Marcellina exchange insults before Marcellina leaves the room.

Cherubino, the Count's page, enters. He is a teen-ager who has just discovered womankind, and he is infatuated with them all.[2] He explains to Susanna that he has been caught with his arms around another servant girl, and now the Count is going to send him away. And he cannot bear to leave the Countess, his most recent infatuation.

Susanna hears the Count approaching and hides Cherubino behind a chair. The Count sits in that very chair, of course, and proceeds to propose lovemaking to Susanna by trying to arrange a meeting that night. Basilio is then heard outside. He is a music teacher as well as a sly and devious master of intrigue. The Count goes behind the chair while, shielded by Susanna, Cherubino slips into the chair. Susanna flings one of the countess' dresses over him.

Basilio is suspicious and asks Susanna if she has seen the Count. He makes some insinuations about the Count's interest in her and advises her to warn Cherubino to restrain his affections for the Countess. The

---

[1] The theme of a servant's outwitting a member of the aristocracy was a popular one in *opera buffa*. There was a keen awareness of social class in the eighteenth century, and the seeds of rebellion had been planted by 1786. *Opera buffa* was attended largely by people of the middle class; thus the popularity of the theme.

[2] The part is written for a soprano and thus is sung by a woman. The purpose of this operatic tradition is probably to convey the idea of Cherubino's youth.

A scene from Act One of The Marriage of Figaro. *Cherubino has just been uncovered.*

Count, hearing this, can stand it no longer and leaps out from behind the chair. A delightful trio follows, in which the music offers insight into the characters and their various reactions to the situation. Susanna, for example, sings "Oh, how dreadful! I am ruined!"

In this trio there is one of those operatic situations that must be seen to be appreciated. While Cherubino is being discussed, Susanna becomes faint. The two men almost, but not quite, seat her in the chair in which Cherubino is hiding. Throughout this action, the music and libretto unite into a truly enjoyable scene. It is opera at its lighthearted best. The trio concludes as the Count describes how just yesterday he caught the youth in Barbarina's room (Barbarina is the gardener's daughter). Re-enacting the scene, he pulls the dress from the chair, only to find Cherubino again.

Confusion follows. The Count wants to tell Figaro that Susanna has been unfaithful, but then he remembers his proposals of only a few moments before. The scene is interrupted by the entrance of a group of peasants and Figaro himself, all of whom are singing the Count's praises. Figaro explains that the demonstration is in honor of the Count because he has revoked the laws of feudal privilege. Figaro requests that the Count now bless the marriage of Susanna and himself. Aware of Figaro's ruse, the Count shrewdly suggests that the event be postponed until that evening.

After the peasants leave, Cherubino begs for mercy and is supported by Figaro and Susanna. But the Count is unrelenting and orders the youth to a post in his regiment.

As the act closes, Figaro, in the well-known aria *"Non piu andrai,"* offers Cherubino some parting advice about military life. He tells the young man that he must give up his amorous exploits for the stern duties of war, such as marching through mud and snow. It closes with a brilliant march-like section to the words *"Cherubino alla vittoria, alla gloria militar"* (Cherubino off to victory, to military glory). The curtain falls.

Mozart was a master composer of opera as well as instrumental forms. In his operas, he welds music and drama into an effective whole. His characters have individuality. His melodies are always pleasant and tuneful. He makes a clear-cut distinction between recitative and aria, treating the recitative text with the greatest possible economy. In Mozart's operas, the problem of realism has been largely surmounted by the use of such an unbelievable story that the listener is no longer concerned about reality. He is free to concentrate on the beauty of the music and the amusement the tale provides.

Another important operatic tradition is found in this first act of *The Marriage of Figaro*. Mozart has the ensemble of principal characters sing at the same time, each expressing his own thoughts. Often such ensemble numbers conclude with a resounding full finish, and so this device is well suited to end an act.

Mozart's operas represent the Classical style, wherein the music exhibits good taste and a control of emotions. True, the librettos of his comic operas are sometimes spiced with *double-entendres*, and the singers' emotions are exaggerated for comic effect. But the music is handled with a restraint that contrasts nicely with any incongruities of text or action. Even in serious operas he did not allow the music to become bombastic or sentimental. There is about his operatic writing what might be called the "light touch," an awareness that music can be valid even when conceived as entertainment.

CHAMBER MUSIC

Suppose you were invited to spend an evening listening to chamber music. What would you expect to hear? Music in a small room? In one respect, that guess would not be far wrong. Chamber music is written for performance in a room rather than a concert hall. But there is more to it than that.

Until the Classical period, most music written for instruments other than the keyboard did not clearly indicate the size of the group that should play it. Indeed, until the Baroque period it was not often clear whether a piece of music was to be sung or played or both. As the orchestra became more established and standardized, composers, especially Haydn, began to specify the type of group for which they were writing. Apparently they felt that what was appropriate for an orchestra might or might not be suitable for a smaller number of players. There emerged, then, music for large groups (symphonies, concertos) and *chamber music* for small groups (quartets, trios, etc.). Although their differences were conspicuous, neither type of music was considered superior to the other.

The Classical period saw a thriving of chamber music. The orchestra was coming into being, and differentiation between music for large and small groups was needed in an age of increasing musical specialization. Furthermore, the social milieu encouraged chamber music. The public concert was only beginning to be a factor in musical presentation. Most performances were still for private audiences of the rich and well born. When a host wished to provide after-dinner diversion for guests in his home, he quite naturally felt a small chamber group to be more appropriate than a symphony orchestra.

Musicians to this day have continued to value chamber music, primarily because it permits a refinement and intimacy of expression that cannot be derived from a large musical organization. An orchestra has power and color, while a string quartet provides a sense of involvement and clarity. One medium can be as effective as the other in the hands of a skilled composer.

In chamber music, the number of players on each part is limited to one. When the instrumentation of some chamber groups is considered, this definition may appear to be wrong. For instance, a string quartet consists of two violins, one viola, and one cello. There are, however, two distinct violin parts. As long as each has a different part, there could be three or more violins and the work would still be considered chamber music.

Voices are not customarily involved in chamber music, although early chamber works were influenced by vocal style. In the Renaissance, madrigals could be either sung or played on string instruments. Such music was described as being "apt for voyces or viols," and it suggested the intimacy and grace of private performance—a feature of later chamber music. In the twentieth century, Stravinsky, Schoenberg, and others have written for voice in chamber compositions. Since the Renaissance, however, and particularly during the Classical period, chamber music has been understood to be instrumental. In the present discussion, therefore, the term "chamber music" will presuppose an instrumental idiom.

Listening to Chamber Music

The techniques for listening to chamber music are essentially the same as those required for listening to music of any type. However, since chamber music is performed by a small group, it lacks the tonal power of a full orchestra or chorus with their lush, colorful sounds. Chamber music cannot compete in sheer mass of sound or richness of color. For this reason, it cannot rest its case to any degree on a sensuous basis, and the listener should not expect it to do so.

Chamber music must instead stand on its musical qualities. Hence the listener must approach it on a more sophisticated level. Such an approach requires attention to two factors. First, one must consider what is happening in the music itself. The composer's musical ideas and his treatment of them in the composition are the warp and woof of chamber music. When he writes, he is well aware that each part will appear more prominently because there are fewer parts. The listener, then, should notice how the musical material is handled under these conditions.

The second factor requiring attention is the skill with which musical details are brought out by the performers. The fewer the number of players, the more closely they must listen to one another and execute their parts together. This feeling of oneness in musical performance is called *ensemble*, the French word for "together." Chamber music is traditionally performed without a conductor, so the sensing of tempos, phrasing, and dynamics is the responsibility of each player. Although one person is acknowledged to be the final arbiter (for example, the first violinist in a string quartet), the cues and nods that start and stop the group are so subtle that they can be seen only by a keen-eyed observer. That is why the word "ensemble" can refer not only to the unified performance of the players but also to the chamber group itself.

For some reason, concert music is far better known than chamber music, perhaps because more knowledge and attention is required for successful chamber-music listening (and performing). Also, until comparatively recently it was difficult to find good recordings of chamber works. The situation was self-perpetuating: since there was a limited audience, few chamber groups could earn a living by means of their performance, and so the potential audience was left unreached. Today, chamber ensembles are found in residence at many universities, while other groups can now at least make a living by giving concerts. The chances of your hearing chamber music performed well are increasing, and it is an area of music that is gradually achieving proper recognition.

The advantages of hearing live performances of music were pointed out in Chapter 5. In the case of chamber music, the advantages become almost necessities. When a small ensemble is heard live in a home or small recital hall, something is added to the listener's enjoyment. Perhaps the closeness to the performers provides a sense of involvement that is essential to chamber-music listening. Possibly the fact that the sound comes from a group seated only a few feet away makes for better aural comprehension than when the sound is reproduced mechanically through a loudspeaker. In any case, chamber music is best heard at close range.

FRANZ JOSEPH HAYDN

One man who had much to do with the delineation of chamber and orchestral music during the Classical period was Franz Joseph Haydn (1732–1809). He was born in the same year as George Washington, in the town of Rohrau in eastern Austria. His father was a wheelwright, so Haydn, unlike Mozart, did not have the advantage of early musical training. An uncle, with whom Haydn went to live at the age of six, gave him his first musical instruction. At eight he became a choirboy at the Cathedral of St. Stephen in Vienna, where he gained musical experience but little theoretical instruction. When his voice changed, he was dismissed. For the next few years he lived a precarious existence doing odd jobs and teaching, as well as studying musical theory on his own initiative. In 1761, at the age of twenty-nine, Haydn was taken into the service of Prince Paul Anton Esterházy (Ester-hahzy), head of one of the richest and most powerful noble families in Hungary.

The next year Nicholas Esterházy succeeded his brother Paul Anton. Nicholas, besides being rich and powerful, was also a connoisseur of music. Most of the time he lived at a country estate, the sumptuousness of which rivaled the French Court at Versailles. On the estate were two

Esterházy palace in Eisenstadt.

beautiful concert halls and two theaters, one for opera and one for marionette plays. The prince himself played the baryton, a complicated monstrosity with six strings to be bowed and up to another forty that sounded as a result of the vibrations of the bowed strings. Accordingly, Haydn wrote over two hundred pieces having a part for baryton. Needless to say, the instrument has long since passed into oblivion.

Like Bach and other musicians of the time, Haydn not only composed but also conducted the performances, trained the musicians, and kept the instruments in repair. Unlike Bach, Haydn had twenty-five *good* instrumentalists and a dozen or so fine singers.

Haydn's contract was typical. It called on him "to produce at once any composition called for" and to smooth out all difficulties among the musicians. He was expected to present himself twice daily in the antechamber to await orders.

For the most part, Haydn's experience with the Esterházy family represented the patronage system at its best. Haydn liked them and they him. He once said, "My prince was pleased with all my work, I was commended, and as conductor of an orchestra I could make experiments, observe what strengthened and what weakened an effect, and thereupon improve, substitute, omit, and try new things; I was cut off from the world, there was no one around to mislead me, and so I was forced to become original."

After Haydn had been with the Esterházys for thirty years, Prince Nicholas died. Haydn subsequently made two visits to London in the 1790s. For each trip he composed six symphonies. The twelve are known as the London symphonies: numbers 92 to 104. They represent Haydn at his orchestral best. After the London trips he returned to work for a while for Nicholas Esterházy II, who was not so interested in music as his father had been. Haydn then wrote mainly vocal works, including two oratorios, *The Creation* and *The Seasons*. He gradually retired from his life of creativity and died in 1809.

Haydn was recognized during his lifetime as a great composer by the public and other musicians. He admired and was in turn admired by Mozart. The two learned from each other's music, a fact especially evident in Haydn's string quartets written after 1781. Beethoven also regarded Haydn with esteem.

Haydn is sometimes referred to as the "father" of the symphony, the string quartet, the modern orchestra, and instrumental music in general. Although such claims are exaggerated, they give some indication of his significance. What Haydn did was to work out a better balance for the new forms. For example, he developed the finale of the symphony. Prior to Haydn, the fourth movement had been no more than a frothy little section. Haydn exchanged it for a movement in sonata or rondo form. While it still did not have the scope of the first movement, it nevertheless revealed musical substance and provided better overall balance.

Franz Joseph Haydn. Painted by John Hoppner during one of Haydn's visits to London.

THE STRING QUARTET

One of Haydn's contributions to music was the shaping of the string quartet, probably the most significant grouping in the history of chamber music. Early in the eighteenth century, compositions called *divertimentos* were common. As the name implies, they were diversionary, innocuous little pieces. They could be played by either a quartet or a string orchestra. Haydn took the divertimento, deleted one of its two minuets, and gave it more musical substance. He called these new works *quartets* rather than divertimentos.

The change did not occur quickly; it was stretched out over much of Haydn's adult life. The quartets show this evolution toward a more sophisticated content. Two will be examined closely for purposes of comparison.

Haydn's String Quartet, Op. 3, No. 5

This work was written in the early 1760s. Its first movement is in sonata form, which in itself represents a real advance over the divertimento. However, the movement is filled with happy, carefree themes that receive little development. The first theme is:

and the second:

The entire exposition can be performed in about one minute, and the development in only about half a minute.

This movement illustrates the elusive nature of musical quality. There is nothing wrong with this music. It does not contain poorly placed sounds, nor is it incoherent. On the other hand, there is little here to merit our attention; there is little that Haydn didn't do better in his eighty-two other quartets, or that other composers of the Classical period haven't done better. The movement is enjoyable but hardly meritorious.

The second movement is a different story. Here Haydn writes a charming solo for the first violin. He designates the movement "Serenade," the title under which it is often played today as an independent piece. The theme of the Serenade begins:

It is a simple melody, played over an even simpler accompaniment of plucked strings. Several points are worth remembering about this movement. (1) The first violin alone has the melody. The second violin, viola, and cello never do more than provide accompaniment. (2) The sound reminds one of a music box; it is refined and fragile. (3) The movement

suggests calm and objective beauty, not a passionate love scene. The satisfaction that comes from hearing it is like the satisfaction that comes from
looking at a rose or a fine piece of china. Thus the melody reveals the attitude of the Classical period.

Contrast this melody in your mind with the Air from the Bach
suite discussed in Chapter 8. Bach's melody has long over-arching phrases;
Haydn's is composed of short fragments. Bach's has a continuous-sounding
bass line; Haydn and other Classical composers dropped the idea of a
continuous bass. Bach's chords are more complex than Haydn's. So the
Baroque air and the Classical serenade are quite different-sounding pieces.

When each of the four instruments plays a musically significant
line, the musical possibilities are much greater, of course. The lack of
interesting musical parts for the second violin, viola, and cello, therefore, is
one mark of the lack of musical sophistication in this particular string
quartet. The three lower instruments are relegated to an inconspicuous role
in each movement. For example, here is the beginning of the third, a
minuet:

Notice that the viola and cello have only a few background notes. The second violin occasionally supports the first violin, but generally its contribution is one of accompaniment.

The quartet closes with a lively movement in sonata form. It is much like the first movement in length, complexity, and musical quality.

Haydn's String Quartet, Op. 76, No. 3

This work, by contrast, represents maturity in the development of the string quartet. It was written in 1797, thirty-three years after *Opus 3, No. 5,* and after Haydn's successful journeys to London.

The first movement is again in sonata form. The exposition takes about two minutes (without repeats) and the development section about one and a quarter minutes. Length does not necessarily indicate quality, of course, but it is significant to notice that with maturity of style came the need to develop musical ideas more completely. In this movement the themes are not as frilly as those in *Opus 3, No. 5;* they now have more substance. All four instruments have important parts. For instance, in measures 5 to 7 of the example on page 231, the instruments play identical rhythmic figures (dotted sixteenth and thirty-second notes) at different times in an ascending scale pattern.

Also, Haydn modulates into more remote keys and modulates more frequently than he did in the earlier quartet. The music is more difficult to play, but it is more substantial, more worthy of hearing.

Theme and Variation. For the second movement, Haydn revised a melody he had given to Austria as a national anthem. It is still the Austrian national anthem, and it is also sung in many churches under the title "Glorious Things of Thee Are Spoken." The entire quartet is sometimes called the "Emperor Quartet" because the original title resembles the English "God Save the King" in its wording. The melody is hymn-like but a little more flowing than a chorale. It is constructed of two repeated phrases with contrasting phrases inserted between the two.

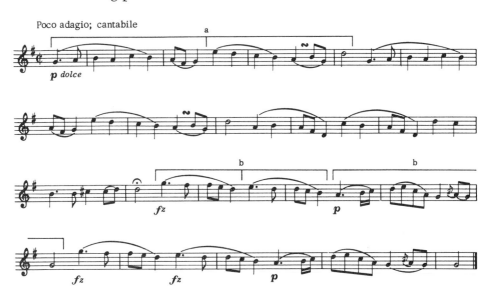

Again the classical ideal of balance is evident. Brackets have been drawn over the two main ideas.

The movement is a *theme-and-variation,* which is, simply, a series of variations on a given melody. Haydn is especially helpful to the listener in this movement because he has one of the instruments continue to play the melody while a variation is introduced.

Variation I presents the melody in the second violin, while the first violin plays a contrapuntal line that embellishes the melody:

In Variation II the melody is in the cello, supported by the second violin. While this is happening, the first violin plays a countermelody that is quite rhythmic:

The counterpoint becomes increasingly complex.

Variation III presents the melody in the viola, with other instruments playing contrasting parts against it:

Variation IV finds the first violin again playing the melody, some of the time an octave higher than before. The other three instruments play an intricate, chordal accompaniment:

Notice that several accidentals appear in the accompaniment. As you can probably hear, the harmony has been changed; other chords were used in the original presentation of the theme. A four-measure concluding section is added to this final variation.

In the fourth variation Haydn uses two compositional techniques that deserve mention. Throughout four measures the cello holds one long note, a D.

The D cannot be consonant with all the notes played in those four measures, although it is consonant with most of them. Its presence, therefore, emphasizes the alternation occurring between consonance and dissonance as the harmonies change. The technique of maintaining a long tone against the changing harmonies of other parts is called *pedal point* or, more briefly, a *pedal.* The name comes from a device often found in organ music—the holding of a certain note by the pedal. The sustained sound of the held note adds unity to the music. As he hears the tone, the listener anticipates that the held note will resolve in a musically satisfying manner, which it does.

The other technique concerns the range in which the instruments are asked to play. In the next example, all four instruments play in their upper range. The cello even plays a portion of its phrase in treble clef.

When string instruments are played in a high register, the sound tends to be clear but intense and exciting. The effect is used by Haydn as the climactic point of the entire movement.

Most examples of theme-and-variation form are not so easy for the listener to follow. Not often does the composer keep the melody intact and sounding in some part. Indeed, later composers wrote variations that were so remotely related to the original theme that no discernible relationship was left. Haydn, however, treats the theme imaginatively without obscuring it. He employs two devices in doing this: he adds contrapuntal parts and he changes the harmony. He might also have varied the rhythm or the pitches of the melody itself. (This latter technique is extremely common, and a delightful example of its use can be found in Mozart's variations —K. 265—on "Twinkle, Twinkle, Little Star," which he knew as the French folk song "Ah! Vous dirai-je, Maman.") Although in this movement Haydn chose not to exploit every possible means of altering the theme, all four variation techniques—melody, harmony, counterpoint, and rhythm—are effective and are used frequently by composers. Furthermore, such devices often appear in combination with one another.

The final two movements of this quartet maintain the standard of excellence that is evident in the first two movements. Typically, the third movement is a minuet and trio, and the fourth movement is a fast finale.

THE SONATA

The sonata (not to be confused with sonata form) is a sizable work in three or four movements. The movements correspond to those found in the symphony or concerto, except that the minuet or third movement is often omitted. In tempo, form, and key relationships, each movement of the sonata tends to resemble its counterpart in the symphonic realm. In this respect the sonata, symphony, string quartet, and concerto all reveal a common ancestry in the early Baroque sonata.

During the Classical period, the use of the word "sonata" became more precise. A Baroque sonata had been almost any kind of instrumental piece; a Classical sonata was usually a composition for two instruments: a piano and one other instrument. This designation still holds true today. In this type of sonata, the two parts are considered to be of *equal* importance. In no sense is the piano accompanying the other instrument. As a matter of fact, the piano part often contains the more important musical idea, while the other accompanies. Since the presence of the piano is assumed, the sonata is called by the name of the other instrument. So a violin sonata is for violin and piano.

Because the sonata is ensemble music, the players perform with the music before them. The custom of memorizing has come to be associated with virtuoso display, as when a soloist performs a difficult concerto. In chamber music, however, the individual must be subordinate to the ensemble, and so feats of memory would seem inappropriate. Furthermore, the complexity of the various lines and the number of players involved (two persons for a sonata, more in other ensembles) make the memorized performance more hazardous and susceptible to error.

One type of sonata is customarily played from memory, and that is the solo sonata. Bach wrote several for violin, and more recent composers have also cast a string or woodwind instrument in the role of soloist with no accompaniment whatsoever. But the instrument most commonly associated with the solo sonata is the piano. Music of this type is vast and varied. More will be said about the piano sonata in the next chapter.

OTHER COMMON CHAMBER-MUSIC GROUPS

Almost every conceivable combination of instruments has had chamber music written for it. Certain groups are more frequently found, however. The most common have been mentioned: the sonata and the string quartet. Another likely string group involves two violins, two violas, and one or two cellos. The woodwind quintet (clarinet, oboe, bassoon, flute, and French horn) was not common in Haydn's time, but it is a standard chamber ensemble today. Brass ensembles have the least standardized instrumentation. Perhaps the quintet (two trumpets, French horn, trombone, and tuba) has most frequently drawn the attention of composers.

It is not unusual to find one nonstring instrument added to a string quartet. For example, a work for clarinet and string quartet is called a "clarinet quintet," though only one clarinet is present. If a piano plus a string quartet is called for, the work is a "piano quintet." A "piano trio" is a piano plus violin and cello. Apparently the presence of strings is taken for granted, so the unusual instrument is designated in the naming of the group.

In one sense, opera and chamber music represent the extremes on the continuum running from dramatic to absolute or non-dramatic music. Both Haydn and Mozart, however, display in their works a similar sense of taste and proportion and high regard for musical craftsmanship. Few composers can resist the lure of writing chamber music and opera. Neither should a student of music ignore it.

SUGGESTIONS FOR FURTHER LISTENING

GLUCK: *Orfeo ed Euridice*

HAYDN:
Oratorios: "The Seasons"
                "The Creation"
Quartets, Op. 64, Nos. 1–6
Quartets, Op. 74, Nos. 1–3
Quartets, Op. 76, No. 4, "Sunrise"
Quartets, Op. 77, Nos. 1 and 2
Symphonies, Nos. 88–104

MOZART:
Operas: Così Fan Tutti ("So Don't They All")
                Don Giovanni ("Don Juan")
                Die Zauberflöte ("The Magic Flute")
Quartet No. 14 in G Major, K. 387
Quartet No. 15 in D Minor, K. 421
Quartet No. 19 in C Major, K. 465
Quartet No. 20 in D Major, K. 499
Quartet No. 1 in G Minor, K. 478 (Piano)
Quartet No. 2 in E-Flat Major, K. 493 (Piano)
Quintet No. 5 in G Minor, K. 516
Quintet in A Major, K. 581 (Clarinet)
Serenade No. 10 in B-Flat Major for Thirteen Wind Instruments, K. 361
Sonata in B-Flat Major for Violin and Piano, K. 454
Trio in E-Flat Major for Clarinet, Viola, and Piano, K. 498

BEETHOVEN:

Quartets, Op. 59, "Rasumovsky"
Septet in E-Flat Major for Strings and Winds, Op. 20
Sonata No. 9 in A Major for Violin and Piano, Op. 47, "Kreutzer"
Trios Nos. 4 and 5, Op. 70 (Piano)
Trio No. 6 in B-Flat Major, Op. 97, "Archduke" (Piano)

Beethoven

11

Leonard Bernstein has written about Beethoven:[1]

Ever since I can recall, the first association that springs to anyone's mind when serious music is mentioned is "Beethoven." When I must give a concert to open a season, an all-Beethoven program is usually requested. When you walk into a concert hall bearing the names of the greats inscribed around it on a frieze, there he sits, front and center, the first, the largest, the most immediately visible, and usually gold-plated. When a festival of orchestral music is contemplated the bets are ten to one it will turn out to be a Beethoven festival. What is the latest chic among young neo-classic composers? Neo-Beethoven! What is the meat-and-potatoes of every piano recital? A Beethoven sonata. Or of every quartet program? Opus one hundred et cetera. What did we play in our symphony concerts when we wanted to honor the fallen

---

[1] From *The Joy of Music*. Copyright © 1954, 1955, 1956, 1957, 1958, 1959 by Leonard Bernstein. Reprinted by permission of Simon and Schuster, Inc.

in war? The *Eroica*. What did we play on V Day? The *Fifth*. What is every United Nations concert? The *Ninth*. What is every Ph. D. oral exam in music schools? Play all the themes you can from the nine symphonies of Beethoven!

Ludwig van Beethoven is such a giant in the musical world that in this book he alone has a chapter to himself. His attainments seem to require this; he was so great and distinctive a composer that he doesn't fit well into groupings with other composers. The man and his music merit special attention.

First, his life. Beethoven was born in 1770 into the family of a ne'er-do-well musician in Bonn, Germany. His father, a drunkard, observed the boy's talent and nourished dreams that he might have sired another prodigy, who like the young Mozart would bring in a good income from his performances. So young Ludwig was pushed into music study, especially piano, viola, and organ. He also sang in the Chapel choir at Bonn. Although talented, he never became the prodigy his father had hoped for. At the age of twenty-two, Beethoven set off for Vienna to make his fortune in the world of music. His finances were limited, and he kept a detailed account of his

"Liberty Leading the People," painted in 1830 by Eugene Delacroix.

expenditures. One entry of twenty-five *groschen* was for "coffee for Haidn and me."

Beethoven's entry about his contact with Joseph Haydn reveals his lack of formal, academic schooling, and comes from the period during which he studied composition with the old master. He also studied with several other teachers, making a name for himself as a pianist and winning friends and admirers among the aristocracy of Vienna. Within a decade he had established himself as a leading composer and performer—one whose services were in demand.

The musical training he received from Haydn and others was steeped in the Classical style of the times, which made a lasting impression on him. But there were other influences. One was the revolutionary spirit that was awakening in Europe. The spirit of independence was burning not only in Beethoven's music but in the works of other artists as well. Delacroix's painting "Liberty Leading the People" (page 240) is an example of revolutionary art. The American and French revolutions both occurred when Beethoven was still a young man, and so he was inevitably affected by these forces.

Then there was Beethoven's own personality. Were he alive today he would probably identify himself with humanitarian causes and social protest groups. He would insist on his rights as a person and on those of others. Two events give support to this view of the man. His *Symphony No. 3*, entitled *Eroica*, the "heroic symphony," was originally dedicated to Napoleon. When Beethoven heard that Napoleon had declared himself Emperor, the composer, disappointed to learn that his idol was just another ambitious soldier-politician, angrily tore up the dedication. In its place he wrote: "To the memory of a great man." Another example of Beethoven's belief concerns his Ninth Symphony. As early as 1792 he had thought of setting Schiller's *Ode to Joy* to music. The ethical ideals of the poem—the universal brotherhood of man and its basis in the love of a heavenly Father —had strong appeal to Beethoven. In short, his beliefs were more nineteenth than eighteenth century in character.

Beethoven is probably the first composer in history to be considered a "personality." His great and independent spirit fills his music. Haydn's music is sometimes difficult to distinguish from Mozart's, and Bach's from Telemann's. But Beethoven's mature works sound like no one else's music. And his personal life reflected this same desire for independence. He took orders from no one. He was successful enough at selling his music that he could remain free from worry about deadlines or patrons. He could afford to be a man unto himself.

In appearance he was described as "a short, stout man with a very red face, small piercing eyes, and bushy eyebrows, dressed in a long overcoat which reached nearly to his ankles. . . . Notwithstanding the high

Ludwig van Beethoven composing his Missa Solemnis. *An 1819 painting by Josef Stieler.*

color of his cheeks and his general untidiness, there was in those small piercing eyes an expression which no painter could render. It was a feeling of sublimity and melancholy combined."[2]

       Beethoven's personality was also affected by a hearing loss that eventually led to complete deafness. The condition was evident by the time he was twenty-eight, and became progressively worse. After the first performance of his monumental Ninth Symphony, Beethoven did not acknowledge the applause because he could not hear it. His attention was attracted by a tug on the sleeve, whereupon he turned and bowed to the cheering audience.

---

[2] From a description by Sir Julius Benedict (1823), quoted in Alexander Wheelock Thayer, *Life of Beethoven* (Princeton, N.J.: Princeton University Press, 1964), p. 873.

In 1802 he wrote a letter to his brothers, to be read after his death. In it he describes the anguish caused by his lack of hearing:

> I must live like an exile; if I approach near to people a hot terror seizes me, a fear that I may be subjected to the danger of letting my condition be observed. Thus it has been during the last half year which I spent in the country . . . what a humiliation when one stood beside me and heard a flute in the distance and *I heard nothing* . . . such incidents brought me to the verge of despair; but little more and I would have put an end to my life. Only art it was that withheld me, it seemed impossible to leave the world until I had produced all that I felt called upon to produce.[3]

His deafness caused him to lose contact with others and to withdraw into himself, becoming more irritable, morose, and suspicious of people. His final compositions were products of this period of his life. They tended to be more personal, meditative, and abstract. His output of new works during the last fifteen years of his life was not large.

You may logically wonder how it was possible for the deaf Beethoven to write entire symphonies. The process becomes understandable when you look within your own experience. You can recall melodies and the sounds of person's voices in your memory, even though physically you hear nothing. A trained person can "think out" a sizable amount of music in his mind. And Beethoven was obviously a well-trained musician with more than average abilities!

There is a second reason for his success despite his disability. It has to do with the way he composed. It was his custom to write down themes in a sketchbook. Then he would work over the themes, revising and rewriting them, making slight alterations and trying them out to determine their suitability for the piece he had in mind. This trial-and-error process might be resumed intermittently over a period of years. So the thematic material for many of his later compositions had been worked out when he was still able to hear fairly well. The sketchbooks have been preserved, and they are fascinating evidence of the metamorphosis of a musical idea.

Beethoven poured strenuous effort into each measure of his music, for he was not the "natural" that Mozart was. Beethoven is reported to have compared the writing of a particular work, his opera *Fidelio*, with the bearing of a child. And well it could be so compared. His manuscripts look "like a bloody record of a tremendous inner battle."[4]

---

[3] Thayer, pp. 304–305.

[4] Bernstein, *The Joy of Music*, p. 81.

*This page from Beethoven's manuscript of the Violin Concerto
shows the great struggle he went through to put his
musical ideas into notation.*

Musicologists have assigned three general periods to Beethoven's works. The early period extends to about 1802. In it are included his first three piano sonatas, the Opus 18 string quartets, and the First Symphony—works that resemble the music of the mature Haydn and Mozart. The second period, from approximately 1803 to 1814, was the most productive of his career. It includes seven symphonies (numbers 2 through 8), his only opera, *Fidelio*, the Opus 59 ("Rasumovsky") string quartets, a number of piano sonatas, and his last two piano concertos. The third period encompasses the years from 1815 until his death in 1827. This was a time of domestic troubles and deafness, during which he wrote the last five piano sonatas, the *Missa Solemnis*, the Ninth Symphony, and the last quartets. As you can see, his life and work bridge the transition from the Classical period to the Romantic period.

THE PIANO

In Mozart's time, only one generation before Beethoven, the piano was essentially a drawing-room instrument. Its tone was light and delicate, and composers wrote for the instrument accordingly. During Beethoven's lifetime, many improvements were made in the piano. Probably the most important was the addition of metal braces to the frame across which the strings were strung. (Later the frame was made of cast iron.) These braces permitted heavier strings, since the frame could now withstand the greater tension required to bring such strings up to pitch. In turn, the greater tension and heavier strings gave the piano more power. The combination of Beethoven's forceful music and a more powerful instrument inevitably enabled the piano to gain a prominent place in the concert hall.

The piano of today has changed only slightly since the beginning of the nineteenth century. The key action has been made a bit more responsive, and a pedal has been added to permit certain sustaining effects, but these improvements are not major ones.

As is also true of the organ, the type of piano construction affects the musical results. The grand piano is superior to the upright in structural design. In order to fit inside the case of an upright, the low strings have to be shortened and tuned with less tension. Hence the upright or spinet lacks the volume and consistency of tone found in the grand piano. The smaller the instrument, the more serious is the loss of tone quality. Concert music such as a Beethoven sonata is, understandably, shown off to best advantage when performed on a grand piano of high quality.

Beethoven's Piano Sonata, Op. 53 *("Waldstein")*

Beethoven's instrument was the piano. It was as a pianist that he became known, and his compositions for the instrument constitute some of his greatest contributions to music literature. In 1804 he wrote a solo piano sonata dedicated to Count von Waldstein, a friend and benefactor. This sonata reveals many elements of Beethoven's musical style, and his pianistic style in particular.

First Movement. The first movement is typically in sonata form. The first theme, however, is not typical of other composers' music. It begins with a soft thumping chord that is repeated thirteen times before a note is changed! And when the pattern does end, it leads into two short, motive-like figures (encircled in the example):

The same idea is repeated immediately, but this time the chords are "broken" so that pitches are sounded one after another instead of simultaneously. The theme is interesting in several respects. (1) It is not melodious in and of itself. Its musical value lies in its potential for development. (2) It does not contain notes of much length. Rather, it relies on the sounding of many tones to compensate for the piano's inability to maintain the intensity of tone that Beethoven probably wanted here. (3) It starts softly and works up to—or rather, erupts into—the short melodic figures. This sense of eruption is typical of Beethoven's music. (4) It is highly suitable for the piano but would fail as a vocal melody. The melodic styles for the various instruments and voices were rather well developed even by 1804.

The transition to the second theme illustrates another of Beethoven's techniques. Like Bach, he makes much use of broken chord patterns. Beethoven, however, likes to have the patterns and scales come toward or move away from each other. The simultaneous contrast of pitch direction is called *contrary motion:*

The second theme is in the remote key of E major. (It shares few pitches in common with the original key of C major; hence it is distant or remote.) As you may recall, the practice of Classical composers was to write the second theme in the key that is centered five notes above the original key center. Beethoven is more free-wheeling and moves to the key *three* notes higher. The traditional adherence to key schemes was breaking down even at this date. The theme itself is in complete contrast to the first. It is like a chorale or a quiet song; no throbbing repetition of chords here:

Like the first theme, it is promptly repeated, but with a difference. The second theme is maintained in the left-hand, bass-clef part, while in the right-hand, treble-clef part Beethoven introduces a countermelody in *triplets* (three equal notes to the beat).

As the music moves on, the triplets take over and become the main thought leading to the codetta. Again Beethoven presents the broken chords in contrary motion. The exposition closes with a brief codetta built around a theme of its own:

The development section opens as the exposition began, except for the key. Soon, however, the two motives from the first theme are repeated at different pitch levels and in different keys. As the development progresses, the triplet figure takes over. Most of the notes of the triplets are chord tones sounded in succession.

Beethoven was one of the first to exploit the extreme ranges of the piano. Both lines in the example are in bass clef, and the lower one moves quite low. Also, the chord in the third measure, top line of the example has rather close intervals (spacing of pitches), considering the low pitch level. Mozart seldom does this (partly because the piano in his time had fewer keys and a lighter tone quality), but Beethoven employs the device often. The closeness of low pitches in a chord creates a dark, heavy sound, which Beethoven uses to advantage.

The recapitulation starts just as the exposition did. A seven-measure passage is inserted between the theme and its repetition. The second theme is in A major, the remote key three notes lower than the original C major. Interestingly, the direction of the modulation is inverted; in the exposition, the new key was three notes higher, whereas now it is three notes lower. These modulations create more freshness in the music, although they tend to weaken the effectiveness of the home key by departing so radically from it.

The music moves on to the closing or codetta theme, much as it did in the exposition. But something happens. Instead of stopping after duly completing the closing theme, the first theme starts up again. Soon its two motives are treated to another development. This second development is much like the first, with the addition of rapidly moving scale passages. Actually, the music at this point takes on many of the qualities of a cadenza, although there are no rhythmically free runs until just before the second theme makes another appearance. Even the presence of the second theme is not unlike a cadenza, because in the improvised cadenzas of the Classical period the performer often elaborated on all the themes stated earlier in the movement. Here the first theme is sounded once more, and the movement is quickly brought to an end with a few loud chords.

What has Beethoven done to the coda? He has made of it a sort of second development section, equal in scope to the exposition, development, or recapitulation. No longer is it merely a short wrap-up section. The coda is expanded not only in this sonata but also in other of his works in sonata form. Of all composers, Beethoven seemed most fond of developing a theme. He openly acknowledged a keen interest in theme development, and this outlook is evident in the working out of melodic fragments in his sketchbooks. To accommodate his desire for development, he altered sonata form by increasing the importance of the coda and revising its purpose. Apparently he based this aesthetic judgment on the nature of the themes, the length of the movement, and the effect he wished to achieve. Since the "Waldstein" Sonata still maintains its place in the piano repertoire after a century and a half, Beethoven clearly made the correct decision for this work.

Second Movement. In the second movement Beethoven faced the problem of what to put between two movements of considerable power and size. An extended, involved movement would be too much. There is an unconfirmed story that Beethoven originally wrote a lengthy second movement but was persuaded by a friend to exchange it for a less pretentious one. The story is doubted by some scholars because it was unlike Beethoven to be swayed by the opinions of others. In any case, the second movement is called "Introduzione" to indicate its function as a quiet introductory section to the brilliant and lengthy third movement.

Third Movement. The third movement, a rondo, has a character that differs radically from the second movement. The main theme of the rondo suggests lightheartedness and ease:

The accompanying chords are broken to increase the feeling of fluency. At this point the music sounds quite Classical. The short phrases of the theme, for example, are paired off symmetrically. Before moving on to another section, Beethoven has the theme played three times: first as it is printed in the example; next in a soft, almost dreamy version; and finally in a full and brilliant setting.

The sections that contrast with the main rondo theme do not contain strong melodies of their own. Rather they explore the possibilities of pianistic technique. For instance, this example from the *B* section features simultaneously sounded octaves in the left hand and broken octaves in the right:

Such a passage would hardly be suitable for any instrument other than the piano.

The entire rondo theme is played again. The next section, *C*, is similar to the *B* portion except that it is in the minor mode. The music moves to a chordal section in which a part of the main theme is heard again. The music that follows has a flexible, ethereal quality about it. Most of it is built around two repeated notes or chords that are derived from the first two notes of the theme.

Again the rondo theme is played in a vigorous manner, twice. A technically difficult passage eventually softens to a point of pause, after which the music takes off on a dazzling and lengthy coda based on the rondo theme.

This movement demands some rather athletic piano playing. The music is pleasing, but at the same time it shows off the abilities of the performer. It contains the seeds of virtuoso piano music.

What characteristics of Beethoven's music can be discovered from a study of the "Waldstein" Sonata? Quite obviously it contains elements of Classicism. Traditional forms are followed, and even when these are altered or expanded, balance and proportion are maintained. But there is also evidence of the forthcoming Romanticism. Beethoven's music has dramatic contrasts of mood; its fiery spirit is often set against tender melodies. (For some reason, he is remembered for the volcanic, eruptive, demonic quality of the music, while the calmer beauty is sometimes forgotten.) He exploited the technique of the piano to its fullest, incorporating the range and dynamic contrast of the instrument to create effects hitherto unknown in music.

Beethoven's Symphony No. 7

The attitude toward the symphony changed between the Classical period and the early Romanticism of Beethoven's time. The change is reflected in the symphonic output of orchestral composers. Haydn completed one hundred and four symphonies. Mozart in his short lifetime wrote fifty-two (although the last is numbered 41). Beethoven wrote only nine. The decreasing number of new symphonies indicated neither a decline in their popularity nor a lack of interest on the part of composer or audience. On the contrary, it meant that the symphony had become a more serious and lengthy work, making stringent demands on the composer's time and abilities. In scope, the Classical symphony might be compared to a short story, the Beethoven symphony to a novel. Only in the last twenty-five years has a composer of repute—Shostakovich—composed more than nine symphonies.

First Movement. As might be expected, Beethoven's *Symphony No. 7* is much longer than the Mozart symphony studied in Chapter 9. It has about it a more pretentious air. It begins not with a wistful melody, as Mozart's did, but with heavy chords interspersed among quiet passages in the winds. This opening is followed by long scale lines that remind one of giant staircases. At last there is a gentle melody played by the woodwinds:

Despite the fact that several musical ideas have been introduced, the exposition has not yet begun. All of the material heard thus far is a part of the introduction, a section consuming the first three and a half minutes of the movement.

The first theme of the exposition is almost dance-like, probably to contrast with the heavy introduction:

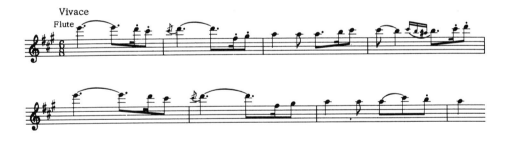

The second theme is similar in character:

Beethoven frequently writes a melodic fragment to be passed around among the instruments.

In the example, the three-note figure is sounded repeatedly in the cellos and basses, while entrances are made sequentially by the oboe, clarinet, bassoon, oboe again, and the flute.

Another passage illustrates Beethoven's handling of repeated notes and contrast. The entire orchestra plays *fortissimo*—very loudly. Suddenly the number of instruments is cut in half and the remaining performers are directed to play *pianissimo*—very softly.

At the end of the codetta and the beginning of the development, another of Beethoven's musical characteristics can be seen: a sense of humor and playfulness. The image of Beethoven that has been handed down through generations is of the indomitable, stern, and angry individualist. But Beethoven had another side. In his personal life he was something of a practical joker, especially before deafness closed in on him. And the lighter side of his nature is evident in his music. Early in this movement,

when the first theme is repeated in the exposition, the music is not only joyful, it is rollicking. Near the end of the exposition, the strings play a quick note just prior to the longer note, and the progression of chords that ends the codetta leaves the listener "up in the air," so to speak. After two measures of silence, the chords with the playful note are heard again, marking the start of the development section.

The development stresses the same rhythm () found in the exposition, this time played in long scales that are reminiscent of the introduction. Throughout this portion of the movement you can hear repeated chords and the tossing around of musical ideas between instruments.

After the recapitulation, a long coda is encountered, much as was found in the "Waldstein" Sonata. For the first time in the main portion of the movement, Beethoven drops the almost continuous use of the characteristic rhythmic figure mentioned above. It is interesting to observe what he inserts in its place. Remember the device called "pedal point" (described in Chapter 10)? Beethoven here chooses a variant of that idea.

Violoncello

Instead of only one note held through a number of measures, a short melodic figure or ostinato is substituted. In this example the ostinato appears ten times. The more conventional pedal-point idea is found in the repeated notes of the woodwinds.

Second Movement. The second movements of Mozart's *Symphony No. 40* and Beethoven's *Symphony No. 7* are similar in this respect: both are extremely beautiful and melodious movements that begin with unpromising, almost monotonous themes. The Beethoven slow movement is built around a persistent pattern:

The top notes in the melody change little in pitch; the harmony underneath provides most of the interest. Soon other ideas are injected into the music. A melody in the viola and cello, which seems like mere accompaniment, eventually becomes a countermelody to the original theme:

Allegretto

Viola, Violoncello

The two ideas are played together several times in different sections of the orchestra. The music grows slowly in intensity until it reaches a climactic point, and then it begins to soften and fade away.

Beethoven was a master at planning long portions of music. He leads the listener to the climax of the music in a most gradual and enticing way. He gives the listener the unmistakable feeling that the music is building up to something. This is certainly one of the reasons for the success of this movement, which, by the way, was wildly applauded at its first two performances—so much so that it had to be repeated before the next movement was played.

After the first long section, the mood changes and the key moves from minor to major. The clarinet and bassoon play a quiet theme over a rippling triplet accompaniment in the violins:

This section again anticipates the Romantic style that was evolving and that was to predominate for the rest of the century. The four measures contain essentially the same figure presented twice. However, in its second appearance Beethoven has changed and added one note to give it more "passion," more intensity—a Romantic characteristic.

Soon the triplets change back to minor and their gentle quality is transformed into a brusque, vigorous sound leading back to the theme. This time the accompaniment is busier than it was earlier in the movement. The strings bandy a figure back and forth:

As the music progresses, the sixteenths lead into a fugue-like portion whose "subject" is derived from the main theme. Like a regular fugue, the section ends with a solid playing of the main theme.

The *B* section of the movement returns, and a coda, again derived from the main theme, closes the movement.

Third Movement. During the Classical period, the third movement of a symphony was expected to be a minuet. But Beethoven was to

change that. He retained the meter and form of the minuet but radically
increased its tempo. Whereas the minuet had been more stately and relaxed, with a moderate tempo of *"one* two three" in each measure, the new
speeded-up version was more fun-filled. It moved at a zestful pace, which
enabled four consecutive measures, for example, to be counted *"one, one,
one, one."* This new type of third movement Beethoven called a *scherzo*
(*scare*-tzoh). The word in Italian means "joke." Beethoven did not label the
third movement in this particular symphony a "scherzo," but it does contain
all the attributes of his scherzos.

The *a* theme of the *A* section is:

Remember as you look at the music that it moves along at the speed of one
quick beat to the measure.

Notice that most of the notes in the scherzo have a dot over or
under them. This marking tells the performer to play the notes in a short,
bouncing style. In this section Beethoven again surprises the listener with
occasional pairs of loud, abrupt chords.

The *B* portion of the three-part *A B A* movement (the section that
was formerly the trio in the traditional minuet) is slowed down and
changed considerably here, to suggest a more calm atmosphere:

The theme is played against a pedal tone held by the violins. Later each
phrase of the theme is answered by the flute in conversational style. As in
Mozart's trio in the G Minor Symphony, the French horns have an important part. This portion of the Beethoven movement stresses rapid dynamic
changes, so that a fast crescendo is followed by a fast decrescendo. As was
true of the trio in the Classical minuet, there is a contrasting melody in this
B portion of the movement. Beethoven lengthens the movement by returning to the slower *B* section before the movement closes.

Fourth Movement. Beethoven's plan for the entire symphony is now three-fourths revealed. The first movement with its heavy introduction leads into happy, dance-like music. The second movement, except for its lyric middle part, is somber. The third movement is a bounding scherzo. Traditionally the role of the fourth movement was to provide a flashy, rapid conclusion to the symphony. Beethoven writes a quick-moving and suitable ending, but there is a surprising element—the boisterousness of the music. All the roughness and fun-loving aspects of his personality seem to burst forth.

The movement begins with two attention-demanding sets of chords. Then the first theme is introduced. The theme itself is not particularly attractive:

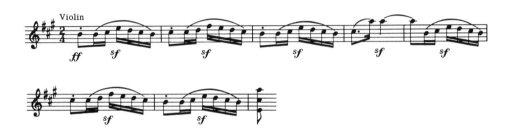

It is played against more chords in the orchestra. The chords, like the first ones, are built on E. But the music is not in the key of E; it is in A, and E is the dominant of A. So Beethoven delays resolution to the tonic chord until twelve measures after the movement begins. It is like a trick played on the listener; for many measures one is fooled about what the key is. To add to the rollicking nature of the music, the chords are written to emphasize the second beat of each measure instead of the expected first beat. The mark *sf*, an abbreviation for *sforzando,* means that the note is to be played with force or a "punch," and it is often seen in Beethoven's music. It is one way in which he indicates his wish to pound out or wring everything he can from the music. The repeated notes and accents give his music a sense of drive that is unmistakable.

The second theme is different. It is coquettish and playful, in contrast to the rough sounds and pounding chords of preceding passages:

Even so, the mood lasts only a few measures before a loud clap of sound is heard. As the music progresses, Beethoven treats the second theme as an object to be passed playfully among the instruments.

Early in the development section, the violins and low strings answer one another in a phrase that sounds almost like an exchange of laughter. After some working over of the first theme, the rhythmic idea of heavy chords on the second beat takes over. Usually it is combined with the quick rapping of chords that began the movement. The motive appears more than thirty-five times as it works its way through changes of harmony. Finally the rapping motive that began the movement becomes a link leading to the recapitulation.

The coda is one of Beethoven's longest. It continues to exploit the motive from the main theme. By passing it from one string section to another and devising a steady bass line that inches its way ever lower, he enables the music to build to a tremendous climax. The progress toward the point of passion begins slowly and builds for about sixty-seven measures, or one minute, until it reaches an animal-like outburst. After a short period of relative quiet, the music explodes once more before the movement ends.

And so Beethoven completed another composition that in its inimitable style is distinctively his. In it can be found the many qualities that mark his music as great: the persistent repeated notes, the unexpected changes of mood and startling chords, the abundant use of motives, the magnificent scope of the movements, the scherzo, the tossing of a musical idea from one section to another, the coda that becomes a second development section, and the sense of drive and vigor.

Beethoven's Egmont Overture, Op. 84

In 1810 Beethoven was commissioned to write an overture and incidental music for a performance of the tragic play *Egmont,* by the German poet and dramatist Goethe (*Geh*-tuh). In Beethoven's day, music was often performed incidentally in conjunction with a stage play, as well as before the opening curtain and between acts. Beethoven, von Weber, Mendelssohn, and other composers received many commissions to write in this manner for the theater. Thus there exists a sizable body of music written for use with dramas. Generally only the overtures are still heard today.

The term "overture" was discussed in Chapter 8, at which time it referred to the introductory movement in a Baroque suite. The overture in those days often had a slow beginning section, which was followed by music of a fugal nature. In many respects, Beethoven's overture resembles Bach's. It too has a slow introduction followed by a rapidly moving section, although Beethoven's music is less contrapuntal.

In Goethe's drama, Egmont is a nobleman and heroic leader of the Netherlanders. In his fight against Spanish tyranny he is killed, victim of the oppressor's brutality. But the triumph of liberty appears in a vision to him before he dies. A human and romantic touch is given the drama by Egmont's love for Klärchen, a lovely girl who adores him.

Beethoven may have tried in *Egmont Overture* to associate the music directly with the events contained in the drama *Egmont;* no one knows for certain. Whatever his intent, the overture now stands on its own musical merit, because the play is seldom performed and is not generally known today.

Egmont Overture begins in a slow tempo. In typical Beethoven style, it starts with a loud, commanding sound. After somber chords, the oboe and woodwinds enter with a tender melodic line:

After about two and a half minutes, the tempo becomes more brisk. The theme at this point is typical of Beethoven:

It is built on chordal patterns. Furthermore, it is definitely instrumental in that it wends its way down two octaves—a wider range than is normally practicable in vocal music. The accompaniment for the theme is also characteristic of Beethoven: a row of repeated notes.

After a transition that grows out of the repeated notes, followed by some repetition of the theme itself in the violins, a second theme enters. It is constructed of material found in the slow introduction but this time played at a much faster speed:

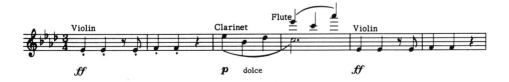

The last example amply illustrates the contrast of volume and mood for which Beethoven is so well known. In fact, the music takes on the air of a conversation. The rough sounds of the strings are answered by the lighter tones of the woodwinds. A rather abrupt modulation into a foreign key adds further musical interest.

After some solidly convincing chords, the music proceeds to a short development section. The first five notes of the first theme provide a pattern that is played by the various woodwinds in turn. The lyric quality of the music is suddenly broken at eight-measure intervals by two brusque chords—a Beethoven characteristic that is becoming familiar to you now.

The music then moves to a recapitulation. The contrasting second theme is repeated in the coda. This time the answering violins sound as though they are pleading, possibly a reference to events in the play to follow. Up to this point, the *Egmont Overture* has been not too complex a work. The development portion, for example, is not as extensive as was encountered in movements of the "Waldstein" Sonata or the *Symphony No. 7*. The present overture is typically in sonata form: introduction, the statement of two contrasting themes, a development, a recapitulation, and a coda built on the foregoing themes.

But to this structure Beethoven adds a second coda, one that is not related thematically to the remainder of the overture. Here again you can hear another favorite technique of Beethoven: the long buildup to a climactic point. The music begins ever so softly, almost like the rumble of a distantly approaching thunderstorm. Many familiar Beethoven devices are unloosed: the *sforzandi,* the timpani roll, the twisting line in the lower strings. The effect of this coda might be compared to the gradual appearance of a bright vision. Perhaps it is intended to relate to Egmont's vision of the triumph of liberty. But no one can be sure what Beethoven had in mind, since he did not indicate such associations in the musical score.

During his career, Beethoven wrote many overtures, seven of which merit attention yet today and maintain a perennial place in the standard orchestral repertoire. In addition to *Egmont*, they are *Prometheus, Coriolan, Leonore No. 1, Leonore No. 2, Leonore No. 3* (Beethoven's three unsuccessful attempts to find an overture that would not overwhelm his opera *Fidelio*), and *Fidelio* (the overture he finally arrived at for his only opera). Although Beethoven had a flair for the dramatic, he seemed more at ease when writing *apart* from theatrical forms. His abstract works (especially those in the large forms of symphonies, concertos, and sonatas) contain all the dramatic elements of suspense, buildup, and surprise. But he achieves these elements in sheerly musical terms, without recourse to the trappings of the stage.

If a man of Beethoven's complexity can be summarized at all, it might be said that he lived at a favorable time in history. He inherited the objective, organized style of the Classical period, but the emerging revolutionary spirit of the times and his own personality provided him with strong Romantic inclinations. Thus Beethoven stands in the musical world with one foot firmly planted in Classicism and the other in Romanticism. This position gives his music a nearly ideal temperamental balance.

SUGGESTIONS FOR FURTHER LISTENING—BEETHOVEN

Concerto No. 3 in C Minor for Piano and Orchestra, Op. 37
Concerto No. 5 in E-Flat Major for Piano and Orchestra, Op. 73
Concerto in D Major for Violin and Orchestra, Op. 61
Overtures
Sonata No 14 in C-Sharp Minor for Piano, Op. 27, No. 2, "Moonlight"
Sonata No. 23 in F Minor for Piano, Op. 57, "Appassionata"
Sonata No. 9´ in A Major for Violin and Piano, Op. 47, "Kreutzer"
String Quartet No. 1 in F Major, Op. 18
String Quartet No. 9 in C Major, Op. 59, No. 3, "Rasumovsky"
String Quartet No. 15 in A Minor, Op. 132
Symphonies Nos. 2–9
Trio No. 6 in B-Flat Major for Violin, Cello, and Piano, Op. 97, "Archduke"

Early Romanticism

12

To most people, the word "romantic" pertains to the emotion of love. To the scholar, however, romanticism means much more. The word "romantic" comes from "romance," which originally referred to a medieval poem written in one of the Romance languages and dealing with a heroic person or event. Later the word took on the connotation of something far away and strange or something imaginative and full of wonder. Yes, it even included the idea of love—romantic love.

In Beethoven one can see substantial evidence of romanticism, especially in his works written after 1800. And so it was that Romanticism as a musical style started to appear at the beginning of the nineteenth century. By about 1820 or 1825, it had become the predominant style, and it remained so until at least the beginning of the twentieth century.

CHARACTERISTICS OF ROMANTICISM

The Romanticist was fascinated by the unknown and stood in awe of the world. He was impressed by the mystery, not the clarity, of the world and its inhabitants. At times, he was almost mystic. Such a quality is revealed in this passage from Wordsworth's *Lines Composed a Few Miles above Tintern Abbey:*

> . . . that blessed mood,
> In which the burthen of the mystery,
> In which the heavy and the weary weight
> Of all this unintelligible world
> Is lightened:—that serene and blessed mood,
> In which the affections gently lead us on,—
> Until, the breath of this corporeal frame
> And even the motion of our human blood
> Almost suspended, we are laid asleep
> In body, and become a living soul:
> While with an eye made quiet by the power
> Of harmony, and the deep power of joy,
> We see into the life of things.

The Romanticist tended to rely on emotion and imagination rather than on the rational intellect that had been central to the Classical outlook. Feelings replaced reason. Truth became what one *felt* to be true; thus it was wrong to deny one's feelings. Keats said in one of his letters: "I am certain of nothing but the holiness of the heart's affections, and the truth of the imagination. What the imagination seizes as beauty must be truth." Inevitably, Romanticism became distrustful of reason and science. To quote Keats again, this time from *Lamia:*

> Do not all charms fly
> At the mere touch of cold philosophy?[1]

The Romanticist was fascinated by the long ago and far away. During the Classical period, intellectuals had thought of medieval times as the "dark ages"; the Romanticist thought of them as heroic. Literature abounds with examples of this attitude, as in Tennyson's *Idylls of the King,* Keats' *Eve of St. Agnes,* Coleridge's *Christabel,* Scott's *Ivanhoe,* and many more. Eugene Delacroix chose Dante's *Inferno,* a writing from early in the fourteenth century, as the subject matter for his painting "The Bark of Dante" (plate 7). It shows the struggling souls of the wicked Florentines trying to escape from Hell by climbing into the boat with Virgil and Dante. Also evident in the painting is the Romantic artist's fondness for the far away and exotic. In music this trait can be found in works such as Rimsky-Korsakov's tone poem *Scheherazade* and Act II of the opera *Parsifal* by Richard Wagner (*Ree*-kard *Vahg*-ner).

---

[1] That is, science.

7

Delacroix: The Bark of Dante. *(Louvre, Paris. Courtesy of Art Reference Bureau, Inc.)*

8

Corot: *Villa D'Avray*. (Gift of Count Cecil Pecci-Blunt, National Gallery of Art, Washington, D.C.)

"Planting Potatoes" by Jean Francois Millet exemplifies one romantic painter's admiration for the common people and rural life.

Not only was the Romantic man impressed by the unknown forces of the world; he reveled in the struggle against them. Coleridge's ancient mariner was "alone on a wide, wide sea." Delacroix's Florentines struggle helplessly against their fate.

The differences between Delacroix's painting and David's "Oath of the Horatii" (plate 6) are worth noting. In the Romantic painting, the sea and clouds swirl in an awesome way. The twisted, pained bodies are very much involved in the scene. Gone is the formal balance of Classicism. Dante (in the green cloak and red hat) stands about two-thirds of the way to the left of the picture. Gone, too, are the even planes. The bodies of the sinners writhe throughout the scene.

The Romanticist resented rules and restraints. He regarded the Classical period as cold and formal, and was unimpressed by its rational deductions and universal laws. He felt perfectly capable of making his own rules, and he proceeded to do so in his artistic works. He cherished freedom, limitless expression and passion, and the pursuit of the unattainable. After all, what more glorious struggle could there be than the yearning and seeking after the impossible? This search is perhaps best epitomized in the legend of the Holy Grail, which was a favored theme in Romantic literature and operas (particularly Wagner's *Parsifal*).

The Romanticist was also attracted by nature. He had a rural orientation instead of the urban outlook of the Classical period. In Mozart's day the cities—London, Paris, Vienna—were the centers of artistic activity, and hence they attracted the person of creative and artistic bent. To the Romanticist, however, nature had more appeal because it represented a world untainted by man. Sometimes nature was extolled to the point of pantheism—the belief that God and nature are one. The rural interest of the time led to landscape painting, poems on natural phenomena, and works like Beethoven's *Symphony No. 6* ("Pastoral" Symphony). The latter work is intended to convey the moods evoked on Beethoven's visits to the Vienna countryside. Beginning with Jean Jacques Rousseau and the Earl of Shaftesbury, and continuing through the American David Thoreau to the present time, a group of philosophers have expounded the idea of natural goodness, whereby the "artificialities" of civilization are rejected because they corrupt man. Wordsworth summed up the Romanticists' thinking on nature when he wrote, in *The Tables Turned:*

> One impulse from a vernal wood
> May teach you more of man,
> Of moral evil and of good,
> Than all the sages can.

The Romantic painters' fondness for and sensitivity to nature is demonstrated in Jean Baptiste Camille Corot's "Ville d'Avray" (plate 8). Corot lived almost entirely in the nineteenth century, and in this work he painted the beauties and pleasures of picking flowers. No struggle against the forces of the world is evident here.

Because the Romanticist was highly subjective and individualistic, it was almost inevitable that he would become egocentric. Works of art were no longer objective examples of a person's craftsmanship; they were considered instead to be a projection of the creator himself. The Romantic artist felt that a bit of his psyche had been given to the world in his poem or prelude. And this personal work was no longer done for a patron. It was now for posterity, for an audience that someday, somewhere would appreciate its true stature. Some Romanticists were nonsocial, if not anti-social. They withdrew into a world of their own, surrounded by a close circle of friends and admirers. And yet the Romantic era saw the establishment of the concert hall with its large audiences, and some Romanticists thoroughly enjoyed the adulation of the public. In any case, the attitude toward musical creativity changed, and with it came the altered position of the musician and composer in society.

These observations provide a brief introduction to the wonderful and turbulent time called the Romantic period. Several less general charac-

Franz Schubert at age sixteen.
A chalk drawing by his friend
Leopold Kupelwieser.

teristics will be pointed out as they occur in the ensuing discussion of Romantic music.

FRANZ SCHUBERT

Franz Schubert (1797–1828) is generally considered the composer who marks the beginning of the Romantic era. And there is much about his life to mark him as the prototype of the Romantic artist. Born into the family of a schoolteacher in a Vienna suburb, young Schubert's creative talent was evident while he was still a boy. Upon completing school, he tried to follow in his father's footsteps, but he could not accept the routine involved in teaching. He preferred to spend his time composing songs.

Schubert never did adjust well to adult life. He never held a real position of employment; indeed, he made only halfhearted attempts to find one. He had a small circle of friends who appreciated his talents. They housed and fed him when he was in need, which was his normal condition. Unlike Beethoven, Schubert was incompetent in dealing with publishers, who made good profits on his music. He sold some pieces, later worth thousands of dollars, to pay for a meal.

As the years passed, he became lonelier and more discouraged. He was even unlucky in love. His output of compositions never dwindled, however. Finally he contracted typhus and died at the age of thirty-one, leaving the world his clothing, his bedding, some manuscripts valued at ten florins—and a vast store of beautiful music.

Schubert was a versatile composer. He wrote piano works, chamber music, and symphonies. Popular legend has falsely assumed that the familiar *Symphony No. 8* ("Unfinished") was left incomplete because of his death or because of his despair over a lost love. The real reason is less dramatic. The work was probably left unfinished because Schubert never got around to completing it. It is even conceivable that he had said all he intended to say in that particular work. In any event, the symphony was *not* curtailed by his premature death. He went on to compose and complete the C Major Symphony (the "Great"), which was widely esteemed by composers such as Schumann, who exclaimed over its "heavenly length."

In his instrumental works, Schubert tended to be less Romantic than in his vocal works. His vocal music, which included seven Masses and about fifteen operas, was thoroughly Romantic. His six hundred songs did much to assure his posthumous success and immortality.

THE SONG

The songs Schubert wrote are of a special type called *art songs* or *lieder* (*lee*der). *Lied* is the German word for "song"; *lieder* is its plural. Essentially the art song or *lied* was a musical setting of a poem. The order is important here. The composer first selected a suitable poem and then composed music that would best project the mood and thought of the verse. The idea of preserving and amplifying the message of the words is basic to the art song.

Because the setting of the words was so important, the composer was not primarily concerned with a lovely melody. He wanted a good melody, of course; but more than that, he wanted the melody to be expressive of the words. The interest in expression also suggested that the accompanying piano part should be descriptive enough to support the singer's efforts. For instance, in the song *"Die Forelle"* ("The Trout"), the piano gives the impression of a babbling brook. At times the piano is deemed important enough to be given solo passages of its own.

The singer of such music is expected first and foremost to project the idea of the song. He may be called on to sing different roles, as in *"Der Erlkönig"* ("The Erl King") of Schubert. Any mood can prevail in the *lied:* anger, sadness, anxiety, boisterousness, contentment, pity. The demands on the singer who performs art songs are somewhat different from those imposed on the opera singer. In fact, singers tend to specialize in one type or the other. The art song is usually less demanding in a technical sense; the range is narrower and there are few virtuoso passages. But the singer must be versatile in vocal technique and able to project within a brief time span the essence of a character or situation. Because art songs are usually sung in small recital halls, the performer must establish rapport with the audience.

In matters of facial expression and gestures, as well as interpretation, he must seek an ideal balance of good taste and expressiveness. The art song might well be compared to its instrumental counterpart, the chamber ensemble: both are intended to produce a sense of intimacy, refinement, and listener involvement.

Involvement is more complete if the listener understands the words. But many fine art songs have a foreign text, and this fact hinders their popularity. For reasons pointed out in the discussion of Handel in Chapter 7, the placement of words in the music is a delicate and crucial matter. When a word is translated, the syllable pattern is almost certain to be changed, either in accent or in number of syllables, and this necessitates an alteration of the original rhythmic notation. There is also a universal problem in translation: many words have shades of meaning that cannot be accurately translated. Not surprisingly, then, most art songs are sung in their original language.

Added to the translation problem is the fact that many poems that Schubert and others set to music are not of high literary quality. Some of them are overly sentimental, almost maudlin. Some of those about love seem a trifle silly and unrealistic to contemporary Americans who have grown up with unflowery popular love songs. Also, part of the difficulty for the modern-day listener is the imagery of which Romantic poets were fond. The Erl King, for example, is a poetic image of the call of death—an image not so well known to present listeners as it was to Schubert's audiences.

Despite the obstacle of translation and the quaintness and obscure imagery of some of the texts, art-song literature is filled with fine music that is well worth knowing. The study of three of Schubert's *lieder* will show the musical possibilities available to the art-song composer and will reveal Schubert's skill in writing for the solo voice and piano combination.

Schubert's "Die Forelle" (*"The Trout"*)

This song typifies the Romanticist's interest in nature. But it is a rather unrealistic type of admiration. (Any trout fisherman knows that stirring up the water will either frighten the fish away or make it more difficult for them to see the fly.) At any rate, the sympathies of the poet are entirely with the living trout; the observer is not thinking about how good a trout tastes when properly cooked. The text is:

In einem Bächlein helle,	Within a sparkling streamlet
Da schoss in froher Eil'	that sang its merry song,
Die launische Forelle	I marked a silver trout
Vorüber wie ein Pfeil.	Like an arrow, speed along.
Ich stand an dem Gestade	Beside the brook I lingered
Und sah in süsser Ruh	And watched the playful trout

Des muntern Fischleins Bade	That all among the shadows
Im klaren Bächlein zu!	Was darting in and out.
(last two lines repeated)	

Ein Fischer mit der Ruthe	With rod and line there waited
Wohl an dem Ufer stand,	An angler by the brook,
Und sah's mit kaltem Blute,	All eager, he, to capture
Wie sich das Fischlein wand.	The fish upon his hook.
So lang' dem Wasser Helle,	While clear the water's flowing,
So dacht' ich, nicht gebricht,	So thought I to myself,
So fängt er die Forelle	His labor will be fruitless:
Mit seiner Angel nicht.	I'm sure the trout is safe.
(last two lines repeated)	

Doch endlich ward dem Diebe	The angler loses patience,
Die Zeit zu lang.	He stirs the stream,
Er macht das Bächlein tückisch trübe,	And makes the limpid, shining water
Und eh' ich es gedacht	All dull and muddy seem:
So zuckte seine Ruthe	"I have him," quoth the stranger
Das Fischlein zappelt d'ran,	As swift his line he cast:
Und ich mit regem Blute	And heeding not the danger,
Sah die Betrog'ne an.	The trout was caught at last.
(last line repeated)	

The piano accompaniment attempts to picture in sound some aspects of the scene—the flowing brook, the leaping fish, and the muddying of the water. The song is enjoyable but not profound.

The stanzas of the poem are sung to basically the same music. Most songs we know today are strophic: hymns, popular songs, and many familiar pieces such as "America."

Schubert later took the melody of this song and used it as the theme for a set of variations in his Piano Quintet, Opus 114, which is logically called the "Trout" Quintet:

Schubert's "Gretchen am Spinnrade" (*"Margaret at the Spinning Wheel"*)

This song is completely Romantic in content and style. As Margaret spins at her wheel, she sings of her lost love:

Mei - ne Ruh_____ ist hin,_____ mein Herz_____ ist schwer; ich
All my rest_____ is gone,_____ my heart_____ is sore; I'll

fin - de, ich fin - de sie nim - mer und nim - mer - mehr.
find it, no more_____ find it nev - er and nev - er more.

Meine Ruh' ist hin,	All my rest is gone,
Mein Herz ist schwer;	My heart is sore,
Ich finde, ich finde sie	I'll find it no more,
Nimmer und nimmermehr.	Find it never and nevermore.
Wo ich ihn nicht hab',	If he is not near,
Ist mir das Grab,	My grave is here,
Die ganze Welt ist mir vergällt.	The world is stress and bitterness.
Mein armer Kopf ist mir verrückt,	My poor, weak head is tempest-tossed,
Mein armer Sinn ist mir zerstückt.	My poor weak senses seem quite lost.
Meine Ruh' ist hin,	All my rest is gone,
Mein Herz ist schwer;	My heart is sore,
Ich finde, ich finde sie	I'll find it no more,
Nimmer und nimmermehr.	Find it never and nevermore.
Nach ihm nur schau' ich	'Tis he alone
Zum Fenster hinaus,	From the window I seek,
Nach ihm nur geh' ich	'Tis he I leave the house
Aus dem Haus.	To meet.
Sein hoher Gang, sein' edle Gestalt,	His noble form, his bearing so high,
Seines Mundes Lächeln,	And his mouth so smiling
Seiner Augen Gewalt,	And his powerful eye,
Und seiner Rede Zauberfluss,	His magic words which bring such bliss,
Sein Händedruck, und ach, sein Kuss!	His hand, his clasp, and O! his kiss!
Meine Ruh' ist hin,	All my rest is gone,
Mein Herz ist schwer;	My heart is sore,
Ich finde, ich finde sie	I'll find it no more,
Nimmer und nimmermehr.	Find it never and nevermore.
Mein Busen drängt sich nach ihm hin.	My bosom strains to meet his clasp,
Ach, dürft ich fassen und halten ihn!	O! might I seize him with eager grasp!

Und küssen ihn so wie ich wollt',	And kissing him as I would kiss,
An seinen Küssen vergehen sollt',	In his embraces I'd die with bliss!
O könnt ich ihn küssen,	Ah! could I but kiss him
So wie ich wollt',	As I would kiss,
An seinen Küssen vergehen sollt'!	In his embraces I'd die with bliss!
(last line repeated)	
Meine Ruh' ist hin,	All my rest is gone,
Mein Herz ist schwer!	My heart is sore!

The text is from Goethe's *Faust,* that favorite tale of so many Romanticists. It emphasizes the pain of love, an aspect that especially attracted Romantic writers. To bolster the words of Goethe's poem, Schubert has the piano supply the motion of the spinning wheel with continuous moving notes, and he chooses a minor key to impart the necessary tinge of sadness. The music for "All my rest is gone . . ." is repeated each time the words occur in the poem. The vocal line on the word *Ruh* (rest) has a sighing sound that adds to the pained character of the music. The song builds to a point of excitement beginning with the words *"Mein Busen drängt."* The contour of the line moves up by half steps until it reaches a high point on the word *"küssen,"* thereby emphasizing the idea of excitement and eagerness. Again, Schubert has worked out the music to amplify the thought of the text.

Schubert's "Der Erlkönig" ("The Erl King")

Schubert wrote this song when he was only eighteen. Again he chose a text from Goethe. The prevailing mood of the work is one of fear and suspense, engendered by the mythical king of elves. According to the legend, whoever is touched by him must die. The singer is required to be narrator, father, child, and Erl King—quite an assignment.

Wer reitet so spät durch Nacht und Wind?	Who rides so late through night and wind?
Es ist der Vater mit seinem Kind;	It is the father with his child.
Er hat den Knaben wohl in dem Arm,	He holds the boy within his arm,
Er fasst ihn sicher, er hält ihn warm.	He clasps him tight, he keeps him warm.
"Mein Sohn, was birgst du so bang dein Gesicht?"	"My son, why hide your face in fear?"
"Siehst, Vater, du den Erlkönig nicht?	"See, father, the Erl King's near.

Den Erlenkönig mit Kron' und
Schweif?"
"Mein Sohn, es ist ein Nebel-
streif."

"Du liebes Kind, komm, geh' mit
mir!
Gar schöne Spiele spiel' ich mit
dir;
Manch' bunte Blumen sind an
dem Strand,
Meine Mutter hat manch' gül-
den Gewand."

"Mein Vater, mein Vater, und
hörest du nicht,
Was Erlenkönig mir leise
verspricht?"

"Sei ruhig, bleibe ruhig, mein
Kind;
In dürren Blättern säuselt der
Wind."
"Willst, feiner Knabe, du mit
mir geh'n?
Meine Töchter sollen dich
warten schön;
Meine Töchter führen den
nächtlichen Reih'n
Und wiegen und tanzen und
singen dich ein."
"Mein Vater, mein Vater, und
siehst du nicht dort

Erlkönigs Töchter am düstern
Ort?"
"Mein Sohn, mein Sohn, ich seh'
es genau,
Es scheinen die alten Weiden so
grau."

"Ich liebe dich, mich reizt deine
schöne Gestalt,
Und bist du nicht willig, so
brauch' ich Gewalt."

"Mein Vater, mein Vater, jetzt
fasst er mich an!
Erlkönig hat mir ein Leid's
gethan!"

The Erl King with crown and
wand."
"Dear son, 'tis but a misty
cloud."

"Ah, sweet child, come with me!

Such pleasant games I'll play
with thee!
Such pleasant flowers bloom in
the field,
My mother has many a robe of
gold."

"Oh father, father, do you not
hear
What the Erl King whispers in
my ear?"

"Be still, my child, be calm;

'Tis but the withered leaves in
the wind."
"My lovely boy, wilt go with
me?
My daughters fair shall wait on
thee,
My daughters nightly revels
keep,
They'll sing and dance and rock
thee to sleep."
"Oh father, father, see you not

The Erl King's daughters in yon
dark spot?"
"My son, my son, the thing you
see
Is only the old gray willow
tree."

"I love thee, thy form enflames
my sense;
And art thou not willing, I'll
take thee hence!"

"Oh father, father, he grasps my
arm,
The Erl King has done me
harm!"

Dem Vater grauset's, er reitet geschwind,	The father shudders, he speeds ahead,
Er hält in Armen das ächzende Kind,	He clasps to his bosom the sobbing child,
Erreicht den Hof mit Müh' und Noth:	He reaches home with pain and dread:
In seinen Armen das Kind war tot!	In his arms the child lay dead!

The music, unlike that in the two preceding examples, does not repeat itself. New lines of melody follow one another until the song ends. The term for this type of song is *through-composed*. The accompaniment adds to the mood with an agitated triplet figure and a foreboding bass pattern:

Dissonance is heard as the child expresses fear, whereas the father's music has a reassuring quality about it. Notice how effectively Schubert ends the song. The piano stops and the singer declaims, "In his arms the child"—a pause to allow anticipation to build up—"lay dead."

These three songs of Schubert typify the art song of the Romantic period. Their texts are uneven in quality and a trifle dated. But they have melodic appeal, especially "The Trout," and their accompaniments enhance the mood of the music in a beautiful and effective way. When Schubert combines text, vocal line, and accompaniment, something of artistic worth is created. That "something" is not duplicated elsewhere in the world of music. Folk songs and operatic arias do not achieve the same kind of expression; they have other virtues. The art song is the acme of the expression of specific ideas in connection with music.

FRÉDÉRIC CHOPIN

Frédéric Chopin (Show-pan, 1810–1849) was the son of a French father and Polish mother. He showed considerable talent at an early age, and received his musical education at the Conservatory in Warsaw. Before he was twenty, he set out to make his way in the world. Shortly after his departure from Poland, the Poles revolted against the Russians and their Tsar. In time the Russians crushed the revolt, an event that caused Chopin considerable anguish.

Frédéric Chopin.
A rare daguerreo-
type made in 1849 shortly
before his death.

He traveled extensively and then reached Paris, the city that was to become his adopted home. His skill as a pianist and composer made him a sought-after musician. Soon he began to move in a circle of artistic friends —the painter Delacroix, musicians like Liszt and Berlioz, writers like Victor Hugo, Balzac, Lamartine, Alexander Dumas, and Heinrich Heine. Through this group of friends Chopin met Mme. Aurore Dudevant, who wrote under the pen name of George Sand. She had an unusual personality and a penchant for smoking cigars and wearing masculine clothing. Although she was considerably older than Chopin, they lived together for several years, and her domineering personality seemed to suit Chopin's need to be governed. The years were productive ones for him.

In time his health began to fail, and the relationship with Mme. Dudevant became strained. Finally they parted in bitterness, and with this event his creative energy seemed to abate. Liszt wrote, "Chopin felt and often repeated that in breaking this long affection, this powerful bond, he had broken his life." At the age of thirty-nine, Chopin died of tuberculosis. Symbolically, his heart was returned to Poland, and the rest of his body stayed in Paris.

PIANO MUSIC

In the early Romantic period, there tended to be two differing concepts of piano music. They were by no means mutually exclusive, but they were distinctive enough to be noticeable. Composers such as Liszt, who is discussed later in the chapter, exploited the powerful sound of the instrument and dazzled the listener with technical display. Others, like Chopin, tended to treat the piano in a more intimate manner. Although Chopin wrote some works in which the piano is called upon to roar, most of his piano pieces seek to enchant the listener with their lyric beauty. Chopin —unlike the born showman Liszt—was by nature a shy man. He was not at ease nor at his best before a large audience; he preferred the atmosphere of the salon. Since he was not primarily interested in concert-hall music, he was not drawn to the composing of concertos. Rather he seemed to seek in his music the same intimacy of expression that one finds in chamber music.

Romantic composers did not wish to be bound by the strict forms that Mozart and Haydn had used so ably. To replace the rondo, sonata form, and others, the Romanticists created many free, short forms—the ballade, impromptu, fantasie, étude, prelude, berceuse, scherzo, and nocturne.

The *ballade* (bah-*lahd*) and *berceuse* (bair-*serz*) are song-like pieces. The ballade is longer and more sophisticated, and is supposedly reminiscent of the ballade poems of the middle ages. An *étude* (*ay*-tood) is a piece that comes to grips with a particular technical problem. Its name is French for "study." In the hands of a composer like Chopin, an étude is far from being a dull exercise, however. It is an attractive piece of music—a melodic study suitable for concert performance. An *impromptu* is supposed to convey the spontaneity its name implies. A *fantasie* is a completely free and imaginative work. The scherzos by Chopin are not as playful as are Beethoven's. Instead, they are longer and more serious, although the typical meter and tempo are retained. The *nocturne* (meaning "night song") was the name given by the Irish composer John Field to piano pieces with a song-like melody. Chopin adopted the title from Field and wrote several works under the designation. Other piano compositions were derived from dance forms—mazurka, polonaise, waltz.

These pieces were intended to have about them the air of improvisation. They were to sound as though they were an inspiration—a momentary feeling that had been put into sound. The impression of improvisation is illusory, however, because Chopin and his contemporaries labored carefully over each measure of their respective works.

There is one feature of Romantic music, and of Chopin's piano works in particular, that cannot be observed in the printed score: the use of *rubato* (roo-*bah*-toh) in playing the music. Rubato is a style of performance in which the player deviates slightly from the exact execution of the rhythm;

a fraction of time is "borrowed" from one note in order to lengthen another. In fact, the word originally meant "robbed" in Italian. Chopin as a performer was often criticized for his use of rubato. Some listeners charged that he could not keep a steady beat. Undoubtedly he could, but apparently he preferred not to in much of his playing. He adhered to the romantic ideal of freedom of expression, and this was manifest in a certain amount of tasteful rubato. Even today there is disagreement among pianists about how much rubato is appropriate when playing Chopin. Good performing artists agree, however, that rubato must be subtle. It must not call attention to itself nor impede the rhythmic flow of the music unnecessarily.

Chopin's Prelude, Op. 28, No. 4

To examine Chopin's music, let us begin with an extremely simple but moody prelude, a short piece only twenty-five measures long. The work is definitely homophonic; it is a melodic line with throbbing chords in the accompaniment.

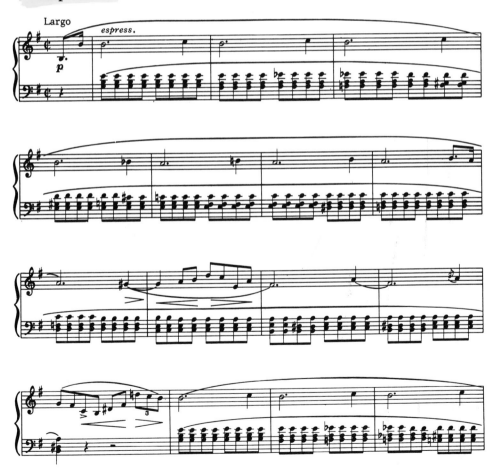

The melody is the epitome of simplicity, and the accompaniment changes little; the entire first measure consists of one chord sounded eight times. But in the handling of such simple elements, Chopin demonstrates his shrewd aesthetic judgment.

Look again at the first three measures. The first complete measure has no change until another note is sounded on the fourth beat. As with Mozart's delaying the resolution of a chord (a device discussed in Chapter 9), Chopin heightens interest by withholding any changes as long as possible, but not so long that the effect is overdone. In the second measure, the harmony changes after four soundings of one chord. To have sounded the chord eight times would have been too much, and would probably have caused the listener's interest to wane. In the third measure the harmony again changes after four soundings of a chord, and then changes after only two. Melodic interest is created solely by the movement to the quarter-note C, which is usually a dissonant tone in the chord pattern when it appears in this piece.

In measure 2 there is another dissonance—a suspension, which was discussed in Chapter 8. The top note in the bass-clef part, E, is held after the chords change, so that it is no longer consonant. This dissonance is retained for four playings of the chord, or half a measure. Bach usually resolved a suspension in less time. But Chopin nurses all he can out of the situation. By manipulating consonance and dissonance over a span of time, he creates some wonderfully attractive but brooding music. This same compositional device reappears later in the Prelude.

If you listen to the chords as they progress, you will sense some of the color and interest Romantic composers achieved in their harmonies. The development of harmony was, in fact, one of their notable contributions to music. No longer do the three basic chords (tonic, dominant, and subdominant) constitute so great a share of the harmony. All sorts of chromatic alterations appear. Foreign modulations become the rule rather than the exception. Often a basic three-note chord has a fourth note added on top to further extend its alternate-note pattern. (In musical terminology, the result is called a *seventh* chord, because the interval between the root and the uppermost chord tone is a seventh.)

This Prelude also demonstrates Chopin's artistry in elaborating on a melodic idea. He often repeats melodic phrases, but with embellishment. In measure 9 the figure arches up and down briefly. In measures 16 to 18 the faster-moving notes consume three measures instead of one, as they did the first time. In these measures, the music reaches a climactic point and is decorated by a five-note turn, such as was mentioned in Chapter 9. Chopin achieves a romantic effect by gliding up to a high note, and thus his use of the turn differs from Mozart's.

The *Prelude, Opus 28, No. 4* illustrates several aspects of Chopin's composing technique. But none is more impressive than the total effect of this short work. Its notes ooze a kind of pained and moody loveliness that is typically Romantic.

Chopin's Polonaise, Op. 53

The *polonaise* was originally a courtly dance, somewhat like a promenade. It was developed in a regal Polish court two hundred and fifty years before Chopin wrote his well-known Polonaises. Although other composers wrote such works before Chopin, his name is most often linked to the form. He wrote thirteen in all, and considered them to be expressions of his Polish sympathies.

The Opus 53 *Polonaise* is a stylized version of the old *polonaises*, just as the dances in the Baroque suite are stylized. It begins with a sizable introduction, followed by the majestic theme:

The melody is full of embellishments. At one point the rhythm seems to stop as a sweeping run is played. The theme is repeated but—as usually happens in Chopin's music—additional notes are added. A short contrasting section is heard, and the first theme appears again.

At this point the music modulates from A-flat major (four flats) to E major (four sharps), which is a foreign modulation by any standard. Then come the rapidly moving notes an octave apart in the bass. The chugging bass line grows over some seventeen measures into a roaring torrent. This piece is one in which Chopin abandons his usual introspective style.

After a repetition of this section, the music takes on a rhapsodic character. Part of the melodic idea used in the section is derived from the contrasting portion. This leads again to the original theme. Thus the piece has a loose three-part, or *A B A,* form. Even though Chopin follows a scheme, as did Mozart and Haydn, his music does not give the same impression of formality.

Bach, Handel, Mozart, Haydn, Beethoven, and Schubert were all extremely versatile composers. They wrote successfully in nearly every medium, vocal and instrumental, solo and ensemble. Chopin was different. He was one of the first "specialist" composers, who tended to limit their writing to one or two areas. Although Chopin attempted a few other media, the bulk of his effort was directed toward his piano works, and through them he earned his reputation as an outstanding composer.

FRANZ LISZT

Franz Liszt (1811–1886) was a man as varied and complex as the Romantic period itself. He grew up on a Hungarian estate of the Esterházy family, the son of a steward and a simple Austrian woman. He was sent to Paris to study under a scholarship arrangement provided by a group of Hungarian noblemen.

Franz Liszt.
Early daguerreotype.

Paris in the 1830s was enamored with virtuoso music, especially that of the sensational Italian violinist Nicolo Paganini (1782–1840, Pah-ga-*nee*-nee). On March 9, 1831, Franz Liszt attended a recital by Paganini. The dazzling violin virtuoso left an indelible impression on the nineteen-year-old Liszt. He was overwhelmed by the conviction that he could do for the piano what Paganini had done for the violin. He could provide it with a new richness of technique and sound. The next morning he cancelled all his concerts and began to retrain himself. He spent hours practicing technical maneuvers such as octaves, trills, scales, and arpeggios (playing the notes of a chord successively rather than simultaneously). He returned again and again to hear Paganini's recitals and to take notes on the incredible feats the master could perform. He even imitated some of the visual aspects of Paganini's appearance: the black, tight-fitting clothes, the tossing hair, and the facial expressions.

As Liszt was well aware, the select audience of the eighteenth-century drawing room had been replaced by the mass audience of the nineteenth-century concert hall. And the new audience demanded spectacular performances by colorful personalities. Liszt seized upon the opportunity by becoming the outstanding piano virtuoso of his day and by writing music that provided abundant opportunity to demonstrate his extraordinary performing talents.

Traditionally the keyboard soloist had performed with his back to the audience. Liszt was one of the first to turn to the sideways position familiar today. In so doing, he provided a visual experience as well as an auditory one. His chiseled profile fascinated the audience, especially the ladies, as he crouched over the keys, alternately caressing and pounding them.

And speaking of ladies—Liszt's life was much involved with them. Although he never married, he had many an affair. One musicologist has painstakingly catalogued over twenty such friendships. He lived for one summer with George Sand and for several years with the novelist Countess Marie d'Agoult. Their relationship produced three children, one of whom, Cosima, subsequently became the wife of Richard Wagner. Later, in Weimar, Liszt lived with the Princess Carolyne von Sayn-Wittgenstein, who assisted him in several of his literary efforts.

Behind the image of the sensational artist, which Liszt did not discourage, there was a musician of depth and a man with a generous heart. He had deep admiration for Beethoven and his music. On one occasion he tried to play an all-Beethoven recital but had to abandon his plan because of the increasing clamor of the audience for flashier numbers. During his thirteen-year stay in Weimar, where he was court conductor to the Grand Duke, he was able to help several musicians, such as Wagner and Berlioz, to get their new works performed. He was also a talented and dedicated teacher, often receiving no pay for his teaching. He was amazingly free of envy in his dealings with other musicians and artists. He was strongly religious and wrote a number of compositions for the church. In the last years of his life he took minor orders in the church and was known as Abbé Liszt. But his fame had already been established, and he was deservedly recognized throughout Europe as a musician of spectacular talent.

Liszt's La Campanella

Liszt's admiration for Paganini led him to transcribe some of Paganini's violin music for the piano. Liszt transcribed six works in all, of which *La Campanella* is probably the highlight. Paganini called the piece *La Clochette* (The Little Bell). Liszt retains the bell effect by sounding a high D-sharp repeatedly throughout the piece.

Transcriptions were very popular in the early Romantic era. They offered the new mass audience the opportunity of hearing technically stunning variations on opera melodies and other works not originally intended for the piano. Since there were no recordings in those days, and few orchestras (none that traveled), a piano recital was often the listener's only contact with quality music.

La Campanella is a typically Romantic composition. First, it is virtuoso music through and through. Even a good professional pianist does not undertake it lightly for public performance. Second, it demands of the player the full range of techniques developed in the Romantic period. And the period has properly been called the "golden age of the piano," because the musical potential of the instrument was realized during that time. Third, it is an attempt to make the piano more orchestral in sound and concept. The very name of the piece suggests that the piano is to be descriptive of something nonpianistic.

While the piece is technically awesome, it is musically rather superficial. It is a set of scintillating variations on a simple two-measure phrase, which is stated and then repeated twice with a concluding phrase:

The technical devices employed are too numerous to cover fully here. A few will suffice to show the scope of technique found in the piece. When a nonpianist hears rapidly repeated notes played on a piano, he assumes that the player is rapping his finger on the key with tremendous speed. Strange as it may seem, however, it is easier to repeat notes in rapid succession if the fingers are changed with each sounding. Liszt calls for this technique in one variation:

He also calls for an extremely fast execution of the chromatic scale:

The use of alternate hands gives the player more speed and power:

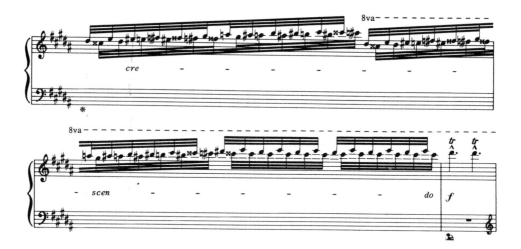

Liszt's exploitation of the range of the piano can be heard in the long trill on the high D-sharp, only a few notes from the top of the keyboard.

From time to time the artistic worth of virtuoso compositions like *La Campanella* is questioned. True, sometimes the construction is superficial and the harmonies repetitious. But not all virtuoso works are sparse in aesthetic content. The bell idea in *La Campanella* is handled imaginatively, and most of the variations are attractive and fresh in sound. Furthermore, virtuoso works offer the listener aural sensations that are not possible in nonvirtuoso music. The high notes of the piano are used in *La Campanella* in a way that is not heard in a Mozart sonata. It should also be admitted that there is a fascination in observing a highly skilled person perform, whether it be a talented athlete or a fine pianist. It is a pleasure to watch an Olympic champion figure-skater or high-diver—to see a person who does something exceptionally well. This is especially true if the observer has tried a little figure skating or high diving and has some appreciation of the skill demanded. Virtuoso music has a rightful place in the repertoire. It should certainly not be the only type of music one likes, however. The weakness of nineteenth-century audiences was that, in general, they took little interest in other kinds of performance, so they missed much that music has to offer.

PROGRAM MUSIC

At the beginning of this chapter it was pointed out that the Romantic composer spurned the formal rules and compositional schemes of the eighteenth century. Having rejected the past, he then faced the problem of finding something to replace the old forms. After all, form had been the means of unifying a work and making it into a coherent structure. To fill this function, composers devised three general techniques, two of which have been discussed earlier. One was the emphasis on works that were short enough not to require a formal scheme in order to appear cohesive. Another solution was to follow the old forms loosely but to incorporate Romantic melodies and harmonies into the music while doing so. Chopin's *Polonaise Opus 53* with its *A B A* form is an example of this type of compromise.

A third answer was *descriptive or program music*—music that the composer specifically intends to be associated with nonmusical ideas or objects. Since program music is instrumental, these associations must be contained within the music itself; there is no vocal text. In rare instances there may be a part for narrator. But by and large the program (the story that is being depicted) is evident only insofar as the composer chooses to explain it through conventional means.

It should be understood that the composer is not attempting to present some tale literally and precisely. No orchestra can describe every detail of a scene in which the heroine is tied to a railroad track by the villain. Without prior knowledge of the program, the listener would probably recognize little more than the increasing sense of excitement in this musical melodrama. If he were to hear a train whistle, with high notes for the screaming victim and low notes for the chuckling villain, he might imagine the scene more accurately. But the quality of such music would be so poor that further speculation is best avoided.

Good program music has substance in and of itself and can stand without being associated with a story. Its musical qualities determine its success or failure, not its program. Sometimes, in fact, programmatic titles were added after the music had been completed. The composer merely uses the story or program as a stimulus for musical ideas. In most cases, all he tries to convey are general moods rather than literal incidents. If the story involves a shipwreck on a stormy sea, the composer writes music that *to him* seems suitable for depicting such an event. A listener not knowing the program might imagine the music to be a struggle between two giants or a passionate love scene. But as long as he responds *in essence* to the music, its program is effective. The excellence of the music itself is the factor that determines the success of program music. It is a type of music that strives to be expressive, a characteristic discussed in Chapter 4.

The idea of relating nonmusical subjects to music was hardly new with the Romanticists. Renaissance and Baroque composers had made such associations in some of their music. But the nineteenth century saw unprecedented interest in this type of writing. Program music was for Liszt and Berlioz what sonata form had been for Mozart and Haydn. It provided some ideas and guidelines for a sizable musical composition, and yet no two program works had the same form. The emphasis was more on the mood of each portion of the music rather than on the composer's skill in filling out predictable forms.

Program music was written under several different names in the nineteenth century. Some works were called overtures even though they were not written to precede an opera. Mendelssohn's *Hebrides (Fingal's Cave)* is an example of such an overture. Some program works were written as incidental music for plays. Mendelssohn's music for *A Midsummer Night's Dream* is one program work of this type. But the main effort of Romantic composers was directed toward the writing of the *tone poem* or *symphonic poem*. Liszt was the first to use the term in 1848. It refers simply to a long orchestral work whose contrasting sections are developed from a mood or scene suggested by the particular program being followed.

Liszt's Les Préludes

Les Préludes is undoubtedly Liszt's best-known tone poem. It was written first as an overture to a choral work, and it was given a name and program after it had been completed. Liszt choose to associate the work with Alphonse de Lamartine's *Méditations Poétique*. The program that Liszt attached to the score contains this quotation from Lamartine's poem:

> What is our life but a series of preludes to that unknown song whose first solemn note is tolled by Death? The enchanted dawn of every life is love. But where is the destiny on whose first delicious joys some storm does not break? . . . And what soul thus cruelly bruised, when the tempest rolls away, seeks not to rest its memories in the pleasant calm of pastoral life? Yet man does not long permit himself to taste the kindly quiet that first attracted him to Nature's lap. For when the trumpet sounds he hastens to danger's post, that in the struggle he may once more regain full knowledge of himself and his strength.

The lines of the poem are pure Romanticism, from the personification of death and its description as "that unknown song" to the exaltation of love and nature, which is also personified.

Les Préludes begins with a three-note germinal idea, one that seems to indicate impending trouble. It is marked with a bracket and X's.

The full orchestra then takes up the idea and plays a longer melody and accompaniment, both of which expand on the original motive:

The "love" theme that follows also contains the opening motive:

As one would expect, Liszt writes the love music to sound as rich and warm as possible. A second theme is heard in the section depicting love. It too contains the pattern of the motive at the beginning of the measure.

The poem speaks next of a storm and a tempest, so the music suggests upheaval and turbulence. The strings scurry up and down the chromatic scale while the brasses bark out foreboding chords.

The calm of pastoral life is represented in a section embodying some of Liszt's best writing. The motive is now woven into an idyllic theme played by the horn and woodwinds:

A shepherd-like melody is then combined with the theme containing the original motive:

This music evolves into a robust closing section that depicts the final triumph of man. Again the motive is incorporated into a theme that suggests a call to battle:

In the closing section, Liszt's weakness as a composer begins to show: his music seems a little trite and obvious. There is not quite enough imagination in the composition to maintain a high level of musical interest. Although the closing section may be somewhat lacking in substance, the pastoral section preceding it exhibits real craftsmanship and sensitivity.

Liszt's music has had an army of imitators and has been exploited under circumstances that did not help its status. Snatches of his works have cropped up in radio and television and in numerous animated cartoons. These frequent playings of Liszt's music have robbed it of some of its freshness for modern-day listeners. Such incongruous appearances of his music are also unfortunate in that they obscure the more worthy aspects of his writing.

One of these aspects, apparent in *Les Préludes*, is Liszt's considerable skill in *theme transformation,* the technique of taking a motive or theme and transforming it into an entirely new melody. The original motive in *Les Préludes* assumed several widely differing characters in the course of the tone poem. Theme transformation should not be confused with theme development or theme and variation, which was discussed in Chapter 10. Variation involves keeping the theme intact to some extent (perhaps only its harmony or rhythm) through a series of musical treatments. Transformation is a freer concept, in which only a few characteristic intervals are preserved, sometimes interspersed with new material.

Theme transformation provides music with some degree of unity, although the listener may not be aware of it. Since tone poems often lack traditional formal structure, the employment of elements of a theme in several guises helps provide a better sense of organization. Composers other than Liszt have exploited this technique—Brahms was the master craftsman in its use.

ROBERT SCHUMANN

One cannot study early Romantic music without paying respect to three outstanding composers in addition to Schubert, Chopin, and Liszt. One of the three, Hector Berlioz, was mentioned in Chapter 4.

Another fine composer was Robert Schumann (1810–1856). He wrote many works for piano, and these represent his better compositions. He also composed several symphonies and chamber works and many songs. One song cycle, *Frauenliebe und Leben* (Woman's Love and Life), is especially melodious and sensitively conceived.

Schumann is remembered not only as a composer but also as the founder and editor of a respected journal, *The New Magazine for Music*. The journal promoted the concepts of the new Romantic music and was influential in bringing this music to the attention of the public.

Schumann's fame and success were partly attributable to his wife, Clara Wieck Schumann. Clara was herself an outstanding pianist, and she did much to promote his works. Their romance had about it many storybook qualities, including her obstinate father and a nine-year age difference between Robert and the young Clara. Their marriage was a happy one, but Schumann's musical productivity gradually declined. He suffered the tragedy of a mental breakdown and died at the age of forty-six.

FELIX MENDELSSOHN

Felix Mendelssohn (1809–1847) was born into a famous and wealthy family. His grandfather, Moses Mendelssohn, was a distinguished philosopher. His father was a banker with a knowledgeable interest in art. They were converted to Christianity when Felix was a child, and added the name Bartholdy to the name Mendelssohn to indicate this change.

Felix grew up hearing good music performed in his own home. Upon occasion his father employed instrumentalists to play in his home, and Felix thus enjoyed a privilege that is rare among composers—the opportunity to hear his instrumental compositions performed at any stage of their development. With all the benefits of a fine education, he became a successful pianist, composer, conductor, and organizer of concerts. (Whereas the custom had been for the orchestral conductor to stand inconspicuously among the players, Mendelssohn was one of the first conductors to stand in front of the orchestra.) Under his direction, the Gewandhaus Orchestra at Leipzig became the finest in Europe. It was he who revived the interest in Bach's music by organizing a performance of the *St. Matthew Passion*. He made ten journeys to England to conduct or perform. Like Schumann, he was happily married. However, after the death of a sister to whom he was deeply attached, he died of a stroke at the age of thirty-eight.

Mendelssohn's music is eminently listenable, if not profound. He wrote several successful symphonies, and his *Concerto for Violin and Orchestra* is one of the most frequently performed works for the instrument. He wrote for piano, generally in a rather light vein. His vocal works are especially enjoyable to hear. He followed the oratorio tradition of Handel in England by writing *St. Paul* and *Elijah*, the latter being one of his finest works. Both of these oratorios are in English.

THE DIRECTION OF ROMANTICISM

This chapter opened with a discussion of the general characteristics of Romanticism. At this point it might be wise to review the observations gained from listening to the music discussed in the chapter.

Immediately evident in Schubert's songs and Chopin's piano pieces is a fondness for the short, expressive work that embodies a moment of feeling. Form, balance, and organization are secondary to the craftsmanship that enables the music to express some distinct emotion.

Since expression was so valued in the Romantic period, it was inevitable that homophonic music predominated. Polyphony may be a more sophisticated form of music, but it does not permit the flexibility of expression that is possible when a single line is developed to its fullest. There is some contrapuntal writing in *Les Préludes*, but appearances of this technique are more limited in Chopin's and Schubert's music.

Schubert and Chopin concentrated instead on creating interesting and colorful harmonies. In the early Baroque era, harmony had been a rather perfunctory accompaniment to a line of recitative. But by the nineteenth century, harmony had evolved into a rich and varied counterpart to the melodic line itself. Modulations were frequent and were no longer confined to closely related keys. In short, harmony was handled with skill and imagination.

The melodic line of the Romantic composer often had unique beauty of its own. Another distinguishing feature was its ability to express a mood. This feature was in clear contrast to the Classical ideal of the well-designed melody and to Beethoven's search for a theme that was suitable for later developmental treatment.

The music of the composers cited in this chapter exemplifies the Romantic preoccupation with the unknown and the surmounting of obstacles. From Gretchen's aching heart to man's struggle for fulfillment in *Les Préludes*, Romantic music has a wonderful time encountering hardship. Perhaps human beings need to undergo emotional ups and downs every now and then. Whatever the reason, the Romanticists enjoyed their emotions and reveled in the chance to grapple with adversity.

The Romantic emphasis on feeling encouraged a freer interpretation of the music. Rubato became a standard component of performance, and music was, ironically, carefully written to sound extemporaneous.

Composers tended to concentrate their writing efforts on the instruments or styles they knew best. Some limited themselves almost exclusively to one area. Chopin confined his efforts largely to the piano, Paganini to the violin, and Wagner to opera.

The piano became to the Romantic period what the organ had been to the Baroque. A rich literature was written for it, and virtuoso techniques of playing developed.

The need of the Romantic period for new means of organizing long works of music brought forth the tone poem, or symphonic poem. It represented a close relationship between literature and music, and it stimulated the musical imagination of the composer, resulting in varied and attractive music. In such a context Liszt was able to write a *Faust Symphony* full of demonic sound, and Berlioz was able in his *Symphonie Fantastique* to pour out the personal fantasies experienced as a result of his unrequited love for a beautiful actress.

Romantic musicians were generally concerned with the other arts and with philosophy. They were familiar with the writings of Goethe and Lamartine, and they often knew the writers personally, even intimately. Liszt wrote a number of literary works, including a book on gypsy music and another entitled *Life of Chopin* (the latter book, unfortunately, containing inaccuracies of fact). Schumann's literary bent led him to edit his music magazine. Wagner wrote lengthy treatises on music, art, and philosophy. Romantic composers believed strongly in a unity of the arts. This attitude culminated in the music dramas of Wagner, discussed in Chapter 13. The Romantic period, for all its uniqueness, was not yet full-blown.

SUGGESTIONS FOR FURTHER LISTENING

BERLIOZ:
Damnation de Faust, Op. 24
Overtures
Symphonie Fantastique, Op. 14

CHOPIN:
Concerto No. 1 in E Minor for Piano, Op. 11
Concerto No. 2 in F Minor for Piano, Op. 21
Short works

LISZT:
Concerto No. 1 in E-Flat Major for Piano
Études after Paganini
Faust Symphony
Hungarian Rhapsodies
Mephisto Waltz

MENDELSSOHN:
Concerto in E Minor for Violin, Op. 64
Elijah, Op. 70
Incidental music, A Midsummer Night's Dream, Op. 21 & 61
Octet in E-Flat Major for Strings, Op. 20
Symphony No. 3 in A Minor, Op. 56 ("Scotch")
Symphony No. 4 in A Major, Op. 90 ("Italian")
Trio No. 1 in D Minor, Op. 49 (Piano)

SCHUBERT:

"Die Schöne Müllerin," Op. 25
Incidental music, Rosamunde, Op. 26
Quartet No. 14 in D Minor, "Death and the Maiden"
Quintet in C Major, D. 956
Quintet in A Major, Op. 114, "The Trout"
Symphony No. 8 in B Minor, "Unfinished"
Symphony No. 9 in C Major, "The Great"
Trio No. 1 in B-Flat Major (piano), *Op. 99*
Wanderer Fantasie for Piano, Op. 15
Winterreise, Op. 89

SCHUMANN:

Carnaval, Op. 9
Concerto in A Minor for Cello and Orchestra, Op. 129
Concerto in A Minor for Piano and Orchestra, Op. 54
Frauenliebe und Leben, Op. 42
Kinderscenen, Op. 15
Symphony No. 4 in D Minor, Op. 120

Late
Romanticism

13

The Romantic composers of the second half of the nineteenth century tended to be a more sophisticated, less colorful lot than the generation that had preceded them. Late Romanticists like Brahms and Strauss were able to build on the work of Liszt and Schubert. No longer was there a preoccupation with new departures or a turning away from the Classical past. Since the later composers were more distant in time from the Classical period, they did not feel the need to prove that their compositions were indeed different from the earlier style. They freely employed features of both the Baroque and Classical periods and yet introduced some innovations of their own.

The late Romantic composers were generally less able performers than their predecessors. Tchaikovsky did not perform publicly and was a notoriously poor conductor, almost ruining the first performance of his Sixth Symphony. Richard Strauss and Brahms did not concentrate on public performance either, although both were skilled conductors and Brahms had a fluent piano technique. The late Romantic composer thought of himself as a composer first of all; his other skills were secondary.

PETER ILICH TCHAIKOVSKY

Until early adulthood, Tchaikovsky (Chy-*koff*-skee, 1840–1893) seemed destined to follow his father's footsteps by working in a governmental position. At the age of twenty-three, however, he decided to become a musician, so he resigned his job and entered the newly founded Conservatory of St. Petersburg (now Leningrad). He did well. In three years he had finished his course and was recommended for a teaching position in the new Conservatory of Moscow. He stayed there for twelve years and taught harmony.

Throughout his life, Tchaikovsky was plagued with serious personal problems, which caused anguish in his sensitive nature. He once described his existence as "regretting the past, hoping for the future, without ever being satisfied with the present." He married a Conservatory student, a rather unstable girl who was madly in love with him. He could feel only pity for her and despair for himself. The marriage proved to be disastrous. Finally, on the verge of a complete mental breakdown he went to live with his brothers in St. Petersburg.

At this point in his life entered Nadezhda von Meck, a wealthy widow who, though a recluse, successfully ran her inherited business empire and the lives of her eleven children. She was impressed by the beauty of Tchaikovsky's music and decided to support him financially. There was, however, one unusual twist to the arrangement. So that she could be sure she was supporting a composer and not a personal friend, she stipulated that they should never meet. And so it was. For thirteen years Mme. von Meck and Tchaikovsky carried on intense and devoted contact—all by letter.

In 1891 he accepted an invitation to America, where he participated in the opening of Carnegie Hall in New York. According to his letters, he liked Americans and was gratified by the fact that they appreciated his music. In 1893, while in St. Petersburg to conduct his Sixth Symphony, he contracted cholera and died at the age of fifty-three.

Tchaikovsky's Symphony No. 4

The *Symphony No. 4 in F Minor, Op. 36*, received its first performance early in 1878. It is the earliest of his symphonies to have maintained a prominent place in the orchestral repertoire. The First, Second, and Third Symphonies are rarely played, but the Fifth and Sixth, like the Fourth, are popular with concert audiences today.

First Movement. Because of the voluminous correspondence with Mme. von Meck, Tchaikovsky's thoughts on this symphony have been preserved. The work opens with a regal introduction. He wrote that it represents "fate, that ominous power, which prevents the craving for happiness from achieving its end. This power is overwhelming and unconquer-

*Peter Ilich Tchaikovsky
at the age of thirty-nine.*

able; nothing remains but submission, and vain lamentations." These lines indicate how closely his philosophy paralleled that of the early Romanticists.

The opening music does sound overwhelming and ominous:

The mighty sounds of the trumpets and horns instill in the listener a tremendous sense of expectation. After such an introduction, it would seem impossible for anything except a great symphony to follow. Tchaikovsky does not disappoint his listeners. The first theme is a tortured, twisting line that is fascinating to hear:

poco cresc.

f

Although the movement is basically in sonata form, a short development of the first theme is started immediately, thus delaying the presentation of the second theme by almost four minutes.

The first theme has an intricate rhythmic pattern. The meter signature is $\frac{9}{8}$, indicating three stressed and regularly spaced beats in each measure: <u>1</u> 2 3 <u>4</u> 5 6 <u>7</u> 8 9. The theme, however, moves so that its points of rhythmic stress occur unevenly: <u>1</u> 2 <u>3</u> 4 <u>5</u> 6 7 <u>8</u> 9. The effect is one of *syncopation,* in which an accent occurs where one is not normally expected or is absent where it *is* expected. Like other aspects of rhythm, syncopation evokes a certain amount of physical response from the listener, the degree of response depending on the degree to which the syncopation is emphasized. Its effect is to nudge the listener by departing from the momentum of predictable motion. Like a skipped heartbeat or a stumble in one's gait, this technique interrupts the expected rhythm and comes as a mild surprise. Romantic composers were certainly not the first to use syncopation, but they exploited it with considerable imagination.

Tchaikovsky does more than manipulate the rhythm of the melody. He adds further interest by varying the rhythm of the accompanying chords. The low strings and horns come in on beats 2 and 4, to contrast strikingly with the accents in the melody. After six measures of entrances on beats 2 and 4, the accompanying chords shift their emphasis to beats 2, 5, and 8. But still they do not correspond with the accents of the melody, because the melody now reverts to the normal stress on beats 1, 4, and 7. The result is a highly complex rhythmic structure. The numerous changes of accent tend to weaken the sense of beat, and so the music does not call forth a simple "foot-tapping" response. But the sophistication and intricacy of the rhythmic treatment is appropriate to the melody, and the music is effective.

When the second theme is finally reached, the character of the music changes. Whereas the first theme was agitated and pained, the second is calm and placid. In the first theme the strings did much of the work; in the second the melody is played by the woodwinds. The rhythmic complexity of the first is exchanged for simpler patterns in the second, although there are still moments of emphasis apart from the main beats. Also introduced is a motive of descending chromatic notes, which will reappear later in this symphony:

Soon the cellos add a countermelody that has the rich sound associated with Romantic music:

The second theme and its countermelody are extended, and then a part of the first theme enters quietly in the woodwinds. The give-and-take between the strings and woodwinds continues, while the timpani tap out a subtle beat that begins slowly but gradually gains speed as it leads to a monumental climax. At the peak of intensity, the strings play a chord pattern in long notes while the winds sound the agitated notes reminiscent of the first theme:

After a few moments, the horns blare out the long tones while the strings and woodwinds play the rhythmic figure. The orchestra is brilliant, full of color and power. Tchaikovsky here achieves a fine union of sensuous appeal and musical craftsmanship. It is this type of climactic passage that has won him a place in the hearts of concert audiences.

The introductory music is heard again. This time it heralds the beginning of the development section. The first theme is fragmented and passed among the sections, modulating as it goes. Later in the development, the violins and violas introduce this melody:

The same phrase, which is occasionally shortened, is played eight times, at successively higher pitch levels. The impression of anxiety and tension is thus increased until the music sounds as though it would burst.

The recapitulation starts with a frenetic outburst of sound on the first theme, which is shorter and less involved than it was in the exposition. The music further parallels the exposition by duplicating the increasing intensity of the earlier climactic portion. This time, however, Tchaikovsky does less with his ideas and reverts to repetitive chord progressions in the agitated rhythmic passage.

The third appearance of the introductory music marks the start of the coda, which features a chorale-like melody and a section in which the tempo is nearly doubled.

In this work you can see the magnitude of a mature Romantic symphony. Although sonata form has been generally preserved, its scope has been expanded into a movement of over twenty minutes in length, and it contains more thematic material and more extensive digressions between themes. You need only recall the first movement of Mozart's Fortieth Symphony to be impressed by the transformation that has taken place in the symphony during those ninety years. In fact, to get the most from your study of music, you should listen again to the first movement of each symphony. Notice that while each composer couches his ideas in essentially the same form, Mozart's piece is radically different from Tchaikovsky's. As you listen, try to remember the basic aural "flavor" of each work.

Second Movement. Tchaikovsky wrote Mme. von Meck that this movement expressed "that melancholy feeling one has when sitting home alone." And the music does certainly suggest melancholy! With only the barest accompaniment, the oboe begins a pathetic but beautiful melody:

The music moves to a contrasting theme, and then returns to the first melody, giving the first portion of the movement an *a b a* pattern. When the *a* theme returns, however, it is treated contrapuntally by the cellos, violins, and woodwinds.

The middle or *B* part of the movement is in major. Gone is the melancholy of the *A* section.

Remember the motive of rapidly moving notes played in the first movement by the woodwinds? As the sad melody of the A section returns in the violins, the woodwinds start tossing this motive about. The idea of incorporating the same motive or melody into more than one movement is called *cyclical* treatment of themes. It was a favorite device of late Romantic composers because it helped unify the various movements of a long work. It was an effective substitute for the Classical forms, which were used less frequently.

Third Movement. The Fourth Symphony received a generally lukewarm reception at its first performance. The only portion that generated any enthusiasm was the third movement, in which the strings play *pizzicato* (*pit*-si-*cah*-toh) throughout its length. Pizzicato is the technique wherein the strings are plucked by the fingers instead of bowed. The sound of a plucked note is short and chopped off, in complete contrast to the warm and sustained tones that are possible when the instrument is bowed. In 1878 it was a novel idea to exploit pizzicato so extensively, but since that time many composers have followed Tchaikovsky's lead.

The form of the movement is readily apparent because various sections of the orchestra are responsible for particular themes. The strings start with their pizzicato part. This is A of a large three-part form. The B portion begins with a long note by the oboe. The first part of B is played by the woodwinds, the second by the brasses. Then both groups combine. This music is reminiscent of portions of Tchaikovsky's more familiar *Nutcracker Suite*. The piccolo, a nineteenth-century addition to the orchestra, has prominent solo passages in this section. The pizzicato portion of the movement reappears and the entire orchestra performs the coda, in which Tchaikovsky demonstrates his ability to build musical intensity and excitement.

Whether he was conscious of it or not, Tchaikovsky revealed a certain understanding of psychology and aesthetics in his handling of build-up and listener expectation. According to one theory of psychology, a listener usually assumes certain outcomes in a musical work he is hearing for the first time. When the music progresses generally as he expected, he finds satisfaction in having anticipated correctly. A few small surprises along the way do not upset him; in fact, they probably attract his interest. But if he is consistently wrong, if he expects mighty chords and gets only the plaintive sound of an oboe, he feels tricked and foolish and will quite naturally tend to dislike the work. Tchaikovsky puts out the proper musical "bait" to suggest increasing intensity and then leads the listener, with just a few delays and surprises, to the expected climactic moment.

For about three-fourths of the coda, he builds to a climax by interjecting rapid exchanges of melodic fragments and by increasing the pitch level and volume. The climax is reached, and the last portion of the coda settles down gently from its high level of intensity. The listener is not dropped abruptly from excitement into nothingness. He is guided down in a satisfying manner.

Fourth Movement. For sheer orchestral fireworks, few symphonies exceed the fourth movement of Tchaikovsky's Fourth Symphony. The music begins like a clap of thunder and seems to shoot forward with lightning speed:

After only a few moments, a completely different kind of theme is heard. It is plaintive, like the opening theme of the second movement:

This little tune is a Russian folk song entitled "The Birch Tree." The entire song is only four phrases long, in the form *a a b b*. Tchaikovsky is not generally considered to be a nationalistic composer, and so his use of a folk song here is not typical of his writing.

Tchaikovsky may have been a romanticist, but he and other Romantic composers nevertheless hold thematic development in high regard. In the development section of this movement, he (1) treats the melody in a variety of ways, (2) provides contrapuntal contrast to a movement that is predominantly homophonic in texture, (3) creates a transition leading back to the opening theme, and (4) delays the return of the theme a bit, so that its reappearance will be more rewarding—the "absence-makes-the-heart-grow-fonder" technique.

This development section, like many in symphonic music, may to some listeners sound disjointed and not particularly melodious. Such a section is, however, essential to the symphonic idea. The purpose of development is to manipulate musical ideas so that the original themes can be heard in a new light as the music progresses. Continuous melody, no matter how beautiful it may be, doesn't develop, doesn't vary. Long works made up entirely of luscious melody would be comparable to eating rich, creamy fudge day after day for breakfast, lunch, and dinner.

Like Liszt, Tchaikovsky has not been accorded the status of first-rate composer by some musicians, who feel that his music occasionally lacks subtlety and becomes routine. But lay listeners respond easily to its beauty and excitement, to its lush harmonies and well-designed, eminently singable melodies. Perhaps this judgment of his music is the more valid one.

JOHANNES BRAHMS

Johannes Brahms (1833–1897) was basically out of character with his time. He was by nature more suited to the Classical period, with its interest in formal balance and good taste. But he was born into the middle of Romanticism, both chronologically and geographically. The blend of his rational personality with the emotional Romantic world proved to be exactly the right chemistry to bring about beautiful and lasting music.

Like Bach, Mozart, and Beethoven, Brahms was the son of a musician, a somewhat shiftless string bass player in Hamburg, Germany. Young Brahms got his start by playing piano in the dance halls in the poorer sections of town. He demonstrated considerable talent, and by the age of twenty was serving as piano accompanist to one of the better violinists of the day. He showed talent in composition as well and soon went to study with Robert Schumann. The Schumanns took the shy young man into their home. Schumann in his magazine spoke highly of Brahms' work, and before long Brahms found himself known throughout the musical world. He was of much help to the family when Schumann suffered a mental collapse and had to be hospitalized.

At first Brahms admired and then grew to love Clara, who was fourteen years older than he and mother of seven children. Because he had the highest regard for her husband, his ailing benefactor, the situation caused him much conflict. After Schumann died, Brahms should have felt free to follow through on his love for Clara and marry her. She was no longer the unattainable ideal. But somehow he could not bring himself to take a step that would have obligated him and limited his freedom. Later in life, Brahms was to fall in love with other women, but he chose never to marry.

Brahms reacted in a similar way to employment. He never accepted a position that made heavy demands on him. The one position he coveted—the conductorship of the orchestra in his native Hamburg—eluded him throughout his life; apparently the directors of the orchestra could not forget that he started out as a waterfront musician. Most of his adult life, therefore, was spent in Vienna, where for short periods of time he directed various choral groups and a music society. Most of his income came from the sale of his compositions and from conducting.

*Johannes Brahms when
a young man.*

Brahms was every bit a human being. He scrimped on buying food for himself but never failed to eat heartily if invited to someone's home for dinner. He was brusque, especially as he grew older, but he was also fond of children and enjoyed a good laugh. He had a caustic wit. To some elderly ladies who were singing Haydn's *Creation,* he pleaded "Why do you drag it so? Surely you took this much faster under Haydn."

Brahms was aware that he had extraordinary talent as a composer, and this was partially the reason for his wanting to be as free as possible. Unlike Beethoven, he left no rejected versions of his music for posterity to find. He wanted the world to know only his best work, and so rough sketches were carefully destroyed. It is said that he burned as many of his compositions as he allowed to be published.

Brahms composed almost every type of music, and wrote with consistently high quality—symphonies, concertos, chamber music, piano works, songs, and choral music. One of his greatest compositions, *A German Requiem,* was written early in his career. This work for chorus, orchestra, and soprano and baritone soloists is one of the most profound in all music literature.

In spite of his demonstrated skill in writing in both the choral and strictly instrumental idioms, Brahms was not attracted to either opera or tone poems, and therefore he attempted neither. His coolness toward opera may have been partly due to the excessive competition raging between the followers of Brahms and those of Wagner. In the second half of the nine-teenth century, music lovers evidently felt obliged to choose sides between the two men. The division concerned aesthetics as much as it did personal-ities. The Wagnerites, with composer Anton Bruckner as leader, held that music was a medium for the expression of emotions and ideas. Brahms, with the support of the eminent critic Eduard Hanslick, promoted the idea that music was an end in itself. Since there is truth in both views, the dispute has never been resolved to everyone's satisfaction. Brahms handled the matter quite sensibly: he ignored it as best he could and went about his composing.

Brahms' Symphony No. 4, Op. 98

Brahms wrote only four symphonies, but each has a prominent place in the orchestral repertoire and is frequently performed today. He approached the writing of a symphony with utmost seriousness. After some labor on what was to have been his first symphony, he decided that the material wasn't properly symphonic, so he reworked it as his first piano concerto. Finally, at the age of forty-three, he did bring out his First Symphony. He completed his Fourth Symphony nine years later, in the summer of 1885. By this time his reputation was unsurpassed, and there was a constant demand for his music.

Before Brahms finally released a work, it was his custom to invite a few close friends, especially Clara Schumann, to look it over and offer suggestions. The Fourth Symphony underwent similar scrutiny before Brahms deemed it ready for presentation to the public. Hans von Bülow, the most famous conductor of his time, referred to Brahms' drive for perfec-tion in a letter to a concert agent: "J. Brahms proposes to rehearse a new Symphony round about October. If he is satisfied with it—you know how he repolishes and no amount of revision is too much for him—then I am sure he would not be adverse to take it on the Rhine and to Holland with us." When the symphony was first performed, Brahms himself conducted it. The work was a great success on the tour, although later audiences in Vienna received it more coolly.

First Movement. The first theme has a sweep that is typical of Brahms:

This theme appears in many guises throughout the movement. For instance, in the next few measures the same idea appears at *twice* its original speed. This technique of shortening all the note values proportionately is called *diminution.* Usually the pitch relationships in the new phrase closely resemble those in the original phrase. But here Brahms chooses to alter the melody somewhat as he presents the rhythm in diminution:

At the end of the development section the same idea appears at *half* its original speed; the note values have been lengthened by means of *augmentation.* Now Brahms retains the melodic line but alters the rhythmic relationships. Despite that alteration, the phrase strongly resembles the opening theme, and the lengthened note values suggest augmentation:

At another place the theme is varied and exchanged between the first and second violins:

Elsewhere it is exchanged between strings and woodwinds:

One could go on for pages showing the countless ways Brahms varies, develops, and transforms this theme. The entire movement is filled with fragments and suggestions of it. Almost from the time the theme appears he is developing it and blending it into the structure of the music in such a way as to create a symphonic masterpiece. Perhaps most noteworthy is the fact that throughout the symphony he maintains the melodious sounds of the Romantic era. His music displays much intellectual content without becoming pedantic.

The second theme combines two melodic ideas. One is played by the horns and some of the woodwinds. It sounds somewhat like introductory music, and perhaps it is, because soon a highly romantic melody starts in the cellos and horns:

The short, martial notes of the woodwinds appear extensively from this point on.

A third theme appears later in the movement but is not quite so pervasive:

The first movement is constructed along the familiar plan of sonata form.

     Second Movement. The techniques of theme transformation, variation, and elaboration that Brahms uses so ably are especially well suited to slow movements. Each second movement of Brahms' four symphonies seems incomparably beautiful.

     This movement shows the gradual weakening of key center that took place in the late Romantic period. The two horns that begin the movement seem to be playing in C major, when in fact those few measures are centered around a mode—one of the tonal patterns that had seldom been employed since the Renaissance. When the strings repeat the theme, they place it squarely in E major. Such momentary vagueness about the key provides some inkling of the abandonment of key center that occurred within twenty-five years after the writing of this symphony.

     The theme is:

     Brahms' inventiveness is shown in the fact that the second four notes are the inversion of the first four. The melody is well suited for development because the group of four notes seems ready-made to serve as a motive.

     The strings start out by playing it pizzicato. While they are sounding the melody, the clarinet is playing a smooth version of the same line. The theme is developed a bit and varied before a new theme is introduced.

     The second theme is another romantic, passionate melody played by the cellos. Notice that it is high in the range of the cello, to provide more intensity:

     Both first and second themes are heard again before the first theme returns to close the movement.

Third Movement. The spirit of this movement is one of heartiness and vigor. In one respect, at least, Brahms might be compared with Robert Browning: both men displayed a sturdy nineteenth-century optimism. For example, Browning says in *Rabbi Ben Ezra:*

> Grow old along with me!
> The best is yet to be,
> The last of life, for which the first was made:
> Our times are in his hand
> Who saith, "A whole I planned,
> Youth shows but half; trust God:
> See all, nor be afraid!"

Brahms indicates the tempo as *allegro giocoso* (joyfully fast). In the opening measures two themes are presented simultaneously, one of which is nearly the inversion of the other:

The rhythmic figure ♪♪♩ appears throughout the movement and contributes to the overall heavy, robust German sound.

This movement differs from a Beethoven or Mendelssohn scherzo in that it has two-beat rather than three-beat meter, but it is similar in style and spirit.

Fourth Movement. The form of the fourth movement is called a *passacaglia* or *chaconne*. Scholars have never quite agreed on which it is, and Brahms did not say what he thought about the matter. The passacaglia was mentioned in Chapter 8 in connection with Bach's outstanding organ work in that form. The word "chaconne" (shah-*cone*) denotes a similar structure. The forms were most prevalent during the Baroque era. Both are based on the principle of variation, wherein a melody or harmonic progression, usually about eight measures long, is repeated many times and a new variation occurs simultaneously with each appearance. Both types are in a moderate three-beat meter and begin with a clear statement of the theme or chord progression on which the work is to be based.

The difference between a passacaglia and chaconne, if any, is sometimes described in this way: a passacaglia consists of variations on a

melody or theme, and a chaconne consists of variations on a certain prescribed harmonic progression. It is difficult to distinguish between the two
terms, however, because composers have used them interchangeably. Furthermore, a given melody often implies a certain harmony; and conversely,
a given harmony often suggests a melody, which then seems to fit all
subsequent appearances of the harmony. And so the two factors—melody
and harmony—are not easily isolated, nor should they be. Although separate definitions may be elusive, the passacaglia/chaconne principle is easily
heard in the music itself, and its purpose is clear: to provide unity through
recurrence of the theme or chord pattern and to sustain interest through the
use of continuous variation.

The theme of this particular movement is a solid melody eight
measures long, with one note per measure:

There are some thirty-five variations and coda. An examination of the first
few variations will show how the music is organized.

In the second variation the theme is played pizzicato by the
strings and by the trombones on the second beat of each measure, following
a pedal-tone chord in the horns that occurs on the beat.

The third variation continues the theme on the second beat of the
measure in the low strings but adds smooth contrapuntal lines in the woodwinds:

In the fourth variation the strings sound the theme on the first
beat of the measure, still in pizzicato style. The winds play a contrapuntal
part in an abrupt, biting manner:

The character of the fifth variation is quite different. The cellos
and string bass play the theme with the bow, while the violins contribute a
broad, romantic countermelody:

The sixth variation adds more instruments to the accompaniment, varies the violin countermelody, and retains the theme only in the pizzicato notes of the string basses:

In the eleventh variation, Brahms makes effective use of simple chords, as he did in the third movement.

At the beginning of the thirteenth variation, the speed at which the notes of the theme are sounded is slowed to one-half the original tempo. This augmentation is achieved by a change of meter. The theme is present largely by implication in the harmony, which serves as accompaniment to a free-sounding flute solo. The fourteenth variation consists of melodious lines in the woodwinds, while both the fifteenth and sixteenth variations are in chorale style.

The return of the theme to its regular tempo is easily heard, because it is the same clear-cut statement that occurred at the beginning of the movement. This return indicates that the music is actually a combination of two forms. First, it is a passacaglia/chaconne. Second, it is a large three-part form, with a slower middle section that emphasizes harmonic settings. Following the slow center section there are another sixteen variations. Generally these are a bit more difficult to follow than those in the first portion of the movement. Included among them are rescorings of variations heard earlier (No. 28 is in the style of No. 6, and No. 29 is No. 7 rescored). Pedal point is used extensively in variation No. 27, and canon in No. 31.

The coda consists of another four settings of the theme. The number of measures becomes irregular and the theme is more disguised, but the listener can sense the relationship of the coda to the theme.

Brahms was fortunate to be able to please both the public and the trained musician. Because of its beautiful sounds, his music can be enjoyed in blissful ignorance of the compositional techniques being employed. On the other hand, because of his skill at writing, his music offers much reward to the listener who seeks to know *why* it sounds good. Perhaps these are the traits that make his music timeless in its appeal.

Richard Strauss at the age of 24, when he was appointed to a position in the Munich Court Opera and composed Don Juan.

RICHARD STRAUSS

Richard Strauss (*Ree*-kard Strouse, 1864–1949) was born of a musical family but was related neither to the Johann Strauss family of waltz fame nor to Oskar Straus, composer of operettas. Richard's father was a horn player in the orchestra at Munich, and his mother was daughter of a wealthy brewer. From his parents he apparently inherited a love of music and a good business sense.

From childhood Strauss displayed unusual musical talent. In his early twenties he was already writing his famous tone poems, and he soon established himself as an outstanding musician. In those days he was considered a radical, an "angry young man." His works were in the general style of Wagner, who had been dead over five years when Strauss wrote *Don Juan,* his first successful tone poem. His music is highly colorful and expressive, sometimes almost blatantly so. Probably it was this quality, rather than any musical innovations, that earned him his early reputation. Until 1900, Strauss confined his compositions largely to tone poems. Six are standard orchestral fare today: *Don Juan, Death and Transfiguration, Till Eulenspiegel's Merry Pranks, Thus Spake Zarathustra, Don Quixote,* and *Ein Heldenleben* (A Hero's Life).

After 1900 Strauss turned to opera. His first successful opera, *Salome* (1906), was a German setting of Oscar Wilde's decadent version of the Biblical story. Although portions of the story are gruesome, especially the scene in which Salome sings to and kisses the decapitated head of John the Baptist, Strauss was able to write music of sufficient artistic merit to prevail over the purely sensational aspects of the story. Strauss' next opera, *Elektra,* is based on a version of Sophocles' play by a Viennese dramatist named Hugo von Hofmannsthal, with whom Strauss collaborated on several operas. Since the opera dwells on the emotions of hatred and revenge, Strauss seized the opportunity to experiment with bold and innovative harmonic writing. In both *Elektra* and *Salome,* the action involved such excesses of bloodletting that the public began to wonder if Strauss could surpass his reputation for producing the macabre. Evidently he could not, or he chose not to do so, because for his next opera, *Der Rosenkavalier* ("The Cavalier of the Rose"); he switched style completely. The story is poignantly humorous, centering about the decadent elegance of the powder-and-wig world of the eighteenth century. The music is romantic and sensuous rather than innovative.

By the end of the First World War, Strauss' creative career was largely behind him. He continued to live in his villa in the Bavarian Alps and write operas until his death in 1949, but he never again saw much success. During the latter years of his life he was treated somewhat as a relic. He was regarded no longer as a daring radical but as a wealthy and outmoded conservative.

Strauss' Don Juan

Strauss wrote *Don Juan* in 1888 when he was twenty-four years old, just three years after Brahms had finished his Fourth Symphony. The literary work that inspired Strauss was a poem by Nicolaus Lenau. Don Juan is the legendary hero whose life has become the prototype of gay abandon and sensuality. There is almost no form of depravity in which he does not indulge as he bounds from one mistress to another. In Lenau's version of the story, Don Juan's escapades are part of his idealistic search for the perfect woman, an explanation that seems hardly credible in light of his conduct. Nevertheless, the harm he has brought to others begins to weigh upon him, and his concern for the pleasure of the moment leaves him increasingly dissatisfied and bored with life. Finally he is challenged to a duel by Don Pedro, the son of a nobleman whom Don Juan has killed. Don Juan battles gloriously and has Don Pedro at his mercy. At that moment he realizes that victory is worthless and that defeat would relieve him of the tedium of living. He allows Don Pedro to kill him.

Strauss included only three excerpts from Lenau's poem at the front of the score. Nothing else is indicated about the program. So the listener can fill out the details to suit himself, and this process may in fact make the music more enjoyable. Like all good program music, however, it can stand very well without literary association.

Despite the fact that Don Juan is a tone poem, it is in a rather loose sonata form. Although many Romantic composers disclaimed the Classical forms they often used at least the basic outline of some of them. The most important theme, which might be called the "Don Juan" theme, is a composite of motives that are developed later in the work. The profusion of melodic ideas is in itself a commentary on Don Juan's nature: impatient for adventure, full of vitality and power, lusting for love and life:

Later:

The first amorous episode suggests lighthearted flirtation:

Soon comes the first true love scene. The winds sound a radiant chord, the solo violin plays sweetly, and this lovely theme appears:

It grows more passionate as the music progresses. When hearing this portion of the work, you may find it helpful to concentrate your attention on the soaring violin line rather than on the intricate accompaniment provided by the remainder of the orchestra. The "Don Juan" theme is heard again as the hero awakens from the oblivion of this love and sets out for new adventures.

His next conquest is less willing. Don Juan pleads with her, and the gasping tones of the flute seem to indicate her halfhearted resistance. She soon weakens, and a second beautiful love theme is heard:

This theme has about it an air of sadness and regret, and there follows the inevitable feeling of boredom. The music reaches a soft, quiet climax, ending with a touch of hopelessness.

Here another "Don Juan" theme appears, played by the four horns.

Presently Don Juan runs to a carnival (in Lenau's version it is a masked ball). The section juggles a theme of its own with motives from the original "Don Juan" theme. After awhile the music becomes increasingly solemn, reflecting Don Juan's feelings of depression. In this condition he sees the ghosts of his previous mistresses, and their melodies reappear.

Then comes the challenge of the duel. Don Juan responds, and the music grows ever stronger, reinforced by the second "Don Juan" theme played again by the horns. The pitch level is three notes higher than it was in its first appearance, and this change adds to the exhilaration of the music. There is a short return of the opening music, which gains in driving force.

Suddenly there is a deathly halt—apparently the moment in which Don Juan decides to give up. The music shifts to minor and the trumpet jabs out a dissonant note. In shuddering sounds, Don Juan's life is ended.

In this tone poem, Strauss associates motives and themes with specific ideas and characters. What was begun with Liszt and Berlioz has been refined and further adapted. Wagner exploited this technique to its fullest in his operas, which will be discussed shortly.

Strauss wrote for a large orchestra. Not only are many instruments required, but most of them play most of the time. This scoring gives the music a thick, heavy sound. Early in *Don Juan* when the solo violin plays, the listener can't help wondering if the orchestra won't soon overwhelm the single instrument. It doesn't; Strauss manages to make the important lines come through.

Strauss' favorite instrument seemed to be the French horn, his father's instrument. He wrote concertos for it and featured it prominently in most of his compositions. In *Don Juan* the horns have the heroic melody. Throughout his writing for French horn he showed its capabilities and thereby promoted the use of the instrument.

GERMAN ROMANTIC OPERA

In the nineteenth century, opera tended to divide into a German type and an Italian type, both of which differed from their eighteenth-century predecessor. German Romantic opera began with Carl Maria von Weber (*Vay*-ber, 1786–1826). In 1821 he wrote *Der Freischütz* (The Free-Shooter), an opera based on German folklore and Romantic ideals. The story concerns a marksman who receives from the black huntsman (that is, the devil) seven magic arrows, six of which do as he wills but the seventh as the devil wills. The devil also gets the soul of the one who receives the arrows. Besides mysticism, the opera features peasants, rustic scenes, and hunting horns. Weber completed two more operas before his early death. Although they are seldom performed today, they exerted a significant influence on Richard Wagner (1813–1883), one of the musical giants of the Romantic era.

RICHARD WAGNER

It is hard to know where to begin or end in discussing the music of Wagner. Entire books have been written on one or another of his operas. In fact, each of his operas has a score the size of a large book. His music is awe-inspiring, profound and pompous, fantastic and forceful. He was a complex musician and a complex personality, with one of history's most massive egos.

As no opera composer before him, Wagner consciously tackled the dilemma of balance between music and drama. In his lengthy philo-

Richard Wagner.

sophical discourses, he often indicated his belief that poetry and music should be one. To meet his artistic goals, he set about creating a vastly different kind of opera, one that he called "music drama" instead of opera.

The music drama necessitated a new and different approach to the concept of libretto. And so Wagner wrote his own texts. The topics were mythological because he felt that such stories best appealed to the emotions. For poetry he revived an old German alliterative form, of which the following is an example:

> Die *L*iebe bringt *L*ust and *L*eid
> Doch in ihr *W*eh auch *w*ebt sie *W*onne.
> (Thus *l*ove doth *l*ighten *l*oss,
> For 'tis from *w*oe she *w*eaves her *w*onder.)

Wagner's favorite libretto themes were not only mythological. They were also rich with philosophical overtones: the struggle between good and evil, the contest between the physical and spiritual, and the idea of redemption through love. Because these overarching themes are present, the characters in the music dramas are not personalities but more nearly symbols or pawns being pushed about by irrevocable forces. In this respect, Wagner approaches the drama of the ancient Greeks.

Next, Wagner refined a technique that Weber had used and that Richard Strauss was later to utilize in *Don Juan*. The technique is to associate a musical motive with a particular character, emotion, or idea; the concept is called *leitmotiv* or "leading motive." As soon as various motives are established, Wagner weaves them in and out of the music at appropriate times to enhance the intrigue of the plot and yet provide unity. Such use of motives also permits the orchestra to assume a more vital role in the music drama, since it can expand on persons and ideas referred to in the text.

Since the division of music into recitatives, arias, and choruses breaks into the forward motion of the drama, Wagner eliminates these forms as independent sections. Instead he creates a flowing, melodious recitative to serve as an unending melody. The vocal line emphasizes the expression of the words being sung. With its continuous interweaving of motives, the orchestra contributes to the impression of never-ending motion. It is incorrect to say that there are no arias in Wagner's music dramas; there are. But they are woven into the continuously flowing music.

To heighten the impression that a musical work is "seamless," Wagner uses much chromatic harmony. That is, by making half-step alterations of chords, he weakens the "magnetic pull" of chords toward a tonic. The absence of a strong tonic means that the music seldom arrives at a cadence point or musical "stopping place." So the feeling of key is nebulous. This harmonic practice led inevitably to music with no semblance of key center whatever—the atonal music of the twentieth century.

Wagner does not treat the orchestra as mere accompaniment for the singers on stage. In his works the importance of the orchestra equals, if not exceeds, that of the singers. In a real sense his orchestra is symphonic, both in its size and in its ability to stand virtually without the vocal parts. In fact, many portions of his operas are performed today as concert pieces without singers. Probably Wagner's greatest genius was his ability to exploit the full resources of the orchestra. He made it produce effects that had previously never been dreamed of—brilliant light as well as dark, somber colors; overwhelming force and sensuous intimacy.

Wagner's "Siegfried's Rhine Journey"

Wagner's most ambitious achievement was a cycle of four complete operas entitled *Der Ring des Nibelungen* (The Ring of the Nibelung). The four operas in the cycle are *Das Rheingold* (The Gold of the Rhine), *Die Walküre* (The Valkyries), *Siegfried,* and *Götterdämmerung* (The Twilight of the Gods).

The story of the cycle of operas is built around some gold supposedly guarded by the Rhine maidens in the Rhine river. The gold is stolen and a curse put on it. (In Romantic operas, the direction of events often hinged on curses and magic potions.) The curse states that if the possessor will renounce love, he will rule the world. The result is a chain of misfortunes affecting all the characters in the drama. The story inspired American Albert Pinkham Ryder's murky painting "Siegfried and the Rhine Maidens," which appears on page 318.

In the Prologue to *Götterdämmerung*, the three Fates or Norns (weavers of destiny) are spinning. When their thread breaks, a terrible catastrophe is predicted. The Fates vanish. At this point, a section of the opera called "Siegfried's Rhine Journey" begins. It is often performed as a concert orchestral number without singers.

The first leitmotiv represents "fate":

There is a short section picturing dawn, and soon the leitmotiv for "Siegfried, the man (or hero)" is heard in the brasses:

Siegfried is the hero in the opera. He has fallen in love with Brünnhilde, the daughter of Wotan, king of the gods. She has given up her divine status because of her love for Siegfried. Here is her leitmotiv:

Brünnhilde's lietmotiv is the basis for a section labeled "Sunrise and the transition to full daylight." The concert version of the music often leaves out the conversation between Siegfried and Brünnhilde. The substance of it is that she is sending him forth to carry out further heroic deeds.

"Siegfried and the Rhine Maidens," painted by the American Albert Pinkham Ryder (1847–1917).

As Siegfried sets out on his journey toward the Rhine, Brünnhilde watches, and her leitmotiv is heard again. Siegfried's leitmotiv appears in a transformed version that indicates "adventure":

A leitmotiv indicating her love is also sounded in the orchestra:

In the opera, the curtain is lowered at this point to mark the end of the Prologue.

The music continues, however. Leitmotivs from earlier operas are brought back and are sometimes combined with other leitmotivs. In Wagner's *Ring*, even the Rhine has its own leitmotiv, which is heard as Siegfried approaches it:

The combined leitmotivs for the Rhine maidens and the gold remind the listener of this curse:

The concert version ends with a closing based on Siegfried's motive. In the opera, the music continues further into Act One.

This brief summary deals with only one small portion of one opera, and that opera is only one of four in *The Ring of the Nibelung*. But the foregoing excerpts offer some insight into Wagner's style. It is hard to assess his music. Some of the time it is brilliant and superbly imaginative. At other times, it is slow-moving and repetitive. The sheer length of his productions makes the task of evaluation difficult. For instance, the *Ring* cycle requires over twelve hours for performance, and it contains more than ninety motives, the exact number depending on how one chooses to count them. For the listener who is unfamiliar with Wagner, the best way to learn about his music is to concentrate on specific short sections, like "Siegfried's Rhine Journey." Attention to the significance of the motives will make the music more meaningful. Besides *The Ring of the Nibelung*,

Wagner's best-known operas are *Tannhäuser, Lohengrin, Tristan and Isolde, Die Meistersinger von Nürnberg* (The Mastersingers of Nuremberg), and *Parsifal.*

Another of Wagner's accomplishments was the theater he built at Bayreuth (By-*royt*). Designing the proper type of theater in which to present his music dramas became Wagner's consuming passion during the latter part of his life. He did more than write his own librettos based on his own stories and compose his own music; he also planned and directed the staging. The Bayreuth theater is wedge-shaped, with the stage placed at the point. The orchestra and conductor are easily seen, and the stage is equipped to handle all the effects required by the dramas. Although the productions are long and the solo roles are difficult to learn, Wagner did not include a prompter's box as an aid to the singers. A Wagnerian music festival is still held annually at Bayreuth, and his descendents still manage the theater.

ITALIAN ROMANTIC OPERA

At the beginning of the nineteenth century, Italian opera was couched in the style found in Mozart's *The Marriage of Figaro*. Gioacchino Rossini (1792–1868) even based his opera *The Barber of Seville* on the same characters found in Mozart's opera. With Vincenzo Bellini (1801–1835), Italian opera reached a high point of interest in melody. The arias in his operas, such as *Norma*, emphasize beautiful singing (*bel canto* in Italian) through technically demanding melodic lines, cadenzas, and ornamentation. Gaetano Donizetti (1797–1848) also contributed to the *bel canto* style of opera. Although these early operas often lacked convincing dramatic qualities, the brilliance of the soloists' lines and the loveliness of the melodies make for highly enjoyable listening.

Italian opera composers seem not to have been influenced by Wagner. They used almost none of his compositional or philosophical ideas. Perhaps the German and Italian temperaments are too dissimilar to embrace the same styles. Or perhaps the reason was more political in its basis: this was the period during which Italy was trying to achieve liberation from Austria. It is doubtful if anything Germanic would have been welcome in Italy during that time. Whatever the reason, Italian opera maintained its own flavor and style, as well as a long tradition.

GIUSEPPE VERDI

The chief name associated with Italian Romantic opera is that of Guiseppe Verdi (*Vair*-dee, 1813–1901). Verdi brought about significant changes. His characters are neither stock roles, as had been found in the Classical period, nor symbols, which they tended to be in Wagner's music dramas. They are more like real persons who react to situations as average people would. Verdi also improved the quality of music in the recitative. No longer was recitative merely the necessary filler between arias or ensembles. His recitatives are melodious and expressive, more like the ideal formulated by the founders of opera. And Verdi lets the orchestra contribute to the mood of the words.

Verdi made another contribution to Italian opera: he insisted on having a good libretto. The usual libretto for earlier operas had been a not-too-carefully prepared version of a mediocre story. Verdi selected the finest literature—Schiller, Victor Hugo, Dumas, Shakespeare. Then he collaborated with the librettist whenever possible to ensure maximum quality.

Verdi's career was long and magnificent, spanning more that fifty years. His last opera, *Falstaff*, was completed when he was seventy-nine! Of the twenty-seven operas he composed, the following are perennial favorites with opera-goers: *Rigoletto* (1851), *Il Trovatore* (1853), *La Traviata* (1853), *Un Ballo in Maschera* ("The Masked Ball") (1859), *La Forza del Destino* ("The Force of Destiny") (1862), *Aïda* (1871), *Otello* (1887), and *Falstaff* (1893).

GIACOMO PUCCINI

Giacomo Puccini (1858–1924) was not so sophisticated a composer as Verdi. He did possess, however, a wonderful gift of melody and an instinct for what would be successful on stage. These abilities have won for his operas a popularity equal to that accorded the works of Verdi.

Puccini belonged to a group of opera composers who stressed *verismo* (realism). Thus he drew material from everyday life, rejecting heroic or exalted themes from mythology and history. He was fond of parallel chord movement and selected chords for their particular sound as well as for their harmonic function.

Puccini's best-known operas include *La Bohème* (1896), *Tosca* (1900), *Madame Butterfly* (1904), which is a story about the marriage of an American naval lieutenant and a Japanese girl, and *Turandot* (1926), which was completed by a friend after Puccini's death.

Puccini's La Bohème

In true *verismo* style, *La Bohème* (The Bohemians) is a story of hippie life on the Left Bank of the Seine in Paris. The setting provides a composer with ample opportunities to inject emotionalism into the music.*

---

* The libretto plus musical examples for the first act of *La Bohème* appears in *Scored for the Understanding of Music.*

Giacomo Puccini about 1908.

The curtain rises on the ramshackle garret in which live four young Bohemians: the poet Rodolfo, the painter Marcello, the philosopher Colline, and the musician Schaunard. Rodolfo and Marcello try to work but can think of little except the bitter cold. It is Christmas Eve and they can't afford fuel for a decent fire. Colline and Schaunard come home shortly and flourish a little of that rare item—money. The landlord, evidently aware of their good fortune, soon comes asking for the rent. By the use of a little chicanery, they are able to get rid of him. They decide to celebrate at the Café Momus, so they leave in high spirits—all except Rodolfo, who is finishing some writing and plans to join them shortly.

There is a knock at the door. It is Mimi. Her candle has gone out, and she cannot see to get up the stairs to her apartment. She is also weak and out of breath, so Rodolfo gives her a little wine and offers her a chair. As he helps her search for the key she dropped on the floor, a draft of wind blows out their candles. They grope in the dark for her key. He finds it and, thinking quickly, slips it into his pocket without telling her. As they continue feeling along the floor, Rodolfo's hand meets hers and he exclaims "Che gelida manina!" ("How cold your little hand is!"). Then begins one of those glorious arias and a duet that exemplify Romantic opera at its best. First, Rodolfo tells Mimi about himself and his lonely life as a poet. In the aria he joins with the orchestra in a luscious Puccini melody:

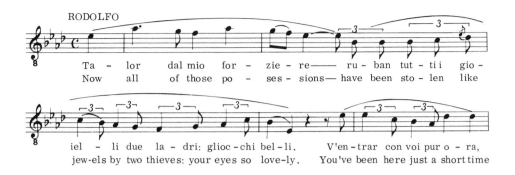

Ta - lor dal mio for - zie - re—— ru - ban tut - ti i gio -
Now all of those po - ses - sions— have been sto - len like

iel - li due la - dri: glioc-chi bel-li. V'en-trar con voi pur o - ra,
jew-els by two thieves: your eyes so love-ly. You've been here just a short time

Mimi responds with an equally beautiful aria, *"Mi chiamano Mimi"* ("I'm always called Mimi"). In it she describes her simple life and her flower embroidery:

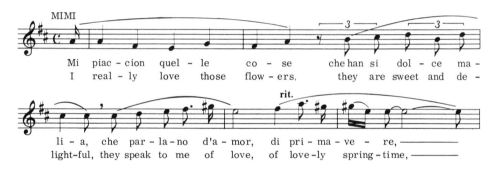

Mi piac - cion quel - le co - se che han si dol - ce ma -
I real - ly love those flow - ers, they are sweet and de -

li - a, che par - la - no d'a - mor, di pri - ma - ve - re,——
light-ful, they speak to me of love, of love-ly spring - time,——

The aria continues with another lovely melody, a phrase that appears later in the opera:

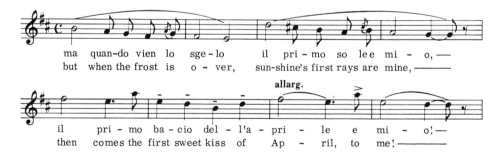

ma quan-do vien lo sge - lo il pri - mo so le e mi - o, —
but when the frost is o - ver, sun-shine's first rays are mine, ——

il pri - mo ba - cio del - l'a - pri - le e mi - o! —
then comes the first sweet kiss of Ap - ril, to me! ——

Rodolfo's friends return to the courtyard outside, urging him not to dawdle. He goes to the window and directs them to return to Momus and reserve a table. Upon the departure of the friends, Mimi and Rodolfo break into a duet in which they speak of the new love that binds them together. Some of the melodies previously introduced in the arias are heard again.

A scene from Act One of La Boheme. *The spotlight shines dramatically on Mimi and Rodolfo as they sing a duet.*

The curtain falls with Mimi and Rodolfo embracing as they sing "Amor."

The realism problem is ever present, even in *verismo* opera. Rodolfo and Mimi tell about themselves briefly, they are interrupted for a few moments, and then—suddenly—they are expounding on their love for each other. Musically, the course of events is well conceived: an aria by the tenor, an aria by the soprano, a short break, and a duet in which they join forces. The scene would not be good opera if the love between the two were allowed to grow more naturally over a period of weeks, or hours at least.

The scene between Rodolfo and Mimi also illustrates the smooth transition between recitative and aria. No longer is there a clear demarcation, particularly now that the recitative has assumed melodic and expressive interest.

For a small, frail girl, Mimi engages in some rather robust singing. Again there is a break with reality that the listener must accept if he is to enjoy the opera. The full, vibrant singing style associated with opera is a musical necessity. The characters in most operas, including Puccini's, react to their environment and emotions on a grand scale. Their responses are exaggerated. Although ordinary persons are reluctant to make declarations of love, especially to people they don't know well, the characters in an opera proclaim their feelings promptly and with magnified intensity. Such a telescoping of emotions and actions is good theater. Ordinary individuals do feel deeply, but they are unlikely to express their feelings with the overt forcefulness of Rodolfo and Mimi. The typical listener, then, responds to opera because he has experienced emotions similar to those depicted on stage, but the timing, degree, and manner of expression are different.

To convey the necessary power and intensity of expression, the singer must produce an "operatic" tone. Anything less will leave the listener cold and unmoved. The vocal style of popular-song artists, even good ones, is inappropriate and inadequate for opera. Most of the currently popular singers lack tonal power, a fact that is usually covered up by amplification systems and recording devices. And then there is the matter of sheer singing ability. Opera singers certainly outclass popular singers when it comes to breath control and endurance, wide pitch range, richness of tone, control of dynamic level, and technical know-how. If a popular singer were to attempt Rodolfo's role, it would be comparable to putting a twelve-year-old boy into the starting lineup of a professional football team.

Opera has acquired some traditions regarding the type of voice and the character to be portrayed. The heroine is almost always a soprano. In most stories she is young and beautiful, so the higher, lighter voice is more suitable. The leading male role is usually sung by a tenor. He is young and frequently sings duets with the soprano, often doubling her note one octave lower. This puts his notes near the top of the male range, and thereby gives the voice quality greater intensity. If there are older people or villains in the plot, the female parts are usually written for mezzo-sopranos or contraltos, the male roles for baritones or basses. Often they are supposed to sound ugly; Madame Flora in *The Medium*, an opera presented in Chapter 15, is an example of this.

The rest of *La Bohème* is equally beautiful and not long. The second act is a delightful scene at the Café Momus in which Musetta, Marcello's former love and notorious flirt, sings a bewitching waltz. In Act Three, Mimi and Rodolfo have broken apart. There is a hint of impending doom because of Mimi's worsening tubercular condition.

In Act Four the setting is again the garret, and there are several musical and dramatic similarities to the first act. This time Musetta enters, saying that Mimi is downstairs, too weak to climb them—an ironic parallel to events of the earlier act. Mimi is helped into the room, and the friends leave quickly to get medicine and medical help. Rodolfo and Mimi recall their first meeting. The old themes are heard, but the music is no longer robust. It is pathetic and shattered. The friends return. They talk quietly among themselves, hoping Mimi can sleep. Suddenly they realize she is dead. "Mimi! Mimi!" Rodolfo cries. The orchestra strikes the chords heard in the love music of the first act. But this time the music is weighted with grief. The curtain falls on a gripping note.

FRANCK, FAURÉ, AND SAINT-SAËNS

César Franck (1822–1890) was a quiet, devout man who taught at the Paris Conservatory and served as organist at St. Clotilde. His compositions caused little stir during his lifetime, partly because he did not travel in the fashionable social circles, partly because his best writing came late in life, and partly because his works were a little too advanced for the audiences of the time. Franck's orientation as an organist was evident in his compositions. He wrote extremely beautiful and complicated harmonies, involving extensive chromatic alteration of chords and unusual modulations.

His D Minor Symphony is cyclical, with themes reappearing in each of its three movements. Completed in 1888, when he was sixty-five, it is his only symphony. The first movement is in sonata form, with a three-note motive as the theme. The second movement features the English horn in an important solo—in Franck's day a rather daring departure from custom, although Berlioz had written similarly in *The Roman Carnival Overture*. The third and final movement recalls earlier themes, and a canon concludes the symphony. It is an impressive musical work.

Gabriel Fauré (1845–1924) was for many years not fully appreciated outside his native France. Like Franck, he was masterful in his handling of harmony, and his music is subtle and melodious. He wrote many songs and a Requiem, which is frequently performed. He also composed for piano, orchestra, and chamber ensembles, especially those including strings.

Camille Saint-Saëns (1835–1921) was a gifted, intelligent man who could converse authoritatively on many subjects other than music. His outlook toward music was more in the Haydn-Mozart Classical tradition than in the Romantic spirit of his time. In this respect he was like Brahms. Unfortunately, in Saint-Saëns' case this attitude leads to music that at times seems to lack conviction. He tried little that was unique or imaginative.

He did write some interesting works, however. The well-known *Danse Macabre* is one of them. The program that inspired the work is a post-midnight dance of the skeletons and spirits in a graveyard; the event ends with the crow of a rooster. Other quality works are *Introduction and Rondo Capriccioso* for violin, an opera, *Samson and Delilah*, and *Carnival of the Animals*.

The Romantic movement in music covers such a vast array of notable persons that few of them can be studied adequately. Some Romantic composers tended to group themselves according to certain interests, and so the next chapter will examine these men and their music.

SUGGESTIONS FOR FURTHER LISTENING

BELLINI: *Norma*

BIZET: *Carmen*

BRAHMS:
Academic Festival Overture
Concerto No. 1 in D Minor for Piano
Concerto in D Major for Violin
Ein Deutsches Requiem (A German Requiem)
Piano music, especially Op. 116–119
Quintet in F Minor for Piano and Strings, Op. 34
Sonatas for Clarinet and Piano
Sonatas for Violin and Piano
Symphonies Nos. 1, 2, and 3
Tragic Overture
Variations on a Theme by Haydn

FAURÉ:
Requiem, Op. 48
Sonata No. 1 in A Major for Violin and Piano
Songs

FRANCK:
Prelude, Fugue and Variation, Op. 18
Sonata in A Major for Violin and Piano
Symphonic Variations for Piano and Orchestra
Symphony in D Minor

LEONCAVALLO: *Pagliacci*

PUCCINI: See page 321

SAINT-SAËNS: See page 328

STRAUSS:
Also Sprach Zarathustra, Op. 30
Ein Heldenleben, Op. 40
Der Rosenkavalier: Waltzes
Salome: Dance of the Seven Veils
Till Eulenspiegel's Merry Pranks, Op. 28
Tod und Verklärung (Death and Transfiguration), *Op. 24*

TCHAIKOVSKY:
Concerto No. 1 in B-Flat Minor for Piano, Op. 23
Concerto in D Major for Violin, Op. 35
Francesca da Rimini, Op. 32
Overture, Romeo and Juliet
Overture, The Year 1812, Op. 49
Serenade in C Major for Strings, Op. 48
Symphonies Nos. 5 and 6

VERDI: See page 321

WAGNER: See page 320

Nationalism, Impressionism, and Post-Romanticism

14

The three "isms" that make up the title of this chapter are distinctively affiliated with the Romantic movement of the nineteenth century. Each basically subscribed to the subjective, philosophical ideas of the time, and each made a significant contribution to the literature of music.

NATIONALISM

Nationalism, when associated with works of art, refers to a deliberate, conscious attempt to develop a mode of artistic expression that is unique to a particular country or region. Often it involves subject matter that is indigenous to only one country, such as a painting of a national event or an opera about a historical character. During the nineteenth century, this attempt at native expression was largely an attempt to break away from the prevailing German-Austrian style. Bach, Mozart, Beethoven, Schubert, Liszt, Schumann, Brahms, and Wagner had long ruled the musical world. To men like Mussorgsky in Russia, Debussy in France, and Grieg in Norway, it was time for a change. They knew that Russians and Frenchmen and Norwegians were as capable of producing good compositions as were the Germans! And they set about proving it.

Several factors in the nineteenth century encouraged nationalistic movements in music. One was the prevalence of Romanticism. It exalted individual feelings and the inherent goodness of man in his natural state. The eighteenth-century man had considered common folk to be untutored and rough; the Romanticist idealized them. He thought of their way of life as good because it was so uncorrupted by the vices of civilization. (It should be noted that almost no Romantic musician *lived* as a peasant. He admired the humble life from a distance.) Furthermore, the life of the common people was a source of subject matter that composers and artists had seldom tapped in the past.

There was another reason for the growing tide of nationalistic art. The nineteenth century was a time of rising political nationalism. The countries of Italy and Germany were finally organized. Wars were pathetically frequent. And in such conflicts, a nation's efforts involved the citizenry to a degree that was unknown in previous centuries. No longer was a war fought by professional soldiers; most of the young men of the nation were involved in one way or another. Nor were sacrifices made for a king who may not have been particularly popular. Now the effort was for France or Germany or Italy. Nationalistic movements in music would probably have occurred even if there had been no political struggles, but the political atmosphere did encourage such music.

In their effort to assert their independence from foreign influence, nationalistic composers often wrote the tempo markings and other musical indications in their native language instead of in the more internationally accepted Italian. So Debussy wrote "Vif" instead of "Vivace," Wagner wrote "Schnell," and some Americans, even today, write "Lively" or "Fast." Such manuscript notation does not effect the sound of the music, of course, but it provides some insight into the composer's thinking and the temper of the times.

THE RUSSIAN FIVE

Until well into the nineteenth century, Russia had little musical tradition of its own. The Tsars imported French and Italian opera as well as French ballet. Mikhail Glinka (1804–1857) was the first native Russian composer to write an opera on a Russian theme. Today he is generally considered the father of Russian music.

More important to the emergence of Russian music was a group of five composers who lived in the latter half of the Romantic period. Their leader was Mily Balakirev (Bah-*lah*-ke-ref, 1837–1910). He himself was not a talented composer, but his contribution was significant. He persuaded the others—César Cui (1835–1918), Alexander Borodin (*Bor*-oh-deen, 1833–1887), Modest Mussorgsky (1839–1881), and Nikolai Rimsky-Korsakov (1844–1908)—that they needn't ape the German style in order to compose great music. He urged them to draw on the musical resources of their native Russia.

Generally the "Five" had little formal training. Balakirev was self-taught, and Cui, an engineer, was not a particularly successful composer. Borodin was a celebrated chemist and an excellent composer. Had he been able to devote more time to composing, his name would be far better known than it is today. His Second Symphony is still performed, as are *In the Steppes of Central Asia* and *String Quartet No. 2*. His greatest work was an opera, *Prince Igor*, which was completed after his death by Rimsky-Korsakov and Alexander Glazounov (1865–1936). Excerpts from Borodin's works furnished the music for the Broadway musical *Kismet*.

Borodin's Polovtzian Dances

Prince Igor is not so much a drama as it is a series of scenes or tableaus. In Act Two there appears a section called "Polovtzian Dances" (Poh-*loft*-zeon). These dances are available in two versions: one is for orchestra alone; the other, more nearly resembling the original, is for chorus and orchestra. The dances themselves are only distantly related to the story line. After a short introductory section, a haunting melody is heard, in a section called "Dance of the Young Girls." (It was incorporated into *Kismet* as the song "Stranger in Paradise.")

The haunting quality of this melody is precisely what marks Borodin's music as nationalistic and Russian. It is inconceivable that Liszt or Brahms would have written that melody—it just isn't Germanic sounding. Nor is there anything Italian, Irish, or American about it. It has the feel of Russia in its sounds. The theme remains fresh and interesting even after its frequent appearances as a popular song.

Its appeal can be partly explained by Borodin's use of harmony and melodic intervals. The melody is in a minor key, but not the minor of Bach, Beethoven, and Brahms. Borodin does not alter the note (E) below the keynote of the scale (F-sharp). He permits it to remain a full step below the keynote instead of raising it a half step, as was common in the minor scale of European music. So the resulting patterns still suggest minor, but with an occasional different interval.

Alexander Borodin.

In this dance, Borodin's chord choice is unusual, too. He moves outside the framework of the dominant-tonic progressions that the listener expects. His harmonies are somewhat unconventional and yet they sound natural and appealing. Borodin's musical insights were instinctively so keen that he could compose effectively even without extensive formal knowledge.

Without pause, the music moves to the "Dance of the Men." It features a brilliant clarinet solo, which is soon taken up by other instruments. As the clarinet finishes his solo, the brasses come in strongly with a vigorous theme reminiscent of the music in the slow introduction. There is a regular beat, but syncopation is frequent:

The music has an unmistakably primitive quality about it. This, too, is a feature of Russian nationalistic music. To the cultured European musician of the day, this music sounded coarse and crude. The nature of the sound can be explained by Borodin's manipulation of the musical material.

In the third measure of this dance the interval C–G appears. Borodin deliberately leaves out the middle note, E, which would have produced a complete chord. He also includes a pedal tone. Although this device was used even before the time of Bach, Borodin's use of it is different. With Bach, the pedal tone was consonant more often than not. The situation is just the reverse with Borodin; until the end of this melody, the pedal tone is almost never a consonant chord member.

The "General Dance" that comes next is novel, even after a hundred years. The rhythm has a barbaric force that impels the music along. Again there are pedal tones and chords with their middle notes missing. The contrasting middle section of the dance is named "Dance of the Female Slaves." The long tone before the three chromatic notes in the melody sounds like some enticing movement of the girls as they dance for the Khan.

The "Dance of the Little Boys" is in a brilliant $\frac{6}{8}$ meter conducted with one beat per measure. Logically, the "Dance of the Little Boys" grows into "Dance of the Men." The rapid notes of the boys' dance are combined with a barbaric melody sung by the men:

The dances are then repeated and combined. First the young girls' music is heard, then it is enhanced with a flashy line of counterpoint in the violins and flutes. The dances of the boys and men are repeated before a second "General Dance" concludes the work. Even this final number is a combination of an earlier dance—the first "Dance of the Men"—with long, sustained notes in the chorus. The music pushes forward to a dazzling conclusion.

Another important member of the "Five" was Rimsky-Korsakov. He was an officer in the navy, with which he sailed extensively; his travels included a trip to the United States. At the age of twenty-seven he was appointed professor of composition and orchestration at the Conservatory of St. Petersburg. Like Berlioz, he wrote a widely used treatise on writing for instruments.

Rimsky-Korsakov represents a phase of Romanticism called "exoticism." Like many other Romantic composers, he felt drawn by the mystery and splendor of Eastern cultures. For example, his best-known work is *Scheherazade,* a tone poem based on the Persian legends in *A Thousand and One Nights.* His "Song of India," from the opera *Sadko,* and "Hymn to the Sun," from the opera *Le Coq d'Or* (The Golden Cockerel) are other familiar works that reveal his keen interest in the Orient. Rimsky-Korsakov also wrote nationalistic music and worked avidly to advance the cause of Russian music.

Mussorgsky's Boris Godunov

Of the "Five," the most original was Mussorgsky. He chose an army career and later became a clerk in the engineering department. He was perhaps the most technically inept of the composers with whom his name is linked, but he is the one whose music best represents the Russian character. His opera *Boris Godunov* (*Goh*-duh-noff) uses a libretto derived from a play by Pushkin.

Boris Godunov does not follow as concise a plot as do most operas. Pushkin's play contained twenty-four scenes. Mussorgsky adapted the libretto himself, using only seven scenes and changing them extensively. The story concerns Tsar Boris, who ruled from 1598 to 1605. For many years it was believed that he had instigated the young prince Dmitri's murder in order to gain the throne. Although recent scholarly research has indicated that Boris was innocent of this crime, the murder is presumed to have taken place before the action of Mussorgsky's opera begins, and it is central to the rest of the plot. The opera describes Boris' mental torment (stemming from his feelings of guilt) and finally his death. There is a scheming adventuress who seeks, with an ambitious pretender to the throne, to capture the Kremlin. The real losers are the people, who must inevitably suffer from the greed and ambition of those who would be Tsar.

Study of the music will point up Mussorgsky's musicianship and his flair for the dramatic. The Prologue features the people of Russia, who are the real heroes of the opera. Afraid for the future, they pray for a ruler for their land. To encourage a greater public clamor for himself, Boris sends one of his lieutenants to tell the crowd that Boris still refuses to become the Tsar. A chorus of religious pilgrims approaches and sings before the curtain falls on the Prologue.

The "Coronation Scene," which follows, is one of the most famous in all opera. It takes place in a courtyard of the Kremlin. The Cathedrals of the Assumption and the Archangels flank the stage.

The orchestra opens with moody and ponderous music, containing dissonant intervals and distant modulations. In music, one of the most

Modest Mussorgsky.

dissonant and awkward intervals occurs when an octave is divided into two equal segments, each containing three *whole* steps (six half steps). The persistent bass "chord" heard in the first two measures of this scene is made up of only that interval. Furthermore, the orchestra alternates between a chord built on A-flat and another on D, two notes that are themselves a distance of three whole steps apart. How unconventional and nationalistic in its sound, how unlike the music of Europe! A few measures later, the higher-pitched instruments present an imaginative contrapuntal line.

From a porch on the Cathedral comes the cry "Long life to thee, Tsar Boris Feodorovich!" The crowd then shouts its praises to him, singing this Russian folk song in a stirring manner:

The text is: "Like unto the bright sun in the sky, Glory! Glory! Is the glory of Russia's Tsar Boris! Glory! Long may you live and reign, O Tsar, our father!"

The Coronation Scene from Boris Godunov.

Mussorgsky's innovative ideas can be observed in this passage:

If you take the notes of each part on the words "Tsar, our fa-," you'll find that they form a scale: A-flat B-flat C D E F-sharp A-flat. But what kind of a scale is that? It has no half steps as do all major and minor scales; it contains only whole steps. So it is called, logically, a *whole-tone scale.* In 1872, when Mussorgsky was writing this opera, whole-tone scales had not often been encountered in serious musical compositions. The unusual effect of this tonal pattern was not lost on Mussorgsky, and in his genius he employed it in just the right musical situation. No wonder that twenty years later Claude Debussy had only highest praise for Mussorgsky and *Boris Godunov.* Debussy himself exploited whole-tone scales quite extensively.

When Boris finally appears in the opera, he is clearly a troubled man. Already the feelings of guilt for ordering the murder of the youthful heir are gnawing at his soul. The text of his solo is:

My soul is sad!
Strange, dark forebodings and evil presentiments
Oppress my spirit.
Oh, Holy Saint, oh my Almighty Father!
Look down from heaven on the tears of thy sinful servant,
And send down thy holy blessing upon my reign!
May I be honest and merciful as Thou,
And reign in glory over my people.

Boris' words are indicative of the probing treatment Mussorgsky gives this complex personality in the opera.

Finally Boris agrees to order the coronation celebration. As he sings the words of invitation to the feast, the quality of the music changes.

Now let us go to kneel
Before the tombs of Russia's former monarchs.
Then all the people are summoned to a feast;
All, from the boyars to the blind beggars,
All are invited, all shall be my honored guests.

"Glory! Glory! Glory!" shout the people. "Long may you live and reign, O Tsar, our father!" At this point the bells of the Moscow cathedrals begin to peal. Mussorgsky calls for a period of silence in the music, so that each conductor may direct the sounding of all the bells at his disposal for as long as he desires. The chorus then repeats the words and music with which they began the scene.

Throughout the "Coronation Scene" a virile, masculine quality is evident. Mussorgsky's admiration for the vigor and strength of his people has found its way into his music. The role of Boris must be sung by a genuinely bass voice to give the impression of a mighty man, the leader of all Russia. To have given this part to a lyric tenor would have been a terrible mistake. The best singer for the role of Boris is the one who gives the impression that he is six and a half feet tall, weighs at least two hundred and fifty pounds, and could bend steel rails with his bare hands.

Boris' solo is extremely expressive and flexible. It suggests both an aria and a recitative because the union of words and music seems perfect. For example, his prayer sounds almost like chant, which is completely natural and appropriate, since chant is a predominant feature of Russian Orthodox worship.

The chorus parts illustrate another aspect of Russian music: rhythmic flexibility. As was demonstrated in the African children's song in Chapter 2, the metrical pattern is broken when the text calls for it. This practice of Mussorgsky's forecasts the metrical freedom that would be exploited in twentieth-century western music.

At the end of the scene, Mussorgsky anticipates the use of polymeters in twentieth-century music.

The bass-clef orchestral parts sound as though they are in $\frac{2}{4}$ meter, because alternate beats are emphasized. But the $\frac{3}{4}$ meter signature is retained, and the choral parts adhere to it. So the effect is that of two different meters occurring simultaneously. This technique is called *polymeter*. It and its close relative polyrhythm, which was also described in Chapter 2, will appear far more frequently in twentieth-century art music, too.

The innovations in harmony and the freer rhythms made Mussorgsky's music fresh and different. In fact, in 1872 it was so innovative that it was looked on with suspicion. Even Mussorgsky's friends and admirers had trouble understanding everything he did. *Boris Godunov* was twice rejected for performance by the Imperial Opera. Only after two reworkings and a performance of three scenes at a benefit concert was it performed in its entirety and published. After Mussorgsky's death in 1881, Rimsky-Korsakov served as musical executor of his estate. He had the bulk of Mussorgsky's music published, but only after he had made many "improvements"; that is, he rewrote the orchestrations and harmony to sound a bit more conventional.

It is interesting to observe how Mussorgsky handles the drama-music dilemma mentioned in the preceding chapters. The drama within each scene moves at a nearly normal pace. For example, when Boris invites the crowd to the feast, his singing of the line is not much slower than would be the speaking of such a proclamation. His aria occurs at a logical point, and the fact that he makes a short speech is also to be expected. Although the action within the opera moves at a rather realistic pace, long periods of time elapse between scenes, and geographical distances occur from scene to scene, so that the episodes lead into one another in only a loose fashion.

Mussorgsky wrote in other mediums in addition to opera. He was an especially good art-song composer. One of his most unusual and popular songs is entitled "The Flea." His tone poem *Night on Bald Mountain* is descriptive and somewhat eerie. *Pictures at an Exhibition*, originally for solo piano, was orchestrated by Maurice Ravel. It is an exciting work in either form, a musical description of a series of paintings created by Victor Hartmann, an artist friend of Mussorgsky's. The music ranges in mood from the twittering "Ballet of the Chickens in Their Shells" to the massive finale, "The Great Gate of Kiev."

OTHER NATIONALISTIC COMPOSERS

The desire to write music native to one's own country was by no means confined to the Russians, although the movement was most pronounced in that country.

Bohemia (what is today part of Czechoslovakia) produced two nationalistic composers in Antonín Dvořák (Da-*vor*-zhock, 1841–1904) and Bedřich Smetana (*Smet*-nuh, 1824–1884). Throughout most of the nineteenth century, Bohemia had been a part of the Austrian empire. The Bohemians found outlets for their nationalistic aspirations in a revival of their

language and music. The style of Dvořák and Smetana does not differ substantially from the prevailing Romantic style of the time. Bohemia was too
steeped in the German-Austrian culture to create new styles. So its nationalism found a voice in folk melodies and native subject matter. Music
from Smetana's opera *The Bartered Bride* is frequently performed today,
and much of it is delightfully Bohemian. Dvořák also arranged native
dances and wrote several operas. His Fourth Symphony makes skillful and
charming use of folk-like melodies.

Much of Dvořák's fame with American audiences stems indirectly
from his trip to America in 1892. He was captivated by the distinctive
elements of American folk tunes, and he set out to write in that style
himself. The melodies in his *Symphony No. 9* ("From the New World")
were not existing American folk tunes; rather, they were an attempt to
reflect the vigor and vitality of America—the New World. He also wrote a
string quartet designated by the adjective "American."

Edvard Grieg (1843–1907) was the leading proponent of Scandinavian music. Among his well-known works are the *Peer Gynt* Suites,
which were originally written as incidental music for Ibsen's play. He also
wrote a highly successful and melodious Piano Concerto, as well as many
shorter piano pieces and chamber works.

Jean Sibelius (1865–1957), mentioned in Chapter 1, also exhibited nationalistic tendencies, especially in the early part of his career. One
of the themes from his *Finlandia* was made the national anthem of his
native Finland. He also used native themes as the basis for program works
such as *The Swan of Tuonela* and *Pohjola's Daughter*.

The music of Edward Elgar (1857–1934) enjoys perennial popularity among his fellow Englishmen and the musical world at large. His
music is not conspicuously different from that of other Romantic composers,
nor is it particularly nationalistic, but it is melodious and varied. It has an
appeal that was to blossom in the twentieth century in the works of his
English successors Ralph Vaughan Williams and Benjamin Britten. Elgar,
incidentally, is the composer of *Pomp and Circumstance,* the stately march
that has become standard fare at graduation exercises. More typical of his
writing, and more worthy of attention, is his *"Enigma" Variations.* On the
score, before each variation, he has inscribed anagrams, initials, and other
clues to indicate which family member or friend is being represented in
each variation. Guessing the intended identities is the puzzle or "enigma"
for which the work is named. This composition would be little more than a
clever gimmick were not the music so listenable and well-constructed in
itself.

Nationalism in Italy was evident primarily in its operatic tradition. Italian nationalism in instrumental music did not come to the fore until
the twentieth century, with the works of Ottorino Respighi (Res-*peeg*-ee,
1879–1936). His familiar *Pines of Rome* and *Fountains of Rome* are avow-
edly nationalistic, and his use of coloristic effects is typically Romantic.

In other countries, too, the tide of nationalism has been prominent in the twentieth century. The United States is one such country. Its music will be discussed in Chapter 16. Spain is another. Composers such as Isaac Albéniz (Al-*bay*-nez, 1860–1909), Enrique Granados (1867–1916), and Manuel de Falla (de *Fy*-ya, 1876–1946) exploited the incomparable rhythm of Spanish dances. Although their careers extended into the twentieth century, their works, like Respighi's, are essentially Romantic in character.

IMPRESSIONISM

The predominant style of French music at the end of the nineteenth century and the beginning of the twentieth was *impressionism*. In one sense it represented French nationalism, because it was a conscious attempt to break away from the influence of German music. French composers also wrote program works based on French stories. But impressionism made more of a mark in the musical world.

Impressionism is an artistic viewpoint. It is based on the belief that experiences in life are largely impressions of sensations rather than detailed observations or artificial experiences. For example, when we enter a room we don't note every imperfection or the placement of each small article. Under normal circumstances, we are content to gain a general impression of the room and to disregard the unnecessary details within it.

Impressions are not stationary. A cloud may reveal an interesting and distinctive shape, but within a minute or two it has changed somewhat. People move about, too. They do not normally pose in the manner traditionally required by portrait painters. And so impressionistic painters caught people at a particular moment in a casual, unposed situation.

Impressionist painters also experimented boldly in the treatment of light, since lighting conditions markedly affect the visual impression of a scene. Realizing that a view changes as the light conditions change, impressionist artists attempted to capture a scene quickly. They would make several rough sketches of a landscape. Perhaps they would make one early in the morning, another at noon, and yet another at sunset, and then they would finish the scenes as necessary in the studio. Their most frequent subjects were landscapes and casual views of people. Claude Monet's "Rouen Cathedral, West Facade, Sunlight" (plate 9) demonstrates the impressionistic style of painting.

Writers and poets worked along similar lines. Some, including Mallarmé and Verlaine, were known as symbolists because they were more interested in mystery and broad truths than in reality. Symbolism appealed to these writers because a symbol hints at a truth without actually stating it. Here again is the characteristic vagueness of impressionism. Lines in a poem were intended to convey an impression through the sounds and rhythms of the words. Definite meaning was avoided. According to Mallarmé, "To name an object is to destroy three-quarters of the pleasure in it."

The impressionistic movement was unusual in the extent to which writers, artists, and musicians were united by common attitudes. Many of them knew and admired one another's work. They exchanged ideas. Perhaps the impressionist view of time was the common denominator among the arts: the painter wanted to capture a fleeting moment on canvas, the author in the printed and spoken word, and the composer in the transitory world of sound. And so they shared in common the subtle nuances of light and shadow, the vague contours, and the veiled thoughts that mark the impressionist. The compositions of Claude Debussy are the epitome of impressionism in music.

CLAUDE DEBUSSY

Claude Debussy (Deb-yew-see, 1862–1918) was born in a small town near Paris, and at the age of eleven he entered the Paris Conservatory. He often revolted against the rules of composition his professors tried to teach him, a trait that lasted throughout his life. When he was twenty-two, one of his compositions won him the Prix de Rome, a coveted award that included a period of study in Rome.

Debussy loved the gaiety and bustle of Paris and he also valued the company of painters and writers, such as Mallarmé, in whose home they often gathered. His early admiration for Wagner faded after a second visit to Bayreuth in 1889, and he developed a strong dislike for German Romantic music and philosophy. Being a writer of articles on music, he articulated his sentiments well. Of that beloved German tradition, sonata form, he wrote that it is "a legacy of clumsy, falsely imposed traditions." He considered thematic development to be a type of dull "musical mathematics," and is reported to have said to a friend at a concert, "Let's go—he's beginning to develop!" Debussy stated his views more seriously in this way: "Extreme complication is contrary to art. Beauty must appeal to the senses, must provide us with immediate enjoyment, must impress or insinuate itself into us without any effort on our part."

He offered another observation to fellow Frenchmen who were tempted to imitate Wagner: "The French forget too easily the qualities of clarity and elegance peculiar to themselves and allow themselves to be influenced by the tedious and ponderous Teuton." His comments regarding the *leitmotiv* principle and *The Ring of the Nibelung* were unfavorable, at best: "The idea of spreading one drama over four evenings! Is this admissible, especially when in these four evenings you always hear the same thing? My God! how unbearable these people in skins and helmets become by the fourth night."

9

Monet: *Rouen Cathedral, West Facade, Sunlight.* (Chester Dale Collection, National Gallery of Art, Washington, D.C.)

10

Kandinsky: *Improvisation No. 30.* (The Art Institute of Chicago, Arthur Jerome Eddy Memorial Collection.)

Claude Debussy.

Debussy, predictably, cast his own opera, *Pelléas et Mélisande,* from a completely different mold. Built on a story by Maeterlinck, it is dreamlike and restrained. In one scene with her lover Pelleas, Melisande unbinds her hair while doves fly about. The text is elusive; nothing is stated clearly. Melisande's words exemplify the effect: "Neither do I understand each thing that I say, do you see . . . I do not know what I have said . . . I do not know what I know . . . I say no longer what I would." The opera has not won a place in the hearts of a majority of the opera-going public, but many critics consider it a masterpiece, and it did establish Debussy as a first-rate composer during his lifetime. The techniques employed in it have fascinated musicians ever since it was first presented in 1902.

World War I profoundly affected Debussy. For a while it caused him to lose all interest in music. The war was not his only torment, however, for he was slowly dying of cancer. In March, 1918, during the bombardment of Paris, he died.

Debussy was a careful workman, and his piano works are held in high regard, perhaps because they reveal a free and sensitive style that is reminiscent of Chopin. Debussy added much that was his own, however: parallel chord movement (forbidden in conventional harmonic writing), chords with added notes, and new colors. He desired that the patterns of his piano works be merged, in performance, to produce a "sonorous halo"—an apt description of impressionism. His "Clair de Lune" (Moonlight) is widely known. Other works representative of his piano writing are *La Cathédrale Engloutie* (The Sunken Cathedral), *Reflets dans l'Eau* (Reflections in the Water), and his several preludes.

His orchestral works, too, are typically impressionistic. There are three Nocturnes, each conveying a distinctive mood: *Nuages* (Clouds), *Fêtes* (Festivals), and *Sirènes* (Sirens). In *La Mer* (The Sea), Debussy writes his impressions of the sea as it might be observed on three different occasions. Also frequently performed are *Ibéria* and the perennial favorite *Prélude à l'après-midi d'un Faune* (Prelude to the Afternoon of a Faun).

Debussy's **Prelude to the Afternoon of a Faun**

As a literary springboard for this work, Debussy turned to a poem by his friend Stéphane Mallarmé. The faun referred to in the poem is not a deer but a mythical creature, half-man and half-goat, who dwells in the forest. His interests are simple and sensual, as you can tell from the story. The faun awakens from a wine-induced sleep, with vague visions of having been visited by three lovely nymphs. Is he recalling a dream or reality? He'll never know. The afternoon is balmy and restful, so he decides to fall asleep again.

This work in some ways resembles a tone poem, but its scope is considerably smaller. The pattern is only loosely *A B A*, and Debussy does not attempt to tell Mallarmé's tale specifically. He tries only to convey the mood of the poem—the impression of a lazy afternoon and an idyllic existence. Accordingly, the music has a dreamy, relaxed beginning and conclusion and a voluptuous center section.

The orchestration of the music contributes to its impressionistic "feel." The flute opens the work with a solo line:

The harp answers with a shimmering effect called a *glissando,* in which the strings are sounded consecutively in rapid, scalewise fashion. The effect is that of nebulous waves of sound rather than individual notes.

Debussy does not call for many full chords from the brasses in his music. The *Prelude* does not even require a tuba, trumpets, or trombones. There are no drums, either. (Such instruments would never be lacking in Wagner's works!) Furthermore, Debussy is economical in his use of instruments. Unlike the individual lines in music of Strauss and Brahms, many of

Debussy's instrumental parts have lengthy passages with nothing but rests.

Debussy knew how to write to get the desired sounds out of the instruments. He does not ask the flute to play its opening solo in its high, brilliant range. Instead, he writes the passage in the lower portion of the flute range, where the tone quality is soft and warm. Near the beginning, he writes a violin accompaniment for the flute solo:

What he wants is a quiet, shimmering sound, and so he directs the violinists to play with the bow over the fingerboard (*sur la touche*), to make the tone softer in quality as well as dynamic level. Then he calls for *tremolo*—short strokes produced by rapid agitation of the bow back and forth across the string. A similar quivering effect by the violins is called for later in the piece. This time it is produced by the fingers of the left hand as they play two alternating pitches in quick succession, in a pattern lasting several moments. The French horns are not given a noble melody, such as was found in *Don Juan;* instead they play a mellow and melodious part. Frequently they are directed to *mute* the sound by inserting the right hand tightly into the bell of the horn. At the close of the piece, Debussy requests the harpist to touch the strings lightly to produce a crystalline, bell-like sound called a *harmonic.*

Debussy heard Javanese and other Eastern music performed at the International Exposition in Paris in 1889. (The Eiffel Tower was built for that Exposition.) The sounds fascinated him, and so he incorporated some of these tonal effects in his compositions. The *Prelude* calls for antique cymbals: tiny metal discs fastened to the thumb and fingers and valued for the bell-like sound emitted when they are tapped against one another.

Two other measures further illustrate Debussy's skill in orchestration (see page 348). The English horn has a short melodic figure, followed by a splash of sound from three flutes and an ascending glissando in the harp. The next measure is similar, but the glissando moves downward. It is impossible to imagine these measures successfully transcribed for piano; too much of the color and sweep of the sounds would be lost.

Debussy emphasizes chords and scales that contribute to the nebulous, impressionistic character of his music. The whole-tone scale, for example, is evident in the clarinet and flute solos occurring about three minutes from the start of the piece. Instead of simple chords containing three different pitches, Debussy employs chords of four and even five different pitches. The music modulates so freely that it cannot be said to center around any one key.

In true impressionistic fashion, the rhythm is blurred and the beat is not easily felt. Never in the piece is the listener tempted to tap his foot. A heavy beat would, of course, have destroyed the dreamy, smooth quality of the music, just as sharp lines would change the character of an impression-istic painting.

The principal melody of the center portion has been marked in the following example to indicate where the beats occur. (When two notes, with no other notes between, *of the same pitch* are connected by a curved line—that is, a *tie*—they are played as one note lasting for the combined duration of both. The dots below the tied notes in the lower line indicate a gentle articulation of each note.)

You can see that many notes in the melody and even more in the accompanying strings (bottom line of the example) do not occur on the beat. Furthermore, on only a limited number of beats do the notes of the melody and accompaniment coincide. When the strings take up the melody a few measures later, the rhythm has become even more intricate. The woodwinds play a figure built out of triplets, the two harps maintain a steady three beats per measure, and the strings present the syncopated rhythm of the melody.

Debussy's care in composing can be seen in the completeness with which he marks each part. For example, in the two measures of full score on page 348, the dynamic markings for each instrument are given as completely as possible. By giving attention to such details (which late Romantic composers typically did), he is able to achieve the maximum musical effect with the minimum number of instruments and little dependence on instrumental doubling. A far cry from the traditions of the Baroque era, when players were responsible for filling in much of the music as they played, and when entire pages would appear without a dynamic marking on them.

Debussy tried to break with the past. He wanted to write music that differed substantially from the prevailing Romanticism. In some ways he succeeded. His music is different; no one can for long confuse it with the music of Brahms or Wagner. In other ways he fell short of his goal. His music is still basically Romantic. This result is to be expected, since Romanticism and impressionism are so similar in outlook: the emphasis on subjective feeling, the fondness for mystery, and the desire to recreate a mood. But by breaking with rules of the past, Debussy pointed to the new paths that more recent composers have pursued.

MAURICE RAVEL

The fact that Maurice Ravel (1875–1937) followed Debussy both chronologically and stylistically has tended to place him in the background despite his many fine compositions. He did have the good fortune to be born into the family of a mining engineer who had once aspired to be a musician himself. So the father encouraged his talented son's musical education. Like Debussy, Ravel studied at the Paris Conservatory. Although he was a composer of some merit, the professors at the Conservatory four times denied him the coveted Prix de Rome, an award for which he was highly qualified. The arbitrary nature of these decisions caused a public furor that eventually led to the resignation of the Conservatory's director.

A French patriot, Ravel drove an ambulance along the front lines during the First World War. After the war he was recognized as France's leading composer, and he toured the United States in 1928. Eventually his polished post-impressionistic compositions became dated in a world whose tastes had changed since the turn of the century. As he grew older, he became more despondent and depressed. At about the age of sixty, he acquired a rare disease of the brain and slowly lost his speech and motor coordination. In desperation he agreed to a dangerous operation, from which he never regained consciousness.

One of Ravel's best-known orchestral works is his *Bolero,* which draws its rhythm and spirit from the Spanish dance of the same name. He wrote it in 1928, and its fame derives from its hypnotic melody, its gradual crescendo that proceeds uninterrupted from beginning to end, and its two-measure rhythmic pattern that is reiterated without pause throughout the entire seventeen-minute work. Ravel declared that someday he would hear a fruit vendor singing it in the street, and his prediction actually came true. Other works include the *Concerto in G Major for Piano, Concerto for the Left Hand, Daphnis et Chloé, La Valse, Rapsodie Espagnole* (Spanish Rhapsody), and *Ma Mère l'Oye* (Mother Goose)—a ballet from which he compiled music for a suite.

Originally written for Diaghilev's Ballet Russe, *Daphnis et Chloé* was rewritten by Ravel into two suites. The second of these is an enormously exciting work that presents music from three scenes in the ballet. "Daybreak" offers a musical impression of rippling brooks, the songs of birds, and shepherd's tunes. "Pantomime" portrays a mythical meeting of the shepherd with Pan and the nymph Syrinx. The invention of a simple musical instrument, the Pan's pipe, is represented by a long flute solo. The final scene of the Suite is the "General Dance," which suggests a fiery, pagan ritual and emphasizes the unusual meter of $\frac{5}{4}$.

Impressionism is a rather narrow concept, and its potential has seldom been realized in the hands of anyone but Debussy and Ravel. Its love of the subdued is quickly consumed, so that a composer has no place to go, save to other styles. It does represent French elegance, however, and is a

Maurice Ravel.

fascinating style of music that easily finds favor with today's listener.

To understand impressionistic music, one must realize that its appeal is delicate, refined, and sensual. Debussy and Ravel were marvelously skilled not at developing themes but at creating beautiful sounds, luscious chords, and elegant nuance. Its beauty does, in Debussy's words, "appeal to the senses."

To the musician, one technical contribution of impressionism is especially significant: it treated dissonance freely. And with successful results! For centuries composers believed that every dissonance had to be prepared and resolved. But impressionist composers proved that some dissonance can be handled differently without shock to the listener's sensibilities. This discovery opened new doors to succeeding generations of composers.

POST-ROMANTICISM

The influence of the Romantic period was so pervasive that it was felt through the early years of the twentieth century. In fact, elements of Romanticism can still be found in music written today, and they will probably always be evident to some degree in artistic works of the future. As might be expected, therefore, a number of composers continued to explore the musical possibilities of the nineteenth-century style even after it had been supplanted by other trends. Three of these men, by dint of their musical keenness, merit a place on any list of outstanding composers.

One is Jean Sibelius, whose *Symphony No. 2* was cited in Chapter 1 and whose nationalistic compositions were mentioned earlier in this chapter. Sibelius' reputation among musicians stems primarily from his symphonies and a violin concerto. The fourth movement of his *Symphony No. 2* is a good example of his style of symphonic writing. He employs vibrant, motive-like themes, ones that seem as sturdy and enduring as the rocks and trees of his native Finland. Then he treats the themes to an enormous amount of development. He is fond of ostinato—those persistent, continuous accompanying figures—and he exploits this device to help build toward climactic moments. He is also a master in writing for the brasses of the orchestra, achieving from them a maximum of brilliance and power.

Sibelius' symphonies are often cyclical. Usually they do not contain traditional forms. The music has a free sound, with many stops and starts and changes of tempo.

In 1914 Sibelius visited the United States, where he conducted some concerts and received an honorary doctorate from Yale University. Although he lived until 1957, almost all of his works were written before 1925. *Symphony No. 2* was completed in 1901. The last years of his life were spent teaching.

Sergei Rachmaninoff (1873–1943) was famous as a composer and pianist during his lifetime. Like several post-Romantic composers, he tended to be in the shadow of someone else's musical style. In Rachmaninoff's case, it was Tchaikovsky. Rachmaninoff at times equalled his predecessor in the writing of lovely, sentimental melodies, although his composing techniques were perhaps not so imaginative. His best works are for piano, with the Second Piano Concerto being the most popular. Like Brahms and Liszt, he drew on a violin caprice by Paganini for his *Rhapsody on a Theme of Paganini*. His solo piano works include two frequently performed Preludes, one in C-sharp minor and another in G minor.

Gustav Mahler (1860–1911) was a successful conductor as well as an excellent composer. He had a strongly vocal outlook on music. Not only did he write many songs; he conceived his instrumental music in a style that is more vocal than instrumental. He followed Beethoven's lead by combining voices and orchestra in several concert works. Mahler believed in the unity of the arts and often combined music, poetry, and philosophical ideas into his compositions. Like Sibelius, he abandoned traditional forms. Instead, his symphonies contain many song-like melodies that are woven together, often contrapuntally, in an intriguing manner. The music sounds so effortless that the listener can easily miss the expertise in his handling of the musical ideas.

Mahler and Anton Bruckner, his teacher, both exhibit one of the traits of Romanticism: a tendency toward musical elephantiasis. Mahler's

Symphony No. 3 holds the dubious distinction of being the longest ever written. It consumes about one hour and thirty-four minutes, with its first movement alone requiring nearly forty-five minutes of performance time. His Eighth Symphony is sometimes called "the Symphony of a Thousand" because it requires so many people to perform it: a gigantic orchestra, additional brass, and male, female, and children's choirs. Amazingly, Mahler does not allow the music to be engulfed; he handles the vast resources with skill and discretion.

Perhaps the length and bulk of these symphonies are omens of the frustration that composers were beginning to feel with the Romantic style. How far can one go in giving vent to feelings without becoming sentimental or bombastic? How much longer than one hour and thirty-four minutes can a symphony be without becoming an intolerable bore? If a thousand performers are augmented, will the music be any better for it? Sibelius and Mahler were able to develop some individuality within the Romantic style. But its resources were fast being consumed. A mood of change was in the air even as the post-Romanticists were composing.

SUGGESTIONS FOR FURTHER LISTENING

BORODIN:

In the Steppes of Central Asia
Quartet No. 2 in D Major
Symphony No. 2 in B Minor

DEBUSSY:

Estampes, for piano
Ibéria
La Mer
Nocturnes
Quartet in G Minor, Op. 10
Sonata No. 1 in D Minor for Cello and Piano
Sonata No. 3 in G Minor for Violin and Piano

GLINKA:

Overture, Russlan and Ludmila

MAHLER:

Songs of a Wayfarer
Symphony No. 1 in D Major
Symphony No. 4 in G Major.

MUSSORGSKY:

Khovantchina: Introduction and Dance of the Persian Slaves
Night on Bald Mountain
Pictures at an Exhibition

RACHMANINOFF:
Concerto No. 2 in C Minor for Piano, Op. 18
Rhapsody on a Theme of Paganini, Op. 43
Symphony No. 2 in E Minor, Op. 27

RAVEL:
Concerto in D Major for the Left Hand
Concerto in G Major for Piano and Orchestra
Daphnis et Chloé: Suite No. 2
Gaspard de la nuit
Introduction and Allegro for Harp, Flute, Clarinet, and String Quartet
Ma Mère l'Oye: Suite
Rapsodie Espagnole
La Valse

RIMSKY-KORSAKOV:
Capriccio Espagnol, Op. 34
Russian Easter Overture, Op. 36
Scheherazade, Op. 35

SIBELIUS:
Concerto in D Minor for Violin, Op. 47
Pohjola's Daughter, Op. 49
Swan of Tuonela, Op. 22
Symphony No. 1 in E Minor, Op. 39
Symphony No. 5 in E-Flat Major, Op. 82
Symphony No. 7 in C Major, Op. 105

Twentieth-Century Music

15

Living in the twentieth century, we are so close to events going on about us that it is difficult to see them in perspective. Furthermore, most of us seldom consider how the changes in society affect the creative artist. For these reasons, it is wise to take a closer look at the character of our time and assess the ways in which it is influencing the fine arts.

MODERN SOCIETY AND THE CREATIVE ARTIST

The modern world is increasingly shaped by technology and machines. Just about every civilized human activity is involved in some way with technology. Not only does this fact have vast economic implications; it affects people's values and thinking. The vast array of goods made possible by technology and mass production in an affluent society has encouraged an attitude termed "materialism"—the placing of primary value on material goods. Materialism holds an important place in Western civilization, especially in America; and in the Soviet Union it is the expressed credo of that society. As someone has said of the average American: "He buys things he doesn't need, with money he doesn't have, to impress people he doesn't like." Whether this is fully apt or not, the description indicates that nonmaterial items such as learning, truth, and beauty usually come out second to the mink stole and the sleek, chrome-trimmed automobile.

Modern society is becoming increasingly urban in its orientation. More and more people live in metropolitan areas, and the urban way of life is being imitated by those living in the country. Nature no longer seems central to existence or to the enjoyment of that existence. Rather, nature is used to achieve other ends, most of which are beneficial to society, as when rivers are dammed to produce electric power and water for irrigation.

Technology has brought the entire world only a few hours away by jet, and instant communication via radio and television has been a reality for years. These advances have made human beings think and act in international terms. Except in newly emerging nations, the ardor of nationalism has abated somewhat. The nations of Europe, which were at war with one another so frequently during the nineteenth century, have now joined into the European Common Market.

Despite the many factors that might be expected to draw the peoples of the world together, international relations have been chaotic in the twentieth century, erupting into two world wars and numerous lesser conflicts. Society has been further shaken by the problems arising from vast increases in population, pollution of water and air, the burgeoning of large cities, the changing way of life caused by technology, the new status of women—the list could be lengthened considerably.

The intellectual climate of the twentieth century differs from that of the nineteenth. Generally, contemporary thought is far more objective and concerned with scientific inquiry. Sometimes, in fact, it is charged that modern man is objective to the point of being cold and calculating, like a machine. This objective attitude is clearly evident in Mondrian's "Composition" (plate 12). Modern man feels that he has outgrown the slushy sentimentality of the Romantic period. He no longer stands in awe of mystery and the unknown. On the contrary, he is exploring the outermost reaches of space and the inmost realms of the mind, confident that science will in time explain nearly everything. Twentieth-century man has not only faced the facts; he has gathered them and placed great value on them.

But in spite of his material comforts and intellectual achievements, contemporary man seems to be less clear about the meaning of his life, and consequently he seems no happier than his predecessors. The old beliefs have largely been rejected, but new understandings and beliefs have not appeared. The results often are feelings of confusion, a desire to escape from reality, or a sense of being hopelessly trapped in the tangle of life. Modern drama illustrates these points well. In Jean-Paul Sartre's *No Exit* the three characters are trapped in their private hell, which is largely of their

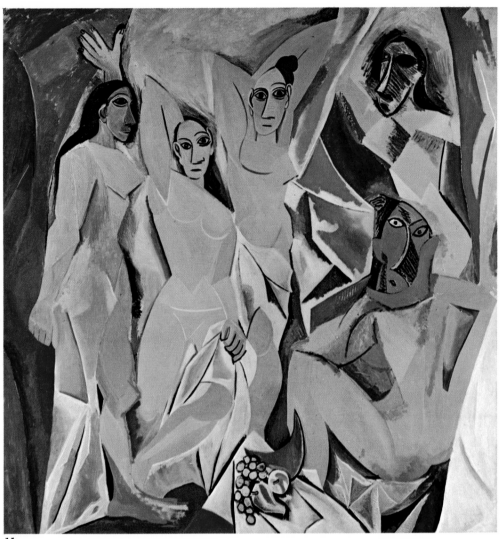

11

Picasso: *Les Demoiselles d'Avignon* (1907, spring). Oil on canvas, 8′ x 7′8″. (Collection, The Museum of Modern Art, New York. Acquired through the Lillie P. Bliss Bequest.)

12

Mondrian: *Composition 8.* (The Solomon R. Guggenheim Museum, New York.)

own making. In Samuel Beckett's *Waiting for Godot* two characters symbolizing mankind wait for Godot, who will take care of their problems. Godot never shows up.

There is a fear that man is becoming dehumanized and depersonalized; people and feelings seem to be lost in the hectic activity of life. This fact has encouraged several counter-intellectual movements—a faddish interest in oriental philosophies and religions, astrology, and pseudo-psychological-philosophical theories of self-fulfillment, for example.

Coupled with the difficulty of finding meaning in life is the change that modern man sees all about him. But change to what? For what reason? Who knows? Who cares? Sometimes change seems to be esteemed for its own sake. Some of the results of this are seen in the existentialist philosophy and in the "God is dead" theology.

The creative artist is especially sensitive to what he sees about him. He often mirrors the feelings of the times in which he lives. He reacts to circumstances as he finds them and thus gives expression to the prevailing attitudes. Creative artists do not, of course, all react alike. Some become cynical and discouraged; others withdraw along an escapist route that ignores society. Still others become "commercial," bowing to mass taste in order to get a fair share of society's material comforts.

With advances in transportation and communication, the creative artist is usually internationally minded. He knows the work of other writers, painters, and composers. Hence international styles in architecture, art, and music.

Since sweeping changes characterize the life and thinking of the twentieth century, it should not be surprising that contemporary music exhibits many differences from the music that preceded it. As examples of it, the music of four twentieth-century masters will be discussed: Igor Stravinsky, Arnold Schoenberg, Bela Bartók and Dmitri Shostakovich.

IGOR STRAVINSKY

Igor Stravinsky was born in 1882. His father was the leading bass at the Imperial Opera in St. Petersburg (Leningrad). The boy studied piano, but not intensively, because his parents wanted him to become a lawyer. He studied law at the University of St. Petersburg and simultaneously studied music with Rimsky-Korsakov.

Stravinsky soon became associated with Sergei Diaghilev, the man who commissioned Ravel's *Daphnis et Chloé*. Once each year for several years, Diaghilev brought Russian music and ballet to Paris with great financial and artistic success. He must have had an uncanny sense of taste and showmanship. In 1910, after hearing only one of Stravinsky's compositions, he assigned the twenty-five-year-old composer to write a new

Igor Stravinsky. This photograph was taken when he was eighty-four years old.

ballet. It was *The Firebird*. Its music is usually heard today in a suite that Stravinsky himself arranged. *The Firebird* was so successful that it earned for the young composer the chance to write a second new ballet, *Petrouchka*, for the next season. Like *The Firebird*, *Petrouchka* is based on a Russian legend. Again Stravinsky was given another commission, and the work he created startled the musical world.

Stravinsky's The Rite of Spring

The third ballet by Stravinsky was *Le Sacre du Printemps* (The Rite of Spring). The production was conceived by Diaghilev, partly as a means of holding the interest of the Paris audience. He had in past years presented classical ballets and Russian legends, and so, with his keen artistic judgment and calculated showmanship, he decided to capitalize on the

Parisians' interest in primitive art. African sculpture and masks had attracted the attention of artists such as the German painters Kirchner and Marc, as well as Picasso in Paris. Diaghilev chose to depict prehistoric rites culminating in the sacrifice of a human being—hardly typical of the stories usually associated with classical ballet.

On opening night the ballet and its music literally caused a small-scale riot. The audience was split between those who were cheering and those who were shouting slurs at the new production. Objects were hurled into the orchestra pit and onto the stage. Pandemonium reigned. No one, not even the dancers, could hear the music. The choreographer stood in the wings yelling out the rhythmic pattern so that the dancers could stay together.

How could any serious work, written in good faith, cause such violence among a fashionable audience? Although probably no one on that famous evening in 1913 thought about it at the time, the disagreement was one involving aesthetics. The audience was accustomed to ballets that presented pleasant music amid beautiful scenery. Their main expectation of art, music, or ballet was that it be lovely. In *The Rite of Spring*, the dancers were clothed in dark brown burlap. Their gestures were rough and angular, lacking the grace and charm of classical ballet movements. The music seemed brutal to the point of vulgarity. The very basis of hallowed artistic beliefs was being assaulted! What Stravinsky had created was a musical work that has much impact on the listener but not one that is pretty or lovely in the conventional sense.

Similar changes of viewpoint can be seen in modern art. In Picasso's "Les Demoiselles d'Avignon" (plate 11) can be seen the emergence of bold, almost blatant expression. Like Diaghilev's production of *The Rite of Spring*, its lines are sharp and angular and the impact almost brutal. Rouault's "Christ Mocked by Soldiers" (page 360) shows the force with which the modern artist can express himself. No loveliness here either.

The Rite of Spring opens with an orchestral "Introduction." The scene is a primitive forest. All sorts of strange and eerie sounds are heard, buzzing and bubbling. The bassoon begins in its highest range with a haunting, hooting quality. Its melody is neither tuneful nor constructed out of motives. Its pitches are confined to a narrow range and its rhythmic pattern is irregular, with frequent stops and starts.

What Stravinsky has written is indeed a melody; it has a logic of its own. But it certainly isn't like a well-fashioned theme from Brahms. Modern melodies are often different from their predecessors in other eras.

In the "Dance of the Adolescents," which follows, Stravinsky

"Christ Mocked by Soldiers," by Georges Rouault (1932). (Collection, The Museum of Modern Art, New York). This painting illustrates the savage expressive power of some artistic works of the twentieth century. Notice the treatment of the face of Christ. In spite of the insults of the soldiers His expression is calm.

unleashes the potent power of rhythm. The effect resembles the wild beating of savage drums. The strings achieve this by playing a dissonant chord with short bow strokes, each punctuated by a rest. Suddenly eight horns (four more than are normally called for) enter to add to the barbaric sound. This new sensational effect is produced by an irregular pattern of accents.

Between the accented chords there is sometimes one beat, sometimes two, three, four, or five beats. Gone is the underlying steadiness of beat that had prevailed for three hundred years. The irregular rhythms used by Stravinsky and some other composers had their roots in the rhythms of non-literate cultures. It was a milestone in the course of Western music.

As the chords bump along in their irregular way, several short primitive-sounding tunes are heard:

The tunes encompass only a few pitches, as though they are being played on a crude flute or pipe with a limited number of holes.

The "Dance of Abduction" is even wilder. A scampering tune is played by the woodwinds and answered by a horn call. The timpani have a prominent part that contributes to the violent mood. The meter signatures change with dizzying frequency. At one point they occur in this order: $\frac{7}{8}$, $\frac{3}{4}$, $\frac{6}{8}$, $\frac{2}{4}$, $\frac{6}{8}$, $\frac{3}{4}$. Polyrhythm, the superimposing of two or more rhythms, is also evident. No wonder the premiere audience could not sit passively; they had to react in an overt, physical manner.

"Round Dances of Spring" brings some relief from the frenzy that precedes it. The tempo is slower and the flutes and other woodwinds play a clearer, sweeter melody, which somewhat resembles an American Indian tune in its simplicity:

Later the orchestra takes up the melody. Some of the dissonance and parallel chord movement of Debussy can be heard here. The effect is beautifully primitive.

The music becomes energetic again in the scene entitled "Games of the Rival Tribes." Stravinsky expresses the idea of competition musically by pitting one section of the orchestra against another, each with its own distinctive music. Then, in the manner of a contest or debate, the "tribes" answer each other. The music is often *bitonal,* occurring in two keys at once.

Bitonality, or *polytonality,* is another contribution of modern music. Actually, the simultaneous use of different tonal centers had been evolving for some time. In *The Rite of Spring* it is a fine device for suggesting restlessness. The pounding chords of the earlier "Dance of the Adolescents" also exploited polytonal chords. In the example on page 361, the bass-clef chord is F-flat A-flat C-flat, and the treble clef part has the chord of E-flat G B-flat D-flat. Every letter of the musical alphabet is represented in these seven notes. Although they can be aligned to form a legitimate minor scale starting on A-flat, their effect when played as indicated is strongly dissonant and polytonal.

The "Entrance of the Sage" brings back the main thematic material with a thick orchestration.

Act One ends with "Dance of the Earth." It too suggests violence and upheaval. The low-pitched instruments play an ostinato line, but, because of the dense quality of the music, the individual lines tend to become lost. To be fully appreciated, the ballet must be seen with this portion of the music.

The second and final act of the ballet depicts the sacrifice of a young maiden to the Chosen One so that the God of Spring may be satisfied. In style it is similar to the first act.

To the listener hearing it for the first time, *The Rite of Spring* may sound like a jumble of random notes. It may even seem that the instrumentalists could play anything they wanted, and no one, not even Stravinsky, would know the difference. Such an idea is, of course, incorrect. Stravinsky carefully planned everything in the score. Like Debussy, he writes detailed directions for the playing of each part. He goes so far as to tell the timpani player when to change from hard to soft sticks, the French horn players when to tilt the bells of their instruments in an upward direction, and the cellists when to retune a string so that a chord can be played on open strings to achieve a more raucous effect.

As is true of so many modern works, the listener after several hearings can begin to sense the logic and coherence of the music. The tonal patterns that were revolutionary nonsense at first now begin to take on sensible shapes. They start to acquire musical meaning. When the listener becomes thoroughly familiar with *The Rite of Spring*, he realizes that not just any notes will do. In fact, he may begin to sense that not a single note could be altered without somewhat affecting the quality of the music. Whether Stravinsky's music is heard as nonsense or logic depends on the listener's familiarity with the particular work and/or its style. Therefore, the suggestion made in Chapter 4 for the repeated hearing of new music becomes a necessity in the case of twentieth-century compositions. The only way to assimilate and understand the syntax of today's music is to hear it often enough so that its techniques become familiar.

The Rite of Spring is such a gigantic masterpiece of barbarism that other composers have shied away from emulating it. In some ways, it is a mutant form of Romanticism. But in its rhythmic innovations, its brutal dissonances, and its irregular melodic lines, it opened up a new world for composers.

The year 1913 was the last before World War I, which seriously curtailed artistic activity in Europe. During the war Stravinsky moved to neutral Switzerland. The revolution in Russia cut off his income, and the ballet company had disbanded. He lived quietly in Switzerland for five years, recovering from a serious illness.

After the armistice, he returned to France. At that time Paris was rich with artists and writers—Picasso, Valéry, Gide—who were expressing Neo-Classical sentiments in their works. Stravinsky became a French citizen and traveled widely as a conductor and pianist. In 1931 he came to the United States to lecture at Harvard University. When World War II prevented his return to Europe, he settled in Hollywood and became an American citizen in 1945. Although none of Stravinsky's later compositions have caused riotous premieres, he has retained his esteemed position as one of the greatest composers of this century. On his eightieth birthday he was the honored guest of President Kennedy at the White House, and on another occasion he was the subject of a special one-hour program presented on a national television network.

NEO-CLASSICISM

Stylistic periods seem to move in either of two directions: toward emotional and subjective expression or toward intellectual objectivity. The

Baroque period was more emotional than the Renaissance, and it was followed by the objectivity of the Classical period. Then came the most subjective style of all, the Romantic. The inevitable direction of music after Wagner and Debussy was toward more objectivity. And so there evolved an attitude called *Neo-Classicism*. It sought to duplicate the restraint of the Classical period and to view artistic endeavor in a more dispassionate light. Neo-Classicism is exemplified in the sensitive painting "The Lovers" by Picasso (page 365).

On this matter Stravinsky's position was straightforward and consistent: "What is important for the clear ordering of the work, for its crystallization, is that all the . . . elements . . . should be properly subjugated and finally subjected to the rule of law before they intoxicate us . . ." For him, writing a musical composition is like solving a problem; it is a task to be done by applying the intellect. Therefore music is meant to express nothing save the composer's ability to contrive interesting tonal and rhythmic patterns. This Neo-Classical position is one that Stravinsky has followed generally since the 1920s. His intellectually oriented music earned him a reputation as leader of a trend euphoniously named the "Back-to-Bach" movement. Several Baroque forms such as the concerto grosso were revived during this time, and there was a renewed emphasis on counterpoint and the linear aspect of music. And so the allusion to Bach is not entirely inappropriate. The clarity of Baroque music held considerable appeal for the Neo-Classicist.

Stravinsky has written in several styles and has freely borrowed themes and elements associated with other composers. After the tumult of *The Rite of Spring*, he composed *Pulcinella*, which incorporated melodies of the eighteenth-century composer Pergolesi. This was followed by works based on the styles of such varied composers as Bach, Rossini, Tchaikovsky, and Grieg. Following World War II, Stravinsky composed some works according to the twelve-tone technique, which will be discussed later in this chapter. Despite the superficial changes of style, Stravinsky has remained true to his objective conception of music. Since a piece of music is something a composer makes, it is essentially an object rather than a representation of his soul. Therefore a person's compositions need not be in a consistent personal style. The skill of composition is paramount, the composer's personality irrelevant. How contrary are these beliefs to the tenets of the Romantic age!

Stravinsky's Octet for Wind Instruments

The Octet, written in 1923, shows how far Stravinsky has moved from the large instrumentation and the startling innovations found in *The Rite of Spring*, written only ten years earlier. The Octet has an unusual instrumentation: a flute, clarinet, two bassoons, two trumpets, and two

"The Lovers," by Pablo Picasso, a painting that demonstrates the balance and restraint typical of the Neo-Classical style.

trombones. In describing the Octet, Stravinsky writes that he sought "to establish order and discipline in the purely sonorous scheme to which I always give precedence over elements of an emotional character." And he succeeded. The music has a "dryness" about it that stamps it as being a truly Neo-Classical composition.

Memories of Bach are called forth immediately. The Octet opens with an introductory section called "Sinfonia," a term often used by Baroque composers. It even contains the dotted rhythms typical of most Baroque overtures, including the Overture of the *Suite No. 3 in D Major* by Bach, which was discussed in Chapter 8. But other aspects of the rhythm are more contemporary. The irregular meters found in *The Rite of Spring* are still employed in the Octet, changing in the Sinfonia from $\frac{2}{8}$ to $\frac{3}{16}$ to $\frac{3}{8}$ to $\frac{2}{4}$.

The main theme of the movement proper is this:

Notice that the line is angular, unlike the smooth sweep of Romantic melodies. It has a wide leap between the second and third notes, a leap of a seventh, which is not a customary melodic interval. The sixth measure contains an extra note and a change of meter. The theme receives much contrapuntal treatment and some development.

A second, contrasting theme is played by the trumpet:

The theme is heavily syncopated and shows Stravinsky's consciousness of jazz, an idiom that is found in some of his compositions.

The second movement is restrained, detached, and comfortable, with a trace of melancholy. It is a theme and variations. The flute presents the theme first, and then the clarinet joins in:

The accompanying chords come after the beat and are played in a "dry" (short and biting) style. Then the brass instruments have their turn with the melody.

The trombone starts the theme for the first variation, accompanied by rushes of sound from low to high notes. The second half of the theme is played by the flute, bassoons, and trumpet in short afterbeats.

The second variation is march-like, and some of it sounds like the Italian song *Funiculi-Funicula*. (This is probably *not* what Stravinsky had in mind when he wrote it.) Later in the variation the woodwinds play in a more delicate style.

An interlude containing material from the first variation is next. Its quiet, pastoral quality affords some contrast between the second and third variations.

In the third variation, the bassoons play a melodic figure with short, crisp notes. Other instruments play gay figures contrapuntally against the melody.

After an unaccompanied flute solo, which serves as an interlude, the last movement begins:

The music is contrapuntal. Notice that the bassoon goes up and down the scale. The part is unmistakably ostinato in character. Later the trumpet provides a jazz-inspired melody. The ending of the Octet seems to fade away in rhythmic fragments.

Admittedly, the Octet is not an immediately appealing work to many people. Although it doesn't assault their ears and artistic beliefs, as did *The Rite of Spring*, it does appear to be cold and mechanical, or "nuts and bolts and razor blades," as one critic has said of Stravinsky's music. His works and those of many other contemporary composers should be approached more as interesting and skillfully produced objects than as means to subjective and emotional musical experiences.

The discussion outlined in Chapter 3 is pertinent here. Because twentieth-century music is so often in an unfamiliar style, it forces frequent reconsideration of basic aesthetic questions. If a listener is to understand the Octet, he must listen to it with the same mental set as Stravinsky. He should not expect a sumptuous Romantic melody or spine-tingling climactic moments. Rather, he should listen for the "clear ordering" of the sounds that have been "properly subjugated and finally subjected to the rule of law," to quote Stravinsky again. This approach will yield the maximum musical understanding of the Octet and similar works.

ARNOLD SCHOENBERG

If Stravinsky's Octet is an attempt to reincarnate the past, Arnold Schoenberg (*Shurn*-bairg, 1874–1951) represents a new direction. Strangely enough, however, he didn't intend to be a revolutionary. Born in Vienna, Schoenberg began studying violin at the age of eight. He was an avid participant in amateur chamber-music performances, and he also attended concerts frequently. After his father's early death, he went to work as a bank clerk. He had little formal music training at an advanced level, but he had for many years exhibited an interest in composing. This interest became increasingly stronger, and so he decided to make music his life-work. First he spent two years in Berlin as a music director in a cabaret; then he returned to Vienna as a teacher, theorist, and composer. His career was interrupted for two years while he served in the Austrian army in World War I.

In 1925 he was appointed professor of composition at the Berlin Academy of Arts. His stay in Berlin ended with the coming to power of Hitler. Although Schoenberg had been converted from Judaism to Catholicism, he left Germany and came to the United States, becoming an American citizen in 1940. He taught at the University of California at Los Angeles until his retirement. His musical activities continued until his death in 1951.

Prior to 1908 his music stood firmly in the tradition of Wagner and Mahler. His best-known composition of the period is *Verklärte Nacht* (Transfigured Night), a tone poem for string orchestra. The literary work that inspired the music is pure Romanticism. As a couple walks through the woods, the woman confesses that she has been unfaithful. The man assures her that he still loves her, and her gratitude transfigures the night. Schoenberg also wrote the tone poem *Pelleas und Melisande* in 1902. Interestingly, at that time he was a far more conservative composer than Debussy.

Another Romantic Schoenberg work is *Gurrelieder*—songs of Gurre, a mythological Scandinavian castle. It shows the influence of Mahler in the size of the performing group. The score calls for an increase in the number and variety of instruments in almost all sections of the orchestra. A bass trumpet and an iron chain are required, as well as five solo voices, three male choruses, and a mixed chorus. No wonder the composition is seldom performed!

Around 1908 Schoenberg began to turn toward smaller groups of instruments. He started to write more contrapuntally and to employ much more chromaticism. Slowly he developed a style of music called *atonal*— that is, music with absolutely no feeling of key or home note. Such a step meant breaking away from the very foundations that had undergirded the music of previous centuries. When Debussy introduced unresolved disso-

Arnold Schoenberg.

nance and Schoenberg developed atonality, it was as though the musical universe had been turned upside down.

If a composer throws out tonality, with what does he replace it? Schoenberg tried several ideas but slowly arrived at what is variously called *twelve-tone, tone row, dodecaphonic,* or *serial music.* The principle is relatively simple. The composer arranges the twelve tones of the chromatic scale in any order he chooses. This is the "row"—a series of intervals that form a unique melody. It is not a chromatic scale, because the notes are not lined up so as to progress by equidistant half steps. The pitches in the row need not all appear within the range of a single octave, either, and so wide interval leaps are sometimes encountered. No tone in the row can be repeated until all the twelve tones have been heard, because such repetition would emphasize one particular note. There is no special importance attached to any tone in the row, and so all are equally significant. Hence there can be no tonic or tonal center.

While the tone-row technique may appear limited at first glance, it has been calculated that there are 479,001,600 different tone rows available. And each row can be treated in countless ways. It can appear vertically in chords as well as horizontally in melodies. The row can be transposed, or it can be moved to a different octave. It can be subdivided into phrases of different lengths.

Most of Schoenberg's twelve-tone works are for piano or chamber groups. The *Variations for Orchestra* is his only composition for full orchestra in this style. It is perhaps the most accessible work in the twelve-tone idiom for the listener who is unaccustomed to the sound of such music.

Schoenberg's Variations for Orchestra, Op. 31

The introduction to the work is very soft, with violin tremolo and nebulous notes in the woodwinds. The fluttering sound of the flute is actually called "flutter tonguing." Like Stravinsky, Schoenberg employs frequent meter changes and polyrhythm.

After a restrained climax, the music quiets down. The flute plays a graceful line, while the lower instruments sound the notes B-flat A C B-natural, which in German is written B A C H.[1] Bach elaborated on these notes in his last great work, *The Art of Fugue,* and other composers have used the figure since. The B A C H notes become important later in Schoenberg's Variations. The opening melodic figures return, a rather conventional compositional device. Up to this point, all the music has been based upon the row, although the row itself has not been presented as a melody. Therefore, the listener has not yet been made conscious of the row.

Here are the pitches of the basic row for this piece:

There are four customary forms in which the row can be presented: (1) the original, (2) retrograde (backwards), (3) inversion (upside down), a technique that was discussed in Chapter 8, and (4) retrograde inversion (upside down and backwards).

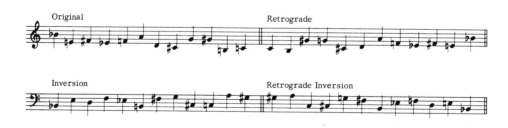

---

[1] In German the note B indicates B-flat, while B-natural is written as the letter H. This system stems from an old tradition in which the awkward interval of the augmented fourth (see discussion of Mussorgsky in Chapter 14) was avoided.

Here is the row, with its rhythmic element, as it first appears played by the cellos:

Then it is heard in retrograde inversion and transposed upward. Next the retrograde of the original appears, and the inversion is transposed. When put together, the theme is:

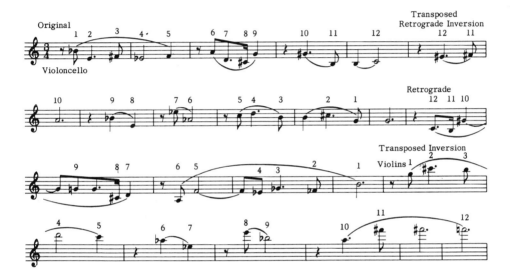

The structure of the music is planned with exceeding care. For example, the chords are derived from one version of the row. The number of tones in the melodic phrases corresponds to the number of tones in the chord.

In the first variation, which is only twenty-three measures long, the theme in its original form begins in the bass clarinet and then proceeds to other instruments. The accompanying parts are not chords but dashing, quick, and colorful lines.

The second variation, again twenty-three measures long, is muted in quality and contrapuntal in texture. There are some canons between various instruments. Toward the end the trombone sounds the B A C H motive.

The third variation is filled with busy notes that are superimposed over a rugged, vigorous rhythmic figure played by the four horns.

The fourth variation is longer and more graceful. As in the second variation, only solo instruments are playing; that is, there is only one instrument per part. The quality is appealing and not harsh. The theme is treated in a shimmering way by the harp, celeste, and mandolin, while being accompanied by new counterthemes.

The row is almost hidden in the string-bass part in the fifth variation. The music seems to be a struggle between opposing melodic and rhythmic patterns. The B A C H motive can be heard popping in and out of the music.

The sixth variation is quiet in character. The solo cello plays the row, while the flute, English horn, and bassoon have significant melodies that are derived from a transposed inversion of the row.

The seventh variation is the softest of all. The row is almost obscured again, being sounded by the piccolo and glockenspiel in single notes in conjunction with a short figure in the solo violin.

The eighth variation is active and strident in character. It has a persistent rhythmic pattern in eighth notes in the bass and an aggressive pattern superimposed above it. The row is heard near the end in the flute, clarinet, and violin parts.

The ninth variation opens with the piccolo playing the theme. The row is in its original form but the rhythmic pattern is new.

The finale is far longer than any of the variations. The B A C H motive predominates. It tends to divide itself into three parts. One has the flutter-tonguing and is in the character of the beginning of the entire work. A graceful center section follows. The fast tempo resumes, and the work closes after a final statement of the B A C H theme. The final chord contains all twelve tones of the row.

It must be admitted that tone-row compositions present problems for many listeners. The idea of the row itself is comprehensible and can be heard easily enough, but does the listener recognize the row when it is turned upside down and played backwards? Is the retrograde inversion any better, musically, than a new countermelody would be? Is the relationship between the original melody and its retrograde or inversion apparent enough to be meaningful to the listener?

A few suggestions may help the listener derive more satisfaction from hearing twelve-tone music. Since the logic of the tone row is radically different, one of the most helpful things to do is to listen to a section of a work many times. Some familiarity with the style is essential.

Because the row is altered to a considerable extent during the course of a composition, and because it is sometimes nearly hidden among other sounds, memorization of the row itself is usually of limited value. Instead, the listener should concentrate on the changing timbres Schoenberg achieves. This feature of his music is often overlooked because of the attention given his tone-row technique.

The idea of manipulating timbre so fascinated Schoenberg that in some of his works he employed an unusual technique to exploit this aspect of music to its fullest. He gave it the wonderful German name of *Klangfarbmelodie*. It is a system wherein changes of tone color are made along with changes of pitch. Schoenberg was influenced by contemporary art and was himself a good painter. He even exhibited works with his friend

Wasily Kandinsky as well as with Paul Klee, another artist. Schoenberg attempted to adapt some of their ideas in his music. In turn, Kandinsky may have tried to emulate the abstract nature of music in giving his works such general titles as "Composition No. 4" and "Improvisation No. 30" (plate 10). In this color plate you can see bold contrasts of color and non-representational shapes and lines.

Schoenberg vigorously denied that his music is cold and intellectual. He considered his music to be packed with emotion. In view of the rigid intellectual nature of tone-row composing, his claims may seem to be inaccurate. But his music contains a great amount of activity within a short span. It appears that he has speeded up the dimension of time, causing the sounds to be more concentrated and hence more exciting. What took.Schubert perhaps one minute, Schoenberg packs into a few seconds. Certainly he is no longer conceiving of music in the rambling dimensions of the Romantic period.

Schoenberg has had a significant influence on the direction of twentieth-century music. In the course of his teaching, he gathered about him a group of enthusiastic and brilliant pupils, including Anton von Webern and Alban Berg. His pupils—one might almost call them disciples—followed his teachings devotedly. And there was something about him that inspired such confidence. He was completely dedicated to his ideals and he persisted in them despite the neglect of much of the "official" musical world. He was one of the first composers to be sustained largely by university appointments. (Jean Cocteau, a leader of French anti-romantic music, once accused Schoenberg of being "first and foremost a blackboard musician.") The security offered him by a university position allowed him to pursue a musical style without regard to public acceptance.

Schoenberg's personal success as a composer is perhaps not so important in the long run as the new ideas of composition that he unleashed. Their effects have not yet been fully realized, nor will they be for many years to come.

BELA BARTÓK

Bela Bartók (1881–1945) composed works that are essentially an outgrowth of the mainstream of music. Although thoroughly familiar with the music of his experimental contemporaries, he was influenced by them only to a small degree.

Bartók's father was director of an agricultural school in Hungary, and his mother was the boy's first music teacher. After she was widowed, she became a schoolteacher, moving frequently with her son. Finally they settled in Pressburg, where he began serious study of piano and composition. In 1899 he enrolled as a student at the Royal Conservatory in Budapest. He became an excellent pianist and gave concerts throughout Europe.

Bela Bartók.

During much of his life, piano teaching was his main source of income.

Bartók first became noted throughout the world, however, not as a pianist or composer but as a collector of Hungarian folk songs. He made a significant contribution to musicology through his compilations and analyses of the folk music of his native land and other countries. One of the facts that his research uncovered was that the type of music traditionally considered "Hungarian" and used by Brahms and Liszt was really gypsy music, as performed in the cafes of Europe, rather than the music of the Hungarian people.

In 1907 Bartók became a professor of piano at the Royal Conservatory and spent most of the next thirty years in Budapest. He received little recognition until the late twenties, when his works began to earn attention outside of Hungary.

After the rise of Hitler and the subsequent collaboration of Hungary with Nazi Germany, Bartók felt impelled to leave his homeland. In 1940 he came to the United States to live. He had to leave much of his worldly goods behind, and his health was failing. He was appointed to a position at Columbia University, primarily to continue his folk-music research. He did receive a few commissions for compositions. ASCAP (the American Society of Composers, Authors, and Publishers) provided him with medical care, and jazz musician Benny Goodman also aided him. In 1945 he died of leukemia, with his true stature as a composer still not fully appreciated.

Bartók displays in his early works an unabashed admiration for Richard Strauss and Debussy. In 1911, two years before Stravinsky wrote *The Rite of Spring,* Bartók began composing rude, barbaric works. In his piano compositions written during this period, he treats the instrument percussively. Instead of the rolling, luscious sounds found in Chopin, he has the pianist bang out thick, dissonant chords.

Bartók composed his greatest music between 1926 and 1937. His *Mikrokosmos* is a set of 153 piano pieces in six volumes, arranged so that the music progresses from simple pieces for the beginner to works of awesome difficulty. In this collection he employs nearly every pianistic device and displays a wide variety of composing techniques. *Music for Strings, Percussion, and Celesta* also stems from this period.

Most significant, however, are his string quartets—Nos. 3, 4, and 5. In them he achieves a striking union of modern and Classical elements. They are particularly well designed. For instance, *String Quartet No. 4* contains five movements. The themes in the various movements are related to one another in this manner:

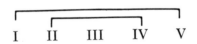

The outline becomes something of a musical arch and represents a certain ideal balance. The harmonies in this quartet are usually dissonant, and the rhythm tends to be violent and pounding, making the character of the work rather wild even though traditional forms appear in it. There is much counterpoint in the quartet, and Bartók includes several modal melodies, probably a result of his study of folk music. Although some of the melodies are folk-like, Bartók did not normally draw on folk tunes for his compositions.

During the latter years of his life, Bartók's mood appeared to mellow. His music became less dissonant, less violent. Besides those already mentioned, his most frequently performed compositions include *String Quartet No. 6,* the well-known *Concerto for Orchestra,* and the *Piano Concerto No. 3.*

Bartók's Concerto No. 3 for Piano

Bartók completed the *Concerto No. 3* in 1945, just before his death. It was in one sense an insurance policy for his wife. He wanted to compose a work that would be easily accepted by concert audiences so that she might receive some income through its performances.

First Movement. The first movement is in sonata form. The first theme, vigorous and rhythmic, begins immediately in the piano:

Instead of rich, full chords, Bartók has the pianist play a single line doubled at the octave. The effect is clear and concise. The jogging, syncopated rhythm is easily heard because there is no thick accompaniment to obscure it.

After a transition featuring a variety of scale and rhythmic patterns, the second theme enters:

It is thoroughly pianistic and would be completely inappropriate for another instrument or for voice. The theme suggests a series of tonal clusters, and it has several subordinate fragments.

There is a codetta in which the music achieves a climax of sound and then tapers down into a two-note figure that reminds one of a cuckoo call.

The development presents new material. The piano has a florid part while the woodwinds play a song-like melody. The effect would be Romantic were it not for the fact that Bartók's orchestration and harmonization retain that certain coolness associated with twentieth-century music. For a few measures the piano does break forth in true nineteenth-century style. Fragments of the first theme are worked into the latter half of the development section.

The first theme is treated dissonantly in the recapitulation. Bartók seems to be seeking dissonance of tonal color rather than tension, however. Because of the dissonance, the theme in the recapitulation gives a different impression than it did in the exposition.

The coda embodies the same ideas as the codetta. After the series of "cuckoos," it ends quietly with a colorful figure in the piano. As in the Stravinsky Octet and the Schoenberg Variations, this movement concludes without need of a flashy Romantic ending. The music just stops when the composer is finished.

Second Movement. The second movement of this concerto is quite striking. It opens with an introductory section primarily for strings. The music is constructed with such extreme simplicity that it seems to achieve its impact by deliberate understatement. The piano enters with a phrase in chorale style:

The strings repeat the chord patterns of the introductory music, and the piano follows with another phrase of the chorale. With each exchange between strings and piano, the intensity of the music increases.

In the middle section, the music shifts radically in tempo and mood. It begins to sound like a summer night in the woods! There are twittering and chirping noises that sound like insects. Aside from a few muted horn effects and some piano runs, the musical ideas are carried by the high woodwinds, including the piccolo, with a little help from the xylophone.

This section is further evidence of the modern composer's fascination with timbre. As was mentioned in Chapter 1 and in connection with

Schoenberg, timbre is a facet of music that has been mined extensively in this century. And sounds *are* fascinating! Bartók's changes of color are achieved with conventional instruments, although more recent composers have moved beyond him into new areas of tone production, some of which are described in Chapter 17.

The chorale melody played by the piano in the first section returns in the woodwinds, giving the movement a large three-part, *A B A* form. This time, however, there are no string interludes. The winds play the chorale melody while the piano provides a line of counterpoint in a style reminiscent of Bach. At the long tones at the ends of phrases, the piano embellishes the chord in a free style. Eventually the strings are added to the orchestral part until the music reaches a point of intensity that can be described only as "passionate." The piano has the final climactic passage, and the strings close the movement with the same music that began it.

The final piano solo in the second movement aptly illustrates the modern composer's use of dissonance to achieve motion through greater or lesser tension. Sometimes people have expressed disappointment in modern music because they feel it is ugly. One of the reasons it isn't pretty, according to standards of past eras, is that modern music contains so many more dissonances. The concept of dissonance is, however, a relative matter. As was mentioned in Chapter 6, composers in the early Gothic period generally avoided notes a third apart because they considered the interval to be too harsh. Today, harmonizing at the third is about as conventional as one can get. The history of music exhibits a tendency toward more and more dissonance. Bach used a little more than Josquin des Prez, Brahms used more than Bach, and so on. The ultimate amount of dissonance is the sounding of all twelve tones in the chromatic scale at the same time, which Schoenberg did at the end of the *Variations for Orchestra*. Charles Ives, an American composer discussed in the next chapter, has specified that a stick 14¾ inches long be pushed down on the piano keyboard so that all notes beneath the stick are sounded simultaneously. A few other composers call for "elbow chords," in which the pianist pushes down the keys beneath his elbow and forearm. The levels of dissonance produced by such means can well be imagined.

Not only is dissonance relative to the prevailing norms of a particular period; the impression of dissonance is also affected by the musical context in which it appears. A dissonant sound is more conspicuous in a simple setting than in a more pungent context. This matter is not left to chance. A good composer knows how to manipulate intervals and tones so that he controls the amount of dissonance at any given moment. Bartók did this with considerable skill. The final piano solo is shown on the next page. Notice that the music achieves a peak of tension, much of it caused by dissonance, and then gracefully relaxes chord by chord to consonance. Although Bartók is using a greater degree of dissonance than did Bach or

Brahms, he is adhering to the same principle that guided his predecessors in their handling of it: greater dissonance resolves to lesser dissonance.

Sust. means "sustaining pedal."

Third Movement. The third movement is in rondo form, one of the favorite forms of the Classical period. The A theme, which recurs throughout the movement, is this:

A rhythmic pattern played by the timpani serves as a transition to the B section, which is fugal in character:

This section leads directly back to a short statement of A. Another timpani transition introduces the C portion of the rondo, which is, again, highly contrapuntal.

The return of *A* is its longest appearance yet encountered, since it is treated to some development. The movement ends with a brilliant coda.

To a greater extent than Stravinsky and Schoenberg, Bartók represents direct evolution from the music of the nineteenth century. He is free in his manipulation of tonality, but he does not abandon it. His style is more restrained and concise than were the styles in the Romantic era, but he does not go to the extremes of either Stravinsky or Schoenberg. He uses Classical forms when it suits his musical purposes. At all times he seems to be more concerned with musical effectiveness than with theories or systems. Because of his keen imagination and craftsmanship, he ranks as one of the finest composers of this century.

DMITRI SHOSTAKOVICH

Dmitri Shostakovich (b. 1906) received all of his musical training in Russia, and he has spent very little time outside the country. He was born in St. Petersburg (Leningrad), and his mother, like Bartók's, was a well-trained pianist. At thirteen he entered the Conservatory at St. Petersburg. In 1925, at the age of nineteen, he finished his First Symphony, which is a remarkably mature and individual work that has become a part of the repertoire of most symphony orchestras. His career was off to an auspicious start.

In 1934 he ran into trouble with the Communist Party over an opera entitled *Lady Macbeth of Mzensk.* It was accused of being "formalistic," a vague charge meaning that the music did not contain enough propaganda or that it was too much like music of the Western world. He publicly promised to do better in the future. In 1937 he brought out his Fifth Symphony, an outstanding work that will be discussed shortly.

During World War II, Shostakovich was not permitted to serve in the armed forces because he was considered so valuable a citizen. He spent the war years in Leningrad, where he remained even through the long seige of that city, writing his Seventh Symphony and serving as a volunteer fireman.

He had another falling out with the Party in 1948 when he was again accused of "musical formalism." A public apology and a new opera extricated him from the predicament. He is now revered in his native land, where he enjoys substantial royalties from his compositions.

Shostakovich's Symphony No. 5

This symphony is probably Shostakovich's most representative work. Its first movement is in sonata form, beginning with a violent-sounding theme treated canonically:

Dmitri Shostakovich.

A second portion of the first theme soon appears:

The next theme has a wide range and is presented over a throbbing rhythmic background:

Throughout the movement these themes are varied and combined with each other. The first movement is long by modern standards.

The second movement is intriguing, filled with humor and occasional satire. The cellos and string basses begin it in waltz tempo, but what they play is too jovial, too fat to be a waltz in the graceful Viennese tradition. It reminds one of music for a dancing bear in a circus. The tiny E-flat clarinet wheezes out a little tune as though it were trying to take itself seriously. The bassoons burp out notes of the shortest possible length, and the solo violinist slides around on a glissando. A peculiar march starts up in the horns; instead of conventional two-beat meter, however, there is an extra beat in each measure, so that the music hobbles along with a quite unusual gait. At the very end, when the heavy chords suggest that something important is about to happen, a meek and plaintive oboe is heard, sounding as though it were apologizing for being there. The whole movement is filled with ideas, instrumentation, and rhythms that are incongruous when combined.

Some writers have attempted to draw a relationship between this satirical movement and Shostakovich's feelings toward the authorities after his public censure, although Shostakovich has denied any such connection.

The third movement is impressive. Like Bartók's Third Piano Concerto, it begins slowly with warm sounds from the strings. The themes have a chant-like quality about them:

The third theme is introduced by the oboe:

Throughout this portion of the music, the extremely transparent nature of Shostakovich's writing is evident. At times, only one instrument is playing. After a while, the first two themes are heard from the strings. The music then winds up to a tremendous climax of intensity and the strings move higher and higher with an excited tremolo. At the climactic point the second part of the first theme is heard coming through the orchestra, its notes doubled by the xylophone. The cellos come in full force on the third theme. The movement closes with the same music that began it.

The fourth movement opens with savage fury. After a pounding passage in the timpani, the brasses blare out this theme:

It is followed by an excited, dance-like melody:

The music continues at a torrid pace. One of its many exciting moments is when the trumpets sound this counter pattern against a melody played by the rest of the orchestra:

The center section introduces the element of contrast by presenting a solo horn playing in augmentation the theme indicated for the violins in the musical example above. Then other melodies are played, some of them over ostinato-like accompaniments. The second theme (second example above) appears in the violins in notes four times the length of the original, or in double augmentation.

The longer notes and the different accompaniment give the melody an entirely new character.

The opening theme is heard again, rounding off the three-part form of the movement. Shostakovich's fondness for pedal point can be seen in the coda. The first three notes of the first theme are retained as a sort of motive:

While the brasses sound the closing notes (which are reminiscent of the musical phrase "How Dry I Am"), the rest of the orchestra continues to drive home a single note.

Shostakovich's music is not so modern as that of the three composers discussed earlier in the chapter. (Tone-row compositions and other newer styles of music are not permitted by the Soviet government.) The ending of the Fifth Symphony, for example, is probably too heroic to suit most modern composers. Nevertheless it is a fine work—not necessarily because of innovative or advanced ideas but because of the composer's obvious skill at writing and his strong gift of melody.

OTHER TWENTIETH-CENTURY COMPOSERS

With Stravinsky, Schoenberg, Bartók, and Shostakovich come a host of excellent composers who for one reason or another have not achieved the prominence of the four just mentioned. In most cases it is because they have not been so prolific or have not exerted as much influence on the course of twentieth-century music.

Russia

The Revolution in 1917 shook Russian music as well as all other phases of national life. Stravinsky left Russia following the Revolution, never to return except for an occasional visit.

Another fine composer, Serge Prokofiev (Pro-*ko*-fee-eff, 1891–1953), left Russia on a tour as a concert pianist immediately after 1917. He traveled and lived in Paris until 1932, when he returned to Russia and accepted the restraints imposed on his work by the Soviet government. As a young man, he wrote violent works in an effort to reject the Romantic style. His best compositions were written after his return to Russia. They are numerous and embrace a wide variety of styles. In addition to the purely patriotic works not heard outside of Russia, his compositions include the delightful *Peter and the Wolf*, the film music for *Lieutenant Kijé*, the ballet *Cinderella*, and the opera *War and Peace*, plus many symphonies, concertos, and chamber works. These latter compositions are lyric and quite listenable. They are modern but often contain strongly Romantic overtones.

Paul Hindemith.

Germany

Paul Hindemith (1895–1963) was recognized as a theorist as well as a composer, and he worked with a variety of compositional styles. At first he was a brash and wild expressionistic composer, then a Neo-Classicist and a member of the "Back-to-Bach" movement, and finally a reactionary. His last years were spent teaching at Yale University. He was a prolific composer who wrote for every medium. One of his musical contributions was an idea called *Gebrauchsmusik* ("everyday" or "useful" music). *Gebrauchsmusik* consists largely of a series of technically undemanding chamber works. His best-known orchestral composition is the symphony *Mathis der Maler* (Matthias the Painter), derived from his opera about Matthias Grünewald, an early sixteenth-century painter. The music is in three movements, each one representing a scene from the Isenheim (*Ee*-zen-hime) Altar in Colmar, Alsace. One of the paintings is reproduced on page 386. Hindemith wrote in a contrapuntal style that reminds one of an updated version of some of Bach's works.

"Entombment," by Matthias Grünewald, from the Isenheim Altar. This was one of the paintings used by Hindemith as a basis for Mathis der Maler.

England

The twentieth century has produced several first-rate English composers. The foremost is Ralph Vaughan Williams (1872–1958). Vaughan Williams helped revive interest in English folk music and also contributed to the improvement of music in the Church of England. For vocal texts he drew on the works of England's finest poets. He also incorporated themes from Elizabethan composers into such works as *Fantasia on a Theme by Thomas Tallis.* In short, he wrote *English* music, thereby shaking off the domination of the German Romantic style. As he grew older—he composed well into his eighties—his music became more modern and more complex in character. His Sixth Symphony, an important work, is a far cry in its style from his early folk-like compositions, such as *Fantasia on "Greensleeves."*

Another outstanding contemporary English composer is a man with the wonderfully appropriate name of Benjamin Britten (b. 1913). His natural musical ability has been compared to Mozart's. Britten began composing at an early age and is remarkably facile at working out music in his mind. He has written for every medium and for varied levels of musical sophistication. *A Young Person's Guide to the Orchestra* is an immensely

Benjamin Britten.
Courtesy of Yousuf Karsh,
Ottawa, Canada.

popular work for novice listeners. Britten has toured the United States frequently and at one time seriously considered living here.

Britten's forte is the composition of vocal works, especially operas. Among his successful operas are *Peter Grimes* (1945), *The Rape of Lucretia* (1946), *Let's Make an Opera* (1948), *Billy Budd* (1951), *The Turn of the Screw* (1954), *Noye's Fludde* (Noah's Flood, 1957), and *A Midsummer Night's Dream* (1960). He has also written for voices and instruments: *Serenade for Tenor, Horn, and Strings* (1943), *Nocturne*, for tenor and small orchestra (1958), *The Ceremony of Carols*, for boys' voices and harp (1942), and the *War Requiem* (1962).

France

Following World War I, France went through a violently anti-Romantic reaction. The informal spokesmen for the new music were a poet, Jean Cocteau, and an eccentric musician, Erik Satie (Sah-*tee*, 1866– 1925). Satie reacted to past music in his own inimitable way by writing little compositions entitled *Three Pieces in the Shape of a Pear, Three Flabby Preludes for a Dog,* and *Dried Embryos.* He filled his scores with sly

"The Six." Jean Cocteau (seated); left to right: Milhaud, Auric, Honegger, Tailleferre, Poulenc, and Durey.

directions: "Play like a nightingale with a toothache" and "With astonishment." The purpose of such titles and directions was to ridicule the seriousness with which Romantic and impressionistic composers had approached their craft.

From this stream of irreverent thought came a group of French composers known as "The Six," so named by a critic who likened them to the Russian "Five" (see Chapter 14). The most important of these composers were Darius Milhaud (Mee-yo, b. 1892), Arthur Honegger (On-eh-gair, 1892–1955), and Francis Poulenc (Poo-lahnk, 1899–1963). These men progressed beyond the Cocteau-Satie phase into mature composers in their own right.

In 1914 Milhaud went to Brazil to serve as secretary to the French ambassador. His acquaintance with Latin American music made a lasting impression on him. He returned to Paris after the war by way of the United States. On this trip another world of music was opened up to him—jazz. He wrote of his visits to night clubs in Harlem:

> The music I heard was absolutely different from anything I had ever heard before, and was a revelation to me. Against the beat of the drums the melodic lines criss-crossed in a breathless pattern of broken and twisted rhythms . . . Its effect on me was so overwhelming that I could not tear myself away.

Although hindered by arthritis, he toured extensively. In World War II he fled France for the United States, where he taught for several years at Mills College in California. He now lives alternately in America and France.

Milhaud is a prolific composer. His opus numbers reached three hundred by the time he was sixty. He has written in every medium. Most of his music is characterized by a French lightness and charm. He is fond of bitonality. Some of his works show the influence of the jazz he heard in Harlem, especially his ballet *La Création du Monde* (The Creation of the World), written in 1923. Its story is similar to Stravinsky's *The Rite of Spring*. The similarities stop there, however. Instead of a huge orchestra, Milhaud writes for a seventeen-piece jazz band.

Honegger was more conservative than Milhaud. While Milhaud was writing his early irreverent works, Honegger was writing the tone poem *Pacific 231*, descriptive of a train. By that time, 1922, tone poems had become strictly passé. Throughout his life he proceeded to write as he wished, without being unduly influenced by changing compositional fashions. His most successful works are of large scope, involving chorus, soloists, and orchestra. *Roi David* (King David, 1921) is the best-known of these. Later he wrote more purely instrumental numbers, including symphonies and chamber works.

Poulenc's music most nearly expresses the Cocteau-Satie attitude. Most of his works are intended to be charming and pleasant, even gauche in a well-mannered way. He wrote nothing for full orchestra, preferring instead to write songs, vocal works, and some chamber music. He also wrote two operas: *Mamelles de Tirésias* (1947) and *Les Dialogues des Carmélites* (1953). The two operas are entirely different. *Mamelles* is a surrealistic farce in which people change sex and babies are born in incubators. It also spoofs some well-known composers and old-fashioned music. *Les Dialogues* is serious and devout—the story of a Carmelite nun who chooses death rather than return to the outside world.

Latin America

The Brazilian Heitor Villa-Lobos (1887–1959) was encouraged by Milhaud in 1915 while the latter composer was with the embassy. Villa-Lobos was a man of tremendous energy who adopted ideas from many composers and styles. His greatest inspiration was the music of the Brazilian people. Although his 2000 works are of uneven quality, many of them are fascinating and unique. His *Bachianas Brasileiras* and *Choros* (he wrote ten of each) are filled with rich sound that alternates between being romantic and blatant.

Heitor Villa-Lobos.

Carlos Chávez (b. 1899) is Mexico's leading composer. His *Symphonie Indee* utilized genuine Inca music, and his *Toccata for Percussion* is an exciting, rhythmic work.

TWENTIETH-CENTURY OPERA

No one opera can serve as an example of all the divergent types that have been written in this century. But at least one outstanding work can be studied with profit, and a few generalizations can be drawn from that study.

Menotti's The Medium

The Medium by Gian-Carlo Menotti was first performed in 1946 in New York. It was commissioned by and premiered at a university (Columbia), and it was not at first affiliated with a commercial opera house.

Menotti was born in 1911 in Italy, but he has lived in America since the age of sixteen. His many successful operas include *The Old Maid and the Thief*, *The Telephone* (a short comic opera that is often coupled with *The Medium* on the same program), *The Consul*, *The Saint of Bleecker Street*, and *Amahl and the Night Visitors*, the latter work having been commissioned for television. He writes the librettos as well as the music for his operas.

The cast of *The Medium* is small. There are only six characters, one of whom is a mute, and three have rather minor roles. There is no chorus. The presentation, then, contrasts sharply with the large casts and choruses found in most Romantic operas. Other differences can be observed. Only one stage setting is required for the opera's two acts. Furthermore, the entire opera encompasses less than one hour of performance time. This length is a distinct reversal of Romantic tendencies, since three or more hours is not an unusual length for a Romantic opera. (*La Bohème* is an exception.)

Menotti's orchestra is also much smaller. The piano is given a prominent part in the accompaniment, whereas it formerly had only limited use in the orchestra. Gone are the lush sounds of yesteryear, although the orchestra does provide coloristic effects to augment the meaning of the singer's words. For instance, at one point in this opera, Madame Flora is sick with fear. As she wails out the word "afraid," the strings sound rapidly repeating notes as though to suggest trembling.

The story, which takes place in New York, is about a devious old lady (Madame Flora, known to her family as Baba) who dupes bereaved

Gian-Carlo Menotti on the set of his television opera Amahl and the Night Visitors.

people into thinking that she can serve as a medium between themselves and the dead. She is assisted in this hoax by her daughter Monica, a sheltered girl of seventeen, and by a mute orphan, Toby, whom she once picked off the streets of Budapest.

The curtain opens on Madame Flora's weird and shabby parlor. The apartment is arranged according to the stage sketch shown. Monica sings to Toby as they indulge in one of their fantasy games, in which he is an oriental king. Madame Flora enters, irked that nothing is ready for the evening seance. Quickly all is made ready—the wires that move the table, the lights, and the curtain behind which Monica imitates the voices of the dead loved ones. Mr. and Mrs. Gobineau enter; they have been attending seances for two years. Soon Mrs. Nolan arrives. It is her first experience with Madame Flora, and she is understandably nervous. The Gobineaus and Mrs. Nolan exchange information about the tragedies that have brought them there.

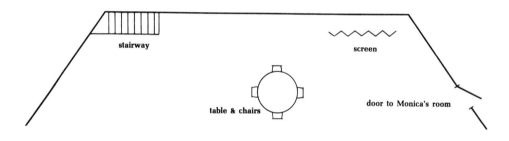

Finally the seance begins. The lights are dimmed and an eerie wailing is evident. Soon a haunting motive ("Mother, Mother, are you there?") is heard coming from behind the screen, where Monica is impersonating Mrs. Nolan's daughter:

Monica and Mrs. Nolan converse for a while, and Monica sings some wonderfully warm, reassuring melodies:

What is death but a sweet-er change, there's no part - ing, there's no end.

She encourages Mrs. Nolan to give away her daughter's personal effects, no doubt mostly to Madame Flora. She mentions a locket. "I have no locket," says Mrs. Nolan. Suddenly the image behind the curtain begins to disappear, and Mrs. Nolan runs to the screen. She is stopped and calmed down.

Next it is the Gobineaus' turn. They talk with their two-year-old son and take comfort from his happy laughter. Suddenly Madame Flora screams. A cold hand has touched her throat! But who or what? The persons involved in the seance were touching hands at all times. Toby and Monica were behind the screen. Madame Flora abruptly ends the seance and rudely dismisses the customers. As they slowly climb the stairs, bewildered and accusing, they sing a chant-like melody to her: "Why be afraid of our dead?" As the act closes, Monica is trying to calm her mother by singing an old gypsy ballad. Madame Flora, terribly shaken, mumbles superstitiously and whispers her rosary in a distracted manner.

The actions of the second act parallel the events of the first. So does some of the music. A week has passed. Monica sings a song, actually an aria, and improvises a dance for Toby. Suddenly the game is no longer childish. Monica asks "Toby, what is it you want to tell me?" Toby, the mute, doesn't need a tongue; the orchestra answers for him with intense, impassioned chords that can only mean love. As Monica's aria continues, she sings both Toby's role and her own. Throughout the scene, much tenderness is added by Monica's gentle caressing of Toby's head. Her lines end "Why, Toby! You're not crying are you? Toby, I want you to know that you have the most beautiful voice in the world!"

The mood changes abruptly, of course, when Madame Flora enters, disheveled and carrying a bottle; she is obviously still tormented by memory of the hand that touched her throat at the seance. She pulls every known trick—emotional blackmail, bribes, threats, and love—to get Toby to admit that he was responsible. Toby's inability to answer only frustrates her further. Toby can neither admit nor deny any guilt, and his silence contributes eloquently to the rising tension of the opera. Madame Flora sings "Toby, you know that I love you," but the orchestral accompaniment is tense and dissonant. It seems to reveal the falseness of the words. Before she is through with Toby, she loses her temper and begins whipping him.

The doorbell rings. Still breathless, Madame Flora answers. It is the Gobineaus and Mrs. Nolan, arriving for their weekly seance. To ease her conscience, she offers to return their money and explains how she tricked them. But they refuse to believe her! Mrs. Nolan has even found the locket! They plead for another seance, but in a rage Madame Flora orders them out. Then, despite Monica's pleadings to the contrary, her mother orders Toby to leave and sends Monica to her room.

Madame Flora seats herself at the table. The haunting "Mother, Mother" motive is heard. Her shouting cannot seem to stop it. She tries to reassure herself: she has seen many horrors in her lifetime, and *they* have never bothered her. She prays. She laughs at her fears. She prays again. Finally, she becomes drowsy and lays her head on the table.

Silently Toby re-enters the apartment. He tries Monica's door but it is locked. He opens a trunk but the lid drops, making a sharp noise. Madame Flora wakens as Toby scampers behind the screen. "Who's there?" she cries. "Speak out or I'll shoot!" Toby's muteness is eloquent. Madame Flora fires. Silence. Then blood begins running down the white curtain. Finally Toby's body falls headlong into the room. Madame Flora unlocks Monica's door, exclaiming "I've killed the ghost!" Monica, horrified, sees what has happened. She cries for help and then runs down the stairs and out into the night. Madame Flora kneels over Toby's lifeless form, still demanding an answer: "Was it you? Was it you?"

Here the opera ends, with its tensions unresolved. The audience has looked on the tangled emotions of persons under stress. As in other modern operas, considerable psychological depth is imparted to the characters. People are seen to be complex mixtures of fear, gullibility, tenderness, guilt, and childishness. No longer are their emotions simple ones like love and anger. Their feelings are sometimes mixed and their motives uncertain. Freudian thinking has, in effect, moved onto the opera stage. *The Medium* might be described as a "psychological opera." Madame Flora, it can be said, is suffering from hallucinations caused by extreme feelings of guilt. But whatever the clinical analysis, the human tragedy lies in the fact that, in attempting to solve her problems, she compounds them. Menotti treats her tortured existence with both insight and compassion.

Menotti and several other twentieth-century opera composers have faced the economic realities of opera production. Their operas are small in scope, and the trappings of the stage are sparse. These composers know that there is little chance for a *new* opera with a huge cast and extensive scenery to be produced. It is just too expensive. Opera companies can hardly make ends meet even when they confine themselves to the standard repertoire. Besides, these modern opera composers are not at all sure that the grandiose opera is what they want to write or what the public wants to hear. They think that perhaps opera comes across best in a more intimate situation, in a setting more closely resembling the chamber-music environment. Although a few operas on a large scale are still being written and produced, with varying degrees of success, there does seem to be a trend toward the smaller, more down-to-earth opera.

THE TWENTIETH CENTURY IN REVIEW

At this point a summary of the changes that have occurred in modern music may be helpful. Twentieth-century music is, first of all, more objective, more intellectual, more fascinated by techniques. It is judged more on its craftsmanship and impact than on its loveliness or lyrical character. Modern composers have sought to create music that has more of an impact on the listener than ever before, with results that have often seemed barbaric and blatant. Some twentieth-century music is cynical and irreverent, as the Cocteau-Satie attitude illustrates.

To achieve desired sounds, composers are manipulating musical elements in new ways. They are disregarding the long-hallowed adherence to a steady beat and are exploiting the driving, dazzling power of rhythm as never before. Tonality is treated freely or is completely abandoned. This approach has produced melodies and harmonies so different that they can no longer be judged by past standards. Chords, for example, are often built in patterns quite different from the old "every-other-note" arrangement. Extreme dissonances are commonplace and no longer need to be resolved. Homophonic music has toppled from its place of prominence, and polyphonic-contrapuntal music has returned with renewed force. New tonal effects are being achieved with instruments. Composers, by and large, are highly specific in their orchestrations.

Many old forms are being revived; some, like the concerto grosso, have not been used widely for a century and a half. New forms are tried, too, and new combinations of instruments and voices occur frequently. New sources of music are tapped—the folk music of Europe and Latin America as well as jazz—and are reset in the context of twentieth-century music.

What a monumental century for music this has been—and it is not yet over. Nor have all the composers and styles been mentioned. One important area, music in the United States, is the subject of the next chapter.

SUGGESTIONS FOR FURTHER LISTENING

BARTÓK:
Concerto for Orchestra
Music for Strings, Percussion, Celesta
Roumanian Folk Dances
String Quartets

BERG:
Concerto for Violin and Orchestra
Lyric Suite
Wozzeck

BRITTEN:
Ceremony of Carols, Op. 28
Serenade for Tenor, Horn, and Strings, Op. 31
War Requiem, Op. 66
Operas: see page 387

CHÁVEZ:
Symphonie Indee

HINDEMITH:
Mathis der Maler
Symphonic Metamorphosis of Themes by Weber

HONEGGER:
Pacific 231

KODÁLY:
Háry János Suite

MILHAUD:
Cheminée du Roi René
Création du monde
Scaramouche Suite, Op. 165b

ORFF:
Carmina Burana

POULENC:
Gloria in G Major
Sextuor for Piano and Woodwind Quintet

PROKOFIEV:
Classical Symphony in D Major, Op. 25
Concerto No. 3 in C Major for Piano, Op. 26
Lieutenant Kijé Suite, Op. 60
Symphony No. 5, Op. 100

SCHOENBERG:
Five Pieces for Orchestra, Op. 16
Concerto for Piano and Orchestra, Op. 42
Verklärte Nacht, Op. 4

SHOSTAKOVICH:
Quintet for Piano and Strings, Op. 57
Symphony No. 1, Op. 10
Symphony No. 7, Op. 60

STRAVINSKY:
Firebird Suite
Petrouchka Suite
Symphony of Psalms
Symphony in C Major

VAUGHAN WILLIAMS:
Fantasia on a Theme by Tallis
Symphony No. 5 in D Major

VILLA-LOBOS:
Bachianas Brasileiras No. 5
Chôros No. 1 for Guitar

WALTON:
Belshazzar's Feast

American Music

16

Music in America had a slow start, for several reasons. The nation began as a loose confederation of small, struggling settlements, isolated from the mainstream of European life by three thousand miles of ocean. Physical survival was the uppermost drive. Lacking was the stimulation of contact with recent artistic creations. Furthermore, in those early days there could be no truly American music, since the settlers came from other lands and were steeped in the traditions of English, Dutch, or German music. The Puritan influence, too, was strong in the colonies. Rightly or wrongly, these devout people thought that art and theater were inimical to religious piety. At best, art and music were mere diversion; at worst, they were products of the devil. The only music permitted was the unaccompanied singing of psalms and hymns. Not surprisingly, then, the first book published in America was the *Bay Psalm Book*, in 1640. The first edition had no music, and none was added until the ninth edition in 1698.

The most sophisticated music written in America before the Revolutionary War was the product of the Moravian communities around Bethlehem, Pennsylvania. These people had come from the Moravian area of

Germany, bringing with them a rich musical heritage. Besides music for church services, they also wrote chamber works. Musicologists are still discovering some of this fine music. There were several active composers in the Moravian community, but John Frederick Peter (1746–1813) was the most skilled. He came to America in 1770.

The first native-born American composer was an amateur, Francis Hopkinson (1737–1791), a friend of George Washington and a signer of the Declaration of Independence. His most famous song was "My Days Have Been So Wondrous Free." In 1788 he published some songs, for which he also wrote the words. He dedicated the book to Washington, whose reply was humble, especially with regard to his own musical ability: "I can neither sing one of the songs, nor raise a single note on any instrument to convince the unbelieving. But I have, however, one argument which will prevail with persons of true estate (at least in America)—I can tell them that *it is the production of Mr. Hopkinson.*"

If Francis Hopkinson's compositions did not sound particularly different from English music at the time, the works of William Billings (1746–1800) did. Billings was a tanner by trade, but he had an insatiable drive to write music. And he was a firm believer in American music for Americans! He explained in his first collection, *The New England Psalm Singer* (1770), that he would follow his own rules for composition. One of the techniques he used in his hymns was "fuguing," which was a high-class name for simple imitation. Billings was not particularly modest in making claims: "[Fuguing] is twenty times as powerful as the old slow tunes. Each part striving for mastery and victory. The audience entertained and delighted. Now the solemn bass demands their attention; next the manly tenor. Now here, now there, now here again! O ecstatic! Rush on, you sons of harmony."

Whatever Billings lacked in training was offset by his native musical ability. Despite some crudities, his music has a quality that has fascinated many musicians and lay people, especially in this century. The tune "Chester" is one of his best known. A version of it from Billings' *Singing Master's Assistant* is shown on page 401. The melody is in the tenor part, which is the third line from the top. The music is extremely plain and unadorned. "Chester" was destined to reappear in the annals of American music, specifically in the twentieth-century music of William Schuman.

Billings was the only ray of American light to appear in a long night of European-dominated music. Even our national songs had their roots in Europe. The origin of "Yankee Doodle" is unknown, but it was first printed in Glasgow in 1782. The British sang it to ridicule the Yankees, who promptly took it over as their own song by adding new verses. The melody of "The Star-Spangled Banner" was adapted from a popular English drinking song, "To Anacreon in Heaven," which was composed by John Stafford

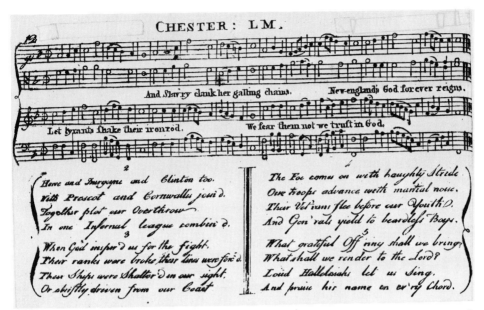

"Chester" by William Billings, as it appears in his Singing Master's
Assistant. *The initials L. M. in the title mean "long meter" and indicate that there are eight syllables in every phrase of the text.*

Smith (1750–1836). The words were written as a poem by the American
Francis Scott Key as he watched the British bombard Fort McHenry in
1814. It was not officially made the national anthem until 1931. "America" is
sung to the same tune as the British national anthem "God Save the King,"
which was written by the English composer Henry Carey (1685–1743). The
words as sung in this country were contributed by the American Samuel
Francis Smith (1808–1895) at the suggestion of Lowell Mason.

THE NINETEENTH CENTURY

The name Mason is an important one in American music. Lowell
Mason (1792–1872) wrote many hymns, including "Nearer, My God, to
Thee," and conducted the Handel and Haydn Society in Boston. His most
significant achievement was the establishment of music in the curriculum of
the public schools in 1838. He also spread the idea of music for the masses
by organizing "conventions" for the training of music teachers. He made
several lengthy trips to Europe to study. Two of his sons founded the piano-
manufacturing company of Mason and Hamlin, and a third son became a

famous music teacher. Mason led a campaign against the "gospel song," which came into being after the decline of Billings' "fuguing tunes." As part of this effort, Mason published a large number of music collections.

Not only did America import much of its music; it imported musicians as well. Many European virtuosos found it profitable to tour the United States. The most sensational of these was the singer Jenny Lind, who was advertised by her brilliant promoter, P. T. Barnum, as "the Swedish Nightingale."

An American piano virtuoso was Louis Moreau Gottschalk (1829–1869). He was a handsome man who cultivated some of the mannerisms of Liszt. He often left his white gloves on the piano for his female admirers to fight over. He wrote sentimental works with such tearjerking titles as *The Last Hope* and *The Dying Poet*.

Louis A. Jullien (1812–1860) chose a different approach. He kept his white gloves on as he conducted with his jewelled baton. He played some good music, including works by American composers. But his biggest success was a number entitled *Firemen's Quadrille*, during which, as flames burst from the ceiling, he brought the local fire department into the hall to dramatically quench the blaze.

For sheer spectacle he was matched only by Patrick Gilmore (1829–1892), a bandmaster who organized supercolossal extravaganzas. One was the Great National Peace Jubilee in Boston in 1869. The performers included a chorus of ten thousand and an orchestra of one thousand, with cannons and one hundred firemen pounding anvils in the "Anvil Chorus" from Verdi's *Il Trovatore*. The only way for Gilmore to top that was to organize a World Peace Jubilee. For this he brought Johann Strauss from Europe to lead his *Blue Danube Waltz*. Although the orchestra was held down to one thousand players, the chorus was increased to twenty thousand singers. Strauss later described, in a letter home, his feelings of terror as he stepped before the group.

From Jullien's orchestra emerged a young German violinist named Theodore Thomas (1835–1905). In 1862 he organized his own orchestra. He maintained high standards of performance and sought to educate the audience, and in so doing he laid the foundation for the symphony orchestras of today. He traveled widely throughout the United States and was for a while the conductor of the New York Philharmonic. Later he organized the Chicago Symphony and was its conductor for many years.

The revolutions in Europe, and especially in Germany, in the mid-1800s brought thousands of immigrants to America. Many were musicians who soon became affiliated with orchestras and opera companies throughout the country. The European immigrants constituted an interested audience for the German symphonic music that Thomas performed for them.

Stephen Collins Foster (1826–1864) was a native American composer both by birth and by compositional style. He was not a Southerner, as many people erroneously believe. He was born in Lawrenceville, Pennsylvania, of a middle-class family. His parents did not consider music a suitable career for a man, and so they did nothing to encourage him. He was a dreamer and a failure at almost everything he undertook—work, marriage, and serious musical compositions. But he was a genius at writing popular songs. He wrote about two hundred of them, particularly for minstrel shows. "Beautiful Dreamer," "My Old Kentucky Home," "Old Folks at Home," "De Camptown Races," "O Susanna," and others are still popular today.

Late in the nineteenth century a few capable American composers began to write longer and more sophisticated works. Most of these composers lived around Boston, and almost all of them had studied in Germany at one time or another. Consequently, much of their music sounded like works of the European masters with whom they had studied. The "Boston" or "New England" group included George W. Chadwick (1854–1931), Horatio Parker (1863–1919), Arthur Foote (1853–1937), and John Knowles Paine (1839–1906), who taught Foote. Little of their music is heard today.

Edward MacDowell (1861–1908) had excellent musical training. He studied at the Paris Conservatory when he was eleven years old, and was a classmate of Debussy. He also played for Liszt at Weimar in 1882. After his return to America, he was for eight years a professor of music at Columbia University. Most of his works are for piano, with *Woodland Sketches* and the ever-popular "To a Wild Rose" being representative of his style. He also wrote four piano sonatas and two piano concertos. His *Suite No. 2* ("Indian Suite") was a landmark, because it was one of the first American works to use music from native sources.

THE TWENTIETH CENTURY

Soon after the turn of the century, the popularity of German Romanticism began to wane in America, only to be replaced by attempts to imitate impressionism. The best-known "American impressionist" was Charles Tomlinson Griffes (1884–1920). At first he wrote in the German tradition, but he later switched to the Debussy-Ravel style. "The White Peacock" from *Roman Sketches* is still a frequently performed number of his. Charles Martin Loeffler (1861–1935), who immigrated to America from Alsace at the age of twenty, also wrote music of a somewhat impressionistic nature.

Thus as the twentieth century began, American music was in a dormant state. All around was a rich heritage of folk music in the songs of the Negro, the lumberjack, the sailor, the cowboy, the Indian, and the mountaineer, as well as the ballads and folklore brought to America by its myriad peoples. But aside from the American MacDowell, only the Bohemian Dvořák had chosen to draw on musical resources of this country. American composers apparently had feelings of inferiority about the quality of their own culture. Not only did it seem necessary for all serious musicians to study in Europe; it was considered advisable to pattern new compositions on European models.

However, one composer in America was writing modern, innovative American music prior to World War I. And at the time, virtually no one had heard of him. The name of Charles Ives meant nothing.

CHARLES IVES

Ives (1874–1954) was born in Danbury, Connecticut, the son of a bandmaster. His father was no ordinary town band leader. He encouraged his son to listen carefully and try to write different tonal effects. "Stretch your ears," was his advice. And so young Ives experimented with various acoustical effects, such as new tunings for the piano, or two bands playing different music while marching toward and away from each other. He attended Yale as a music student, and upon graduation went to New York, where he literally made a fortune in the insurance business. He had a country home in Connecticut. In the evenings he would sit at his desk and compose for relaxation. As he finished a page of music he would stack it on the floor near him. When the stacks became too high, he would carry them out to the barn for storage. Because he had no need for money, he did not feel the need to have his works published and sold. In fact, for a long time no one knew about them; they just sat there in the barn.

Shortly after the turn of the century, Ives was writing novel harmonies and rhythms that did not appear in Europe until a decade or more later. He was using such ideas as polytonality, dissonant counterpoint, atonality, polyrhythm, chords with added tones, unusual melodic intervals, and something called *sprechstimme*, which is a kind of singsong speech that Schoenberg used in several of his works.

Ives' *Symphony No. 3*, written between 1901 and 1904, won him the Pulitzer Prize in 1947. Another work that is often played is the *Piano Sonata No. 2* ("Concord"), which contains fragments of several well-known tunes heard in Concord, Massachusetts between 1840 and 1860. The fragments Ives selected, the manner in which he employed devices such as polytonality, the character of his melodies, and his use of instruments produced music that was in no sense a copy of Stravinsky or Milhaud. It was American music. At long last, the seed planted by Billings, the tanner, was flourishing in Ives, the insurance man. But until the 1930s, no one knew it.

Charles Ives.

American music came of age shortly after World War I. Soon it would equal that being written anywhere in the world. The music of three esteemed American composers will serve to exemplify the new music of our land: Aaron Copland, William Schuman, and Alan Hovhaness.

AARON COPLAND

Aaron Copland was born in Brooklyn in 1900 of Russian-Jewish immigrant parents. He attended the New York City public schools, worked in his father's department store, and took his first piano lessons from his older sister. After graduation from high school, he studied piano and harmony in New York and spent much time studying scores at the public library. In 1921 he went·to the American School of Music at Fontainebleau in France. The teacher there was a remarkable woman named Mlle. Nadia Boulanger (Boo-lahn-zhay). Copland became the first of a long list of young American composers to study with her. When she was invited to give some concerts in the United States, she asked Copland to compose a work for performance on her tour. The work he provided was the *Symphony for Organ and Orchestra*. It was given its first performance in New York in 1925. Thus his career as a composer was launched.

Aaron Copland.

Copland became interested in jazz in the late twenties, and several of his compositions show the jazz influence. *Music for the Theater* and *Symphonic Ode* are from this period. His works in the early thirties tend to be more abstract, as revealed in his *Piano Variations* and *Short Symphony*. In the late thirties he showed the influence of the *gebrauchsmusik* ideal in *The Second Hurricane* and *Outdoor Overture*, both of which were written for performance by school groups. *A Lincoln Portrait* is a tremendously exciting work. It contains a part for narrator and is centered on the quotations of Abraham Lincoln. *El Salón México* is a rhythmic rhapsody on Mexican tunes.

In three of his works, all ballets, Copland exploits American folk music: *Billy the Kid* (1938), *Rodeo* (1942), and *Appalachian Spring* (1943–1944). In them he reaches a happy medium between retaining the interest and respect of the trained musician and at the same time pleasing the public. Not many twentieth-century composers have been able to accomplish this!

Since the late 1940s his music has become a bit more intellectual, and he has worked to some extent with tone-row principles. Copland has traveled widely, his journeys taking him to South America and the Far East. With Roger Sessions, another able American composer, he organized a series of concerts to promote new music in America. He is the author of several very readable books for the musical layman. He has lectured at many universities and has written several film scores.

Copland's Appalachian Spring

This ballet concerns the courtship and wedding of a Shaker couple in rural Pennsylvania in the early nineteenth century. It was written for the outstanding choreographer and teacher Martha Graham. Copland draws on several Shaker melodies to serve as themes. The overall spirit of the ballet is calm and hymn-like, as befits the character of the people being portrayed. The music is usually heard as a concert suite arranged by the composer.

Copland provides a synopsis of the score. The opening section is marked *Very Slowly.* His words continue, "Introduction of the characters, one by one, in a suffused light."[1] The bride enters, then the groom, a neighbor, and a revivalist and his flock. The music is built around a motive derived from the major chord. Soon a hymn-like melody emerges:

Notice that the distance between many of its tones is four or five steps. These intervals add to the open, sturdy sound of the line. Notice also that Copland writes the tempo directions in English.

"2. *Fast.* A sudden burst of unison strings in A-major arpeggios starts the action. A sentiment both elated and religious gives the keynote to this scene." The theme is a lively one that could come from no other country than America:

Copland soon combines the high, rapidly moving notes with the long notes in the trombones and basses. The flute has a lovely obligato part.

"3. Duo for bride and her intended—scene of tenderness and

---

[1] *Appalachian Spring,* copyright 1945 by Boosey and Hawkes, Inc. Used by permission.

passion." Here Copland depicts with taste and skill the sensitivity and sincerity of feeling that pervades the scene.

"4. *Quite fast.* The Revivalist and his flock. Folksy feeling—suggestions of square dances and country fiddlers." The music here is as American as baseball and the Liberty Bell.

"5. *Still faster.* Solo dance of the bride—presentiment of motherhood. Extremes of joy and fear and wonder." Again the music is beautifully sensitive and expressive.

"6. *Very slowly* (as at first). Transition scene to music reminiscent of the introduction." Some of the music heard in this section is derived from Section 2.

"7. *Calm and flowing.* Scenes of daily activity for the bride and her farmer husband. There are five variations on a Shaker theme." The Shaker song Copland has chosen is "Simple Gifts." It appears first in the clarinet:

The theme is perfectly suited to the needs of the music. The words to the folk song give an even better clue to the character of the Shaker religious sect.

> 'Tis a gift to be simple,
> 'Tis a gift to be free,
> 'Tis a gift to come down where you ought to be.
> And when we find ourselves in the place just right,
> 'Twill be in the valley of love and delight.
>
> When true simplicity is gained,
> To bow and to bend we shan't be ashamed.
> To turn, turn, will be our delight
> 'Til by turning, turning we come round right.

Copland treats the theme to old-fashioned contrapuntal devices such as augmentation, canon, and new lines of counterpoint. The theme ends in a mighty hymn.

"8. The bride takes her place among her neighbors." The section is a quiet coda that balances the Introduction. The neighbors depart, and the newlyweds remain "quiet and strong in their new house." The music closes with a serene passage for strings, which sounds "like a prayer."

The story for the ballet *Appalachian Spring* is thoroughly American, and Copland's music is equally native to our land. There is something about the way the sounds are organized that can never be confused with Russian, Spanish, or German music. So in the twentieth century the United States was finally to produce its nationalistic music.

Appalachian Spring sounds simple and uncomplicated. Think back to Schoenberg's *Variations for Orchestra* or Stravinsky's *The Rite of Spring* to realize the differences between those works and Copland's. There is more technical sophistication in Copland's music than is immediately noticeable, but it does sound less complex than its European contemporaries. And this is not entirely due to the demands for simplicity in the story. Most of Copland's works have this quality, and it can be observed in the music of many other American composers. The lines are bolder and more clear-cut, imparting a straightforward quality to the music.

WILLIAM SCHUMAN

William Schuman was born in New York City (in 1910), and entered the music world as a Tin Pan Alley song writer and song plugger. At the same time, he was enrolled in a business curriculum at New York University. He heard his first symphony concert when he was about twenty years old. It made such an impact on him that the next day he withdrew from his business course and quit the job he had taken with an advertising agency. He switched his major to music and for two years attended Teachers College, Columbia University. While teaching at Sarah Lawrence College, he led the college chorus, which familiarized him with the vocal medium. He also studied with Roy Harris.

By the late 1930s, Schuman's music was being performed by major orchestras at home and abroad. In 1945 he became president of the Juilliard School of Music, a position he held until 1961, when he became director of the Lincoln Center for the Performing Arts.

Schuman is equally successful in writing for vocal and instrumental groups. Most of his vocal works date from the early 1940s and include *Pioneers*, based on Walt Whitman's poetry; a "secular cantata" named *A Free Song;* and the short, vivacious "Holiday Song." His instrumental works are better known. They include a number of symphonies and

William Schuman.

chamber works. Several, such as *New England Triptych*, are based on national themes.

Schuman's New England Triptych

In 1956 Schuman turned to the music of that early Boston tanner William Billings. He chose three of Billings' songs to serve as the basis for this orchestral work. The word "triptych" (*trip*-tic) comes from a Greek word meaning "three layers or parts."

In the program notes—Schuman requested that they be included whenever possible—he pays this tribute to Billings:

> The works of this dynamic composer capture the spirit of sinewy ruggedness, deep religiosity, and patriotic fervor that we associate with the Revolutionary Period. Despite the undeniable crudities and technical shortcomings of his music, its appeal, even today, is forceful and moving. I am not alone among American composers who feel an identity with Billings and it is this sense of identity which accounts for my use of his music as a point of departure. These pieces do not constitute a "fantasy" on themes of Billings, nor "variations" on his themes, but rather a fusion of styles and musical language.[2]

The first movement of the Triptych is built from the anthem "Be Glad Then, America." The opening timpani solo is developed further in the strings:

Trombones and trumpets start the main section, which is a free and varied setting of the words "Be glad then, America, shout and rejoice":

The timpani lead into a fugal section based on the theme for the words "And ye shall be satisfied":

The music gains momentum and combines themes as it continues to a climax.

Playing melodic themes on the timpani became possible late in the Romantic period through the addition of pedals, which enabled the player to regulate the tension of the drumheads more quickly and thereby change pitch at will. Schuman's use of timpani in this work is highly effective.

The excitement that can be created by exploitation of rhythm is illustrated in the fugal section of the music. In the following example, the regular beats have a number above them, and the syncopated notes are marked by an X.

The meter changes from $\frac{2}{4}$ to $\frac{3}{4}$ and back to $\frac{2}{4}$. The passage demonstrates that instruments other than percussion can achieve very vigorous rhythms.

The second movement is based on Billings' anthem "When Jesus Wept." The text of the original anthem is:

When Jesus wept, the falling tear
In mercy flowed beyond all bound;
When Jesus groaned, a trembling fear
Seized all the guilty world around.

The tenor drum with snares loosened opens the section. With its hollow sound, it imparts the feel of a funeral procession. The bassoon begins Billings' melody, followed by the oboe.

The melody is a moderately long round. Schuman probably chose these two instruments because their timbres suggest melancholy. The tune would not sound nearly so plaintive if played by a flute or clarinet.

The relationship between the notes of the two lines illustrates a characteristic of modern music. Traditionally, two contrapuntal lines were expected to fit together in a pleasing consonance. But in this setting of "When Jesus Wept," they don't. In fact, they are sometimes downright dissonant. Because twentieth-century composers use dissonance so freely, it is only logical to assume that some of the counterpoint will likewise be dissonant. And so it is. In the musical example below, the notes with an X above them are dissonances that seldom appeared before the twentieth century.

Is dissonant counterpoint good music in this instance? Yes, because it contributes to the painful character of the experience that the music is attempting to express in sound.

After the oboe-bassoon duet, the strings play in the same mournful mood. The duet returns again to round out a three-part form. The funeral cadence of the drum closes the movement.

The final movement is based on Billings' marching song "Chester," and it is dazzling. The tune is played by the woodwinds in a straightforward hymn style. But suddenly the tempo doubles, creating the effect of diminution. Flashy runs are heard, and fragments of the theme appear from time to time. There is even a "fife and drum" duet between the piccolo and snare drum. The percussion instruments add conspicuously to the fireworks that conclude the *Triptych*.

Schuman has written a work that stands in the mainstream of American culture, historically and emotionally. The music, like American life itself, is vigorous, dynamic, and perhaps a bit brash. Notice the prominent place given the brass and percussion. Of course, this instrumentation is partially the result of all the attention accorded to rhythm. But Schoenberg, Britten, and Milhaud do not use anywhere near the same amount of brass and percussion. Only the Russian Shostakovich comes close to it, and even he does not equal the American composers in this respect.

ALAN HOVHANESS

Alan Hovhaness Chakmakjian was born on March 8, 1911 in Somerville, Massachusetts, of Armenian-Scottish parents. From the beginning he seemed destined to bring together the best of two worlds, the old and the new, the occident and the orient. His musical training in his younger years was largely confined to Boston and the New England Conservatory of Music. He did, however, study astronomy and Eastern music and religions. For a while he taught theory and composition in Boston and was church organist at an Armenian church in Watertown, Massachusetts. Early in his career he dropped his long and complicated last name.

Hovhaness began receiving public attention in the late 1940s. Thereafter he received several awards and grants to study music and compose. These grants took him to India, Japan, and Korea. His creative work seems to have increased with these journeys. His opus numbers are well past 200.

Unlike Copland and Schuman, Hovhaness was not interested in creating American music. He typifies the change of many American composers into more cosmopolitan or international styles. In writing about the

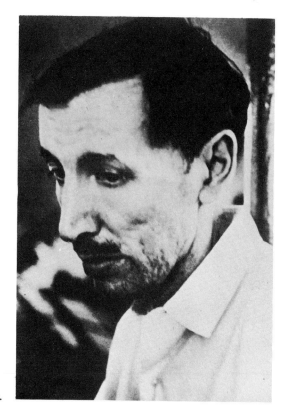

Alan Hovhaness.

Symphony No. 4, which he composed in 1958, he says "I admire the giant melody of the Himalayan Mountains, seventh-century Armenian religious music, classical music of South India, orchestra music of Tang Dynasty China about 700 A.D., opera-oratorios of Handel." His *Symphony No. 4* represents a synthesis of these very different musical styles.

Hovhaness' Symphony No. 4

This symphony is unusual in that it is written for what Hovhaness calls a "wind orchestra." No strings are used, except the harp. The word "band" was not used because the instrumentation is more limited than most band music. (Instrumentation is far less consistent for bands than for orchestras.) This particular score calls for flutes, oboes, English horn, clarinets, bass clarinet, bassoon, contrabassoon, horns, trumpets, and trombones, tuba, and harp, plus four percussion parts. No more than six instruments of any single type are specified.

And Hovhaness does achieve something different from the traditional band sound. The music is filled with what he calls "points of sound" —coloristic tonal effects, mainly from the percussion section. To add even more color to the music, groups of instruments are sounded in contrast to one another in concerto grosso style. The bass clarinet, contrabassoon, marimba, and xylophone—instruments seldom heard from—are given lengthy solos.

The first movement consists of five sections, with the first and third, and the second and fourth having a similar character. Sections one and three are hymn-like and are written for brasses. Sections two and four have an oriental quality and feature solo bass clarinet and contrabassoon. The fifth section is like a fugue. It develops contrapuntally.

The second movement opens with a marimba solo in an irregular rhythmic pattern. The middle section consists of two slow dance melodies. The first one is played by the woodwinds and the harp; the second by the vibraphone and woodwinds.

The third movement opens with a hymn-like melody.

Short interludes for the English horn are inserted between appearances of the theme. The second section is for the trombones, which seem to be Hovhaness' favorite instruments. Oboe interludes are included in this portion of the movement. The third section contains an unusual tonal effect. The melody is in the low trombones.

Copyright © 1967 by C. F. Peters Corporation, 373 Park Avenue South, New York, New York 10016. Reprint permission granted by the publisher.

The passage is accompanied by small "smears" or *glissandi* in the higher trombones. Between the third and fourth section there is an interlude for the chimes and bells, reminiscent of Mussorgsky's "Coronation Scene." The fourth and final portion of the movement is fugue-like and employs a theme that is very similar to the one that opened the movement. The symphony ends in a mighty climax of sound.

OTHER AMERICAN COMPOSERS

Some of the world's finest music written during the past thirty-five years has come from the pen of native-born American composers. The twentieth-century Americans mentioned thus far—Ives, Copland, Hovhaness, and Schuman—are but four of many fine composers.

Ernest Bloch (1880–1959) was born in Switzerland but spent much of his adult life in the United States. He wrote many works based on Hebrew melodic style, such as *Schelomo* (Solomon), a rhapsody for cello and orchestra. Other compositions, such as his First Violin Sonata, are more powerful. His *Concerto Grosso No. 1* is especially good—an early form in a modern setting.

Walter Piston (b. 1894) is more classical in his writing. The music for his ballet *The Incredible Flutist* is often performed as an orchestral suite. Most of his works are instrumental and include several symphonies. For many years he taught at Harvard, and he has written several textbooks in music theory.

Howard Hanson.

Howard Hanson (b. 1896) is one of the outstanding names in American music. He is noted both as composer and teacher, and he served for many years as director of the Eastman School of Music. He has promoted American music in many capacities. His works are romantic and rather heavy in nature, something like Sibelius' music. Hanson's *Symphony*

No. 2 ("Romantic") is a moving work. His opera *Merry Mount* is based on an early American story. He writes well for all mediums.

Virgil Thomson (b. 1896) was for many years the music critic for the New York Herald Tribune. His works tend to be witty, sophisticated, and objective. Not a prolific composer, he cooperated with Gertrude Stein on two operas: *Four Saints in Three Acts,* and *The Mother of Us All.* Some of his film scores are played often, particularly *The Plow that Broke the Plains* and *The River.* He has also written some abstract instrumental works.

Roger Sessions (b. 1896) writes generally in a complicated manner. He maintains that music is a medium for expressing highly serious thoughts (not verbal ones, however). And so his music takes on the characteristic of depth and complexity. His not lengthy list of compositions includes two operas as well as orchestral and chamber music. Like Piston, he was a university professor, teaching first at Boston University, then at Princeton and the University of California.

George Gershwin.

George Gershwin (1898–1937) had little musical training. His early efforts were confined to popular songs and musical comedies. In 1924, when he wrote *Rhapsody in Blue,* he did not feel competent to write for instruments other than the piano, so he had Ferde Grofé do the orchestration. Gershwin's writing style matured rapidly, only to be cut short by death from a brain tumor. Other well-known works include *An American in Paris,* for orchestra, and *Concerto in F,* for piano and orchestra. *Porgy and Bess,* a folk opera, is one of the great American works for the stage.

Roy Harris (b. 1898) is a westerner in education and outlook. He has some interesting ideas about music, and he has written some outstanding compositions. He believes that music should be emotional but not romantic and that emotion is best achieved when the tempo is kept close to that of the normal heartbeat (72 to 80 beats per minute). He feels that the brightness of chords is related to the intervals used and their placement in the harmonic series (see Appendix D). His most successful work is *Symphony No. 5.* It was written in 1937–38 and is in one movement of about 17 minutes in length. Five sections can be heard in the work. Harris describes them: I—tragic, II—lyric, III—pastoral, IV—fugue, and V—dramatic. The fifth section contains themes from the previous sections.

Samuel Barber (b. 1910) is highly regarded as an American composer, as evidenced by his commission to compose an opera for the opening of the Metropolitan Opera House in Lincoln Center. His music frequently shows evidence of Neo-Romanticism, as in the lush *Adagio for Strings.* He is equally successful in vocal or instrumental mediums. Besides having written several symphonies and concertos, Barber combines vocalist and orchestra well in *Knoxville: Summer of 1915.* His opera *Vanessa* is considered one of the best written in the twentieth century.

Elliott Carter (b. 1908) developed slowly as a recognized composer. Since 1950, however, his work has assumed more importance and has received high praise from the critics. Most of his compositions are for instrumental groups. His style is complex and appears to be influenced by the music of Schoenberg and Stravinsky.

Norman Dello Joio (b. 1913) combines old and new elements in his music. His *Ricercari, Variations, Chaconne and Finale,* and *Concerto for Harp and Orchestra* all employ old forms. He also reaches back in music history and selects portions of Gregorian chant for thematic material.

Vincent Persichetti (b. 1915) draws from any source and utilizes any technique that he thinks will contribute to his music. He is especially successful in writing for piano. His seven symphonies are worthy of careful listening, as is his *Quintet for Piano and Strings.*

Ulysses Kay (b. 1917) writes both instrumental and choral works. Probably his best known works in each area are *Sinfonia in E,* written in 1950, and *Choral Tryptich,* written in 1962.

Gunther Schuller (b. 1925) is the leading advocate of what he calls the "third stream" movement, which combines contemporary art music and jazz. Unlike the planned jazz writing of Milhaud and others, actual improvisation by jazz musicians is called for in Schuller's music. Among his works in this vein are *12 by 11, Concertino for Jazz Quartet and Orchestra, Densities I,* and *Night Music.* These four works were written between 1955 and 1962. Prior to that time Schuller wrote abstract instrumental compositions using tone-row techniques, and since 1962 he has turned to opera. The "third stream" concept is an idea that seems logical but in fact is not easy to accomplish. To date it has not caught on in a big way, and even Schuller himself has moved to other types of music.

Lukas Foss was born in Berlin in 1922 and came to America in 1937. His early works were in the style of Hindemith, but later he became interested in improvisation. *Time Cycle* was written for soprano and orchestra with improvised interludes.

The list of American composers could be greatly extended, and most of these men deserve far greater coverage than is given them here. You will find it worthwhile to become as familiar as possible with their music. The foregoing study of the music of Copland, Hovhaness, and Schuman will help you in your listening.

MUSICAL COMEDY

If there is a middle ground between the popular song and serious art music, it is occupied by an American musical development called the *musical comedy*. This form of entertainment enjoys tremendous public interest. Enormous sums of money are spent on musical comedies, and over two thousand such productions have opened on Broadway in the last century.

Historically, musical comedy evolved from the musical revue, in which singing and dancing were strung together without pretense of a plot. Musical comedy is generally less formal than an operetta, and it integrates its parts in a logical, natural way. Musical comedy also tends to favor plot subjects dealing with the here-and-now, such as *West Side Story* and *The Pajama Game;* the operetta is more likely to feature the long-ago and far-away, as in *The Student Prince* and *The Desert Song*.

A line from *The Pajama Game* illustrates the present-day, vernacular quality of musical comedy. The workers at the pajama factory are planning to strike for a 7½¢ raise. They sing: "Seven and a half cents doesn't buy a helluva lot . . . but give it to me every hour, forty hours every week . . ." The musical comedy often comments on the current social scene. *Bye Bye Birdie* spoofs the teenage idol, *West Side Story* comments on the strained relations between ethnic and racial groups, and *Hair* vents feelings against established society and national policies.

The musical comedy is an interesting hybrid of commercial and art music. Because of the large sums of money at stake, a favorable audience reaction is imperative. Therefore the writers and producers make any change that they think will gain greater audience response. Such pressures may hamper artistic freedom somewhat, but they also keep the composer in touch with his audience. The musical comedy has been prevented from drifting off into its own little esoteric world, as has happened with some types of twentieth-century art music.

The need for a favorable audience reaction has led to commendable variety in these shows, and has called forth a great deal of imaginative effort. The need for variety means that every kind of music is being incorporated into this entertainment form. Exciting dance numbers exist side by side with romantic and melodious duets and solos. The latest jazz and the most traditional music are often present in the same musical.

Many talented and creative people are associated with musical comedy, and they necessarily have a keen understanding of the audience and its likes. Although there are disadvantages in writing music mainly to please the public, some composers are able to create show music of artistic worth that can still be understood by a majority of the musical-comedy audience. The music of *West Side Story* contains portions that are opera, and these moments are easily assimilated by the audience.

There is an interesting historical parallel between the American musical comedy and the German *Singspiel* of the eighteenth century, which was similar in purpose and makeup to the musical comedy. Mozart wrote some *Singspiels,* and at least one of them, *The Magic Flute,* is still on the standard operatic repertoire. Perhaps the American musical comedy is becoming an art form of similar longevity. At least it may well be serving as the basis for an even better form of dramatic music.

American music has had a rags-to-riches history. From weak imitations of European styles, American music has progressed to a place of equal prominence in the world. America has developed a body of music uniquely its own. With the tremendous vitality of its cultural life and the increasing attention being paid the arts, music in America should continue to change and expand.

SUGGESTIONS FOR FURTHER LISTENING

BARBER:
Adagio for Strings
Essay No. 2 for Orchestra
Knoxville: Summer of 1915
Symphony No. 1 in One Movement
Vanessa

BERNSTEIN:
Symphony No. 3, "Kaddish"
West Side Story

BLOCH:
Concerto Grosso No. 1 for Strings and Piano
Schelomo—Rhapsody for Cello and Orchestra
Sonata No. 1 for Violin and Piano

CARTER:
Sonata for Flute, Oboe, Cello, and Harpsichord
Sonata for Piano

COPLAND:
Billy the Kid: Suite
Lincoln Portrait
Rodeo
El Salón México
Symphony No. 3

DELLO JOIO:
Fantasy and Variations for Piano and Orchestra

FOSS:
Phorion

GERSHWIN:
An American in Paris
Concerto in F
Porgy and Bess

HANSON:
Chorale and Alleluia
Symphony No. 2, "Romantic"

HARRIS:
Sonata for Violin and Piano
Symphony No. 4, "Folksong"

HOVHANESS:
Fantasy of Japanese Woodprints
Mysterious Mountain

IVES:
Sonata No. 2, "Concord, Mass., 1840–1860"
Songs
Three Places in New England

KAY:
Brass Quartet

MACDOWELL:
Suite No. 2, Op. 48, "Indian Suite"
Woodland Sketches

PERSICHETTI:
Concerto for Piano
Masquerade for Band

PISTON:
The Incredible Flutist (ballet suite)
Symphony No. 4

SCHULLER:
Seven Studies on Themes of Paul Klee
Tripium

SCHUMAN:
Carols of Death
Symphony No. 6

SESSIONS:
Black Maskers: Suite
From My Diary
Symphony No. 1

RANDALL THOMPSON:
Alleluia
Testament of Freedom

VIRGIL THOMSON:
Louisiana Story: Acadian Songs and Dances
The Plow That Broke the Plains

The Present and
Future of Music

17

Perhaps the "elbow chord" and Hovhaness' "sound points" mentioned in the preceding chapter have made you wonder, "What's music coming to? Where can it go from here?" The two questions can be answered virtually at the same time.

It isn't easy to single out any style or type of music that currently dominates the world of art music, any more than it is possible to do so in the case of popular music. With the passing of time a definite trend may become evident, but as of the moment such is not the case. "Pluralism" is again the best word to describe the situation. There are several types of music, each with its own devotees, and each based on somewhat different beliefs and attitudes. To further obscure any current trend, some advocates of one type of music have switched to another type and publicly confessed past musical mistakes. Whether the various types are clearly delineated or not, an examination of them is necessary if one is to understand present and future music.

Anton von Webern.

FURTHER DEVELOPMENT OF TONE-ROW TECHNIQUES

Since 1950, an increasing number of composers have turned to the tone-row principles developed by Schoenberg. This trend can be attributed primarily to the influence of a quiet student of his: Anton von Webern (*Vay*-burn, 1883–1945). Webern, who spent almost all his life in Austria, seemed to exemplify the cross-currents and inconsistencies of the twentieth century. Although the epitome of an intellectual, he is reputed to have said his prayers every night with simple childish piety, often on his knees. At the same time, he was a convinced socialist. His life was ended tragically at the end of World War II; he was fired on as he lit a cigarette outdoors in the dark during a strict curfew.

Webern's music was largely ignored until after his death, but in the 1950s his abilities were recognized. He wrote in the same compositional idiom as Schoenberg, but his works are even more austere and economical. Of his thirty-one compositions, the longest is ten minutes, and his complete works can be performed in less than three hours. His dynamics are usually the softest imaginable, and his frail tone-row melodies are passed note by note from one instrument to another. Only the subtlest combinations and colors are used. The principle of economy in composing

"White on White" (*1918?*) *by Kasimir Malevich.*

was carried to its limit by Webern. If he had written more sparsely, one feels, the music would disappear entirely.

A parallel to Webern's music can be found in the art of a twentieth-century Russian painter named Kasimir Malevich. In 1918 he painted "White on White," which appears on this page. Malevich's painting may be an idea carried to an extreme point, but the principle of calm, objective, abstract art forms holds some aesthetic appeal.

On first hearing, Webern's music sounds like muted chaos. Little blobs of sound appear and disappear at apparent random between gaps of silence. But intensive listening discloses that what at first seems disorganized is actually organization of an intense and compact nature. The musical ideas are trimmed mercilessly to exclude every bit of waste or decoration. Only the absolute essentials remain.

The Webern style of tone-row composition has attracted many young composers throughout the world, and it has won over to some extent such mature composers as Copland, Barber, Sessions, Piston, Britten, and Stravinsky (who has publicly expressed great admiration for Webern). These composers manipulate the rules of tone-row music to suit their purposes. Copland expressed his view by saying that the tone-row technique is an "angle of vision. . . . Like fugal treatment, it is a stimulus that enlivens musical thinking. . . . It is a method, not a style, and therefore it solves no problems of musical expressivity."

New Applications of Tone-Row Principles

The idea of a row has been applied to aspects of music in addition to pitch—duration, dynamics, and articulation. One composer who applies rows to several aspects of his music is the Frenchman Pierre Boulez (Boo-lez, b. 1925), who is currently conductor of the New York Philharmonic Orchestra. In addition to a row of pitches, one of his compositions contains this rhythmic row,

this row of articulations,

and this row of dynamics.

In the 1950s Boulez and several other composers favored such "total control" in composing. By the 1960s Boulez had turned to some very different types of compositions, as we shall see shortly.

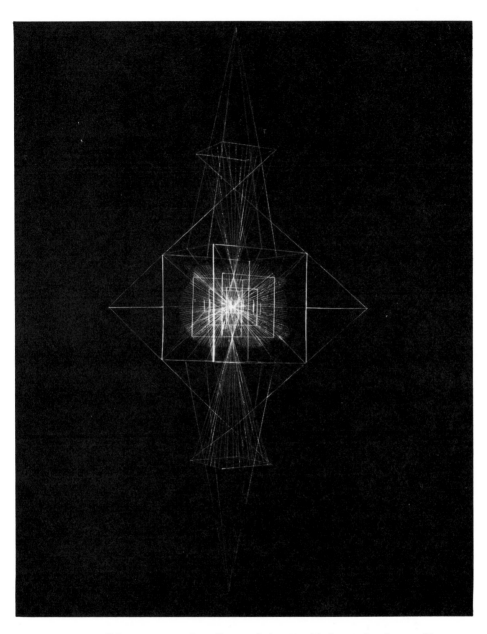

"Variation No. 7: Full Moon" (1949–50) by Richard Lippold.
This work is made from brass rods, and nickel-chromium and
stainless steel wires. It stands 10 feet high.

MICROTONAL MUSIC

Attempts, some as early as 1906, have been made to develop new means of tuning. Generally, these efforts have involved dividing the present half-step into quarter tones. Other intervals have been attempted, too. A Hungarian composer, Alois Hába (Hah-ba, b. 1893), has been a leader in this effort. Most of his compositions date from the 1920s and early 1930s.

To date, such microtonal music has not caught on very well. There are several reasons that might explain the negligible response thus far. Many instruments—all the woodwinds, all brasses except trombone, all keyboard instruments, and the harp—cannot play microtones without engaging in some inconvenient operation such as closing a hole halfway. Widespread adoption of microtonal music, then, would require redesigning of instruments, revision of music notation, and retraining of musicians. Furthermore, there is the question of how subtle a pitch difference is discernible to the ear.

Some music written for electronic instruments manufactures new pitches that are arbitrarily established by the composer. Several of these works reject any kind of scale in which the steps are equidistant from one another. Instead, the proportions of the harmonic series or a mathematical formula are likely to be employed.

MATHEMATICS

Historically, music and mathematics have been closely connected. Since the time of the ancient Greeks, the ratios of vibration frequency and rhythms have been a source of philosophical discourse. The analysis of systems of composing and the calculation of probabilities in the arrangement of music sounds have also received renewed attention.

The Frenchman Olivier Messiaen (Mess-yun, b. 1908) has written a work entitled *Quatre études des rythme*. This piano work contains one piece that uses a melodic series of 36 notes, a rhythmic series of 24 durations, a dynamic series of 7 intensities, and a timbre series of 7 styles of attack. Each of the 36 pitches has a fixed intensity, duration, and timbre.

Yannis Xenakis (Zeh-*nock*-iss, b. 1922) was born in Athens. He studied architecture and then composition in Paris, and he now teaches composition at Indiana University. He believes that musical compositions should be based on the calculus of probabilities. In his music, which he calls "stochastic," it doesn't matter if a particular note is played or not, since the ear cannot perceive every individual sound. *Metastasis*, written in 1955, uses 63 instruments (mostly strings); but it consists of *glissandi* (slides) with only the upper and lower pitch limits specified. The effect is one of a

Yannis Xenakis.

"haze" or rain of sounds. Despite his promotion of "statistical" sound, Xenakis reserves an important place for intuition and emotion.

TIMBRES

The fascination with timbres is both old and new. The diversity of instruments is evidence of the perennial appeal of varied and unique tone colors. When Berlioz wrote his treatise on orchestration, he was indicating an interest in tone quality and acknowledging its importance.

In the twentieth century, interest in varied sonorities has increased even more. There has been further exploitation of the possibilities offered by conventional instruments, as evidenced by Schoenberg's and Webern's *Klangfarbmelodie,* the changing of timbre rather than pitch. The "nature" or "night" sounds heard in the second movement of Bartók's Third Piano Concerto are another example, as are some of the effects in Stravinsky's ballets. Concern for tone quality as well as intricate contrapuntal relationships has been a mark of the tone-row composers.

Even more advanced has been the experimentation with tone sources other than musical instruments. A foretaste of this development was the "prepared piano" devised primarily by the American John Cage (b. 1912). In order to get distinctive timbres, sundry items are placed on the hammers and strings of the piano according to the specifications of the composer. Necessary equipment can include tape, chewing gum, thumb tacks, coins, cloth, paper, and other miscellany. New timbres are indeed the result. The pianist is sometimes instructed to reach into the top of the piano and strum the strings with his hand.

Not surprisingly, most nonconventional instruments are allied with the percussion section. In fact, the advent of the percussion ensemble is a twentieth-century phenomenon. One of the first to feature percussion was Edgard Varèse (Vah-*rez*, 1883–1965), who was born in France but lived in America after 1916. His *Ionisation* (1931) calls for an orchestra of forty-one percussion instruments (including a piano) and two sirens. The result is rhythm and timbre freed from conventional melody and harmony. Other composers have augmented the percussion section with brake drums (which incidentally have a pleasing tone), pieces from metal bed frames, and wooden articles. Sometimes the percussion-centered works feature a singer or reciter, or they may be combined with conventional instruments.

An even more advanced manipulation of sounds and noises was advocated more than fifty years ago by an Italian named Luigi Russolo (1885–1942). He wrote, "We must break out of this narrow circle of pure musical sounds and conquer the infinite variety of noise sounds." He went on to suggest an "instrumentation" of sounds according to six families or types:

1. Booms, thunderclaps, explosions, crashes, slashes, roars.
2. Whistles, hisses, snorts.
3. Whispers, murmurs, mutterings, bustling noises, gurgles.
4. Screams, screeches, rustlings, buzzes, crackling sounds obtained by friction.
5. Noises obtained by percussion on metals, wood, stone, terra cotta, etc.
6. Voices of animals and humans, shouts, shrieks, groans, howls, laughs, wheezes, sobs.

If his ideas seem futuristic today, imagine how startling they must have been in 1913, when he first propounded them!

ELECTRONIC MUSIC

Russolo's general philosophy, if not his specific categorizing, was picked up in the 1950s by a group of French composers (Boulez was one of

Milton Babbitt seated at the controls of the RCA Synthesizer in the Electronic Music Center of Columbia-Princeton Universities.

them), who worked with tape recorders. There are several types of electronic music, of which *musique concrete* is one. Recordings are made of natural sounds and voices—parts of human speech, a fly buzzing, the wind, a motor roaring, a whistle. Then the tape is manipulated according to the desires of the composer. It can be speeded up or slowed down. It can be spliced. It can be recorded through a second or third recorder and the sounds combined. The composition in *musique concrete* is a segment of tape that contains selected and manipulated sounds in a planned sequence.

An American advocate of *musique concrete* is Vladimir Ussachevsky (b. 1911), of Columbia University. He combines natural sounds and sounds from musical instruments, usually percussion, on tape. For instance, from the ring of a gong he may salvage only the last portion, or "afterglow" of sound. Then he may slow down the sound several times. The aural effect is new and may be interesting in a later composition.

Musique concrete has functioned successfully as background for movies, plays, and ballet scenes when eerie and unearthly music is required.

Another type of electronic music consists of sounds produced on electronic devices and then recorded on tape. This music had its beginnings in the Studio for Electronic Music of the West German Radio in the 1950s. The tones produced by the oscillator are said to be "pure"—that is, free

Karlheinz Stockhausen.

from any overtones. All sounds within the limits of human hearing are possible, even those too high or low to be identifiable as musical pitches. This range is considerably larger than the customary eighty-eight tones available on the piano keyboard. Furthermore, every level of volume and timbre can be reproduced. Also possible are synthetic machine rhythms, which are more complex and more accurately executed than those produced by humans.

The oscillator and tape recorder have opened up an entirely new dimension to music. And in so doing they have raised some difficult questions. For instance, how does one notate such music? The example on page 433 shows a portion of *Elektronische Studien II* (Electronic Study II) by Karlheinz Stockhausen (b. 1928), one of the originators of this type of music. Stockhausen says that it is not really a score but rather "working instructions for the electro-acoustical realization of the composition." The top section indicates the pitch and timbre. A new scale of eighty-one steps is used in this composition, and one hundred and ninety-three mixtures are constructed from them. The parallel horizontal lines in the center of the page indicate the time in terms of centimeters of tape moving at a certain speed. The shapes at the bottom indicate the volume.

If you were to hear *Electronische Studien II,* you would not listen to someone perform it in the conventional sense. You or someone else would

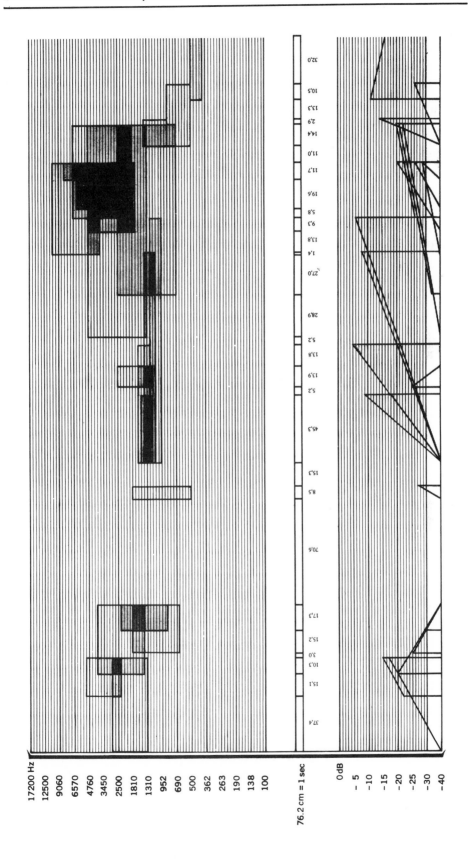

merely push the button to start the machine. If the technician who prepared the tape has followed Stockhausen's directions accurately, you would hear *exactly* the sounds the composer intended. The concept of the performer is thus so completely eliminated that there is no such function even in committing the sounds to a recording. The idea seems revolutionary at first. And yet in the visual arts no one expects to watch a painting being repainted by a "performing" artist. We see just what the original artist painted. The same principle prevails in the world of electronic music.

Several Americans, including Milton Babbitt (b. 1916) and Otto Luening (b. 1900) at Columbia-Princeton Electronic Music Center in New York, are also experimenting with electronic music. There is wide variety in notational systems for electronic music. Stockhausen's is just one example. It is much too soon to guess what direction electronic music will take. Composers, however, are showing much interest in it.

COMPUTER MUSIC

Sometimes one has the eerie feeling that computers and data-processing equipment are slowly taking over men's affairs. It is reassuring to recall that man, after all, makes the computer and tells it what to do. In computer music, a composer sets up a formula to be fulfilled by the computer according to the information supplied it. Whether the computer makes good music depends on the instructions given it. For example, a computer called Datatron was fed the characteristics of one hundred popular songs, along with some of Mozart's comments about melodic design. Within an hour, the computer had turned out four thousand new popular song melodies, something the world may or may not have needed. In this experiment and others like it, the music "composed" by the computer is no worse than that created by humans writing in the same style.

The computer holds more promise as a research tool than it does as an aid to musical composition. But only time can supply the final answer.

CHANCE MUSIC

Chance (or *aleatory*) music is that in which musical events are determined partly by chance and are therefore unpredictable. A clarinet player, for example, might be instructed to play anything he wishes for six beats, or to rest during that time if he chooses. Or the selection of notes may depend on dice throwing. Whatever the system, the exact musical results are unpremeditated.

The chief American proponent of chance music is John Cage. One of his pieces is a piano work written on several different sheets of paper. The player is told to drop the sheets, pick them up at random, and then play the pages in the new order. Cage has also written a work for twenty-four radios and twelve "performers." The performers switch stations according to directions involving the use of a stopwatch. The resulting sounds are clearly a product of chance.

To understand what Cage is trying to achieve (or, more accurately, not to achieve), you need to know his underlying philosophy, even if you don't agree with it. For centuries Western civilization held to the idea of progress, the idea of working toward goals. Through increases in knowledge, which in turn led to such practical outcomes as improved medical care, more food, a shorter work week, etc., it was held that mankind was progressing. But the idea of progress has come under attack in the twentieth century from existential philosophy and from advocates of oriental religious beliefs. The idea of progress is false, they claim; there is only change, not progress. The implications of the only-change, no-goal-toward-which-to-progress position are enormous. It is a little like removing the goal lines and uprights on the football field and ceasing to keep score or time; the game just happens and goes on. About the only assumption that one can make is that the players will eventually tire and stop playing.

This view rejects the idea that art must have meaning. As the poet Archibald MacLeish says:

A poem should not mean
But be.

The use of the Campbell soup can or comic strip character in a painting is not, as some people believe, a comment on the vulgarity of modern civilization. The content of such works is so blatant that no attempt at interpretation can be made, which is the way the artist wants it. A picture is a picture, and that's all. In his book *Silence,* Cage urges the composer to "give up the desire to control sound, clear his mind of music [in the usual sense] and set about discovering means to let sounds be themselves rather than vehicles for man-made theories or expression of human sentiments." The use of chance devices in music is one of the ways Cage and others encourage the listener to listen to sound rather than to seek relationships in the sounds. While at first glance it may seem foolish to determine a work's order by dropping its pages on the floor, such a procedure comes from the consistent application of a philosophical position.

Cage's musical practices, and perhaps parts of his philosophy, have been adopted and adapted by composers such as Stockhausen. In a complete switch from his electronic works of the 1950s, Stockhausen's

Originale (written in 1961) is based on a scheme of simultaneous, incoherent "happenings." The whole effect is something akin to the clowns taking over the circus. In one scene the directions are:

> Pianist and percussionist put on clothes brought in by cloakroom attendant. The pianist takes off his cultic robes and puts on Oriental female costume. . . . When he is ready, he begins to brew up tea at the piano.

It is difficult to predict much of a future for chance music. Although any object can be contemplated for what it is, the trouble with Pop art and chance music is that it lacks the evidence of skillful invention and elegance necessary to make the works aesthetically interesting. Very little unusual talent or devotion is exhibited in a painting of a soup can or in a musical work calling on the performer to manipulate a dial on a radio.

NEW SOURCES

As was pointed out in the beginning of Chapter 15, composers today know more about music around the world than at any time in history. The twentieth century has seen the development of scholarly research into folk and ethnic music. Some composers, such as Bartók in Hungary, have been involved in the collecting of folk music. With all its intellectualism, this century has seen abundant interest in folk material.

Especially fascinating to some composers has been the discovery of oriental music. Messiaen and Hovhaness have been influenced by Indian music, and the native music of South America has found its way into compositions by Milhaud, Messiaen, and Villa-Lobos.

ECLECTICISM—CONSOLIDATION

Although contemporary art music is pluralistic, with composers writing in widely divergent styles, there are some composers who use what they believe to be the best of each style. They own allegiance to no musical system or philosophy, and their compositions cannot be classified in any of the categories previously mentioned in this chapter.

In the opinion of many musicians, the leading composer today is Krzysztof Penderecki (Pen-der-*et*-ski), who was born in 1933 near Cracow, Poland. He is most interested in timbre and tonal effect, but he also uses the tape recorder in some of his compositions. His best known work is *The Passion According to St. Luke*. It was commissioned by the Cologne Radio and first performed in the Münster Cathedral in 1966. The work lasts for over an hour and calls for three soloists, a speaker, three mixed choirs, a boy choir, and an orchestra. The music is built on a tone-row series incorporating the B-A-C-H figure (p. 370), and it uses slides, microtones, "statistical" masses of notes, and tone clusters. The choirs sing, and in addition whisper, hiss, babble, laugh, and even shriek. Penderecki's success lies partly in the fact that much of the time he rations the number of ideas the listener is to hear, so the music is quite open and uncluttered. Also, one does not get the impression that the techniques of composition are more important than the musical effect; techniques are called on to make a musical contribution.

The *St. Luke Passion* is further proof of the interest of many twentieth-century composers in religious and humanitarian themes. Webern, Stravinsky, Messiaen, Stockhausen, and the Austrian-American Ernst Křenek have all written at least one religious composition. Nor is it unusual that a composer from eastern Europe knows and writes in the newest styles. Penderecki's first compositions appeared in the late 1950s— soon after the easing of governmental restraints in 1956.

Other eclectic, experimental composers include the Italians Luigi Nono (b. 1924) and Luigi Dallapiccola (b. 1904), the Pole Witold Lutoslawski (b. 1913), and the German Hans Werner Henze (b. 1926).

THE FUTURE FOR THE LISTENER

In assessing the worth of contemporary music, remember that you are hearing all kinds of works, both good and bad. The "test of time" has not yet been applied, so the less effective pieces still remain in the repertoire. Today, not all of Bach's or Mozart's works are performed; only the better music of these great composers has lasted. Many contemporary works don't sound like much, and they aren't. But time will take care of them, and fifty years from now they will have passed into oblivion.

More music is being written today than at any time in the world's history. The population has increased tremendously since Bach's time, and many more persons have been educated to write music. The "composition explosion" makes it even more difficult for anyone to become knowledgeable about the myriad styles and composers of today's music.

As Chapter 15 pointed out, Schoenberg was a composer who, during most of his life, depended on income from university teaching rather than from the sale of his music. A similar situation holds true for many contemporary composers. In some respects this situation is beneficial. The universities have the services of a skilled composer-teacher, and the composer is freed from the worries of where his next meal is coming from and whether his patron or the public will like his new piece. But the situation also has its minus side. The cleavage between the composer and the public has too often widened into a gulf. As a result, the composer appears to be ever more esoteric and aloof, and the public responds with deadening disinterest. In the meantime, music suffers.

The new and relatively secure position of the composer is not the only reason for a lack of understanding between public and composer. The twentieth century is an age of specialization. While in the past there have been specialists in music and its composition, the trend toward increased specialization is unmistakable. Some compositions written in this century are so complex and their musical intentions so obtuse that one almost has to be a composer in the particular style of the work in order to understand what's going on. This is not a criticism of the artistic worth of complex works, but it is a possible explanation of the inaccessibility of some modern music to persons who are not well-schooled musicians. Even trained musicians cannot spend many hours studying the score, listening carefully to themes or tone rows, and reading the composer's explanation of every work. In any event, there is little doubt that the ever greater specialization of many composers has contributed to the lack of rapport between themselves and much of their potential audience.

Although Bach and Haydn had to write music "on order," as it were, no one wants to return to a situation in which the composer must please the audience or else. The gap in understanding is a situation that is often talked about, but, like the weather, no one seems able to do much about it. An upgrading of school music curricula will help, of course. But it is simply not possible for school courses, under present conditions, to teach all the myriad styles of music in the necessary depth. To do so would require devoting most of the school day to music instruction, a most unlikely possibility.

Perhaps the solution to audience acceptance is not a solution at all but rather a realization that for the forseeable future there will be good serious music for the majority of the concert audience *and* more complex, innovative works for a limited, specialized clientele. This view would relieve the conscientious layman of the obligation to know all styles and works, no matter how difficult and unrewarding they might seem to him. At least he would not need to feel musically delinquent because he liked Copland and Bartók but could not understand Webern and Penderecki. Who knows—perhaps he *will* understand Webern and Penderecki eventually if Copland and Bartók have been grasped first.

Only two predictions can be made with confidence about music in the future. (1) There will be music. Mankind has found sound and its manipulation too fascinating, too satisfying to abandon it completely. In fact, the indications are that music and other fine arts will mean more, not less, in the years to come. (2) Music of the future will differ from music of the past. The creative mind is restless and forever unsatisfied with previous accomplishments. It wants to experiment with new ways, new materials. The truly creative artist is constitutionally unable to make imitations or be content with the efforts of others.

By definition, creativity involves the bringing forth of something new and unique. And so in the art of music, as in any creative endeavor, there will always be something new under the sun. Music, when it is the product of an imaginative and skilled composer, will always be a fascination to hear and a joy to understand.

SUGGESTIONS FOR FURTHER LISTENING

ANTHEIL:
Ballet mécanique

BABBITT:
Composition for Synthesizer

BERIO:
Circles (e. e. cummings)

BOULEZ:
Marteau sans Maitre

CAGE:
Indeterminacy
Sonatas and Interludes for Prepared Piano

COWELL:
Ostinato Pianissimo for Percussion Orchestra

HÁBA:
Fantasy for Violin Solo in ¼-Tones, Op. 9a

HARRISON:
Canticle No. 3 for Percussion

HENZE:
Symphonies

MESSIAEN:
Trois Petites Liturgies de la Présence Divine

NONO:
Epitaffio per Garcia Lorca

PENDERECKI:
Dies Irae
Threnody for the Victims of Hiroshima

STOCKHAUSEN:

Gesang der Jünglinge
Zeitmasse for Five Woodwinds, Op. 5

USSACHEVSKY:

Composition
Sonic Contours
Underwater Waltz

VARÈSE:

Ionisation

WEBERN:

Five Orchestral Pieces, Op. 10

Appendixes

Glossary

(Terms associated with rhythm, pitch, notation, and harmony are defined in Appendix C.)

A cappella—unaccompanied choral music.
Accidental—a sharp, flat, or natural sign written in the music to show a departure from the prevailing key signature.
Acoustics—the science of sound.
Air—a song or melody.
Antiphonal—two groups performing "against" each other and stationed apart.
Appoggiatura—a musical ornament occurring on the beat and consisting of a nonharmonic, dissonant note that resolves to an adjacent harmonic note.
Arpeggio—in "harp" style; a broken chord in which the notes are played one after another instead of simultaneously.
Atonal, atonality—not in any key or tonality.
Bitonal, bitonality—two keys occurring simultaneously.

Cadence—a progression of chords (usually two or three) giving the sense of phrase ending. In poetic usage, it sometimes refers to "beat" or "tempo."

Cadenza—a solo passage of an improvised, free nature, usually found in concertos.

Canon—strict imitation carried on between two or more lines of music for a significant amount of time.

Cantabile—in singing style.

Cembalo—harpsichord.

Chanson—song (French).

Chromatic—melodic movement by semitones.

Clavecin—harpsichord (French).

Consonance—concord; a group of sounds that the listener considers restful or pleasant.

Continuo—a bass line for keyboard in which the player is given only a succession of single notes and other symbols from which he fills out the remainder of the harmony. Also, the instruments that play that part.

Dissonance—discord; a group of sounds that the listener considers restless or unpleasant.

Enharmonic—the characteristic of a pitch whereby it can have two names, as on a keyboard instrument: E-flat is D-sharp.

Ensemble—a group of performers, or the effect of unity achieved when they perform together.

Equal temperament—a system of tuning in which the octave is divided into twelve equal segments or semitones.

Fugal—suggestive of a fugue in style, but not actually a fugue in form.

Glissando—ascending or descending notes occurring quickly. Played on a piano by rapidly moving the hand across the keys; on a harp by plucking many strings consecutively in a single sweeping motion. Other instruments achieve the sliding sound in a variety of ways.

Grace note—an ornamental note preceding another more important pitch, and printed in smaller size. It is quickly performed and does not usually affect the rhythm of the music.

Harmonic—a note produced by lightly touching a string at a proper place to divide it into segments. The sound is high and light in quality. See Appendix D.

Harmonic series—see Appendix D.

Harmony—the effect created when tones are sounded simultaneously.

Homophony—music consisting essentially of a melody with accompanying chords.

Improvisation—music that is performed without prior planning.

Inversion—turning a melody upside down so that an ascending interval descends, and vice versa. Also, rearranging the notes in a chord so that its basic note is no longer on the bottom.

Intonation—the quality of sounding "in tune."

Key—the centering or relating of pitches around a particular pitch. See Appendix C.

Legato—smooth.

Leitmotiv—a motive or theme that is associated with a particular character or idea, especially in the music dramas of Wagner.

Libretto—the text of an opera.

Lied—song (German).

Manual—organ (or harpsichord) keyboard played with the hands, as opposed to pedal keyboard played by the feet.

Melody—a series of consecutive pitches that form a unified and coherent musical entity.

Meter—the pattern created by stressed and unstressed beats in music.

Meter signature—time signature; numbers at the beginning of a musical work that indicate the meter.

Modulation—changing key as the music progresses, usually without a break.

Monophony—a single unaccompanied melody.

Motive—a short melodic or rhythmic fragment that achieves structural importance through its frequent recurrence.

Mute—a device for muffling or damping the sound of an instrument.

Octave—a pitch that has twice or half the frequency of vibration of another. The two pitches, if sounded simultaneously, blend into a sameness of sound.

Opus (Op.)—work. The opus numbers of a composer's music are generally in chronological order.

Ornament—a decorative note, or a rather unimportant melodic figure.

Ostinato—a persistently repeated musical figure.

Overtone series—harmonic series. See Appendix D.

Pedal point—a note sustained above or below changing harmonies.

Pitch—the highness or lowness of a musical tone, as determined by the frequency of its sound waves.

Polyphony—music in which melodies of more or less equal importance occur simultaneously.

Polyrhythm—several rhythms occurring simultaneously.

Polytonal, polytonality—several keys occurring simultaneously.

Range—the upper and lower pitch limits of a voice or instrument.

Retrograde—a theme performed backward, last note first.

Rhythm—the sensation of movement in music; a factor regulated by the duration and strength of the various sounds.

Rubato—a performer's slight deviation from strict interpretation of rhythm.

Sequence—the repetition of a phrase at successively higher or lower pitch levels than the original.

Sforzando—a sudden accent on a tone.

Slur—a curved line grouping notes together and indicating that they are to be performed smoothly.

Staccato—notes disconnected from one another; usually indicated by a dot over or under each note.

Suite—a collection of stylized dances; or music from a ballet or opera.

Suspension—a nonharmonic, dissonant tone that was consonant in the preceding harmony and that eventually resolves downward to become consonant in its present harmony.

Syncopation—displacement of accent, so that accents occur where they are not normally expected and are lacking where they *are* expected.

Texture—the basic setting of the music: monophonic, homophonic, or polyphonic.

Timbre—tone quality or tone color.

Through-composed—a melody without repetition of phrases.

Tonality—key.

Transcribe—to arrange a piece for a performing medium other than the original.

Transpose—to rewrite music or perform it at a pitch level other than the original.

Tremolo—"trembling"; produced in two ways: by rapid back-and-forth motion of the bow on a stringed instrument, or by rapid alternation between two pitches.

Trill—an ornament in which there is a rapid alternation between the written note and the note immediately above it.

Turn—an ornament consisting of several notes that move above and below the main note.

Vibrato—a very slight but rapid fluctuation of pitch.

Musical
Instruments

B

Instruments can be divided into "families" on the basis of similar design and principles of sound production. There are four families: strings, woodwinds, brasses, and percussion.

STRINGS

In a symphony orchestra the strings are the backbone of the ensemble. They constitute fully half of the orchestra.

The violin, viola, violoncello (cello), and string bass have essentially the same design. The main difference among them is one of size and consequently the general pitch level at which they play. The player produces tone by plucking the strings with the finger, or, most often, by drawing a horsehair bow across the strings. If the hair of the bow is examined under a microscope, tiny jagged barbs, like the edges of a sawblade, can be observed. It is these edges that catch on the string to set it vibrating. The player also applies rosin to the bow to help it catch the string better.

Aldanya String Quartet. Andrew Zaplatinsky and Yasuoki Tanaka, violins; Alan de Veritch, viola; Daniel Rothmüller, cello.

The "box" or body of the instrument is largely hollow. The wooden bridge visible on the top of the instrument props up the strings and transmits their vibrations to the body, which amplifies the sound and provides the distinctive tone quality of the instrument.

Extending out from the body of the stringed instrument is the neck, on which is glued the black fingerboard. The player presses the string down firmly on the fingerboard at various spots to change the pitch. The shorter the string—that is, the closer the distance between bridge and finger —the higher the pitch. The four strings are of different materials, thicknesses, and tension. Tension is regulated by the pegs at the scroll end of the instrument. When the player tunes, a tightening of the string produces a higher pitch, while loosening the tension causes a lowering of pitch. The instruments are tuned so that there is a fifth between the pitch of each string and the one adjacent to it; on the string bass the interval is a fourth.

It is possible to play two or even three notes at one time, a technique called *double* (or *triple*) *stops*. The bow in this instance is drawn across adjacent strings in a single stroke, so that they vibrate simultaneously.

As the player controls pitch with the fingers of his left hand, he manipulates volume and phrasing with the bow held in the right hand. The more pressure he applies to the bow, and the faster he draws it over the strings, the louder the tone will be. He can bow smoothly, or he can separate the strokes to produce a variety of styles.

All good string players rock their left hand in slight, rapid motion when playing. This motion creates vibrato, which adds warmth to the tone by causing fast, imperceptible changes of pitch. The mute for stringed instruments consists of a wood or plastic device that is fitted over the bridge. It softens the tone and gives it a more humming quality.

String bass.

The violin is the smallest and highest-pitched of the four instruments. Its range covers well over four octaves from its lowest note, which is G below middle C. There are two sections of violins in the orchestra: first and second. There is no difference in the instruments themselves; the distinction lies in the way the music is written for them. The first violin part is generally higher, more difficult, and more conspicuous in the total orchestral fabric.

The viola is somewhat larger, but it is also held under the chin. Its general range is about five notes lower than the violin's.

The cello is held between the player's knees. It is pitched an octave below the viola. In general its range is comparable to that of a baritone singer, and thus it is especially well suited for warm, melodious passages.

The string bass is known by several other names: contrabass, double bass, bass viol, and the affectionate term "bull fiddle." When playing, the performer either stands or partially rests his weight on a high stool. The string bass is seldom heard alone, although its tone is not unpleasant in the slightest. The instrument contributes substantially to the important low register of the orchestra.

The harp is also a member of the string family. Its distinctive shape and pure, clear tones have earned it a reputation as the instrument most likely to be heard in heaven. All of its sounds are made by plucking the strings with the hands. There are only about half as many strings on a harp as there are keys on a piano. But the harp compensates by means of a pedal mechanism, which can change the length of the strings almost instantaneously to provide any necessary sharps, flats, or naturals.

WOODWINDS

As their family name implies, these instruments use wind to produce the tone and are (or were) made of wood. Their strong point is the varied timbres they provide. In a symphony orchestra one usually finds two flutes and a piccolo, two oboes and an English horn, two clarinets and a bass clarinet, and two bassoons and a contrabassoon. Saxophones are used sparingly in a symphony orchestra.

All woodwinds are alike in that their bodies are hollow tubes. Holes along the length of the tube are opened and closed either by the fingers or by small pads attached to key mechanisms. As the holes are opened moving toward the mouthpiece, or source of air, the pitch gets progressively higher, because the tube is being "shortened." At a certain point a key is opened to permit the instrument to move into a still higher range, and the holes and keys can be used for a new set of pitches. Woodwinds are articulated by the player's tongue, and each instrument can produce only one note at a time.

The flute shed its wooden body early in the twentieth century in favor of a metal one, which is usually of a silver-nickel alloy. The metal construction gives the instrument a more brilliant tone. The flute and its diminutive version, the piccolo, are unique in that they produce sound on the stopped-pipe principle. Many a youngster has made a sound by blowing across an empty pop bottle. The flute operates in a similar way. What happens is that the air going into the pipe collides with the air returning from the stopped end, and a tone results. The flute's range is from middle C up about three octaves, and the piccolo's range is one octave higher.

The oboe is made of wood that, like the wood in the clarinet and bassoon, has been carefully treated to prevent warping and cracking. The distinctive tone of the oboe is produced by a double reed. The reed is similar to bamboo cane. It is shaved, and the two small reeds are wired together facing each other. The instrument does not have a wide range; it extends only a little over two octaves. Its best notes lie around an octave above middle C, where they can be easily heard. The English horn is neither a horn nor is it English in origin. It is basically a large oboe with a bulb-shaped bell.

The bassoon is also a double-reed instrument. It can play from more than two octaves below middle C to at least one octave above it. Its

California Woodwind Quintet. Robert Armer, flute; Russell Howland, clarinet; James Winter, French horn; Sanford Helm, bassoon; Clayton Wilson, oboe.

tone is highly distinctive but not powerful. The range of the contrabassoon is an octave lower, its lowest pitch reaching almost to the lowest note on the piano.

The clarinet has the most varied timbre in its more than three-octave range. Its low notes have a quite different quality than its high notes. It uses only one reed, which is placed on a mouthpiece. Clarinets come in a variety of sizes, but only three are found regularly in the symphony orchestra: the B-flat or A soprano, and the B-flat bass, which looks like a black wooden saxophone.

The saxophone is the newest instrument in the woodwind family. There are eight different-sized instruments in the saxophone family. It is used only occasionally in orchestral music, but is a regular member of concert and jazz bands.

BRASSES

The brasses are simple in construction and are the most uniform of all the instruments. The sound is produced by a "buzzing" or vibrating of the lip membranes on a cup-shaped mouthpiece. This buzzing sound is then amplified through a metal tube with a flared bell at the end. Today all brass instruments have curves in them so that they can be carried more easily. Also, all of the orchestral brasses have some means of changing the length of the tube.

A bugle is not an orchestral instrument, but it can illustrate an important principle of brass playing. The bugle has no valves, and so all its different pitches must be produced solely by changes of tension in the player's lips. This limitation means that the bugle can produce only certain tones, the familiar ones heard in bugle calls. These are identical in pattern with the harmonic series (Appendix D). All brass instruments can achieve

Brass Ensemble, Indiana University. Herbert Mueller and Louis Davidson, trumpets; Abe Kniaz, French horn; William Bell, tuba; Lewis Van Haney and Edwin Baker, Trombones.

different pitches by lip manipulation, but if pitches outside a particular overtone series are desired, the length of the tube must be changed so that a new overtone series is possible—one that contains the desired pitch. This is the function of the valves on most orchestral brasses: by pushing down various combinations of valves, the player opens or closes different portions of tubing so that the air column can be made the desired length for a new overtone series.

As in woodwind instruments, the brasses are articulated by the player's tongue.

Generally an orchestra uses three trumpets, four French horns, two tenor trombones, one bass trombone, and one tuba.

The trumpet is the highest-pitched brass instrument. It has three piston valves, which, when activated, change the length of tube in varying amounts. Its range is not extremely wide, extending from a few notes below middle C up somewhat over two octaves. What the instrument lacks in range it makes up for in power. The cornet is similar to the trumpet except for the conical tapering of its tube or bore. (The trumpet bore is more cylindrical.) Differences in the shape of the bore account for the mellower sound of the cornet. A mute for cornet or trumpet can be inserted in the bell. It dampens the tone and makes it sound more pinched. The most common is a fiber mute, although there are other materials and several variations of the basic mute.

The French horn uses a higher portion of the harmonic series than do the other brasses. This causes the available notes to be closer together in pitch, so extreme accuracy of lip tension is required in order to produce the desired note. The French horn can play more than an octave lower than the trumpet, and its overall range is wider. Its valves, operated by the player's left hand, are of a rotary type. The valve mechanism turns, thus regulating the amount of tubing. The player inserts his right hand into the bell to control the tone somewhat. A mute is occasionally used.

The trombone is an octave lower than the trumpet. It is unique in that it has a slide to regulate the length of its tubing. The trombone has great power. The bass trombone is somewhat larger than the usual tenor trombone and plays a few notes lower.

The tuba is comparable to the string bass in its musical function. It seldom gets to play a solo. Tubas come in several sizes, too.

PERCUSSION

All percussion instruments produce sound by being struck or rattled. They may be further grouped into those that play definite pitches and those that do not. First to be considered are those that can produce definite pitch.

A kettledrum is a large copper bowl over which is stretched a calfskin head. Around the rim is a ring that regulates the tension of the head when the small protruding handles are adjusted: the tighter the drumhead, the higher the pitch. The problem with this procedure is that it takes a minute or two, which means the performer must stop playing for that period of time. Until the middle of the last century, composers had to consider the inconvenience of retuning when they wrote for the instrument. Today there is a pedal mechanism that regulates pitch very quickly. The sticks have padded balls on the end. To permit a variety of tone qualities, the player has available several pairs, all having a different firmness.

Kettledrums do not appear singly. A minimum of two is required, and more are often used, each of a different size and tuned to a different pitch. The name *timpani* is plural, and is synonymous with kettledrums. The timpanist positions the instruments around him in semicircular fashion for ease of playing.

The glockenspiel, xylophone, marimba, and vibraphone are similar. All have tuned bars arranged to resemble a piano keyboard, and the player strikes them with mallets. The glockenspiel is highest in pitch and has metal bars, which produce a light, tinkling sound. The xylophone has wooden bars and produces a dry, brittle tone. The marimba also has wooden bars, but below them hang hollow metal tubes that permit the sound to resonate for a few moments after a bar is struck. The vibraphone also has tubes, but has in addition an electrically powered device that produces a vibrato in the tone.

The piano and celesta are keyboard instruments. The piano tone is produced when a felt hammer, activated when the player pushes a key, strikes the strings. Because of this striking action, the piano is often included among the percussion instruments, despite the fact that its tones are produced by the vibration of strings. The celesta looks like a small spinet piano, but it is essentially a glockenspiel operated from a keyboard. Steel plates are struck by hammers.

The chimes also produce definite pitches. The player hits near the top of a hollow metal tube with a wooden hammer.

Percussion instruments of indefinite pitch are many in number. Most important is the snare drum. It is hollow, with calfskin heads stretched over both top and bottom. On the underside are several strands of wire that rattle against the lower head when they are tightened sufficiently to touch it. These are the snares, and they give the drum its characteristic crisp sound. The snare drum is played with a pair of wooden sticks.

The bass drum is the largest percussion instrument, and it is placed on its side for playing. A single stick or "beater" with a balled head is used to strike it. When hit hard, the bass drum has tremendous power.

The cymbals are large metal discs that are often struck together as a pair. A cymbal can also be suspended from its center and struck with a stick. A gong is a large metal disc of thicker metal than a cymbal. It is suspended from one edge, and is struck with a beater.

The triangle is a three-sided metal frame suspended from one corner. A small metal beater activates the sound. The player can produce single strokes on one of the sides or can produce a more sustained effect by placing the beater inside one of the angles and moving it rapidly back and forth between the two adjacent sides.

The tambourine has a calfskin head stretched over a wood or metal rim, around which are placed small metal discs that rattle. The player shakes the instrument or taps it against his fist. Castanets are hollow pieces of wood or plastic that are clicked against each other.

The percussion player is assigned many unusual instruments. He hits the wood block, cracks a whip (which consists of two large, flat wood pieces snapped together), shakes maracas (hollow, dry "gourds" into which metal pellets have been placed), and even gets to blow on whistles. Most ingenious is the dog bark: a tin can covered by calfskin, from which is extended a string. When the thumb is dragged rapidly along the string, a distinct yelp is produced.

The possibilities for orchestral timbre are almost limitless.

SUGGESTIONS FOR FURTHER LISTENING

FLUTE:
Bach—*Sonatas (7) for Flute and Harpsichord*
Griffes—*Poem for Flute and Orchestra*
Mozart—*Concertos for Flute, K. 313 and 314*

OBOE:
Handel—*Concertos (3) for Oboe*
Mozart—*Concerto in C Major for Oboe, K. 314*
Poulenc—*Sonata for Oboe and Piano*

CLARINET:
Brahms—*Sonatas for Clarinet and Piano, Op. 120, Nos. 1 and 2*
Debussy—*Premiére Rapsodie for Clarinet and Piano*
Mozart—*Concerto in A Major for Clarinet, K. 622*

BASSOON:
Hindemith—*Sonata for Bassoon and Piano*
Mozart—*Concerto in B-Flat Major for Bassoon, K. 191*
Vivaldi—*Concertos for Bassoon and Orchestra*

SAXOPHONE:
Debussy—*Rapsodie for Saxophone and Orchestra*
Glazounov—*Concerto for Saxophone*
Ibert—*Concertino da Camera, for Saxophone and Chamber Orchestra*

TRUMPET:
Haydn—*Concerto in E-Flat Major for Trumpet and Orchestra*
Hindemith—*Sonata for Trumpet and Piano*
Purcell—*Sonata for Trumpet and Strings*

FRENCH HORN:
Hindemith—*Sonata for 4 Horns*
Mozart—*Concertos (4) for Horn, K. 412, 417, 447, and 495*
Strauss—*Concertos (2) for Horn*

TROMBONE:
Hindemith—*Sonata for Trombone and Piano*
Poulenc—*Trio for Trumpet, Trombone, Horn*

PERCUSSION:
Chávez—*Toccata for Percussion*
Harrison—*Canticle No. 3 for Percussion*

HARP:
Handel—*Concertos (2) for Harp, Op. 4, Nos. 5 and 6*
Hindemith—*Sonata for Harp*
Ravel—*Introduction and Allegro for Harp, Flute, Clarinet, and String Quartet*

VIOLIN:
Beethoven—*Concerto in D Major for Violin, Op. 61*
Chausson—*Poèm for Violin and Orchestra, Op. 25*
Prokofiev—*Concerto No. 2 in G Minor for Violin, Op. 63*

VIOLA:

Bartók—*Concerto for Viola and Orchestra*
Berlioz—*Harold in Italy, Op. 16*
Hindemith—*Trauermusik for Viola and Strings*

CELLO:

Bloch—*Schelomo—Rhapsody for Cello and Orchestra*
Dvořák—*Concerto in B Minor for Cello, Op. 104*
Haydn—*Concerto in D Major for Cello, Op. 101*

ORCHESTRA:

Britten—*Young Person's Guide to the Orchestra*

The
Notation
of
Music

RHYTHM

Beat: the pulse or throb that recurs regularly in music and that is accented periodically. The beat is the unit of measurement by which we judge the duration of a musical sound.

Tempo: the rate of speed at which the beats recur.

Meter: the way in which beats are grouped together and measured. Meter requires attention to the heaviness or lightness of the various beats:

Example:
beat beat *beat* beat *beat* beat (suggests a grouping of twos)
beat beat beat *beat* beat beat (suggests a grouping of threes)

Note Values: The passing of time in music is indicated by various kinds of notes, each one representing a particular duration. The duration of a note is always figured in relation to the beat.

Whole note	○	usually lasts for 4 beats
Half note	𝅗𝅥	usually lasts for 2 beats
Quarter note	♩	usually lasts for 1 beat
Eighth note	♪	usually lasts for ½ beat
Sixteenth note	𝅘𝅥𝅯	usually lasts for ¼ beat

The mathematical relationship between these note values is illustrated by the following chart. The arrows here represent the passing of time; they do not appear in actual music.

Consecutive notes may share flags for ease in writing and reading.

♪ ♪ = 𝅘𝅥𝅮𝅘𝅥𝅮   ♪ 𝅘𝅥𝅯𝅘𝅥𝅯 = 𝅘𝅥𝅮𝅘𝅥𝅯𝅘𝅥𝅯

Rest: a sign to indicate silence for a certain period of time. For each kind of note there is a rest with the same name and time value.

▬	▬	𝄽	𝄾	𝄿
Whole rest	Half rest	Quarter rest	Eighth rest	Sixteenth rest

The whole rest may also indicate an entire measure of rest, regardless of measure length. In such case it is called a "measure rest."

Dotted Notes: a dot to the right of a note indicates that the note is lengthened by half of the original note value. In other words, the value of the dot depends on the value of the note preceding it. Assuming in each case below that a quarter note receives one beat, the duration of each dotted note is:

♩. = ♩ + ♪ = 1½ beats   ♪ = ♪ + ♪ = ¾ of a beat

♩. = 2 + 1 = 3 beats   𝅝· = 4 + 2 = 6 beats

Time Signature or Meter Signature: the two numbers at the beginning of a piece of music. The time signature indicates the meter or basic rhythmic grouping of the beats. This grouping is indicated by vertical bar lines in the music itself; the areas marked off by bar lines are called "measures." The *top number* of the time signature tells how many beats are in each measure. The *bottom number* tells what kind of note lasts for one beat. A 4 on the bottom stands for a quarter note, a 2 stands for a half note, and an 8 stands for an eighth note.

The time signature is *not* a fraction; $\frac{3}{4}$ or 3/4 does *not* mean three-fourths, because it does not represent a portion of anything.

Two abbreviated time signatures are seen frequently:

    c (common time)   means $\frac{4}{4}$

    ¢ (cut time, or alla breve) means $\frac{2}{2}$

Meters are of two types. One has beats that are subdivided into twos; it is called *simple* time. The other, called *compound* time, subdivides the beat into threes.

The meter signature for compound time is more complex. Since the common note values are based on multiples of *two*, some type of dotted note must represent multiples of *three*. Furthermore, the meter signature must somehow indicate to the performer that the meter is compound. But a signature such as 2/1½ is impracticable. So the number of beat *subdivisions* is indicated in the top number, and the note value of each of these subdivisions is indicated in the bottom number. Hence $\frac{6}{8}$ means that there are two beats per measure, with a dotted quarter note receiving a beat:

PITCH

Note: a sign placed on the staff to indicate the pitch and duration of a particular musical tone.

Staff: the five horizontal lines and four spaces upon which the notes are written.

Leger Lines: short horizontal lines indicating the pitch of notes too high or too low to be placed on the regular staff. Leger lines extend the range of the staff.

Clef: a sign placed on a staff to show the exact pitches of the notes written on the staff. The two most common clefs are:

treble clef (or G clef, because it curls around the second line, G);

bass clef (or F clef, because it has two dots on either side of the fourth line, F).

The treble and bass clefs indicate definite pitches, all named for letters of the alphabet from A to G:

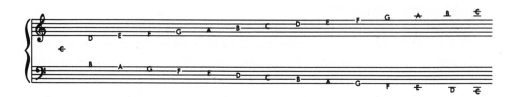

Another clef sometimes encountered in instrumental music is the alto clef (or C clef, because it indicates the position of middle C):

Sharp: (#) a sign placed before a note to raise the pitch one half step.

Flat: (♭) a sign placed before a note to lower the pitch one half step.

Natural: (♮) a sign placed before a note to indicate that it is neither raised nor lowered. This sign cancels a sharp or flat previously applied to the note.

Pitches on the Piano Keyboard

The black keys of the piano are found in groups of twos and threes. All white keys are identified in relation to these groups of black keys. For example, every C on the piano is a white key immediately to the left of a two-black-key group; every F is a white key immediately to the left of a three-black-key group. The white keys are named consecutively from left to right, using the letters A to G:

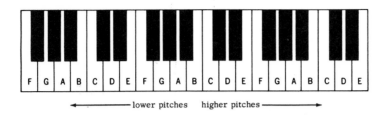

To find the sharp of any white key on the piano, find the black key touching it on the *right*. To find the flat of any white key, find the black key touching it on the *left*. If there is no black key on the side where you are looking, the nearest white key in that direction is the sharp or flat.

On the keyboard below, notice that each black key has two names, such as the key called G-sharp (because it is to the right of G) or A-flat (because it is to the left of A).

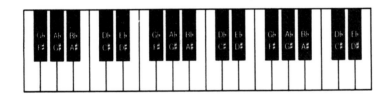

"Middle C," the note midway between the treble and bass staffs, is also the C nearest the middle of the piano keyboard. Using this as a guide, you can look at any note on the staff and find the exact tone it represents.

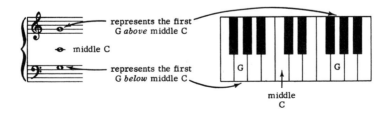

Interval: the difference in pitch between two tones. The name of an interval is determined by the number of letters it includes, counting the lower tone and the higher tone. Examples:

second   fifth   third   octave   prime or unison

Interval names are not to be considered fractions; they are not portions of anything. The name is written in full: "a sixth" rather than "1/6."

Half Step: the smallest interval that can be played on the piano; also called a semitone or a minor second.

Whole Step: an interval of two semitones; also called a major second.

Scale: a series of tones ascending or descending by a specific pattern of intervals; an "index" of the tones that constitute a musical composition or a portion thereof. A scale can be built on any note, which is then called the *tonal center* or *keynote*. A scale usually consists of eight tones, the eighth tone having the same letter name as the first, or keynote. Numbers are often used to indicate the successive steps of the scale:

When eight-tone scales are written, they must utilize each successive line and space—every letter—between the low and high keynote.

Major Scale: a scale having this pattern of whole and half steps:

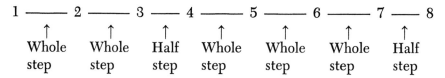

A scale can also be visualized as a flight of steps. The steps are not of equal height—steps 3 and 4 are close together, as are steps 7 and 8.

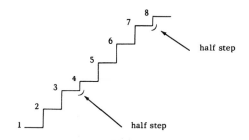

Key: the effect created when several tones are related to a common tonal center. If these tones are rearranged to form a scale, the starting note of the scale (step 1) is the name of the key.

Key Signature: a group of sharps or flats placed after the clef at the beginning of the staff. Every sharp or flat in the key signature applies to its particular note throughout the composition, unless the composer later cancels it with a natural. The key signature indicates the tonal center of the composition.

If the signature is in *sharps,* the last sharp to your right is always step 7 of the major scale; therefore the eighth step, or keynote, is a half step above this last sharp. If the signature is in *flats,* the last flat to your right is always step 4 of the major scale. (If there is more than one flat, the keynote has the same name as the next-to-last flat in the signature.)

Here are the key signatures for all major keys. The order in which flats appear in a signature is exactly the reverse of the order of sharps.

Accidental: a sharp, flat, or natural used within a composition to show a pitch not indicated by the key signature. An accidental remains in effect for one measure; after a bar line it is assumed to be cancelled unless it is specifically indicated again in succeeding measures.

Modulation: changing key within a composition, usually with no break in the music.

Transposition: changing the key of an entire piece, so that it is performed at a higher or lower pitch level.

HARMONY

Chord: a combination of three or more tones sounded simultaneously.

Triad: a chord of three tones, each a third apart.

Root: the tone on which a chord is built.

The harmony most familiar in Western culture is based on a specific type of chord—the triad. In any key, there are three triads that are basic because they occur so frequently. They can be better understood when they are related to the scale:

In any key: The triad built on step 1 is called I or *tonic* triad.
The triad built on step 4 is called IV or *subdominant* triad.
The triad built on step 5 is called V or *dominant* triad.

Although the I, IV, and V triads are the most common, triads can be built on any step of the scale, and are named accordingly: II, VI, etc. (In harmonic analysis, a Roman numeral indicates a *triad;* an Arabic numeral indicates only *one* tone—one particular scale step.)

Chord Function: the role of a chord in a particular key. In the music example above, the G triad (G B D) functions as V. It suggests restlessness, and the listener wants it to resolve to the home triad of C E G, which is I. But in the key of G major, the same G B D triad has a different function; it is the home triad and gives the listener a feeling of repose and rest. The purpose of Roman numerals is to indicate chord function—to tell how a particular chord works in a particular key.

Seventh Chord: a chord of four tones, consisting of a root plus intervals of a third, fifth, and seventh above the root:

The most common seventh chord is the V^7, or dominant seventh chord. The term "seventh" refers to the interval above the root; it does not mean the seventh step of the scale.

Inverted Chord: a chord that does not have its root sounding as the lowest tone. Inversion does not affect the name or function of the chord.

A chord may be sounded in many ways. Here are the three basic methods:

Key of D: I   V   I   I   V   I   I   V   I

Block chords   Arpeggios   Broken chords

MINOR KEYS

Minor Key: the effect created when the third step above the keynote is lowered. Other tones may be lowerd also, but a lowered third step is a consistent feature of music in minor keys.

The basic tone relationships in a minor piece are these:

1   2   3   4   5   6   7   8

This is *natural* (or "pure") minor; steps 3, 6, and 7 are lowered a half step from their position in a comparable major key. In the diagram below, the dotted lines show at what pitch steps 3, 6, and 7 would be heard if the music were major:

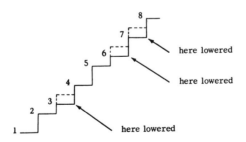

Steps 6 and 7 may be altered in a minor key. Here is one of the altered forms of minor:

1   2   3   4   5   6   7   8

The pattern above represents *harmonic* minor: steps 3 and 6 are lowered as in natural minor, but step 7 is raised so that it is now only a half step away from the keynote. This gives a nice feeling of "leading into" the keynote, but it creates a rather large gap between steps 6 and 7. The following alteration, then, is a compromise:

It is called *melodic* minor: steps 6 and 7 are raised when the notes ascend and lowered when the notes descend. In ascending passages, the raised step 7 serves as a "leading tone," to pull strongly into step 8. When step 6 is raised, the awkward interval found in the harmonic-minor scale is eliminated and the pattern is easier to sing or play—it is more "melodious"— hence the name. In descending passages, these two notes are lowered, so that the music sounds more distinctively minor again, as in the natural-minor form.

The key signature of a minor piece assumes that the notes will conform to the patterns of *natural* minor. Therefore, any deviations from natural minor must be written in the piece as accidentals. Here are the signatures for all minor keys:

Compare the foregoing chart with the chart of major keys on page 463. Notice that *each minor key has three more flats* than the major key built on the same note. These additional flats (or cancelled sharps, as the case may be) indicate the lowered 3, 6, and 7 of natural minor.

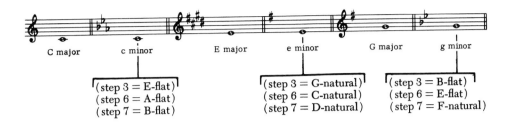

C major   c minor   E major   e minor   G major   g minor

(step 3 = E-flat)   (step 3 = G-natural)   (step 3 = B-flat)
(step 6 = A-flat)   (step 6 = C-natural)   (step 6 = E-flat)
(step 7 = B-flat)   (step 7 = D-natural)   (step 7 = F-natural)

The examples above illustrate major and minor *parallel* keys: they have the same key center but require different key signatures. Think of the scales of each pair as starting on the same horizontal plane on the staff, "parallel" to each other.

As can be observed from the two signature charts, every key signature can represent either a major key or a minor key. The two keys thus related are called *relative* keys: they share the same key signature but have a different key center. Interesting item: the key center of a minor key is always step 6 of its relative major key. Examples of relative major and minor keys:

B-flat major and G minor each have two flats; G is step 6 in key of B-flat major.

D major and B minor each have two sharps; B is step 6 in key of D major.

F major and D minor each have one flat; D is step 6 in key of F major.

The
Harmonic
Series

D

The harmonic series reflects a phenomenon of acoustics: almost every musical tone has several other pitches sounding with it, but so faintly as to be almost inaudible. These pitches are higher than the predominant tone, and they occur in a certain mathematical ratio to it. Here is the pattern for the first twenty-four overtones (also called *partials* or *harmonics*) based on the fundamental note of C:

Notes of the harmonic series are produced audibly whenever a string or air column is made to vibrate not in its entirety but in segments such as halves, thirds, fourths, fifths, etc. The concept is much like the analysis of light: sunlight is composed of many colors that are not usually apparent, but they can be isolated and made distinguishable by focusing the light beam through a prism. In the same way, an apparently simple sound has many components, which can be isolated and used toward musical ends.

As was mentioned in Appendix B, brass instrumentalists rely on the harmonic series to make different pitches. Stringed instrumentalists use the series to play certain high notes called harmonics. By *lightly* touching the string at certain places, the player can sound these pure, high, crystal like tones. He is not shortening the string; he is causing it to vibrate in segments so that a single, isolated overtone is heard. If he divides the string into three segments by pressing lightly at a point one-third of the way along its length, the third overtone is produced. If he divides the string into fourths in the same manner, the fourth overtone is heard, and so on.

The number and strength of the various partials or overtones determine the timbre of an instrument or voice. Only an oscillator produces a completely pure sound with no overtones. Its timbre, therefore, is hollow and dull. Overtones impart richness to the tone quality, and their proportionate strength determines the tone color of a musical sound.

Index

A cappella, 121
Accented beats, 15
Accidentals, 199, 463
Accompaniment:
    aria, 143
    recitative, 139
    song, 268
Acoustics, 99–100
Aesthetics, 55–61, 359
    Debussy's views, 344
    and recreation, 56

Aesthetics (continued)
    in twentieth-century music, 367
    views of Brahms and Wagner, 303
African music, 38–41
    drumming, 39–40
    form, 31, 40
    harmony, 40
    rhythm, 28, 40
Afro-American music, 43–52
Air (see also Aria)
    from Bach *Suite No. 3*, 174–175
Albéniz, Isaac, 343

Aleatory music, see Chance music
Allemande, 172–173
Alto part, 12
Alpert, Herb, 52
"America," 401
American Bandstand, The, 57
American Federation of Musicians, 94
American music:
    current popular music, 52–54
    folk, 41–52
    history, 399–405
Arabian music, 35–36
Arcadelt, Jacob, 125
Aria, 140–145
Armstrong, Louis, 50
Arpeggio, 281
Art and music compared, 65, 76, 83–84
Art song, see Song
Arts councils, 93–94
ASCAP, 93, 347
Atonality, 368–369
Augmentation, 304
Augmentation, double, 383
Ave Maria, 103

Babbitt, Milton, 431, 434
Bach, Anna Magdalena, 162
Bach, Carl Philipp Emanuel, 161
Bach, Johann Christian, 161
Bach, Johann Christoph, 161
Bach, Johann Christoph Friedrich, 161
Bach, Johann Sebastian, 161–164
    The Art of Fugue, 370
    Brandenburg Concerto No. 5, 180–185
    Cantata No. 140, 7–9, 12–13, 151–
        157
    Fugue in G Minor, 167–171
    and Haydn compared, 230
    St. Matthew Passion, 93, 152, 157
    Suite No. 2 from *English Suites,* 176–
        179
    Suite No. 3, 173–175
    Well-Tempered Clavier, 161
Bach, Wilhelm Friedemann, 161
Bach Gesellschaft, 162
Bacharach, Burt, 53
B A C H motive, 370
"Back to Bach" movement, 365
Bacon, Francis, 114
Baez, Joan, 53
Balakirev, Mily, 332–333
Balboa, Vasco Núñez de, 113
Ballad, 41–42
Ballade, 276

Balzac, Honoré de, 275
Bands, 87
Barber, Samuel, 418
Barnum, P. T., 402
Baroque period:
    characteristics, 129–134, 159–161
    instrumental music summarized, 187
    vocal music summarized, 157
Bartók, Bela, 373–375
    Concerto No. 3 for Piano, 375–380
    Mikrokosmos, 375
    Quartet No. 4, 375
Baryton, 227
Basie, Count, 51
Bass clarinet, 451
Basso continuo, 182
Bassoon, 450–451
Bass part, 12, 115
Baton, 92
Bay Psalm Book, 399
Beatles, The, 52
Beaumarchais, Pierre Augustin, 220
Beckett, Samuel, *Waiting for Godot,* 357
Beethoven, Ludwig van, 61, 240–245
    changes in coda, 248
    deafness, 242–243
    Egmont Overture, 258–260
    Fidelio, 243
    and Haydn, 241
    melodic style, 246
    and Napoleon, 241
    overtures, 260
    scherzo, 256
    and Schiller's *Ode to Joy,* 241
    Sonata, op. 53 "Waldstein," 245–250
    style summarized, 258, 260
    Symphony No. 3, 241
    Symphony No. 5, 4
    Symphony No. 6, 266
    Symphony No. 7, 250–258
    techniques of composing, 243
    use of tonality, 247, 257
    Violin Concerto, 244
Beetle Bailey, 62
Beiderbecke, Bix, 48
Bel canto, 320
Bellini, Vincenzo, 320
Belz, Carl, *The Story of Rock,* 57
Berceuse, 276
Berg, Alban, 373
Berlioz, Hector, 19
    and Liszt, 282
    Roman Carnival Overture, 76–79, 81–
        82
    Symphonie Fantastique, 291

Bernini, Lorenzo:
    colonnades at St. Peter's, 131–132
    St. Theresa in Ecstasy, 132, 133
Bernstein, Leonard, 64–65
    on Beethoven, 239, 243
    West Side Story, 419–420
Billings, William, 400
    "Chester," 400–401, 413
    William Schuman on, 410
"Birch Tree, The," 300
Bitonality, 362
Bloch, Ernest, 416
Blood, Sweat, and Tears, 54
Blue note, 45–46
Blues, 45–46
Boccaccio, Giovanni, 114
Böhm, Georg, 186
Bolero, 38
Boogie-woogie, 50
Bop, 51
Borodin, Alexander, 333–335
    Polovtzian Dances, 333–335
Botticelli, Sandro, 112
    The Adoration of the Magi, plate 2
Boucher, François, 190
    Venus Consoling Love, plate 5
Boulanger, Nadia, 405
Boulez, Pierre, 426, 430
Bourrée, 175, 178
Boyle, Robert, 132
Brahms, Johannes, 301–303
    A German Requiem, 302
    as a performer, 293
    and Schumann, 301
    Symphony No. 4, 303–309
    theme transformation, 288
    and Wagner, 303
Brass instruments, 451–453
Brass quintet, 237
Break, in jazz, 47
Britten, Benjamin, 386–387, 413
    A Young Person's Guide to the Orchestra, 80
Broadside, 41–42
Browning, Robert, *Rabbi Ben Ezra,* 307
Bruckner, Anton, 303, 352–353
Brueghel, Pieter, 112
Bugle, 451
Bülow, Hans von, 303
Bunyan, John, *Pilgrim's Progress,* 132
Buxtehude, Dietrich, 186
Bye Bye Birdie, 419
Byrd, William, 125

Cabezón, Antonio de, 126
Cabot, John, 113
Cadenza, 211
Cage, John, 430
    on composing, 435
Camerata, 218
Canon, 78
Cantata, 151–157
Carey, Henry, 401
Carter, Elliott, 418
Celesta, 453
Cello (Violoncello), 449
Cembalo, 181
Chaconne, 307–309
Chadwick, George W., 403
Chamber music:
    common groups, 236–237
    definition, 224
    Haydn's contributions, 223
    listening techniques, 224
    presence of piano in, 237
Chance music, 434–436
Chant, see Gregorian chant
Chartres Cathedral, 110
    sculpture on, 112–113
Chávez, Carlos, 390
Chimes, 454
Chinese music, 34–35
    notation of, 28
Chopin, Frédéric, 274–275
    and Berlioz, 275
    on composing, 22
    lack of versatility, 280
    and Liszt, 275
    Liszt's *Life of Chopin,* 291
    Polonaise, Op. 53, 279–280
    Prelude, Op. 28, No. 4, 65, 277
Chorale, 7, 150–151
    in cantata, 152
Chorale prelude, 171–172
Chorale variations, 171–172
Chord:
    function, 464
    inversion, 465
    pattern, 10
    root, 464
    seventh, 464
Chorus, 145–150
Chromaticism:
    in Mozart, 199
    in Wagner, 316
Clarinet, 451
    in Mozart's time, 210
Classical period:
    chamber music, 224
    characteristics, 190–193

Classical period (continued)
  development of symphony, 195–196
  improvisation in, 211
  melody, 198
  philosophy, 190
Clavier, 175
Clefs, 460
Clemens, Jacobus, 125
Cocteau, Jean, 387
  on Schoenberg, 373
Coda, 202
  Beethoven's changes in, 248
Codetta, 199
Coleman, Ornette, 52
Coleridge, Samuel Taylor, *Christabel,*
  264
Coltrane, John, 52
Columbus, Christopher, 113
Composer:
  income, 95
  and public, 95, 437–438
Composing:
  inspiration in, 20
  methods of, 20
Computer music, 434
Concerted style, 179
Concerto, 209–210
Concerto grosso, 179–185
Conducting patterns, 90–91
Conductor, 90–92
Consonance, 11
Continuo, see Basso continuo
Copernicus, Nicholas, 114
Copland, Aaron, 72, 405–407
  Appalachian Spring, 407–409
  on composing, 20
  on tone-row composition, 426
Corelli, Arcangelo, 186
Cornet, 452
Cornyshe, William, 125
Corot, Jean Baptiste Camille, 266
  Ville d'Avray, plate 8
Corrido, 38
Council of Trent, 115
Counterpoint, 6–9
  dissonant, 412
Counter-Reformation, 132
Countersubject, 169
Country-Western music, 52
Couperin, François, 190
Courante, 173
Crescendo, 18
Cro-Magnon man, 59, 60
Crusades, 109
Cui, César, 333

Culture,
  and ethnic music, 28
  and music, 63
Cyclical form, 299
Cymbals, 454
  antique, 347

da Capo form, 144
d'Agoult, Countess Marie, 282
Dallapiccola, Luigi, 437
Dante Alighieri, *The Divine Comedy,*
  109
David, 26
David, Jacques Louis, 192–193
  The Oath of the Horatii, plate 6
Davis, Miles, 52
Debussy, Claude, 344–346
  harmony, 345, 347
  and Mussorgsky, 338
  orchestration, 346–347
  and oriental music, 347
  Pelléas et Mélisande, 345
  Prelude to the Afternoon of a Faun,
    346–349
  and Wagner's music, 344
"Deck the Halls," 21–22
Declaration of Independence, 191
Dello Joio, Norman, 418
Decrescendo, 18
Delacroix, Eugene, 109, 264–265, 275
  The Bark of Dante, plate 7
  Liberty Leading the People, 240, 241
Descartes, René, 133, 190
Development section:
  reason for, 300
  in sonata form, 200–201
Diaghilev, Sergei, 357
Diderot, Denis, 190
Diminuendo, 18
Diminution, 304
Dissonance, 11
  in Mozart's music, 205–206, 212
  in twentieth-century music, 378
Divertimento, 228
Dixieland, 50
Doctrine of Affects (also Doctrine of Af-
  fections), 152, 180–181
Dominant chord, 464
Dominant key, 169
Donizetti, Gaetano, 320
Dorsey, Tommy, 51
Double, in Baroque suite, 173
Double exposition, 211
Double stops, 448
Dowland, John, 125

Drone, 30
Drums, 454
Dulcimer, 41
Dumas, Alexander, 275
Dunstable, John, 111
Dürer, Albrecht, 112
Dvořák, Antonín, 341–342
   Symphony No. 9, 404
Dylan, Bob, 52
Dynamics, 18
  in Beethoven's music, 253
  terraced, 175

Eclecticism, in twentieth-century music,
   436–437
Education, music, 95–96
Educational Policies Commission, 59
Eisenstadt, 226
Einstein, Alfred, 195
Elbow chord, 378
Electronic music, 430–434
  tuning, 428
Elgar, Edward, *Enigma Variations*, 342
El Greco (Domenikos Theotokopoulos),
   132
  The Holy Family, plate 4
Ellington, Duke, 51
English horn, 450
Ensemble, 225
Equal temperament, 161
Erasmus, Desiderius, 114
  on Socrates, 112
Esterházy, Nicholas, 226–227
Esterházy, Paul Anton, 226
Ethnic music, 26–27
  African, 38–41
  in America, 41–44
  Arabian, 35–36
  Chinese, 34–35
  complexity of, 28
  creation, 27
  European, 32–33
  Jewish, 36–37
  as a musical source, 436
  oral tradition, 27
  Spanish-American, 37–38
Etude, 276
Existentialism, 357, 435
Exoticism, 336
Exposition:
  in fugue, 167–169
  in sonata form, 197–200
Falla, Manuel de, 343

Fantasie, 276
Fauré, Gabriel, 327–328
Fayrfax, Robert, 125
Festa, Costanzo, 126
Field, John, 276
Figured bass, 182
Finale, 208
Five-note turn, 205
Fine arts:
  importance of, 59
  reasons for, 60
Flat, 460
Flute, 450
  types in Baroque, 160
Folk music, 26–27 (see also Ethnic
   music)
Foote, Arthur, 403
Form, 21–22
  in African music, 40
  of aria, 144–145
  Baroque sonata, 179
  chaconne, 307–309
  in concerto grosso, 181
  cyclical, 299
  fugue, 166–171
  in jazz, 47
  minuet and trio, 206–207
  in Non-Western music, 30–31
  passacaglia, 307–309
  in Renaissance motet, 121
  use in Romantic period, 280
  rondo, 212–213
  sonata, 197–203
  theme and variation, 232–235
Foss, Lucas, 419
Foster, Stephen Collins, 403
Fragonard, Jean Honoré, 190
Franck, César, 327
French horn, 452
  in Mozart's time, 210
  R. Strauss' contributions to, 314
French "Six," The, 388–389
Free form jazz, 52
Frescobaldi, Girolamo, 186
Fugue, 166–171
Fuguing, 400

Gabrieli, Giovanni, 129, 186
Galant style, 189
Galileo Galilei, 132
Gavotte, 175
Gay, John, *The Beggar's Opera*, 135–136
Gebrauchsmusik, 385
Genesis, Book of, 59

Gershwin, George, 417–418
  Rhapsody in Blue, 48
Gesualdo, Carlo, 126
Gigue, 173
Gilbert, William, 132
Gillespie, Dizzy, 51
Gilmore, Patrick, 402
Glazounov, Alexander, 333
Glinka, Mikhail, 332
Glissando, 346, 415
Glockenspiel, 453
"Glorious Things of Thee Are Spoken,"
  232
Gluck, Christoph Willibald von, 220
Goethe, Johann Wolfgang von,
  Egmont, 258
  Der Erlkönig, 272
  Faust, 272
Goodman, Benny, 49, 51
Gothic period, 109
Gottschalk, Louis Moreau, 402
Graham, Martha, 407
Granados, Enrique, 343
Greek music, 99–100
Gregorian chant, 101–106
  as religious music, 150–151
Gregory I, Pope, 101
Grieg, Edvard, 342
Griffes, Charles Tomlinson, 403
Grofé, Ferde, 417
Grünewald, Matthias, *Entombment,*
  385–386
Guerrero, Francisco, 126
Guru, 34
Gushe, 36
Gutenberg, Johann (Johann Gensfleisch),
  113

Hába, Alois, 428
Hair, 419
Half step, 462
Hammarskjöld, Dag, 164
Handel, George Frideric, 134–136
  Messiah, 137–150
  oratorios, 136–137
  Water Music, 135
Handy, W. C., 45
Hanslick, Eduard, 303
Hanson, Howard, 416–417
Harmonic progression, 11, 139
Harmonic series, 469–470
Harmonics, 469
  effect on timbre, 470
  on harp, 347
  on violin, 470

Harmony, 10–13
  in African music, 40
  atonality, 368–369
  in Bartók's music, 378–379
  in Borodin's music, 333–335
  in Debussy's music, 347
  elbow chord, 378
  in impressionistic music, 351
  in Jewish music, 37
  in Non-Western music, 30
  modulation, 139
  in Mussorgsky's music, 337
  notation of, 464–465
  in Renaissance motet, 120
  in Romantic music, 278
  tonal center, 139
  in Wagner's music, 316
Harp, 450
Harpsichord, 175–179
Harris, Roy, 418
Hartmann, Victor, 341
Harvey, Ben, 45
Harvey, William, 133
Hassler, Hans Leo, 126
Hawkins, Coleman, 51
Haydn, Franz Joseph, 226–228
  and Beethoven, 241
  chamber music contributions, 223
  "London" symphonies, 227
  Quartet, Op. 3, No. 5, 228–231
  Quartet, Op. 76, No. 3, 231–235
Henderson, Fletcher, 48, 51
Henze, Hans Werner, 437
Hindemith, Paul, 385
Hocking, William Ernest, 59
Hofmannsthal, Hugo von, 311
Homer, 99
Homophony, 10
  in recitative, 138
Honegger, Arthur, 388–389
Hooke, Robert, 133
Hopkinson, Francis, 400
Hovhaness, Alan, 413–414
  Symphony No. 4, 414–415
Hugo, Victor, 275
Humanism, 112

Imitation, 207
  in Renaissance music, 114, 117
  strict, 78, 167
Impromptu, 276
Impressionism, 343–344
Improvisation, 31–32, 211
  in African music, 40
  in jazz, 47

Musical instruments: (see also particular instruments)
Afro-American, 44
American Indian, 42
Arabian, 36
Chinese, 35
folk-ethnic, 32
Indian, 34
orchestral, 447–456
Intellect, in music listening, 71–72
Indian music, American, 42–43
Indian music, 33–34
notation of, 28
Interpretation of music, 87
Interval, 3, 461–462
of a third, 107, 111
Inversion, 183–184, 370
Isaac, Heinrich, 125
Ives, Charles, 404–405
dissonance, 378

James, Harry, 49, 51
Jannequin, Clément, 126
Jazz, 45–52
Copland's use of, 406
harmony, 46
improvisation, 47
melody, 45–46
Milhaud's interest in, 388–389
rhythm, 46
"third stream," 418–419
Jefferson, Thomas, 191–192
Jewish music, 36–37
Joplin, Scott, 45
Josquin des Prez, 114–115
Jullien, Louis A., 402

Kandinsky, Wassily, 66, 373
Improvisation No. 30, plate 10
Kay, Ulysses, 418
Keats, John:
Eve of St. Agnes, 264
Lamia, 264
Kennedy, John F., 191, 363
Kenton, Stan, 52
Kepler, Johann, 132
Kettledrums, see Timpani
Key, 11, 463
Key, Francis Scott, 401
Keyboard, 460–461
Keys:
Brahms' use of, 306
in Classical period, 202–203
major, 462–463

Keys (continued)
minor, 465
parallel, 207, 467
relative, 467
Key signature, 463
King George I, 135
King George II, 137
Kirchner, Ernst Ludwig, 359
Kismet, 333
Klangfarbmelodie, 372, 429
Klee, Paul, 373
Köchel numbers, 195
Krupa, Gene, 49, 51

Lamartine, Alphonse de, 275
Méditations Poétique, 286
Landini, 111
Lasso, Orlando di, 114, 126
Lead Belly, (Huddie Ledbetter), 45
Leger lines, 460
Leibniz, Gottfried Wilhelm von, 133
Leitmotiv, 316
Le Jeune, Claude, 126
Lenau, Nicolaus, 311
Libretto, 220
Lied or Lieder, see Song
Lincoln, Abraham, 406
Lincoln Center, 85–86
Lind, Jenny, 402
Lippold, Richard, *Variation No. 7*, 427
Listening:
attitude, 70–71
emotion in, 71–72
intellect in, 71–72
knowledge in, 79, 81–82
memory, 75–76
planes of, 72–75
sensitivity, 69–70
techniques, 75–80
tests of, 80–81
for themes, 77
to tone-row music, 372
to twentieth-century music, 363
Liszt, Franz, 280–282, 403
admiration for Beethoven, 282
and Berlioz, 282
Faust Symphony, 291
La Campanella, 282–284
Les Préludes, 286–288
Life of Chopin, 291
and Wagner, 282
Liszt (Wagner), Cosima, 282
Liturgy, 101
Loeffler, Charles Martin, 403

Luening, Otto, 434
Luke, Book of, 140
Lully, Jean Baptiste, 186
Lute, 122, 123
Luther, Martin, 112, 151
Lutoslawski, Witold, 437
Lyre, 99

MacDowell, Edward, 403, 404
Machaut, Guilliame de, 111
Machiavelli, Niccolo, 114
MacLeish, Archibald, 435
Madrigal, 122–125
Madrigal, spiritual, 122
Magellan, Ferdinand, 113
Magna Charta, 109
Mahler, Gustav, 352–353
Malevich, Kasimir, *White on White*, 425
Major keys, see Keys, major
Mallarmé, Stéphane, 343, 344, 346
Mannheim orchestra, 196
Manuals, organ, 165
Maracas, 454
Marc, Franz, 359
Marcellus, Pope, 116
Marenzio, Luca, 122, 126
Mariachi band, 38
Marimba, 453
Mark, Book of, 101
Mason, Lowell, 401–402
Materialism, effect on arts, 355–356
Mathematics and music, 428–429
Matthew, Book of, 101
Mazurka, 276
Meck, Nadezhda von, 294
Melody, 3–6
    Beethoven's style of, 246
    in Classical period, 198, 208
    embellishment in Baroque suite, 176–
        177
    in Gregorian chant, 104
    in jazz, 45–46
    Neo-Classical, 366
    in Non-Western music, 30
    in recitative, 140
    in Renaissance motet, 121
    in Romantic style, 290
    and rhythm, 6
    in second movements, 203
    in Stravinsky's music, 359
    Wagner's style, 316
Memorization:
    in conducting, 90
    in solo sonata, 236

Mendelssohn, Felix, 258, 289
    and Bach *St. Matthew Passion,* 93,
        289
    Concerto for Violin, 289
    Elijah, 289
    and Gewandhaus orchestra, 289
    Hebrides Overture (Fingal's Cave),
        286
    *Incidental Music for a Midsummer
        Night's Dream,* 286
    St. Paul, 289
Mendelssohn, Moses, 190, 289
Menotti, Gian-Carlo, 390–391
    The Medium, 391–394
Messiaen, Olivier, 428
Meter, 457
Meter signature, 16, 459
Metronome, 17
Mexican music, 38
Michelangelo Buonarroti:
    The Bound Slave, 129, 130
    David, 112–113
    Sistine Chapel, 112
Microtones, 30, 428
"Mighty Fortress Is Our God, A," 150
Miley, Bubber, 47–48
Milhaud, Darius, 388–389, 413
Miller, Glenn, 51
Millet, Jean François, *Planting Potatoes,*
    265
Milton, John, *Paradise Lost,* 132
Mingus, Charlie, 52
Minor keys and scales, 465–466
Minuet and trio, 206–207
Modes, 30, 104
Modes, rhythmic, 106, 109
Modulation, 139, 463
    in sonata form, 198–199
Mondrian, Piet, 66, 356
    Composition 8, plate 12
Monet, Claude, 343
    *Rouen Cathedral, West Façade, Sun-
        light,* plate 9
Montaigne, Michel de, 114
Monte, Philippe de, 126
Monteverdi, Claudio, 126, 138
    and opera, 219
Monticello, 191–192
Morales, Cristóbal de, 126
Moravian music, 399–400
More, Thomas, 114
Morley, Thomas, "April Is In My Mis-
    tress' Face," 123–125
Morton, Ferdinand "Jelly Roll," 45
Motet:
    Baroque, 157

Motet (continued)
  Gothic, 109–110
  Renaissance, 115–121
Motive, 204
Movement, 4
Mozart, Leopold, 194
Mozart, Wolfgang Amadeus, 193–195
  Concerto for Violin No. 5, 210–213
  concertos, 209–210
  and Haydn, 227
  The Magic Flute, 420
  The Marriage of Figaro, 220–223
  Symphony No. 40, 196–209
  Variations, K. 265, 235
Mueller, John H., 20
Music:
  and art compared, 65–66
  artistic, 24
  and complexness, 28, 67
  and culture, 63, 355
  definition, 2
  evaluation of, 66
  as expression, 74–75
  functional, 23
  functional and art compared, 57–58
  future of, 437–439
  learning about, 61–62
  as a language, 64
  meaning, 64–65
  reactions to, 80
  relation to fine arts, 108
  and religion, 59–60
  as self-expression, 53
  sensuous appeal of, 72–73
  social uses of, 26
  study of, 58
Music drama, 315
Music education, see Education, music
Music, film, 24
Music reading, 62
Music, recreational, 26
Music, religious, 24–25
Music therapy, 26
Musical comedy, 419–420
Musical director, 92
Musical instruments, see Instruments, musical
Musician, professional, 94–95
Musique concrete, 431
Mussorgsky, Modest, 333, 336
  Boris Godunov, 336–341
  and Debussy, 338
  Pictures at an Exhibition, 341
  and Rimsky-Korsakov, 341

Mutes:
  for brasses, 46
  for strings, 347

Nanino, Giovanni, 126
Nationalism, 331–332
Natural, 460
Neo-Classicism, 363–367
New England Psalm Singer, The, 400
Newton, Isaac, 132
New Christy Minstrels, 52
New York Rock and Roll Ensemble, 54
Niles, John Jacob, 42
Nocturne, 276
Nono, Luigi, 437
Non-Western music:
  harmony, 30
  improvisation in, 31–32
  melody, 30
  rhythm, 29
Notation, musical, 457–467
  adequacy of, 86–87
  in electronic music, 432–433
  of Gregorian chant, 103
Notes, dotted, 458
Note values, 458
Noüy, Lecomte du, 59
Numerology, 162–163

Oboe, 450
Obrecht, Jacob, 126
Occupational songs, 43
Ockeghem, Johannes, 126
Oliver, Joe "King," 48, 49
Opera:
  appreciation of, 218
  buffa, 220, 221
  Chinese, 35
  early, 218–220
  use of foreign languages, 216–217
  German Romantic, 314
  Italian Romantic, 320–327
  production cost, 92–93, 217–218, 394
  realism, 216, 218, 223, 314–315, 326, 341
  seria, 220
  singing style, 217, 220, 326, 339
  twentieth-century, 391–394
  voice assignments, 326–327
Opus numbers, 194
Oratorio, 130–131
Orchestras, 87
Organ, electronic, 166
Organ, pipe, 164–166

Ornaments, in keyboard music, 176–177
Ostinato, 50, 254
Overtones, 469
Overture, 173, 258

Pachelbel, Johann, 186
Paganini, Nicolo, 281, 352
  La Clochette, 282
Paine, John Knowles, 403
Pajama Game, 419
Palestrina, Giovanni Pierluigi da, 115, 116
  Sanctus, 117–121
Parallel keys, 467
Parker, Charlie "Bird," 51
Parker, Horatio, 403
Partials, 469
Passacaglia, 172, 307–309
Passion, 157
Patronage, 193
Payola, 54
Peanuts, 58
Pedal, Pedal point, 234–235
  in Borodin's music, 335
  in Shostakovich, 383–384
Pedalboard, 166
Penderecki, Krzysztof, 436–437
Percussion instruments, 430, 453–454
Performance, musical:
  acoustical conditions, 85
  in Afro-American music, 44
  of Baroque music, 178–179
  Baroque string playing, 173–174
  in electronic music, 432–434
  of figured bass, 182–183
  financial support, 92–95
  importance of, 83–84
  live, 84–85
  memorizing, 88, 90
  preparation, 87–90
  of recitative, 138–139
  of Renaissance music, 127
  reviews of, 96–97
  skill of performer, 84
  traditions, 87
Pergolesi, G. B., 364
Peri, Jacopo, *Euridice,* 219
Persichetti, Vincent, 418
Peter, John Frederick, 400
Petrarch, Francesco, 122
Phrasing, 18
Piano, 245, 276–277, 453
  "prepared," 430
  in song, 268

Piano (continued)
  techniques of playing, 246, 283–284
  virtuosity, 258–260
Picasso, Pablo, 359, 363
  Les Demoiselles d'Avignon, plate 11
  The Lovers, 364, 365
Piston, Walter, 416
Pitch, 2–3
  on keyboard, 460–461
  notation of, 459–460
Pizzicato, 299
Plato, 59
Pluralism:
  in current art music, 423
  in current popular music, 52–53
Poe, Edgar Allan, "Annabel Lee," 16
Poetry, in music drama, 315
Polonaise, 276
Polymeter, 340–341
Polyphony, 10, 106–107
  in Baroque chorus, 145, 149
  in Renaissance, 117
Polyrhythm, 40, 361
Polytonality, 362
Ponte, Lorenzo da, 220
Popular music, 52–54
  economics of, 53
  song, 25
Post-Romanticism, 351–353
Poulenc, Francis, 388–389
Prelude:
  Baroque, 172
  to suite, 173
Program music, 285–288
Progressive jazz, 52
Prokofiev, Serge, 384
Psalm singing, 399
Puccini, Giacomo, 321
  La Bohème, 321–327
Purcell, Henry, 186
Pushkin, Alexander Sergeevich, 334
Pythagoras, 99–100, 160–161

Quadrivium, 59

Rabelais, François, 114
Rachmaninoff, Sergei, 352
Raga, 27, 33–34
Ragtime, 45
Ragtime Instructor, The, 45
Rameau, Jean Philippe, 186
Raphael, Santi, 112

Ravel, Maurice, 341, 350–351
  Bolero, 350
  Daphnis et Chloé, 350
Rebab, 31, 36
Recapitulation, in sonata form, 201
Recitative, 137–139
  types, 140
Relative keys, 467
Reformation, 132
Religious music:
  early Christian, 100–101
  Gregorian chant, 101–106
  in India, 33
  Islam, 36
  and jazz, 151
  Judaism, 36
  in twentieth century, 437
Rembrandt van Rijn, 132
  The Descent from the Cross, plate 3
Renaissance period:
  characteristics, 111–114
  madrigal, 122–125
  motet, 115–121
  perspective, 126–127
Respighi, Ottorino, 342
Rests, 458
Retrograde, 370
Retrograde-inversion, 370
Reviews of musical events, 96–97
Rhythm:
  in African music, 40
  in Baroque period, 145
  in Gregorian chant, 104
  in impressionistic music, 348–349
  and meter, 339–340
  in Non-Western music, 29
  notation, 457–459
  in recitative, 139
  in Renaissance motet, 120–121
  in Stravinsky's music, 361
  tala, 34
  in Tchaikovsky's music, 296
Rhythmic modes, 106
Rhythm and blues, 53
Rich, Buddy, 53
Rimsky-Korsakov, Nikolai, 333, 335–336, 357
  Scheherazade, 264, 336
Rock, 52–54
Rockabilly, 53
Rococo subperiod, 189–190
Rolling Stones, 52
Roman music, 100
Romantic period:
  characteristics, 263–267, 332
  definition, 263

Romantic period (continued)
  nationalism, 331–343
  opera, 314–328
  summarized, 290–291
  symphony, 298
Rondo, 212–213
Rore, Cipriano da, 122, 126
Rossini, Gioacchino, 320
  The Barber of Seville, 220
Rouault, Georges, 359
  Christ Mocked by Soldiers, 360
Rousseau, Jean Jacques, 266
Rubato, 276–277
Russian "Five," The, 332–341
Russolo, Luigi, 430
Ryder, Albert Pinkham, 317
  Siegfried and the Rhine Maidens, 318

St. Peter's Cathedral, 131–132
St. Thomas' Church, Leipzig, 162, 164
Saint-Saëns, Camille, 328
Sand, George (Mme. Aurore Dudevant), 275, 282
Sarabande, 173, 176–177
Sartre, Jean-Paul, *No Exit,* 356–357
Satie, Eric, 387–388
Sax, Adolphe, 46
Saxophone, 451
Sayn-Wittgenstein, Princess Carolyne von, 282
Scales, 30, 462
  major, 462
  minor, 465
  pentatonic, 30
  whole-tone, 338
Scarlatti, Alessandro, 186
Scarlatti, Domenico, 186
Scherzo, 256
  Chopin's, 276
Schiller, Johann Christoph Friedrich von, *Ode to Joy,* 241
Schoenberg, Arnold, 368–370, 404, 413
  Gurrelieder, 368
  Variations for Orchestra, 370–373
  Verklärte Nacht, 368
Scholasticism, 109
Scholes, Percy A., 77
Schubert, Franz, 267–268
  "Der Erlkönig," 268, 272–274
  "Die Forelle," 268, 269–270
  "Gretchen am Spinnrade," 270–272
  Symphony No. 8, 268
  "Trout" Quintet, 270
Schuller, Gunther, 418–419

Schuman, William, 409–410
    New England Triptych, 410–413
Schumann, Clara Wieck, 289
    and Brahms, 303
Schumann, Robert, 288–289
    and Brahms, 301
    Frauenliebe und Leben, 288
    as a writer, 288–289
Score, 88–90
Scored for the Understanding of Music,
    77
Scott, Walter, *Ivanhoe,* 264
Seashore, Carl, 15
Secular music, 106
Sequence, 170–171, 183
Serial music, see Tone-row music
Sermisy, Claudin de, 126
Sessions, Roger, 406, 417
Seventh Chord, 279
Sforzando, 204, 257
Shaftesbury, Earl of, 266
Shaker music, "Simple Gifts," 408
Sharp, 460
Shaw, Artie, 51
Shostakovich, Dmitri, 250, 380–381, 413
    Symphony No. 5, 380–384
Sibelius, Jean, 342, 352
    Symphony No. 2, 4–6
Simon and Garfunkel, 52
Sinfonia, 366
Singing style:
    Afro-American, 44
    American Indian, 43
    Arabian, 35
    ballad, 41
    operatic, 217, 326
Singspiel, 420
Sitar, 34
Smetana, Bedřich, *The Bartered Bride,*
    341–342
Smith, Bessie, 48
Smith, John Stafford, 401
Smith, Samuel Francis, 401
Solesmes, monks of, 106
Sonata:
    Baroque, 179
    Classical, 196, 236
    memorization for performance, 236
    trio, 183
Sonata form, 196, 197–203
    Beethoven's changes, 248
    in concerto, 210–211
Song, 268–274
    demands on singer, 268
    role of piano, 268, 270

Song (continued)
    translation, 269
    through-composed, 274
Soprano part, 12
Soul music, 52
Sound, principles of, 1
Spanish-American music, 37–38
Spinoza, Baruch, 190
Sprechstimme, 404
Staff, 460
"Star-Spangled Banner, The," 401
Stockhausen, Karlheinz, 432–434, 435–
    436
Straus, Oskar, 310
Strauss, Johann, 310, 402
Strauss, Richard, 310–311
    as conductor, 293
    Don Juan, 88–89, 311–314
    and French horn, 314
    use of motives, 316
    operas, 311
    orchestration, 314
    tone poems, 310
Stravinsky, Igor, 357–358, 363–364
    The Firebird, 358
    Octet, 364–367
    Petrouchka, 358
    Pulcinella, 364
    The Rite of Spring, 358–363
    views on composing, 364, 366
    on Webern, 426
String bass, 449
String instruments, 447–450
String Quartet, 224, 228–235
String Quintet, 236
Strophic songs, 33
Style, concept of, 107–108
Stylistic periods, comparison of, 214
Stylized dances, 172, 206
Subdominant chord, 464
Subject in fugue, 169
Suite, Baroque, 24, 172–175
Sur la touche, 347
Suspension, 185, 278
Sweelinck, Jan, 126
Swing era, 50–51
Symphony:
    characteristics of fourth movement,
        208
    characteristics of second movement,
        203
    characteristics of third movement, 206
    Classical, 196–209
    historical development, 195–196
    Romantic, 250, 298

Syncopation, 46, 296, 411
Syntax, 61

Tala, 34
Tallis, Thomas, 125
Tambourine, 35–36, 454
Tape recorder, in composition, 19, 430–
   434
Taverner, John, 125
Tchaikovsky, Peter Ilich, 294–295
   as conductor, 293
   Nutcracker Suite, 299
   Symphony No. 4, 294–301
   techniques of composition, 299–300
Telemann, Georg Philipp, 186
Tempo, 16–17
Tempo markings, 17
Tennyson, Alfred, *Idylls of the King*,
   264
Tenor part, 12
Terraced dynamics, 175
Text:
   art song, 269
   ballade, 41
   blues, 47
   Gothic motet, 109
   Gothic secular song, 106
   madrigal, 122
   oratorio, 137
   Renaissance motet, 117
Texture, 10
Theme, 3
Theme and variation, 232–235
   techniques of, 235
Theme transformation, 288
Thomas, Theodore, 402
Thomson, Virgil, 417
Thoreau, David, 266
Tie, 349
Timbre, 19
   affected by harmonic series, 470
   in Bartók's music, 377–378
   in experimental music, 429–430
   Hovhaness' "points of sound," 414–
   415
   jazz, 46
   in tone-row music, 372
Time, 13–17
   beat, 14–15
   measure, 16
   meter, 15–16
   meter signature, 16, 459
   rhythm, 14
   tempo, 16–17
Timpani, 160, 453

Tintoretto (Jacopo Robusti), 112
Titian (Tiziano Vecellio), 112
Toccata, 172
Tombak, 36
Tonality, 11, 130
   in Baroque polyphony, 145
   in Classical symphony, 198–199, 202–
   203
   in minuet and trio, 207
   in late Romantic music, 316
   in twentieth-century music, 362, 368–
   369
Tone color, see Timbre
Tone poem, 285–288, 310, 314
Tone-row music, 369–373
   further applications of, 426
Tonic, 11
Tonic chord, 464
Torelli, Giuseppe, 186
Transcription, 160, 282
Transition, in sonata form, 198–199
Transposition, 88, 463
Tremolo, 347
Triangle, 454
Trio, in minuet, 207
Triplets, 247
Trombone, 453
Troubadours, 106
Trouvères, 106
Trumpet, 452
Tuba, 453
Tune, 3
Tuning (temperament), 160–161
Turn, five-note, 279
Twelve-tone music, see Tone-row music
Twentieth century:
   characteristics, 355–357
   dissonance, 378
   melody, 359, 366
   opera, 390–394
   rhythm, 361, 411
   summarized, 395

Ud, 36
Ussachevsky, Vladimir, 431

Van Eyck, Jan, 109
   Angels Playing, plate 1
Varèse, Edgard, 430
Vatican Council II, 102
Vaughn Williams, Ralph, 386
Verdi, Giuseppe, 320–321
Verismo, 326
Verlaine, Paul, 343

Vibraphone, 453
Vibrato, 46
  on strings, 448
Victoria, Tomás Luis de, 126
Villa-Lobos, Heitor, 389–390
Vinci, Leonardo da, 112
Viola, 449
Violin, 160, 449
Virtuosity:
  in early opera, 220
  in piano playing, 284
  in singing, 143–144
Vivaldi, Antonio, 164, 186
Voices, in fugue, 170

Wagner, Richard, 314–316
  on the arts, 291, 315
  and Bayreuth, 320
  and Brahms, 303
  Der Ring des Nibelungen, 316–319
  harmony, 316
  influence of Weber on, 314
  leitmotiv, 316
  and Liszt, 282
  melodic style, 316
  operas, 320
  opera texts, 315
  use of orchestra, 316
  Parsifal, 264, 266
  "Siegfried's Rhine Journey," 316–319
Waldstein, Count von, 246
Waller, Fats, 51

Waltz, 276
Washington, George, 226, 400
Watteau, Antoine, 190
Weber, Carl Maria von, 258, 314
  Der Freischütz, 314
  influence on Wagner, 314
Webern, Anton von, 373, 424–426
Weelkes, Thomas, 125
Welk, Lawrence, 52
Westminster Abbey, 136
Whiteman, Paul, 48
Whitman, Walt, 409
Whole step, 462
Whole-tone scale, 338
Wilbye, John, 125
Wilde, Oscar, 311
Willaert, Adrian, 126
"Wolf" children, 63
Woodwind quintet, 236
Woodwind instruments, 450–451
Words and music, 149, 269, (see also
  Text)
Wordsworth, William, *Lines Composed
  a Few Miles Above Tintern Abbey,*
  264
  The Tables Turned, 266

Xenakis, Yannis, 428–429
Xylophone, 453

"Yankee Doodle," 400–401

PERIOD	PROMINENT COMPOSERS	NEW LARGE FORMS	NEW SMALL FORMS
GOTHIC 1100-1450	Machaut, Landini	Mass	Motet, secular ballades
RENAISSANCE 1450-1600	Josquin des Prez, Palestrina, di Lasso, Byrd		Madrigal, motet, chorale melody
BAROQUE 1600-1750	Monteverdi, Corelli, Vivaldi, Purcell, Lully, Telemann, Rameau, Bach, Handel	Opera, oratorio, cantata, sonata, concerto grosso, suite	Chorale, fugue, passacaglia, toccata, prelude, overture, chorale variation, chorale prelude, recitative, aria
Rococo 1725-1765	Couperin		
CLASSICAL 1750-1825	Mozart, Haydn, Gluck, J. C. Bach, C. P. E. Bach	Symphony, solo concerto, sonata, string quartet	Sonata form, rondo, theme and variation, minuet and trio, scherzo
ROMANTIC 1825-1900	Beethoven, Schubert, von Weber, Chopin, Liszt, Mendelssohn, Berlioz, Schumann, Franck, Verdi, Brahms, Tchaikovsky, Fauré, Dvořák, Mussorgsky, Borodin, Rimsky-Korsakov, Rachmaninoff, Puccini, Wagner, Grieg, Elgar, R. Strauss, Mahler, Sibelius	Art song, symphonic poem, grand opera and music drama	Short lyric instrumental pieces
Impressionism 1890-1920	Debussy, Ravel		
TWENTIETH CENTURY 1900-	Stravinsky, Schoenberg, Bartók, Berg, Ives, Copland, Shostakovich, Prokofiev, Britten, Menotti, Vaughan Williams, Hindemith, Poulenc, Milhaud, Villa-Lobos, Webern, Penderecki, Cage		Jazz, electronic music, microtonal music, aleatory music, tone row